Filmography of Social Issues

A Reference Guide

Charles P. Mitchell

GREENWOOD PRESS
Westport, Connecticut • London

Library of Congress Cataloging-in-Publication Data

Mitchell, Charles P., 1949–
  Filmography of social issues : a reference guide / Charles P. Mitchell.
    p. cm.
  Includes bibliographical references and index.
  ISBN 0-313-32037-3 (alk. paper)
    1. Social problems in motion pictures. 2. Motion pictures—United States—Plots,
  themes, etc. I. Title.
  PN1995.9.S62M58   2004
  791.43′6556—dc22   2004017893

British Library Cataloguing in Publication Data is available.

Library of Congress Catalog Card Number: 2004017893
ISBN: 0-313-32037-3

First published in 2004

Greenwood Press, 88 Post Road West, Westport, CT 06881
An imprint of Greenwood Publishing Group, Inc.
www.greenwood.com

Printed in the United States of America

The paper used in this book complies with the
Permanent Paper Standard issued by the National
Information Standards Organization (Z39.48-1984).

10 9 8 7 6 5 4 3 2 1

This volume is dedicated to my parents

Charles S. Mitchell (1903–1963)
and
Anna B. Mitchell (1908–2003)

Contents

Introduction   1

America America (1963)   19
American History X (1998)   21
And the Band Played On (1993)   23
As Good As It Gets (1997)   26
Betrayed (1988)   29
Black Legion (1936)   32
Black Like Me (1964)   34
Blue Denim (1959)   37
Border Incident (1949)   40
The Burning Bed (1984)   42
Cell 2455 Death Row (1955)   45
Chicago Calling (1951)   47
The Choice (1981)   50
A Civil Action (1998)   52
Colors (1988)   54
Compulsion (1959)   57
Conrack (1974)   59
Cradle Will Rock (1999)   62
Cruising (1980)   66
Dangerous Child (2002)   68
Dead Man Walking (1995)   71
Divorce His (1973)/Divorce Hers (1973)   73

The Divorcee (1930)   76
Dolores Claiborne (1995)   78
Domestic Disturbance (2001)   82
Driving Miss Daisy (1989)   85
An Early Frost (1985)   87
Environment (1971)   90
Focus (2001)   93
Fourteen Hours (1951)   95
The Glass Wall (1953)   98
Gods and Monsters (1998)   101
Good Morning, Vietnam (1987)   104
Good Will Hunting (1997)   107
The Grapes of Wrath (1940)   111
Green Card (1990)   114
Green Dragon (2002)   117
Guess Who's Coming to Dinner? (1967)   120
I Want to Live! (1958)   123
If These Walls Could Talk (1996)   125
In Cold Blood (1967)   128
Indictment (1995)   130
The Intruder (1962)   133
Iris (2001)   135
Judge Horton and the Scottsboro Boys (1976)   137
Kate's Secret (1986)   140
Key Witness (1960)   142
Kissing Jessica Stein (2001)   144
The Lady Gambles (1949)   146
Lean on Me (1989)   149
Lenny (1974)   152
The Lost Weekend (1945)   154
Mad at the World (1955)   157
The Man Who Played God (1932)   160
The Man With the Golden Arm (1956)   162
Mask (1985)   164
The Men (1950)   167
Modern Times (1936)   170
Monkey on My Back (1957)   173

My Name Is Bill W. (1989)   176
Night Unto Night (1947/1949)   178
No Blade of Grass (1970)   180
No Way Out (1950)   185
Patty (1962)   188
The Perez Family (1995)   190
Philadelphia (1993)   193
The Pride of Jesse Hallam (1981)   196
Prophecy (1979)   198
Pump Up the Volume (1990)   201
Reversal of Fortune (1990)   203
Right of Way (1983)   206
Rock Hudson (1990)   208
Roe vs. Wade (1989)   211
Separate but Equal (1991)   214
Sign of the Ram (1948)   216
Sixth and Main (1977)   219
Sleeping With the Enemy (1991)   222
Slender Thread (1965)   224
A Small Killing (1981)   227
Soylent Green (1973)   229
Stand and Deliver (1987)   232
Stone Pillow (1985)   234
Storm Center (1956)   236
Storm Warning (1950)   238
The Straight Story (1999)   241
The Suicide's Wife (1979)   244
Suspect (1987)   246
Sybil (1976)   249
Ten Rillington Place (1971)   252
Trial (1955)   255
Ultimate Betrayal (1993)   258
The Unfaithful (1947)   261
The Unspoken Truth (1995)   264
Walking on Water (2002)   266
The War of the Roses (1989)   269
West Side Story (1961)   271

The Whales of August (1987)   274
When Innocence Is Lost (1997)   276
Whose Life Is It Anyway? (1981)   279
Woman on the Beach (1947)   281

Index   285

Introduction

I don't seek out social issue films, but I am proud to be in a movie that will make people think.

—Kevin Spacey, actor

It's a myth in Hollywood that you have to have a message.

—Famke Janssen, actress

Messages are for Western Union.

—Samuel Goldwyn, producer

In fact, every movie ever made has a message, only you don't know it if they are good.

—Louis B. Mayer, producer

I think there is a social undercurrent in all my films, but with only one exception, it is never on the surface.

—Roger Corman, producer, director, and actor

Filmmakers, performers, and reviewers have debated the relevance of films with social themes since the early days of silent cinema. One of the first pictures to highlight conditions of life in the slums was *The Musketeers of Pig Alley* (1912), a crime drama by D. W. Griffith. Other early dramas featuring various social concerns included exploitation of women in *Traffic in Souls* (1913), marital infidelity and divorce in *A Fool There Was* (1914), and poverty in *Regeneration* (1915). Perhaps the film that best epitomizes this era is *Intolerance* (1916), the multilevel masterpiece by D. W. Griffith, with episodes in four different time periods. The contemporary story, called *The Mother and the*

Law, is the primary plot of this epic, which also includes episodes from the fall of ancient Babylon, the crucifixion of Christ, and the St. Bartholomew's Day massacre in sixteenth-century Paris. Interestingly, social reformers in *Intolerance* are portrayed as exacerbating rather than relieving the ills suffered by the oppressed poor. A fresh wave of social issue films unfolded in the late 1920s, inspired by such motion pictures as F. W. Murnau's *Sunrise* (1927), King Vidor's *The Crowd* (1928), and Frank Borzage's *Street Angel* (1928). The inclination to include social messages continued into the talking era, although the box office failure of some pictures such as *City Girl* (1931) and *Our Daily Bread* (1934) led to an eccentric industry attitude that became more pronounced over the next thirty years: If a motion picture appears to be preaching to its audience, it is both ineffectual and a box office failure. If the film, however, manages to camouflage its social message, it may be able to reap both critical honors and solid profits. Similarly, the critics developed a love-hate attitude toward social issue films, alternately heaping praise or looking down on them. Filmmakers had to learn to walk a tightrope, balancing their use of social issues with emphasis on other elements, particularly stressing the entertainment value of their products as their most important concern. Their reasoning is that films are a reflection of life, and they would naturally depict the major social themes of their time. One measure of the success of message movies is their overall popularity as reflected in their recognition by the Academy Awards.

Filmography of Social Issues examines twenty specific social themes and shows how they are examined in a hundred motion pictures. The book is intended to serve as a guide for librarians, students, educators, public employees, sociologists, cultural historians, and any individuals interested in motion pictures and how they reflect and comment on the major issues of our time. Some titles may deal with only one of these issues, but frequently they will include more than one category. The entries are all English-language films, primarily American, but also including a few selections from Great Britain and Australia. Most can be located easily for viewing through standard video sources or cable. They were chosen to represent as wide a cross section as possible of different types of films over the last seventy-five years, the earliest one being *The Divorcee* (1930) and the most recent, *Green Dragon* (2002). Some are major studio productions, while others are modest efforts made directly for television. Many are based on actual historical events, such as *Judge Horton and the Scottsboro Boys, My Name Is Bill W, Ten Rillington Place,* and *A Civil Action.* Others are real events that are thinly disguised, as in *Cell 2455 Death Row, Black Like Me,* and *Compulsion.* A few are even based on memorable works of literature by such writers as John Steinbeck (*The Grapes of Wrath*), Arthur Miller (*Focus*), Truman Capote (*In Cold Blood*), and Stephen King (*Dolores Claiborne*). Many different genres are also represented, including film noir (*Woman on the Beach*), science fiction (*No Blade of Grass*), gothic (*Sign of the Ram*), comedy (*War of the Roses*), mystery (*Suspect*), romance (*Green Card*), biographical (*Lenny*), exploitation (*Patty*), and even a musical (*West Side Story*).

The volume is comprised of one hundred entries, each discussing a selected film. Entries are arranged in alphabetical order using a standard format beginning with title and year of release. This is followed by a listing of the principal social themes arranged in order of prominence. Credits appear next, including studio, Motion Picture Association of America ratings, major cast, writer, cinematographer, editor, composer, producer, and director. The credits section concludes with designation of color or black and white (B&W) and running time. The next section is the Overview, which briefly summarizes why the film was selected and its particular significance. The Synopsis provides a brief summary of the main action of the story as presented on screen. The Critique includes various degrees of background information, commentary, analysis, and evaluation. It sometimes indicates additional areas for study that may be helpful to students or individuals doing research.

The social issues examined in the films attempt to represent the principal concerns that interest, affect, worry, and often divide the public. Additional topics, such as the public health system, civil defense, the loss of individuality in modern society, and religious and cultural toleration are occasionally addressed in the films, but are not assigned separate categories. The issues are arranged here in alphabetical order, including a listing of the films relating to each topic. Those films in which the issue is the primary topic are marked by an asterisk (*). A brief commentary follows each list discussing the issue in historical terms and citing additional films relevant to each topic.

Abortion

Blue Denim ★ *The Choice* ★ *If These Walls Could Talk* ★ *Patty* ★ *Prophecy* ★ *Roe vs. Wade* ★ *Ten Rillington Place*

Abortion is perhaps the most divisive of public issues, with most activists divided into two camps, pro-life and pro-choice, which view their opponents with derision and hostility. Some religions have a strong moral prohibition concerning the procedure. Much of the country, however, is in between, usually favoring abortion but desiring that it be subject to limitations such as parental consent for minors. This category also includes the topic of teenage pregnancy. The U.S. Supreme Court decision in the case of *Roe vs. Wade* is the focal point of many abortion films, comparing the situation before and after this landmark decision. The motion picture industry, influenced by the production code, avoided abortion in their storylines prior to *Detective Story* (1951), the first major production to include the issue. The topic slowly began to appear in more films, particularly after *The Cardinal* (1963). This film by Otto Preminger includes a controversial scene in which a young priest (Tom Tryon) refuses to sanction an emergency abortion to save the life of his sister (Carol Lynley), and she dies in the hospital's delivery room. Other films to confront the issue include *The Interns* (1962), *To Find a Man* (1972), and *Cider House Rules* (1999).

Addiction

Chicago Calling ★ *Dolores Claiborne* ★ *The Lady Gambles** ★ *Lenny* ★ *Lost Weekend** ★ *The Man With the Golden Arm** ★ *Mask* ★ *Monkey on My Back** ★ *My Name Is Bill W.** ★ *Reversal of Fortune* ★ *Sixth and Main*

There are three basic categories of addiction films, those dealing with alcohol, drugs, and gambling. Other conditions, such as eating and obsessive/compulsive disorders, are classified under Disabilities. From the earliest days of cinema, alcoholism was treated either in a light-hearted fashion, such as Chaplin's unforgettable drunk in *One AM* (1916) or in a melodramatic style, such as D. W. Griffith's *A Drunkard's Reformation* (1908) or his final film *The Struggle* (1931). Morality plays, such as the Victorian melodrama *The Drunkard*, was satirized by W. C. Fields in *The Old-Fashioned Way* (1934) and by Buster Keaton in *The Villain Still Pursued Her* (1940). A few performers, such as Arthur Houseman, specialized in playing screen drunks. A few serious portrayals occasionally filtered through, such as Fredric March in *A Star Is Born* (1937), Thomas Mitchell in *Stagecoach* (1939), and some early film noirs, but it wasn't until *The Lost Weekend* (1945) that the issue was studied in depth. Other films followed, including *Smash-Up* (1947), *Blind Spot* (1947), *The Bottom of the Bottle* (1956), and *The Days of Wine and Roses* (1962). Nevertheless, the humorous tradition also continued, as demonstrated by Jimmy Stewart in *Harvey* (1950), Jackie Gleason in *Papa's Delicate Condition* (1963), and Dudley Moore in *Arthur* (1981).

Drug addiction appeared sporadically in silent films, such as *Cocaine Traffic* (1914), *Human Wreckage* (1923), and the German sensation, *Opium* (1918). When the production code by the Hays Office became dominant, the topic of drug addiction all but vanished from mainstream films with a few exceptions like *Dragonwyck* (1946). On the other hand, low-budget exploitation films highlighted the topic in *Narcotic* (1933), *Reefer Madness* (1936), *The Devil's Harvest* (1941), and many others, frequently in a highly exaggerated style. Film noir began to tackle the issue in pictures such as *Port of New York* (1949) and *Johnny Stool Pigeon* (1949). News about celebrities including Bela Lugosi and boxer Barney Ross kicking their medically incurred addictions led to greater screen interest. The breakthrough film was Otto Preminger's *The Man With the Golden Arm* (1956). A number of major productions followed, including *A Hatful of Rain* (1957), *Synanon* (1965), and *Panic in Needle Park* (1971). Although many films used the topic as "window dressing" or "hip" comedies (Cheech and Chong, etc.), the number of films that critically dealt with the issue continued to be impressive.

Gambling as an addiction was first thoroughly addressed in *The Lady Gambles* (1949), but other films maintained the effort, including *The Great Sinner* (1949), inspired by the great Russian writer Fyodor Dostoevsky, *California Split* (1974), and *House of Games* (1987).

Aging

Dolores Claiborne ★ *Driving Miss Daisy** ★ *Iris** ★ *Right of Way* ★ *A Small Killing** ★ *Soylent Green** ★ *The Straight Story** ★ *Whales of August**

Films highlighting the problems of the elderly have been relatively few, largely for commercial reasons. The primary motivation for this to change was the fact that many popular screen performers, such as Katharine Hepburn, Henry Fonda, James Stewart, Bette Davis, Hume Cronin, and Jessica Tandy, remained active as they got older. A number of actors and actresses were noted for their performances during the extended twilight of their careers, including George Burns (1886-1986), Edward Everett Horton (1885-1970), Sam Jaffe (1891-1984), A. E. Mathews (1869-1960), Adeline de Walt Reynolds (1862-1961), Ernest Thesiger (1879-1961), Estelle Winwood (1882-1984), and Ian Wolfe (1896-1992).

Stories were specifically adapted for these seasoned veterans. One of the earlier films to tackle the issue was *Make Way for Tomorrow* (1937), an unusual story focusing on an elderly couple cast aside by their ungrateful grown children. Other significant films include *I Never Sang for My Father* (1970), *Boardwalk* (1979), *On Golden Pond* (1981), and, in a lighter vein, *Going in Style* (1979) and *Cocoon* (1985). One of the most controversial films on the topic is the black comedy *Grace Quigley* (1985), in which a woman (Katharine Hepburn), tired of the tribulations of being old, hires a hit man to dispose of herself and her elderly friends.

AIDS

And the Band Played On* ★ *An Early Frost** ★ *Philadelphia** ★ *Rock Hudson** ★ *Walking on Water**

AIDS is provided its individual category because the disease is a recent phenomenon that has impacted on modern society during the last twenty years. In this case, motion pictures have provided a valuable service in promoting a considerable number of films that have given the general public accurate information about the nature of AIDS, its effects, and how it is spread. In a survey of Americans in the late 1990s, over one third of people responding cited motion pictures as their primary source of information about AIDS, a remarkable statistic. Films have been credited with helping the public avoid hysteria and disregard the myths about AIDS that were commonplace in the late 1980s. The first films dealing with the topic were *An Early Frost* (1985) and *Parting Glances* (1986). Additional representative titles are *Longtime Companion* (1990), *The Living End* (1992), and, most prominently, the Academy Award–winning *Philadelphia* (1993). Most of these efforts have concentrated on homosexuals who have been affected by AIDS, but several films such as *The Ryan White Story* (1989) and the documentary *Common Threads: Stories from the Quilt* (1989), have included other victims such as hemophiliacs, stressing the fact that AIDS is not just of concern to the gay community.

Capital Punishment

Cell 2455 Death Row* ★ *Compulsion** ★ *Dead Man Walking** ★ *I Want To Live!** ★ *In Cold Blood** ★ *Ten Rillington Place**

The death penalty has been a frequent plot device in countless films, particularly detective stories. A typical example is *Charlie Chan in London* (1934), in which the famous Chinese inspector (Warner Oland) receives a last-minute appeal from a lawyer (Ray Milland) and his fiancee (Drue Leyton) to save her brother, Paul Gray (Douglas Walton), who is scheduled to be executed in three days for the murder of Captain Hamilton. Since all appeals have been exhausted, only Chan's expertise as a detective can save him. He visits the scene of the crime, the estate of Geoffrey Raymond (Alan Mowbray), Gray's employer. Hamilton, who was an inventor, was murdered in the stable, and the groom, who resides in a room in the stable, apparently commits suicide after being questioned by Chan. Working with the local police, Chan proves the groom was murdered, because the real killer of Hamilton was afraid the groom would reveal too much to Chan. With only a few hours before the execution, Chan sets a trap using himself as bait, by claiming that he located the plans for Hamilton's latest invention, an aircraft motor silencer. Geoffrey Raymond is caught trying to kill Chan, who exposes him as a foreign agent. Gray is saved moments before his execution. The basic outline of *Charlie Chan in London* has been repeated, with numerous variations, in dozens of films. In one of the most clever, *Daybreak* (1948), the hangman himself stops the execution with an unexpected confession.

Besides mysteries, the death penalty is a frequent component in prison films such as *The Criminal Code* (1930), *Two Seconds* (1932), *The Last Mile* (1932), *Front Page Woman* (1935), *We Who Are About to Die* (1936), and *Angels With Dirty Faces* (1938), in which James Cagney pretends to turn chicken on the way to his execution to discourage youths who idolize him from following his criminal path. Horror/fantasy films have depicted capital punishment in pictures such as *The Green Mile* (1999), *The Seventh Sign* (1988), and *The Walking Dead* (1936), in which the wrongly executed Boris Karloff is brought back to life and hunts down the actual killers. Film noir also focused on capital punishment in efforts like *Nora Prentiss* (1947), *Black Tuesday*

(1955), and *Decoy* (1947), in which the prison doctor (Herbert Rudley) is bribed to fake the execution of a mob boss (Robert Armstrong). Other unusual pictures include *The Verdict* (1946), in which police inspector Sydney Greenstreet loses his job for having arrested an innocent man who was executed, *Beyond a Reasonable Doubt* (1956), in which reporter Dana Andrews frames himself for murder to write a journalistic scoop against capital punishment, *One on Top of the Other* (1971), with the closing scene shot in the actual gas chamber at Alcatraz, and *The Player* (1992), a black comedy in which a screenwriter fights to prevent his script against capital punishment from being watered down. The only drawback is that not all these efforts actually explore the reasoning behind capital punishment. Unlike other issues studied in this book, the most compelling arguments against the death penalty were made in France over two centuries earlier in a speech by revolutionary leader Maximilien Robespierre before the Constituent Assembly in May 1791. His motion to outlaw capital punishment, however, was defeated, and after the execution of King Louis XVI in January 1792, Robespierre again made a plea to outlaw the death penalty. Noted lawyer Clarence Darrow studied the French leader's logic and used it in his famous courtroom statements. In *Compulsion*, Orson Welles also used these ideas in perhaps one of the greatest courtroom speeches ever delivered in a motion picture. The most recent film to seriously examine capital punishment is *The Life of David Gale* (2003), the film Kevin Spacey was making when he made his comment cited at the beginning of the introduction.

Censorship

Cradle Will Rock * ★ *Good Morning, Vietnam* * ★ *Lenny* * ★
Pump Up the Volume * ★ *Soylent Green* ★ *Storm Center* *

Censorship has been a rather difficult topic for films to depict, except in a handful of dramas about the newspaper industry such as *Park Row* (1952) or *−30−* (1959). The attempt to censor the teaching of evolution by the state of Tennessee was covered in *Inherit the Wind* (1960), a thinly veiled drama based on the famous Scopes monkey trial of 1925 featuring William Jennings Bryan and Clarence Darrow. The Motion Picture Producers and Distributors of America (commonly called the Hays Office after its first president, Will H. Hays the former Postmaster General) censored films. The office, founded in 1922 to avoid possible government control of film content, was initially a form of voluntary self-regulation. The first production code, issued in 1930, was largely the work of Martin Quigley and Reverend Daniel A. Lord. When Hays appointed Joseph Breen to run the code enforcement division in 1934, the code began to be strictly enforced. The code required each studio picture to obtain a certificate of approval from the office or else pay a fine of $25,000. Joseph Breen succeeded Hays as president in the mid-1940s, and he maintained tight control until the late 1950s, when the code was gradually relaxed and revised. Topics such as homosexuality, drug addiction, prostitution, and censorship itself were all but forbidden by the code enforcement office, which submitted a list of "suggestions" for each film they reviewed before granting a certificate. Since many minor details were objected to, directors began to insert material they knew would be censored in order to slip through other material. Charlie Chaplin, in particular, was often able to outsmart the censors; he was able to include an obscene gesture in *City Lights* (1931) and the most provocative of "forbidden words," camouflaged with double talk, in *The Great Dictator* (1940). The code enforcement office later retaliated by being extreme in their censorship of *Monsieur Verdoux* (1947). Although there is ample material for films about this area of censorship, the film industry has by and large avoided it.

Another form of censorship, blacklisting during the early 1950s, was explored in a number of productions, particularly in *The Front* (1976). Many individuals who were actually blacklisted appeared in this social issues comedy. After 1968, the motion picture code was dropped, replaced by the rating system issued by the reorganized Motion Picture Association of America (MPAA). The Catholic Legion of Decency, an independent rating system, was established in 1934. Other countries developed their own rating systems, the earliest being the British Board of Film Censors, founded in 1912, which classified motion pictures.

Child Abuse/Spouse Abuse

The Burning Bed ★ *Dangerous Child** ★ *Dolores Claiborne* ★ *Domestic Disturbance* ★ *Good Will Hunting* ★ *Indictment** ★ *Sleeping With the Enemy** ★ *Storm Warning* ★ *Sybil** ★ *Ultimate Betrayal** ★ *The Unspoken Truth* ★ *The War of the Roses* ★ *Woman on the Beach*

Both marital abuse and child abuse have been regularly portrayed in films, although usually in a subsidiary role. One of the earliest depictions was *The White Caps* (1906), in which a wife-beater was subjected to intimidation by a group of hooded social avengers. Cecil B. DeMille tackled the subject in *The Golden Chance* (1915), in which a society couple shelter a wife from her abusive husband. The most heinous scene of child abuse was a German soldier murdering a baby in D. W. Griffith's film *Hearts of the World* (1918). Erich von Stroheim tackled the issues in both *Foolish Wives* (1922) and *Greed* (1925), the latter with its unforgettable scene in which McTeague (Gibson Gowland) assaults his wife (Zasu Pitts). Spouse abuse remained a common theme portrayed in films throughout the sound era in theatrical and television films, the most publicized of all being *The Burning Bed* (1984).

Mary Pickford's *Sparrows* (1926) presented a harrowing portrait of abused and exploited children. In later films, the theme of child abuse has been explored in many films in different genres, including *Chinatown* (1974), *Who'll Save Our Children?* (1978), *Missing Children: A Mother's Story* (1982), *Adam: His Song Continues* (1986), *The Children of Times Square* (1986), *Flowers in the Attic* (1987), the remake of *The Haunting* (1999), and *Mystic River* (2003).

Disabilities

As Good As It Gets ★ *Kate's Secret** ★ *The Man Who Played God** ★ *Mask** ★ *The Men** ★ *No Way Out* ★ *Sign of the Ram* ★ *Sixth and Main* ★ *Suspect* ★ *Whales of August* ★ *Whose Life Is It Anyway?* ★ *Woman on the Beach**

Disabilities have been depicted frequently in motion pictures since the silent era. Lon Chaney, for example, specialized in playing physically challenged individuals—blind, crippled, or lacking limbs—who still were strong, even dominant characters. Among the specific disabilities examined in distinguished films are: blindness in *The Light that Failed* (1939), *On Dangerous Ground* (1951), and *A Patch of Blue* (1965); deafness in *Johnny Belinda* (1948), *The Heart Is a Lonely Hunter* (1968), and *Children of a Lesser God* (1986); mental retardation in *Charly* (1968), *Bill* (1981), and *Sling Blade* (1996); mental illness in *The Snake Pit* (1948), *Tender Is the Night* (1962), and *One Flew Over the Cuckoo's Nest* (1975); and individuals confined to a wheelchair in the *Dr. Kildare* film series, *My Left Foot* (1989), and the remake of *Rear Window* (1998) in which quadriplegic Christopher Reeve played the lead. Perhaps the most renowned film dealing with disabilities is *The Miracle Worker* (1962), based on the early years of Helen Keller. Her later years are featured in *Helen Keller, The Miracle Continues* (1984).

Divorce

The Burning Bed ★ *Dangerous Child* ★ *Divorce His/Divorce Hers** ★ *The Divorcee** ★ *Domestic Disturbance** ★ *Fourteen Hours* ★ *The Unfaithful** ★ *The War of the Roses**

According to the late film critic Gene Siskel, divorce has been reflected in films almost like a mirror to society itself. The breakup and dissolution of marriages has figured prominently and regularly in motion pictures beginning with such efforts as *Old Wives for New* (1918), *Don't Change Your Husband* (1918), and *Why Change Your Wife?* (1920). The topic received both serious and light-hearted treatments through the years, some of the most interesting being *A Bill of Divorcement* (1932 & remake 1940), *Dodsworth* (1936), *The Divorce of Lady X* (1938), *Alimony* (1949), *The Marrying Kind* (1952), *The Bigamist* (1953), *The Parent Trap* (1961), *Divorce American Style* (1968), *The Marriage of a Young Stockbroker* (1971), *Breaking Up Is Hard To Do* (1979), *Divorce Wars* (1982), *Mrs. Doubtfire* (1993), and *The First Wives' Club* (1996).

Education/Literacy

Conrack* ★ *Driving Miss Daisy* ★ *Good Will Hunting** ★ *Lean on Me** ★ *The Pride of Jesse Hallam** ★ *Pump Up the Volume* ★ *Stand and Deliver** ★ *Storm Center*

Education has been a popular theme in many films. Traditionally, the plot showcases the efforts of an outstanding teacher, such as Robert Donat in *Goodbye Mr. Chips* (1939), Bette Davis in *The Corn Is Green* (1945), Ingrid Bergman in *The Bells of St. Mary's* (1945), Jennifer Jones in *Good Morning Miss Dove* (1955), Sidney Poitier in *To Sir With Love* (1967), Richard Dreyfuss in *Mr. Holland's Opus* (1995), and Kevin Kline in *The Emperor's Club* (2002). Then there are the more acerbic teachers such as John Houseman in *The Paper Chase* (1973) or Richard Burton in *Absolution* (1981). Other teachers may be sinister like Robert Preston in *Child's Play* (1972), troubled like Laurence Olivier in *Term of Trial* (1962), or unbalanced like James Mason in *Bigger than Life* (1956). Conversely, teaching literacy is depicted infrequently, usually in telefilms such as *The Pride of Jesse Hallam*.

End-of-Life Issues

Dolores Claiborne ★ *Gods and Monsters* ★ *Iris* ★ *Mask* ★ *Night Unto Night** ★ *Reversal of Fortune** ★ *Right of Way** ★ *Walking on Water** ★ *Whales of August* ★ *Whose Life Is It Anyway?**

End-of-life issues take two basic forms: euthanasia and the right to die with dignity. It has been suspected that some members of the medical profession have been quietly performing euthanasia for centuries, although this topic has seldom surfaced in films with a very few exceptions including: *Dr. Cook's Garden* (1971) and *Murder or Mercy* (1974). In *An Act of Murder* (1948), a judge, played by Fredric March, kills his wife to relieve her suffering during her final illness. The right to die with dignity first gained attention as a legal issue in 1975. Karen Ann Quinlan, a New Jersey teenager, lapsed into a coma after taking some tranquilizers and alcohol at a party. When informed that recovery was impossible, her parents sued for their daughter to be taken off her respirator so that she could die with dignity. The case aroused great public interest, and the Quinlans were successful in their case. Ironically, Quinlan continued to breathe on her own and lived for another ten years. In 1977, NBC produced a telefilm, *In the Matter of Karen Ann Quinlan*, with Brian Keith and Piper Laurie as the parents. Several years later, CBS ran another film, *The Miracle of Kathy Miller* (1982), based on a true 1977 event. In this case, Miller was a teenager who was struck down by a car and who lapsed into a coma. After ten weeks, her parents were advised that she had suffered massive brain damage and would remain in a vegetative state. In this case, however, she later awoke from the coma and recovered, becoming an athlete.

These two telefilms were considered by some critics to be polar opposites on the issue. In an unusual move, both films were withheld from syndication after their initial broadcast.

During the past twenty-five years, the concept of living wills—in which individuals would write down the treatment they desired in case they became totally incapacitated—became more prevalent. When former president Richard Nixon lapsed into a coma, his living will was invoked for minimum treatment. Controversy has also arisen about doctor-assisted suicide for individuals facing terminal illness, but the motion picture industry has dealt with this issue only sporadically, perhaps most prominently in *Whose Life Is It Anyway?*

Environmental Issues

A Civil Action ★ *Environment* ★ *Green Card* ★ *No Blade of Grass* ★ *Prophecy* ★ *Soylent Green**

The film industry often treats environmental concerns in dramatic fashion by projecting into the future the consequences of the unchecked misuse of nature. This is the working method of such science fiction and disaster films as *No Blade of Grass* (1970), *Doomwatch* (1972), *Silent Running* (1972), *Quiet Earth* (1985), *Waterworld* (1995), and *The Day After Tomorrow* (2004). For an in-depth study, see my book *A Guide to Apocalyptic Cinema* (Greenwood Press, 2001).

Hate Groups

American History X ★ *Betrayed** ★ *Black Legion** ★ *Focus* ★ *The Intruder* ★ *No Way Out* ★ *Storm Warning** ★ *Trial**

It is an unfortunate fact that the first great motion picture, *Birth of a Nation* (1915), is tarnished not only by racism, but also by a heroic depiction of one of history's most infamous hate groups, the Ku Klux Klan (KKK). Even more unfortunate, the film is believed to have revitalized the KKK, which had previously been moribund. More accurate portrayals of the Klan were given in films such as *Black Legion* (1936), *The Legion of Terror* (1937), and *The Burning Cross* (1947). One sequence of *The Cardinal* (1963) was set in the South where a Vatican envoy was flogged by the Klan. More recent efforts include *The Klansman* (1974), *Attack on Terror: The FBI vs. the Ku Klux Klan* (1975), and *Cross of Fire* (1989). The KKK has been satirized in other films, never more effectively than in *O Brother, Where Art Thou?* (2000).

Other hate groups are also frequently depicted on screen. The Nazi reign of terror in Europe has been the subject of hundreds of films. The Nazi movement in America has also been depicted in *Confessions of a Nazi Spy* (1939), *Strange Holiday* (1942), *They Came to Blow Up America* (1943), *Pressure Point* (1962), and *Roots: The Next Generation* (1979), in which Marlon Brando played the American Nazi George Lincoln Rockwell. The subversive wing of the Communist movement has been depicted in *The Iron Curtain* (1948), *My Son John* (1952), and *Walk East on Beacon* (1953). Islamic radical groups have been portrayed in *21 Hours in Munich* (1976), *Voyage of Terror, the Achille Lauro Affair* (1990), *Executive Decision* (1996), and *The Siege* (1998). Undoubtedly, since the events of September 11, 2001, this group will be closely examined in future films.

Homelessness/Poverty

The Burning Bed ★ *Chicago Calling* ★ *Conrack* ★ *Cradle Will Rock* ★ *The Glass Wall* ★ *Good Will Hunting* ★ *The Grapes of Wrath** ★ *Modern Times** ★ *Sixth and Main** ★ *A Small Killing* ★ *Stone Pillow** ★ *The Suicide's Wife* ★ *Suspect**

Poverty, the underprivileged, and the problems of the lower classes including homelessness have been included in many films in cinema history, although one could justly claim that ninety-five percent of screenplay treatments completely ignore the poor. In silent films, Charlie Chaplin's tramp persona naturally led him to depict the downtrodden in a daily struggle to survive, as opposed to Harold Lloyd and Buster Keaton whose screen images usually depicted ambitious go-getters bound for success. Likewise, Mary Pickford and Lillian Gish often portrayed impoverished heroines facing homelessness, Pickford in *Amarilly of Clothesline Alley* (1919) and *Tess of the Storm Country* (1922), and *Way Down East* (1920) and *The Wind* (1928) for Gish. Another controversial film about poverty was *The Red Kimono* (1925). In the 1930s, the effects of the Depression were portrayed in *I Was a Fugitive from a Chain Gang* (1932), *Hard to Handle* (1933), *Wild Boys of the Road* (1933), *One More Spring* (1935), and *One Third of a Nation* (1938). Alternatively, poverty was depicted in a light-hearted fashion in other pictures including *Hallelujah I'm a Bum* (1933) and *Mrs. Wiggs of the Cabbage Patch* (1934). Several landmark films appeared in the 1940s inspired in part by *The Grapes of Wrath*; these include *Tobacco Road* (1941) and *Sullivan's Travels* (1941). Interest in poverty as subject matter declined somewhat in the 1950s, but was later revived, particularly in social issue telefilms along the lines of *The Children Nobody Wanted* (1981), *Dreams Don't Die* (1982), *Samaritan: The Mitch Snyder Story* (1986), and *Home Sweet Homeless* (1988).

Homosexuality

And the Band Played On ★ *As Good As It Gets** ★ *Cruising** ★ *Cradle Will Rock* ★ *An Early Frost* ★ *Gods and Monsters** ★ *Kissing Jessica Stein** ★ *Philadelphia* ★ *Pump Up the Volume* ★ *Walking on Water*

It took a long time for homosexuality to be portrayed realistically on screen. The production code strictly banned the topic from consideration or even from any reference being made to it. The same was largely true on the world scene, with one notable exception, *Different from the Others* (1919) released in Germany shortly after World War I. This film, directed by Richard Oswald and starring Conrad Veidt, was a remarkably frank and sympathetic treatment of homosexuality, showing how they are persecuted by the laws of the state and how they often became the target of blackmailers. *Different from the Others* was later censored dramatically, and today only a pared-down thirty-five-minute version, less than half the original length, exists. An early German sound film, *Mädchen In Uniform* (1931), was plainly suggestive of lesbianism at a girls' school, and on release, this film was banned from public performance in New York and other states with their own censorship boards. So for many years, the only possible references to homosexuality were veiled, such as the lesbian undertones in *Dracula's Daughter* (1936). But when Lillian Hellman's play *The Children's Hour* was brought to the screen that same year, under the title *These Three*, all the lesbian references had been eliminated. With few exceptions, such as *Well of Loneliness* (1934), exploitation films generally stayed clear of homosexual themes as well. In 1948, Alfred Hitchcock came close to breaking the taboo with *Rope*, a thriller loosely inspired by the Leopold and Loeb case (see the entry *Compulsion*). The characters played by Farley Granger and John Dall are homosexuals, but their relationship is never spelled out.

Gradually, through the 1950s, filmmakers became more open about the subject. Among the first films to explore the topic more fully were *The Trials of Oscar Wilde* (1960), *The Victim* (1962), *A View from the Bridge* (1962), and *Advise and Consent* (1962). *The Children's Hour* (1961) was refilmed with the lesbian inferences restored, and the topic was more openly explored in *The Killing of Sister George* (1968) and *Personal Best* (1982). Other notable films include the controversial *Staircase* (1969) (which starred Richard Burton and Rex Harrison as lovers), *The Boys in the Band* (1970), *A Different Story* (1978), and *Death Trap* (1982). By the 1980s, gay and lesbian films received wide attention, appealing to both general as well as gay audiences. One memorable telefilm was *Welcome Home Bobby* (1986), which concerned a sexually ambivalent teenager (Timothy William) and his father (Tony LoBianco), who could not accept his homosexuality. The issue of AIDS impacted many stories from the late 1980s onward.

Immigration

America America ★ *American History X* ★ *Black Legion* ★ *Border Incident* ★ *The Glass Wall* ★ *Green Card* ★ *Green Dragon* ★ *The Perez Family* ★ *Trial* ★ *West Side Story*

Stories about immigrants and immigration have surfaced periodically in film. One of the earliest pictures was *The Italian* (1915), set among the immigrant community in lower Manhattan. Chaplin made *The Immigrant* in 1917, which includes the ironical scene of the newcomers to America being roped off like cattle moments after they catch sight of the Statue of Liberty. The difficulties faced by immigrants became a popular theme during the 1920s as well, often highlighting Spanish, Italian, Jewish, and Irish immigrants; a typical example is *Mother Machree* (1928). Lon Chaney specialized in playing Asians in *Shadows* (1922) and other pictures. During the sound era, the emphasis shifted to immigrants as background characters or part of a subplot, with a few exceptions such as *Romance in Manhattan* (1934) and *Hold Back the Dawn* (1941). The mass immigration of war refugees became a standard theme in many pictures, including *The Mortal Storm* (1940), *The Glass Wall* (1953), and *Dondi* (1961). By the 1960s, stories about immigrants became more frequently portrayed in social terms, with a few exceptional variations like the musical *Flower Drum Song* (1961) or the animated feature *An American Tail* (1986), in which a family of mice emigrate from Russia. In addition, major films such as the *Godfather* series and the television miniseries *Ellis Island* also focused on the immigrant experience.

Racism/Civil Rights

American History X ★ *Betrayed* ★ *Black Like Me** ★ *Conrack* ★ *Driving Miss Daisy* ★ *Focus** ★ *Guess Who's Coming to Dinner?** ★ *The Intruder** ★ *Judge Horton and the Scottsboro Boys** ★ *Lean on Me* ★ *No Way Out** ★ *Separate but Equal** ★ *Stand and Deliver* ★ *Storm Warning* ★ *Trial*

Racism has probably received more screen treatments than any other specific social issue. *Birth of a Nation* (1915), perhaps the first great film, has remained controversial for its racist portrayal of blacks, particularly in the scenes of blacks in authority in the legislature or carrying out voting abuses. The scene in which teenage Miriam Cooper falls to her death to avoid a black rapist has been cited for provoking racial hatred. Largely ignored by critics, the first all-black film, *Darktown Jubilee*, appeared simultaneously with *Birth of a Nation*. In 1920, black filmmaker Oscar Micheaux made *Symbol of the Unconquered* (1920) about the KKK, which was considered to be a rebuttal to the racism of *Birth of a Nation*. Motion pictures dealing with civil rights and prejudice against Black Americans include *They Won't Forget* (1937), *Lost Boundaries* (1948), *Intruder in the Dust* (1949), *Home of the Brave* (1949), *The Well* (1951), *To Kill a Mockingbird* (1962), *In the Heat of the Night* (1967), *Hurry Sundown* (1967), *Watermelon Man* (1970), and *The Autobiography of Miss Jane Pittman* (1974). *Roots* (1977) and *Roots: The Next Generation* (1979) were two of the most influential television miniseries of all time.

Anti-Semitism has also been a featured theme in many motion pictures including *Crossfire* (1947), *Gentleman's Agreement* (1947), *The Pawnbroker* (1965), and *Skokie* (1981). The persecution of Jews by Adolf Hitler during the

Nazi regime in Europe has been explored as well in numerous films and television miniseries such as *The Holocaust* (1978), *The Winds of War* (1983), and its sequel *War and Remembrance* (1988). Racism against Asians has been examined as far back as *Broken Blossoms* (1919), as well as in later films including *The Hatchet Man* (1932) and *The Crimson Kimono* (1960). In some ways, Asians may have been the victims of greater screen prejudice than were blacks, considering the "Yellow Peril" films of the 1930s as well as *Samurai* (1945), a war propaganda film that unfairly targeted Japanese Americans. This was balanced, however, by the positive depiction of Chinese Americans in the Charlie Chan films (1931–1949), one of film history's most popular series. Reverse discrimination was portrayed in *Bridge to the Sun* (1961), in which the American wife of a Japanese diplomat was the target of racist hostility in Japan. American Indians have been depicted in a hostile fashion in countless westerns. Only a handful of films, such as *Devil's Doorway* (1950), *Seminole* (1953), *The Outsider* (1961), and *Cheyenne Autumn* (1964), focused on the racism faced by the Indians. A host of other motion pictures covered injustice and civil rights abuses encountered by different ethnic groups, the Irish, Hispanics, Greeks, Italians, Eastern Europeans, Russians, Arabs, Gypsies, Polynesians, Filipinos, and Asiatic Indians.

Suicide/Depression

Chicago Calling* ★ *Dolores Claiborne* ★ *An Early Frost* ★ *Fourteen Hours** ★ *Gods and Monsters* ★ *Green Dragon* ★ *The Lady Gambles* ★ *Lost Weekend* ★ *The Man Who Played God* ★ *Night Unto Night* ★ *Pump Up the Volume* ★ *Reversal of Fortune* ★ *Right of Way* ★ *Roe vs. Wade* ★ *Sign of the Ram** ★ *Sixth and Main* ★ *Slender Thread** ★ *Soylent Green* ★ *The Suicide's Wife** ★ *Suspect* ★ *Sybil* ★ *The Unspoken Truth* ★ *Whose Life Is It Anyway?* ★ *Woman on the Beach*

Suicide and attempted suicide has been a key ingredient in theatrical dramas for centuries. It is no accident that the most famous Shakespeare soliloquy, "To be or not to be" from *Hamlet*, deals with suicide and that it has been recited on the screen dozens of times, ranging from Shakespearean productions by Kenneth Branagh, Richard Burton, Mel Gibson, Ethan Hawke, Laurence Olivier, Nicol Williamson, and many others, to film comedies by Charlie Chaplin in *A King in New York* (1957), Clifton Webb in *Dreamboat* (1952), and, perhaps most famously, Jack Benny in *To Be or Not To Be* (1942). Suicide is often a common feature in films in spite of the production code, which did not allow suicide to be shown directly on camera. Directors simply found ways around this prohibition. In melodramas, the suicide route often chosen by villains when their plans failed was only shown in part, such as Basil Rathbone, who takes a swan dive off a high-rise building in *The Mad Doctor* (1941); Leo G. Carroll in *Spellbound* (1944), who turned the gun he was holding on Ingrid Bergman around to shoot himself; or Richard Basehart who leapt from a helicopter at the climax of *The Satan Bug* (1965). Suicide has been played for laughs, such as Harold Lloyd in *Never Weaken* (1921), Buster Keaton in *Hard Luck* (1921), Oliver Hardy in *The Flying Deuces* (1939), and Jack Lemmon in *Buddy Buddy* (1981). In fantasy pictures, suicide forms the basis for a number of films, either with an uplifting message as in *Between Two Worlds* (1944) and *It's a Wonderful Life* (1946), or in a grittier tone in *Orpheus* (1949) or *What Dreams May Come* (1998). At times, suicide is presented in a heroic light, such as films where characters sacrifice themselves to save others. In film noir, suicide was frequently a key component of many story lines, either when a murder is disguised as a suicide as in *A Kiss Before Dying* (1956), or when a villain tries to drive another character to suicide as in *Fear in the Night* (1947) or *Sleep My Love* (1948). Somewhat rarer, a few noirs portray a character so depressed that he decides to kill himself, such as Jack Palance in *The Big Knife* (1955). Despite the genre, suicide or attempted suicide is often accompanied by a degree of critical commentary, either by the characters in the film or by the filmmaker through the method of presentation. Depression, hopelessness, and despair are usually presented as the prime factors leading to suicide. Other causes depicted in films include serious illness and pain, guilt and remorse, or in rare cases, extreme ennui. Finally, juvenile suicide is generally treated with sensitivity, representing the tragic cases, as in *Silence of the Heart* (1984), *Surviving* (1985), and *Dead Poets Society* (1989).

Violence/Gangs

American History X ★ *Colors** ★ *Good Will Hunting* ★ *Key Witness** ★ *Mad at the World** ★ *West Side Story**

Juvenile gang violence was rarely portrayed in silent movies. Many youth gangs were benign, such as the long-running (1925–1944) *Our Gang* series produced by Hal Roach. A Broadway play about a gang of slum toughs, *Dead End*, was brought to the screen in 1938. The youthful actors, including fourteen-year-old Bobby Jordan, sixteen-year-old Huntz Hall, seventeen-year-old Billy Halop, and twenty-one-year-old Leo Gorcey, became very popular. Similar films about troubled youths, such as *Boys Town* (1938) and *Boy Slaves* (1939), were also successful. Additional films were made with the Dead End Kids, including *Crime School* (1938) and *They Made Me a Criminal* (1939), but eventually the social conscious aspects of the concept were dropped as the gang became played for laughs. The gang was later transformed into the East Side Gang and finally the Bowery Boys. By the time the series petered out twenty years after it began, they had completed an amazing eighty-six feature films and three serials. During the same period, other low-budget films began to concentrate on problem teenagers with *Are These Our Children?* (1943), *I Accuse My Parents* (1944), and *City Across the River* (1949), the latter based on

Irving Shulman's best-selling novel, *The Amboy Dukes*, about a gang in the slums of Brooklyn. By the mid-1950s, a virtual tidal wave of films about youth violence appeared, some exploitive but others providing a serious examination of the issue. Marlon Brando caused a sensation as the head of a motorcycle gang in *The Wild One* (1953), as did James Dean as a troubled youth in *Rebel Without a Cause* (1955). Other well-known films from this era include *Blackboard Jungle* (1955), *The Delinquents* (1957), *High School Hellcats* (1958), *The Rebel Set* (1959), and *The Sadist* (1963).

In the later 1960s, many films concentrated on the protest movements; these include *Riot on Sunset Strip* (1967) and the semidocumentary *The Hippie Revolt* (1968). In 1969, *Easy Rider* launched a new era of youth films, as did the nostalgic *American Graffiti* (1973). The significance of gang violence began to reassert itself in the following decades, with the racial and ethnic background of urban gangs given a fresh emphasis.

Women's Rights

The Burning Bed ★ *Dolores Claiborne** ★ *Domestic Disturbance* ★ *Kate's Secret* ★ *Roe vs. Wade* ★ *Sleeping With the Enemy* ★ *The Unspoken Truth** ★ *When Innocence Is Lost**

Although somewhat of a catch phrase, the term "women's rights" combines a divergent grouping of issues that are relevant to women. They include suffrage, equal opportunity in education and employment, equal pay, and equal treatment under the law. Certain protections also need to be granted to women due to pregnancy and motherhood. Finally, women are more often the target of harassment, as well as sex crimes, so the legal framework regarding the prosecution of violators also falls under the classification of women's rights. Films depicting these social concerns can vary greatly from decade to decade. Earlier films were more concerned with gaining the right to vote and with women trailblazing in new endeavors. At the beginning of her career, Katharine Hepburn was often cast in strong roles as an independent and determined young woman; these films include *Christopher Strong* (1933) and *A Woman Rebels* (1936). Later she appeared in a remarkable series of films with Spencer Tracy, usually as a professional in direct competition with him. *Woman of the Year* (1942), *Adam's Rib* (1949), and *Desk Set* (1957) are three of these efforts. Other actresses who secured trailblazing roles for women include Joan Crawford, Bette Davis, and Olivia de Havilland.

It was not until the rise of the telefilm in the late 1970s and early 1980s, however, that women's rights emerged as a popular topic. In fact, the modest budget, time slots (seventy three minutes running time for a ninety-minute slot or ninety-six minutes for a two-hour slot), and topical immediacy seemed ideally suited for women's issues. These films also served as vehicles for many outstanding actresses. Some of these were *Women in Chains* (1972) with Ida Lupino, *I Want to Keep My Baby* (1976) with Mariel Hemingway, *Rape and Marriage* (1980) with Linda Hamilton, *The Women's Room* (1980) with Lee Remick, *The Face of Rage* (1983) with Dianne Wiest, *Victims for Victims* (1984) with Theresa Saldana, and *This Child Is Mine* (1985) with Lindsay Wagner. Cable networks geared toward women viewers, such as Lifetime, have also sponsored telefilms dealing with various women's issues.

In conclusion, I wish to thank my wife, Roberta, for her considerable input to this volume, viewing all the selections, reading the first draft, and making suggestions. Without her contributions, this volume would not have been possible.

America America
(1963)

Principal social theme: immigration

Warner Brothers. No MPAA rating. Featuring: Stathis Giallelis, Frank Wolff, Elena Karam, Lou Antonio, John Marley, Estelle Helmsley, Robert H. Harris, Gregory Rozakis, Salem Ludwig, Linda Marsh, Paul Mann, Joanna Frank, Harry Davis. Written by Elia Kazan. Cinematography by Haskell Wexler. Edited by Dede Allen. Music by Manos Hadjidakis. Produced by Charles H. Maguire. Directed by Elia Kazan. B&W. 168 minutes.

Overview

This epic film by legendary director Elia Kazan tells the story of his uncle's efforts to emigrate to America in the late nineteenth century. Filmed on location in Turkey, Greece, and the United States, this highly personal motion picture is one of the most dramatic immigration stories ever filmed. It received Academy Award nominations for Best Picture, Best Director, and Best Original Screenplay.

Synopsis

The film opens with narration by Elia Kazan, who calls himself "a Greek by blood, a Turk by birth, and an American because my uncle made a journey." His uncle's story is then presented on screen, beginning in 1896 when Kazan's Uncle Stavros, a restless young man tired of the Turkish oppression of the Greeks and Armenians, vows to make his way to America. When he is approached by a young Armenian, Hohannes, who is also trying to come to America, Stavros generously gives him his shoes. When Stavros's father decides that his family should move to Constantinople (Istanbul), he pools all his family's finest possessions and sends his son on the hazardous journey to the capital to scout it out for him. Another traveler, Abdul, a verbose Muslim beggar, joins Stavros on his trek, but little by little he steals his goods. When Stavros tries to escape from his clutches, Abdul goes to the police and claims Stavros stole all his possessions from him. The police take the goods for themselves. Abdul tracks down Stavros and demands the gold coins that he saw the boy swallow when the police arrested him. The beggar announces his plans to kill him after praying to Mecca, but instead Stavros kills Abdul while the Muslim prays.

Stavros continues to make his way to Istanbul, but by the time he arrives there, he is penniless. He goes to the carpet shop run by his father's cousin, who expects to save his business with the funds that Stavros had been carrying. When he finds that all his money was stolen, the merchant writes to the boy's father describing his son's failure. Stavros tries to restore the lost money by working as a laborer, but he is unable to save very much. Finally, Stavros is shot by soldiers on a raid looking for Armenian terrorists. Mistaken for dead, Stavros is loaded onto a cart filled with corpses. He topples off and makes his way back to the carpet shop. The merchant proposes a new plan for gaining money. He will dress Stavros in fine clothes and introduce him to the families of rich Greeks with plain daughters seeking husbands. Stavros undertakes the charade, and he even falls in love with Tomna, his betrothed. He is tempted by the soft life he could live, but he chooses to take his dowry money and book passage to America. He confesses his plans to Tomna, who is heartbroken yet grateful that Stavros has told her the truth. While on the ship, Stavros again meets Hohannes, who is ill with tuberculosis. Hohannes had gained passage with seven other young refugees from a New York businessman in exchange for two years of servitude as a bootblack. Stavros is seduced by the wife of Aratoon Kebabian, a wealthy Greek-American. When he learns of the affair, Kebabian plans to use his influence so that Stavros will be rejected by the American immigration officials and returned to Turkey. Stavros plans to jump ship and try to swim to shore. Hohannes, knowing he has only a short time to live, jumps instead and drowns. The businessman aids Stavros by allowing him to assume Hohannes' identity. The immigration officials give him a new name, Joe Arness, on his immigration papers. The officials are informed that it was Stavros who had been killed. Stavros works hard in New York, and eventually he earns enough money to bring all the members of his family to America.

Critique

America America is a powerful invocation of the promise of America to refugees around the world. The Ottoman Empire is portrayed as oppressive and brutal, with the oppression of the Armenians foreshadowing the even more terrible episodes of genocide to follow. The Muslim faith is not portrayed in a positive light, particularly in their callous persecution of the

Christian Armenians and Greeks. Islam is exemplified by Abdul, the crafty thief who continually quotes Mohammed while he robs Stavros. Finally, as Abdul plans to kill Stavros, he flamboyantly prepares for the event by elaborately bowing and praying in the direction of Mecca. With Abdul's death after their struggle, Stavros loses his innocence. He is no longer the smiling hopeful youth. For the rest of the film he frowns as he endures hardship and adversity to realize his dream of reaching America and bringing his family to this new land. His real crisis of confidence comes when he becomes Tomna's suitor in order to gain the dowry. In one act of humanity, he refuses the larger dowry offered, only accepting the minimum he needs to pay for his passage to America. In his relationship with Tomna, Stavros loses the sympathy of much of the audience, who feel that if he were patient he would have been able to emigrate later, with her. His final passage to the new world involves another sacrifice, the life of his friend Hohannes, who kills himself so Stavros can take his place. The first three-quarters of the film represent a graphic portrayal of the obstacles that may face immigrants wishing to come to America. The final hurdle involves immigration laws, but in this case, American officials eager to welcome the immigrants to America, apply the laws in a tolerant manner. Their recommendation to adopt an American-sounding name is not done sarcastically but with the sincere desire to help the newcomer's transition.

Many moments of *America America* are stunning and poetic, and the cinematography is tremendously effective. The other production values, the acting, and production design are also tremendously striking and even moving. *America America* depicts one breathtaking and true-life example that can serve as a metaphor for the immigration experience as a whole.

American History X
(1998)

Principal social themes: hate groups, violence/gangs, racism/civil rights, immigration

New Line Cinema. R rating. Featuring: Edward Norton, Edward Furlong, Avery Brooks, Stacy Keach, Beverly D'Angelo, Jennifer Lein, Fairuza Balk, Elliott Gould, William Russ, Joe Cortese, Ethan Suplee, Guy Tory, Giuseppe Andrews, Anne Lamblon, Alex Sol, Jim Norton, Paul LeMat; Written by David McKenna. Cinematography by Tony Kaye. Edited by Jerry Greenberg and Alan Heim.

Music by Anne Dudley. Produced by John Morrissey. Directed by Stuart Heisler. Color/B&W. 118 minutes.

Overview

American History X is one of the most intense cinematic examinations of hate movements, their operational methods, and basic influence. It also serves as an excellent study of the cycle of violence. Director Stuart Heisler and star Edward Norton had a falling out over the final cut, but the end product did not seem to suffer. Norton received critical acclaim for his leading role as Derek Vinyard, including an Academy Award nomination.

Synopsis

American History X has an unusual structure: The main plot is depicted in color, and events in the past are shown in black and white. Derek Vinyard, a neo-Nazi with a large swastika tattooed over his heart, is released from prison as the film opens. Derek has served three years for killing a black vandal who had broken into his car. His younger brother Danny (Edward Furlong) emulates him, adopting a skinhead mentality. He thinks nothing of confronting a group of black students in the school lavatory. When assigned to write a paper on a civil rights leader, Danny submits one about Adolf Hitler. His teacher turns to Dr. Sweeney (Avery Brooks), the principal, for help. Sweeney asks Danny to submit another report for their private seminar to be called "American History X." The topic is to be his brother, Derek. Unknown to Danny, Sweeney has been visiting Derek in prison. Under his guidance, Derek has abandoned his radical views and now rejects hate groups. When he is released from prison, Derek is greeted as a hero by other members of the hate group, including their remote charismatic leader, Cameron (Stacy Keach). In a private meeting, Derek rejects Cameron and his neo-Nazi philosophy. As he leaves, Derek is hooted down by the others. He then sits down with Danny to explain why he changed his views in prison. He noticed the skinhead clique in jail were into marketing drugs, and he realized they were merely self-serving phonies. After he was beaten and abused by this group, Derek kept to himself and was befriended by a black convict who saved him from being a target of the black gangs behind bars. Sweeney visited him regularly and helped him gain parole. Together, Derek and his brother remove the Nazi paraphernalia from their bedroom, including their collection of Hitler photographs and white power posters. Danny completes his paper for Sweeney, noting why Derek originally turned to hate groups and how he came to repudiate their message. When Danny returns to school to hand in his paper, he is shot to death in the lavatory by one of the black gang members he confronted at the start of the film. As the end credits roll,

Danny's voice is heard on the soundtrack reading the last paragraph of his paper, concluding with a quote by Abraham Lincoln.

Critique

American History X has a complex structure that unfolds on different levels with numerous flashbacks. First, there is the main plot, how Derek tries to help his brother from following his path with the skinheads. Second, the film is a case study of how hate groups operate and the similarity between both the white and black gangs. That is one reason why Sweeney, the black teacher, relates so closely to Derek; because he had been a black hatemonger in his youth. Third, there is the background story of Derek, how he became a neo-Nazi after his father was killed and how he became an effective youth leader of the neo-Nazis. He delivers a lengthy speech against immigration at one point that seems logical, potent, and inflammatory. Interestingly, the script does not provide a counterbalance to this early outburst, as the reformed Derek is quiet, methodical, and prefers to make his points by his actions. The response to Derek's words only appears at the end of the film, in Danny's paper. The impact of the story is quite powerful, particularly since the expected outcome of the story is that Derek, not Danny, would be killed. The cycle of violence is then complete.

The production values of *American History X* are quite high. Avery Brooks, Edward Norton, and Edward Furlong deliver riveting performances. The various social issues are blended expertly in the script, which has a genuine edge. It is a rare film that manages to stay in the viewer's memory a long time after the picture ends.

And the Band Played On
(1993)

Principal social themes: AIDS, homosexuality

HBO. PG rating. Featuring: Matthew Modine, Alan Alda, Patrick Bauchau, Nathalie Baye, Ian McKellen, Charles Martin Smith, Richard Gere, Anjelica Huston, David Dukes, Alex Courtney, David Marshall Grant, Stephen Spinella, Lily Tomlin, Swoosie Kurtz, Bud Cort, Phil Collins, Christian Clemenson, David

Clennon, Ronald Guttman, Ken Jenkins, Tcheky Karyo, Jeffrey Nordling, Jack Laufer, Donal Logue, Richard Masur, Dakin Mathews, Saul Rubinek, Peter McRobbie, Glenne Headly, B. D. Wong, Steve Martin. Written by Arnold Schulman based on the book by Randy Shilts. Cinematography by Paul Elliott. Edited by Lois Freeman-Fox. Music by Carter Burwell. Produced by Midge Sanford, Sarah Pillsbury, and Aaron Spelling (executive). Directed by Roger Spottiswoode. Color. 155 minutes (original version); 142 minutes (revised version).

Overview

Randy Shilts' book *And the Band Played On* was the first critical study of the development of the AIDS epidemic. Insightful, detailed, and passionately argued, the book generated tremendous interest as well as a number of controversies, particularly with sections of the text that appeared to be critical of some segments of the gay community. HBO decided to turn the book into a docudrama, fictionalizing some characters and having actors portray a number of figures involved in the story. The screenplay also edits in clips of actual news reports and documentary footage of a number of authentic events, such as a moving, candlelight memorial procession in San Francisco. *And the Band Played On* debuted on cable television in a longer version that was later edited down and released to other networks and on home video. It also had a number of theatrical bookings, especially in foreign markets.

Synopsis

And the Band Played On unfolds its story on two levels, first in traditional terms as seen through the eyes of a central protagonist, Dr. Don Francis, a scientist working at the Centers for Disease Control and Prevention (CDC) in Atlanta, and then through a series of short dramatized scenes blended with news clips that illustrate the evolution of the epidemic. The picture actually begins with a brief flashback from 1976, showing his experiences in Africa with a deadly ebola outbreak, a medical catastrophe that had been contained. In 1980, a few isolated cases of immune system failure among homosexual men in New York, San Francisco, and Los Angeles come to the attention of the CDC. Progress is painstakingly slow in gathering information and identifying the characteristics of this new disease, referred to only as "gay cancer" in the homosexual community. The regular media ignores the disease completely, but the number of cases continues to expand at an alarming rate. Overworked and poorly equipped, researches at the CDC begin to make several conclusions. The disease is sexually transmitted, has a long incubation period, and may be a retrovirus. Dr. Robert Gallo, a controversial figure and an expert on human retroviruses, is enlisted to study this possible connection. Dr. Francis develops the theory of "Patient Zero" based on a promiscuous gay flight attendant whose sexual activities might have helped to spread the disease to countless individuals. An attempt to close the bathhouses of San Francisco, which many members of the gay community fear is a direct assault on their lifestyle, fails. In January 1983, the CDC has a workshop that finally gives the disease a name, AIDS, for "acquired immunodeficiency syndrome." AIDS has begun to spread beyond the gay community and is now being publicized in the media. The CDC is concerned that the nation's blood supply might become contaminated from donors with AIDS, but blood bank executives resist any new guidelines to test and monitor the nation's blood supply. Another obstacle occurs because of the rivalry between researchers at the Pasteur Institute in Paris and Dr. Gallo's group, who make rival claims about isolating and identifying the AIDS virus. This threatens to delay progress by tying the matter up in court. Gallo blames Dr. Francis for helping the French researchers and limits his cooperation with the CDC. Once the virus is identified, Dr. Francis proposes a phase two plan for prevention, education, and cure. His request is forwarded to Washington by Dr. Curran, his superior, but his report is turned down as too expensive. Frustrated, Dr. Francis asks for a transfer from the main CDC lab to work directly on the AIDS epidemic in San Francisco. When he arrives on the West Coast, he goes to the hospital to visit Bill Kraus, a long-time gay activist and safe-sex advocate, who is dying from the disease. It is an emotional leave-taking, and the film concludes with Elton John singing "The Last Song," as a lengthy montage shows major celebrities who died from AIDS—Rock Hudson, Liberace, Arthur Ashe, Amanda Blake, and Anthony Perkins—as well as numerous other victims from all walks of life, including young Ryan White. A series of end title cards discusses the fate of various individuals portrayed in the picture. The final card reveals that as of 1993, forty million people worldwide have been infected with AIDS.

Critique

And the Band Played On is a remarkable, powerful, and unique accomplishment, although the script did blunt some of Stilts' sharper criticisms of segments of the gay liberation movement. The major flaw in the production is the strident criticism of President Ronald Reagan. On the other hand, much of the other sentiments of the screenplay are successful and ring true. The best part of the picture is the camaraderie of the members of the CDC research team. Charles Martin Smith is memorable as Harold Jaffe, the research expert on sexually transmitted diseases. Saul Rubinek is outstanding as the beleaguered head of the division. Ian McKellen (as Bill Kraus), Richard Gere (as an unidentified choreographer based on Michael Bennet), Jeffrey Nordling (as the notorious Patient Zero), and Alan Alda, who practically steals the show as the duplicitous Dr. Gallo, give masterful performances. Matthew Modine's bland approach to Dr. Francis, in contrast, seems artificial and stale until his final scene at the bedside of Bill Kraus. *And the Band*

Played On is valuable for discussion and study because of the excellent overview it provides about AIDS, touching base with all the important factors: the initial lack of interest by media and politicians, the lack of government funding, the homophobia of mainstream society, the rivalry and infighting between major research organizations, the hostility of militant gays who spurned any modification of their lifestyle, and the slow response of blood banks to safeguard their supply. The final memorial epilogue is also of great interest. Only a few of these victims are identified by name. Since the celebrities appear together with ordinary individuals (including babies), this technique also helps to illustrate the breadth of the impact of the AIDS epidemic.

As Good As It Gets
(1997)

Principal social themes: homosexuality, disabilities

TriStar Pictures. PG-13 rating. Featuring: Jack Nicholson, Helen Hunt, Greg Kinnear, Cuba Gooding Jr., Skeet Ulrich, Shirley Knight, Yeardley Smith, Lupe Ontiveros, Bibi Osterwald, Ross Bleckner, Jesse James, Lawrence Kasdan, Linda Gehringer, Julie Benz, Harold Ramis, Jill. Written by Mark Andrus and James L. Brooks based on a story by Mark Andrus. Cinematography by John Bailey. Edited by Richard Marks. Music by Hans Zimmer. Produced by James L. Brooks, Bridgit Johnson, and Kristi Zea. Directed by James L. Brooks. B&W. 139 minutes.

Overview

Although considered a romantic comedy, *As Good As It Gets* covers a number of social issues within its storyline, particularly the overcoming of the principal character's homophobia and his coming to terms with his own disability, an extreme case of obsessive/compulsive disorder. The production paid special attention to get the symptoms of this condition (repetitive rituals and phobias) accurately portrayed in the character of Melvin Udall (Jack Nicholson). The film garnered considerable financial and critical success, winning a Golden Globe Award as Best Picture. Jack Nicholson won the Academy Award for Best Actor, and Helen Hunt won the Best Actress award. Greg Kinnear was also nominated as Best Supporting Actor in a role that won him considerable praise for its positive and sympathetic portrayal of a homosexual who faces and overcomes not only prejudice but also medical and financial challenges.

Synopsis

The film opens in a fashionable Manhattan apartment, where Melvin Udall (Jack Nicholson) attempts to lure his neighbor's small dog into the elevator. Failing that, he picks the dog up and throws him down the garbage chute. Moments later, Simon Bishop (Greg Kinnear), a mild-mannered artist, approaches Udall to ask about his dog, Verdell. After his dog is located, Simon attempts to scold Melvin, but instead the irascible man insults and browbeats Simon for disturbing him. However, Simon's agent Frank (Cuba Gooding Jr.) later corners Melvin and warns him that he now owes a moral debt to Simon that he must someday repay. It turns out that Melvin is a popular romance novelist who is bedeviled by many psychological compunctions, including his belligerence to everyone he meets, making an endless string of comments that are anti-gay, racist, or sexist. He is an extremely unpopular and disliked man. He is also a cleanliness freak, refuses to step on any cracks in the street, and unable to eat except at one specific table at a local restaurant. Only one waitress, Carol Connelly (Helen Hunt), a hard-working single mother, has the patience to deal with him. When she takes offense at a comment he makes about her sickly son, she forces him to back down and behave. After Simon is assaulted and badly beaten in a robbery attempt, Frank forces Melvin to care for Verdell. Slowly, the charm and lively antics of the dog begin to win Melvin over and soon he starts to dote on the animal. A crisis develops when Carol takes time off from her job to care for her son, who has a severe case of asthma. Melvin arranges and pays for a specialist to treat the boy, on the condition that Carol returns to her job. The waitress is suspicious but grateful for this unexpected act of kindness. Meanwhile, Simon returns from the hospital, but finds himself penniless due to mounting bills and his inability to work. Most of his friends abandon him, but he is unexpectedly assisted by Melvin, who continues to walk and help care for Verdell. Frank persuades Melvin to drive Simon to Baltimore so he can approach his wealthy parents for assistance. Years earlier, his father disowned him when he learned of his homosexuality. Melvin asks Carol to come along on the trip to serve as chaperone, since he is still not really comfortable around Simon. They reach Baltimore, and take rooms at a hotel. Melvin takes Carol to a fancy restaurant where he tells her that he is now taking some medication to help his disorder because he wants to be a better person, a feeling she inspired in him. Carol is moved by this revelation, but Melvin then makes some inappropriate comments, and she runs off, going to Simon's room at the hotel. She winds up posing for Simon, who finds himself inspired by her and able to draw again. The artist is so delighted that he does not approach his parents for money. When they return to New York, Carol storms off, filled with mixed feelings about Melvin. She is attracted to him, but put off by his attitude and compulsive condition. Simon has been tossed out of his apartment, and Melvin offers to let him to stay in his own spare room. Simon persuades Melvin to go to Carol's house and let her know he loves her. He follows Simon's advice, and Carol becomes convinced that he truly loves her and would also make a good father for her son.

Critique

In essence, the success of this film relies on three fascinating central characters, Nicholson's tormented, caustic romance novelist, Hunt's no-nonsense but caring waitress, and Kinnear's sensitive and troubled artist. In fact, Kinnear's character has equivalent screen time as the others, but at award time he was considered in the supporting category. One could also argue that Verdell (played by six different Brussels Griffon dogs with Jill being the foremost of the group) is the picture's main character for the entire first half of the film, receding in importance only after the road trip to Baltimore commences. Each of the main characters reflects different social issues. Simon is a complex and multilayered character. His homosexuality is a crucial element in the entire story. More precisely, it is Melvin's reaction to Simon's homosexuality that is film's pivotal reaction. Melvin's response slowly moves from private fear and ridicule to acceptance and finally sincere friendship. The most remarkable line in the film occurs in the last scene between Kinnear and Nicholson. When Simon tells Melvin that he loves him, the author sighs and says, "I tell you, buddy, I would be the luckiest guy alive if that did it for me." This transformation seems so honest that it might inspire some audience members to reexamine their own attitudes. The only shortcoming is that Simon seems to be too nice. It is hard to imagine anyone who would not find this earnest, friendly individual appealing. Composer Hans Zimmer provides Simon with a charming melody that resembles the main theme from Prokofiev's *Peter and the Wolf*. This musical bit makes his character seem gentle, naive, and innocent. Compared to Simon, Melvin starts off as the big bad wolf: snarling, grouchy, selfish, and bitter. It takes genuine skill for Nicholson to gain the sympathy of the audience. Although his insults are offensive, they are also witty, so Nicholson manages to make it seem that Melvin is not really anti-Semitic or anti-black, just an equal opportunity misanthrope. It is the dog Verdell who breaks down Melvin's hard-hearted exterior and provides the first step in Melvin's redemption. As a social problem, Melvin's disorder is a tragic handicap, leaving him an outcast. If he did not have his wealth, Melvin would be in dire straits. He had completely shut the door to his own humanity. When Simon returns from the hospital and reclaims Verdell, Melvin sits alone and starts to simultaneously laugh and cry, saying aloud, "It's all because of a dog!" After having his emotions awakened by Verdell, Melvin falls in love with Carol, who hesitates at first to respond because of his obsessiveness. Carol's situation reflects the film's third social issue, the gaps and inadequacies of the modern day medical care system. Just as Simon was healed but bankrupted by his medical treatment, Carol's son is also let down because he is provided with only minimal attention. When her son receives proper treatment due to Melvin's intercession, her rant against HMOs usually provokes a strong round of applause by the audience. In conclusion, *As Good As It Gets* does an excellent job utilizing a number of social concerns without ever being preachy or obvious; it remains a solid example of screen entertainment. This is no small accomplishment.

Betrayed
(1988)

Principal social themes: hate groups, racism/civil rights

United Artists. R rating. Featuring: Debra Winger, Tom Berenger, John Heard, Betsy Blair, Ted Levine, John Mahoney, Jeffrey DeMunn, David Clennon, Robert Swann, Richard Libertini, Albert Hall. Written by Joe Eszterhas. Cinematography by Patrick Blossier. Edited by Joële Van Effenterre. Music by Bill Conti. Produced by Irwin Winkler. Directed by Constantin Costa-Gavras. Color. 127 minutes.

Overview

Betrayed is a thriller about an FBI attempt to infiltrate a violent white supremacist group in the Midwest. An undercover female agent becomes close to one of the suspected leaders, eventually agreeing to marry him. Much of the script concentrates on the lives and thought processes of family members belonging to a hate group, in some ways quite normal but in other ways extremely distorted.

Synopsis

The film opens as Sam Kraus, a Chicago radio shock jock, challenges any anti-Semite to call him on the phone. After his broadcast, Kraus is shot while approaching his car in a parking garage. The killer then spray paints the letters ZOG over the body of his victim. The scene shifts to a large wheat field being harvested by a combine, a large farm vehicle. The driver, a woman named Katie Miller, makes the acquaintance of farmer Gary Simmons, a widower. He invites her to dinner, and she meets Gary's mother and two young children, Joey and Rachel. She finds them all likable people. Later, Katie tells Gary that she has been called away to Texas, where her mother is having an operation. Instead, she goes to the Chicago office of the FBI. She is actually Cathy Weaver, an undercover agent assigned to investigate Gary. She reports that he seems to be a normal family man. She is ordered to return to her assignment. Katie becomes romantically involved with Gary, whom she finds attractive. She even attends church with him and his family. The farmer invites her to join his hunt one evening. Most of the local farmers turn out for this event, acknowledging Gary as their leader. Katie is shocked to discover that they are actually hunting a black man. She reluctantly pretends to join the hunt, but screams in shock when the man is killed. Gary tells her that her reaction is normal, but she must realize they are in a war against ZOG or the "Zionist Occupation Government." Katie reports to the FBI that their suspicions about Gary are correct. They insist she resume her undercover mission. When she returns, Gary seeks her out and makes love to her, asking her to marry him. She moves into his home. The children are overjoyed, particularly now that they no longer have to keep secrets. Even Rachel, the little girl, uses racial epithets against blacks and Jews. Wes, one of Gary's associates, does not like Katie, suspecting she may be a "grasshopper," a spy for the federal government. Gary takes Katie and the kids on an outing to a Ku Klux Klan conference, combining camping, rifle training, and information seminars. When Jack Carpenter, an ultra-conservative candidate for president, shows up at the camp, Gary shouts him down as a phony and not really dedicated to their cause. Katie also learns that Gary is a shooter, a professional assassin, for the group and he had murdered Sam Kraus. They return home, and soon Gary gets another assignment, to kill Jack Carpenter. He also is given papers proving that Katie is an FBI agent named Cathy Weaver. Gary is heartbroken by the revelation. He takes Katie with him when he goes to shoot Carpenter, and before the killing, he tells her that he knows her real identity. Taking aim on Carpenter, Gary challenges her to shoot him. She hesitates, but then kills Gary. A moment later, however, the presidential candidate is shot by a second assassin in another location. Weary, Katie quits the FBI. She travels back to visit Rachel as she leaves church on Sunday. The minister and other members of Gary's family curse her and denounce her, but Rachel greets her warmly. She bids farewell to Rachel as the end credits appear.

Critique

Betrayed had a mixed critical reaction when it initially appeared. In his movie guide, Leonard Maltin gives the film a low one-and-a-half star rating, calling Katie "the stupidest FBI agent in movie history." However, his short plot synopsis misrepresents the basic story, suggesting that Katie fell in love with

Gary after she learned he was a leader in the hate group. In fact, her personal interest in Gary vanished when she discovered his true nature. The most interesting aspect of *Betrayed* is the depiction of the hate group members. This can provide ample room for discussion. For example, one member, Shorty, is a kind-hearted and gentle man, but he has become convinced, after the government took his farm, that the U.S. government is controlled by Jews, blacks, and homosexuals. He felt that by joining the group, he was only defending himself. The haunting question is proposed subtly: How many decent people can be indoctrinated by a philosophy of hatred and violence? The example of Nazi Germany can serve as a warning that many people may be vulnerable to a charismatic leader. By presenting a few members of the hate group as decent, the picture emphasizes the virulent nature of hatred.

The story also shows that there are no simple answers. Gary himself was radicalized by the suicide of his father, who had joined a militia group. When he refused to pay his taxes, the government put a lien on his farm and he hanged himself. Gary had been a war hero in Vietnam, winning the Purple Heart and other medals, and he believed he had a genuine love for America before his ideals became corrupted. At the KKK rally, Gary shows remnants of his original feelings, such as when he lashes out at a neo-Nazi selling photos of Adolf Hitler. Ironically Gary is infected with the same racist ideology as the Nazi leader he despises. Perhaps the most shocking moment in the film, however, is when Katie first overhears innocent young Rachel employ the same racist language as her father.

There are numerous references in the film to actual events. Katie's actual last name, for example, is Weaver, the same as well-known militia leader Randy Weaver of the Ruby Ridge case. By attempting a more realistic portrayal of the followers, not as caricatures but decent people whose views have been perverted, *Betrayed* tackles another theme, how hate groups manage to recruit individuals to their distorted viewpoints. When questioned by Katie, for example, Shorty admits he never actually met a black or a Jew, so his hatred was cultivated by the group and was not the result of personal experience. A final piece of irony is the title. Who was actually betrayed? Was it Gary, who fell in love with Katie, the undercover agent? Could it have been Katie, who in her initial evaluation considered Gary and his family to be true-blue patriots? Or could it be the ideals of America, betrayed by the detestable agenda of hate groups such as the one championed by Gary and his friends?

Black Legion
(1936)

Principal social themes: hate groups, immigration

Warner Brothers. No MPAA rating. Featuring: Humphrey Bogart, Dick Foran, Erin O'Brien-Moore, Ann Sheridan, Robert Barrat, Helen Flint, Joseph Sawyer, Addison Richards, Eddie Acuff, Paul Harvey, Samuel S. Hinds, John Litel, Alonzo Price, Henry Brandon, Egon Brecher, Dorothy Vaughan, Pat C. Flick, Harry Hayden, Dickie Jones, Emmett Vogan, Paul Stanton. Written by Abem Finkel and William Wister Haines. Cinematography by George Barnes. Edited by Owen Marks. Music by Bernhard Kaun. Produced by Robert Lord. Directed by Archie Mayo. B&W. 83 minutes.

Overview

Black Legion was loosely based on a Michigan kidnap-murder case involving a local hate group known as the Black Legion. Warner Brothers studio received numerous threats while preparing the film. The screenwriters used the Ku Klux Klan as the model for their film depiction, and the script followed Klan rituals precisely, even reproducing their oath of allegiance word for word. In fact, after the film was released, the KKK actually sued the studio for copyright violation since the costumes worn by the legion included the Klan symbol, which they had registered in the 1920s with the U.S. Patent Office. The case was dismissed as frivolous. *Black Legion* was regarded as Humphrey Bogart's breakthrough film, the first one in which he was billed as the headline star.

Synopsis

At the opening of the film, Frank Taylor is presented as a typical American, married to Ruth and with a son, Buddy. Frank earns a decent living as a factory worker, but he is ambitious and wants better things for his family. When a foreman's job opens in his division, Frank feels certain he will get it, since he is the worker with the most seniority and he readily admits he is the best at what he does. However, when the job is given to a bright younger worker named Joe Dombrowski, who had invented a system that saved the company a lot of money, Frank becomes embittered. He starts to listen to radio broadcasts denouncing foreign workers who displace Americans at the workplace. A coworker recruits Frank to join the Black Legion, a group of hooded vigilantes, and he swears allegiance to the secret society. The Black Legion conducts a raid on the Dombrowski farm, burning it to the ground and running Joe and his father out of town. Frank now inherits the foreman job. He attempts to get his best friend, Ed Jackson, interested in the legion, but is rebuffed. Frank loses his position after an accident, which happens while he is busy trying to recruit another worker for the Black Legion. When Ruth criticizes her husband for spending all his time with the hate group, he strikes her. She takes Buddy and leaves. While drunk, Frank tells Ed a bit too much about the legion, and his friend threatens to go to the police. Frank warns the legion, and they kidnap Ed, who is killed while trying to escape. When Frank is arrested for his murder, the Black Legion concocts an alibi for him with a phony witness, a former girlfriend of Ed's. Frank breaks down at his trial and incriminates the legion and its members for their criminal reign of terror. Despite his confession and cooperation, Frank is given a life sentence along with the members of the Black Legion who kidnapped Ed. As he is led away from the courtroom, Frank appears to be forgiven by a sorrowful Ruth.

Critique

Black Legion is a tough, uncompromising portrait of American hate groups, although it avoids any actual mention of the Ku Klux Klan itself. Nevertheless, no member of the audience was unaware of the target. The film depicts the tactics and rituals of the KKK in a cohesive and convincing fashion, although one must note that the actual Black Legion was disbanded in 1937 and the KKK itself found the North less than fertile territory. In the South, the hate group was far better established, its tentacles often controlling the local authorities to an extent far unlike the community portrayed in *Black Legion*. Although the script hits hard on the topics of immigrant-baiting and racism, the focus of the legion's hatred are also Catholics. The film might have had an even sharper edge if several blacks or Jews were included among their targets in the plot. The emphasis of the film is not society, but instead the impact of the Black Legion on one family. In those terms, the transformation of Humphrey Bogart from a decent, well-meaning citizen to a vicious hatemonger is both chilling and credible. Undoubtedly, *Black Legion* is one of the most powerful social issue films of the mid-1930s. The film received critical acclaim by most of the major newspapers and magazines of the era, and Humphrey Bogart in particular received the best notices of his career to that time.

Black Like Me
(1964)

Principal social theme: racism/civil rights

Walter Reade/Sterling. No MPAA rating. Featuring: James Whitmore, Sorrell Booke, Roscoe Lee Browne, Al Freeman Jr., Will Geer, Robert Gerringer, Clifton James, John Marriott, Thelma Oliver, Lenka Petersen, P. J. Sidney, Alan Bergmann, Stanley Brock, Heywood Hale Broun, Sarah Cunningham, David Huddleston, Eva Jessye, D'Urville Martin, Walter Mason, Richard Ward, Dan Priest, Raymond St. Jacques, Millie Allen; Written by Gerda Lerner and Carl Lerner based on the book *Black Like Me* by John Howard Griffin. Cinematography by Victor Lukens and Henry Mueller II. Edited by Lora Hays. Music by Meyer Kupferman. Produced by Julius Tannenbaum. Directed by Carl Lerner. B&W. 107 minutes.

Overview

In 1959, Texas author John Howard Griffin wrote a compelling series of magazine articles about his travels through the Deep South after darkening his skin by chemical treatment to experience first hand the everyday conditions encountered by Black Americans. In 1961, the articles were expanded into a book, *Black Like Me*, which drew critical attention and became very influential. The film *Black Like Me* dramatized the book in a hard-edged, gritty style reminiscent of film noir. Although the screenplay fictionalized the story (for instance, John Howard Griffin was changed to John Finley Horton), the events are based entirely on fact. Although the picture had only spotty distribution in the South, it was recognized as one of the most striking film treatments of the topic of racism by the film industry.

Synopsis

Since Negro was the preferred term for African Americans at the time of this film's setting, the term will be used in the synopsis. The credits appear in close-ups beside fragments of a larger design. It only becomes apparent that this is the Confederate flag before the final credit, the director's name, Carl Lerner. The first image in the film proper is a traveling shot of the white line that divides the lanes of a highway. This image recurs throughout the film, and by the picture's end, it is clear that it is meant to represent the color line in America. The scene shifts to the interior of a crowded bus. James Whitmore, skin darkened so that he appears to be a Negro, offers his seat to a middle-aged white woman, who angrily turns down his gesture as if it were an affront. At a rest stop, the driver tells Horton to stay on the bus. Instead, he storms off the bus and starts to hitchhike down the road. When he reaches the next town, he approaches a Negro and asks about finding a room. The man warns him that the town is very inhospitable to black people and arranges for Horton to board at a private home. After settling into his room, Horton watches from the window as a gang of white hot-rodders start to harass Negroes as they walk down the street. He stares at his black face in the mirror as a flashback shows Whitmore as a white Horton, approaching his friend, a wealthy magazine publisher, as they relax by the side of a swimming pool. The publisher is fascinated by Horton's daring idea, to write in diary fashion his experiences as he passes for a Negro in the Deep South. The publisher warns Horton that his plan could be very dangerous if he falls into the clutches of any racists who penetrate his disguise. Horton explains that his skin will be darkened chemically. From this point on, the picture becomes episodic, jumping around between the white Horton's preparations for this assignment and the Negro Horton's encounters with numerous individuals. Most of the Negroes he meets are reserved when encountering white people but open and friendly when dealing with members of their own race. Most of the whites encountered by Horton are hostile, abusive, or insulting. A series of white drivers give Horton a lift, but they all seem obsessed with talking about sex and carnal relations between the races. Horton begins to develop an angry veneer as he experiences racism in many forms. He becomes abrupt with one white driver who tries to chat with him until Horton finally realizes that the man is only trying to be pleasant. Later he encounters a bigoted young white student writing a thesis, and Horton becomes so angry he almost chokes the youth to death. A devout Catholic, Horton has a spiritual crisis and turns to a local priest and reveals that he is passing as a Negro. The priest counsels him, suggesting that his problem stems from his "pride of self." When Horton's articles start to appear, he moves in with a gentle, elderly man whose son has become active in the civil rights movement. He finally shows them one of the articles. They are at first stunned and suspicious as Horton tries to explain his motives and his sincere wish for better race relations. Their discussion is spirited and provides the dramatic climax of the picture. Horton decides to conclude his travels and return home to his wife and children, knowing his skin will return to normal when he discontinues taking the drug. He symbolically crosses the white line in the road as the screen turns to black. The film concludes without any end credits.

Critique

Black Like Me is well intentioned, sensational, and disturbing. The stark cinematography, crisp editing, abrasive atonal music, and dramatic run-down location footage are genuinely remarkable. Griffin's original concept is audacious, and the film accurately depicts many of the events of the book. Only those viewers who read the book, however, can judge if the screenwriters selected the most representative incidents to portray. The most vivid characters in the film include Roscoe Lee Browne as Christopher, a smooth-talking former convict, Will Geer as the nasty, old-school racist, and Richard Ward as Burt Wilson, the shoeshine parlor owner who helps Whitmore to adopt the proper manner as a black man in the Deep South. The impact of the picture rises or falls with the audience's acceptance of Whitmore as a black man; his blue eyes and physical features work against full believability. Another weakness is Whitmore's speaking style, which remains unchanged throughout the film. Whenever he opens his mouth, he sounds like a professor. Yet his conviction and dedication to the role seem total. Several critics have commented that his angry demeanor in the second half of the film is unrealistic, and there is some truth to this. Griffin's anger was internal in the book, but Whitmore's Horton has to express it more externally. The picture has a few weak points. The structure of the story makes everything seem vague, and we are never told what state Horton is in or in which direction he is going. Although set in 1959, the music and popular dance styles are of the mid-1960s. The crude sexual emphasis in the hitchhiking sequences is somewhat overdone and becomes unintentionally funny, but the screenplay saves the sequence with Horton's reaction when a decent man gives him a lift, only wanting to show off the photos of his kids. Whitmore is unconvincing and awkward in his scenes with Mrs. Horton, who disapproves of her husband's endeavors. The scene in which Horton double dates with a black girl, however, is touching and well handled. Several moments of the picture are unforgettable, such as when two thugs pursue Horton through the dark streets and a white motorist refuses to help him. The quiet moments can be just as effective, such as when Horton is walking on the beach and pauses to talk with a young white girl building a sand castle. The child is without a shred of racism, but her mother is frantic when she notices Horton and her daughter together. Another memorable moment is at the bus station, where an elderly female ticket-seller refuses to change Whitmore's twenty-dollar bill and stares at him with pure hatred. Finally, the scene in which some local white thugs stalk Horton and he challenges them to follow him into an alley is one of the most chilling and dramatic scenes in any film from the era. Students might find *Black Like Me* very useful as a snapshot of a point in time, and explore how things have changed in the years since the setting of the movie. It could be used in many ways by students wishing to gain an understanding of the roots of the civil rights movement and of the many levels of discrimination faced by black citizens in the American South in the late 1950s. The film could be viewed on different levels, appealing to both a white and black audience and studied for the different gradations of racism. It could even be useful to consider subtle points, such as language. Are phrases such as "you people" actually code words for racism? How does the personality of Horton affect his overall experience? This film can provide a wealth of material for discussion, including the ways in which society has or has not changed. Ironically, the next time a white character tried to become a black was in *Soul Man* (1986), in which a white student passed for black to gain an unclaimed minority scholarship at a university. Despite its occasional flaws, *Black Like Me* remains a unique milestone in examining the issue of racism in America.

Blue Denim (AKA Blue Jeans)
(1959)

Principal social theme: abortion

20th Century Fox. No MPAA rating. Featuring: Carol Lynley, Brandon de Wilde, Macdonald Carey, Marsha Hunt, Warren Berlinger, Roberta Shore, Nina Shipman, Buck Class, Vaughn Taylor, William Schallert, Michael Gainey, Jenny Maxwell, Juney Ellis, Grace Field. Written by Philip Dunne and Edith R. Sommer based on a play by James Leo Herlihy and William Noble. Cinematography by Leo Tover. Edited by William Reynolds. Music by Bernard Herrmann. Produced by Charles Brackett. Directed by Philip Dunne. B&W. 89 minutes.

Overview

One of the first films by a major studio to tackle the issue of abortion, *Blue Denim* can serve as a sanitized portrait of mainstream America's attitudes toward the issue thirteen years before the *Roe vs. Wade* decision by the U.S. Supreme Court. It is based on a stage play that also starred Carol Lynley. Viewed today, the film seems very old-fashioned, but when it was initially released it was a popular success and was considered to be highly relevant. The film sparked considerable debate and stimulated a wide range of opinion. *Boxoffice*, for example, regarded it as being true-to-life and compassionate, whereas the *New York Times* dismissed it as clumsy and artificial.

Synopsis

The film opens with a quote from Samuel Butler's novel *The Way of All Flesh*: "Youth is like spring, an overpraised season." The plot centers on two typical, middle-class teenagers, fifteen-year-old Janet Willard (Carol Lynley) who has a crush on sixteen-year-old Arthur Bartley (Brandon de Wilde). Both of them are lonely, somewhat naive, and unable to communicate with their parents. Arthur's father is Major Malcolm Bartley (Macdonald Carey), a retired army officer who looks at everything from a military point of view. His mother is mainly interested in Lillian, his older sister, and her engagement to Axel, the local dentist. Janet's father is a widower, a gentle but stodgy college professor who frightens away Janet's friends with his fussy, paternal attitude. As the picture opens, Arthur comes home from school to find that his father has put his elderly dog Hector to sleep. Arthur is hurt that since his father wanted to spare him the painful decision, he did not have a chance to say goodbye to his beloved pet. Arthur retreats to his basement clubhouse, where he rebels by playing poker, drinking beer, and smoking with his wiseguy friend Ernie. Janet later joins them and asks Ernie to forge an excuse slip for her to cut class. She complains that her father refuses to let her wear makeup. After Ernie leaves, Janet pretends to sprain her leg in order to sneak a kiss from Arthur. At the big basketball game, Arthur has a chance to score the winning basket at the end of the game, but he misses the shot. Janet walks him home and consoles him. When they agree to go steady, Janet asks Arthur about his experiences with other girls. He bluffs, pretending he is not a virgin. When she questions him further, he admits to lying. They go into the basement clubhouse and kiss, while the screen blacks out. Three months pass, and Janet learns that she has become pregnant. She explains to Arthur that she could never tell her father about her condition. In desperation they consider their options, such as sneaking off and getting married, but find they are too young to obtain a license. Arthur confides in Ernie, who is always boasting that he has helped other kids in trouble to find a good doctor, but his friend admits he was only bragging. They finally discover that the local soda jerk can arrange for an abortion. The cost, however, is $150. Janet, Arthur, and Ernie pool their money, but can only come up with $58. Arthur attempts to tell his parents about the problem, but they are so deeply involved in Lillian's approaching wedding that they both brush him off. He steals a check from his father and persuades Ernie to forge Major Bartley's signature. The "back-alley" abortion is arranged for the same day as the wedding. Janet is stoic until the car arrives to take her for the procedure. She then breaks down, hugs Arthur, and exclaims that she does not want to go. Arthur pleads to be allowed to accompany her, but is refused. After Janet is driven off, Ernie turns on Arthur, accusing him of cowardess for not enlisting his parents' help. At the wedding reception, Major Bartley is approached by one of the guests, the bank manager, who is suspicious about the check he cashed for Arthur. After the reception, the major tries to talk to his son, who finally admits he is in trouble and begs for help to locate Janet and stop the abortion. After contacting Professor Willard, the major confronts the soda jerk and forces him to reveal where Janet has been taken.

They arrive in time to rescue Janet just after she has been sedated. The doctor warns them of consequences if the law becomes involved. They take Janet home, where the major, his wife, and Professor Willard discuss the situation. Janet awakens and insists that she is responsible for what has happened, and she does not want Arthur to be forced into a marriage that might ruin his future. She decides on leaving town, moving in with her aunt across the country until her baby is born. The next morning, Arthur is stunned to learn that Janet has already left town by train. He tells his parents he is outraged that the decision was made for him behind his back, just like the euthanasia of his dog. He insists that he must take responsibility and marry Janet. His parents give their permission, and Ernie races his friend in the major's car to intercept the train at the next town. Arthur boards the train and finds Janet sitting forlornly. He says, "Where did you think you were going?" and puts his arm around her as she smiles and puts her head on his shoulder while the film draws to a close.

Critique

The various social issues presented in *Blue Denim* are timeless, but the script's approach seems dated even for the 1950s. The film takes it for granted that abortion is wrong, not on moral principles but simply because it is illegal. Ernie, the cool "Eddie Haskell" character is the only one who voices a strong opinion, calling it "murder" at one point. After Janet and Arthur conclude that it is the only possible option that would hide the truth from their parents, the main argument against abortion is largely a matter of health and safety. Later, Arthur becomes convinced that Janet will not survive. The script centers far more on Arthur rather than Janet, even though she logically should be the main focus. The ideal offspring, in the eyes of the Bartleys, is nineteen-year-old Lillian, who seems as bubble-headed as her mother and who is regarded as successful because she is going to marry a man of status. The possible role model for girls is limited and very stereotypical, with education being of only marginal importance. On the other hand, a complete education is essential for a boy to have any chance for success. When discussing the early marriage option, both the Bartleys and Professor Willard seem to convey an attitude that parents never financially help their children once they become married, even if it allows them to complete their education. Another weakness is the fact that little attention is paid to the future of the baby, with options such as adoption never being mentioned. The picture's denouement is far too pat.

Despite the flaws and presence of closed-minded attitudes, however, the script does a fairly good job portraying the generation gap and exploring issues that were almost always avoided in mainstream films. They did this in part by making Arthur and Janet good kids, not wild or troublesome. The parents are not shocked that their children had sex, but rather that they did not come to them at the start. The production standards are fairly good. Carol Lynley, seventeen at the time of the filming, is exceptional and handles her role with great sensitivity, making Janet genuinely believable. Brandon de Wilde was also seventeen when he played Arthur, but he seems far less convincing than Lynley. The most memorable element of the film may be its soundtrack, composed by one of the greatest of screen performers, Bernard Herrmann. In fact, his lyrical and intense musical score is highly reminiscent of one of his greatest compositions, *Vertigo*, completed a year before his work on *Blue Denim*. His music smooths out some of the film's rough edges, making the troubles of the screen characters appear more compelling. Philip Dunne's direction is somewhat erratic, particularly in the scenes with the parents, but his scenes with the principals alone are empathetic and well handled. *Blue Denim* could serve as a focal point for discussion on the issues of abortion, teenage pregnancy, and parent–teenager relationships with a special emphasis on how these attitudes and issues have changed since the time of this picture's release.

Border Incident
(1949)

Principal social theme: immigration

MGM. No MPAA rating. Featuring: Ricardo Montalban, George Murphy, Howard da Silva, Arnold Moss, Charles McGraw, James Mitchell, Alfonso Bedoya, Teresa Celli, Jose Torey, Arthur Hunnicutt, John Ridgely, Sig Ruman, Otto Waldis, Harry Antrim, Tony Barr, Fred Graham, Martin Garralaga. Written by John C. Higgins. Cinematography by John Alton. Edited by Conrad Nervig. Music by André Previn. Produced by Nicholas Nayfack. Directed by Anthony Mann. B&W. 96 minutes.

Overview

Border Incident is one of the first films by a major studio to focus on illegal immigration along the Mexican-American border. It foreshadows major concerns by incorporating the red tape of legal immigration, the needs of the agriculture industry for cheap labor, the exploitation of immigrants, and cooperation between the American and Mexican governments. The film was also filmed largely on location along both sides of the Mexican border.

Synopsis

A lengthy narration provides the background for *Border Incident*. Mexican workers known as *braceros* apply for work permits to enter the United States, but it is a slow, sometimes cumbersome procedure that can take six weeks. Instead, many Mexican laborers cross the border illegally, some using their own resources and some smuggled in by criminal organizations. These immigrants face many hazards. Those crossing on their own are often robbed and killed by bandits. Those brought in by others often find themselves cheated and exploited. The story focuses on one particular case in which two top undercover agents, American Jim Bearnes (George Murphy) and Mexican Pablo Rodriguez (Ricardo Montalban) work together to crack a sinister gang that victimizes illegal immigrants. Pablo poses as a poor bracero who wants to cross over the border. Jim poses as a crook on the run who infiltrates a gang working the smuggling racket. The illegal operation turns out to be headed by a wily rancher, Owen Parkson (Howard da Silva). The story concentrates on the inhuman treatment experienced by the Mexican workers who fall into Parkson's clutches. Parkson discovers Jim's identity and orders him killed, crushed to death by a tractor. Pablo escapes from the ranch and gets a message through to the American immigration officials. He is recaptured by Parkson's gang, who plan to dispose of him and other troublesome workers by throwing them in quicksand in an isolated location nicknamed the "Canyon of Death." American lawmen conduct a raid at the canyon just in time to save Pablo. Parkson and his henchmen are killed in a shootout and by quicksand. Jim Bearnes is awarded a posthumous medal, and Pablo Martinez is also cited by both the American and Mexican governments for his work in cracking the Parkson gang. However, constant vigilance must be maintained to prevent other groups from emulating Parkson. The film ends noting that the story was based on an actual case.

Critique

By focusing its plot on the plight of migrant workers, *Border Incident* raises numerous concerns beyond the limits of the central plot, the adventures of the two undercover agents. The film is very bleak in tone, like many film noirs, with a particularly hard edge as demonstrated by the dramatic killing of one of the film's two leads late in the picture. The choices faced by the braceros wishing to enter America are difficult. To enter by the legal route involves much paperwork and many weeks of waiting at the border crossings. Even after entering America, their life is difficult, although the law offers them a handful of basic protections and a wage of seventy-five cents an hour. The illegal route risks death and conditions beneath human dignity. Their wages are only a third of the legal workers', as they become totally reliant on the ranchers who exploit them. *Border Incident* portrays greed rather than racism as the root of the exploitation, as a number of Mexicans are included among the parasites who ruthlessly smuggle human cargo. The film tries to include an upbeat ending, but the prospects for the braceros are not really improved. Like the drug trade, other vultures are ready to step in whenever one criminal organization like the Parkson crowd is brought down. No explanation is ever given as to why the legal process is so drawn out and complicated. The script never faults these Mexicans for turning to illegal options. No one in the Immigration Department seems to realize how their system is failing both the citizens of the United States and Mexico, practically driving honest immigrants into the clutches of criminals. This message is clearly at the heart of *Border Incident*, but government officials turn a blind eye to it. *Border Incident* can serve as a launching point for discussions about how the system has or has not changed for immigrants, and how the situation could possibly be improved or remedied.

The Burning Bed
(1984)

Principal social themes: women's rights, child abuse/
spouse abuse, divorce, education/literacy,
homelessness/poverty

Tisch Productions. No MPAA rating. Featuring: Farrah Fawcett, Paul LeMat, Richard Masur, Grace Zabriskie, Penelope Milford, Christa Denton, James Callahan, Gary Grubbs, Virgil Frye, Dixie Wade, Deena Michaels, Jeremy Ross. Written by Rose L. Goldemberg based on the book by Faith McNulty. Cinematography by Isadore Mankofsky. Edited by Richard Fetterman and Michael Stevenson. Music by Charles Gross. Produced by Carol Schreder, Jon Avnet, and Steve Tisch (executive). Directed by Robert Greenwald. Color. 98 minutes.

Overview

Based on an actual case, *The Burning Bed* was one of the most important telefilms ever to deal with women's rights and spouse abuse. Playing a victim of battered woman's syndrome, it was the most critically acclaimed performance of Farrah Fawcett's career. After suffering a beating, her character poured gasoline on the bed in which her former husband slept, ignited it, and killed him. She was acquitted of a murder charge using a defense of temporary insanity. *The Burning Bed* was broadcast by NBC on October 8, 1984, and it received a large number of Emmy Award nominations. *The Burning Bed* was named as Best Feature at the first International Television Movie Festival.

Synopsis

The film opens as Francine Hughes (Farrah Fawcett) is fleeing from her burning house with her three children in March 1982. Shortly afterward, she is charged with murder. Her court-appointed attorney, Aryon Greydanus (Richard Mauser) meets with her but finds her dazed and unresponsive. He pleads with her to cooperate, and she finally begins to tell her story, going back to the mid-1960s when she met the volatile Mickey Hughes (Paul LeMat). She fell in love with him, even though she felt he was somewhat of a bully. They marry and eventually had three children, Christy, Jimmy, and Nicole. She becomes terrified of his physical abuse, which began to grow in intensity. She applied for a divorce, gaining custody of her three children. Mickey then has a terrible automobile accident. When Francine visits him in the hospital, he was entirely covered in bandages. She decides to help with Mickey's rehabilitation, even moving into the small house adjacent to the Hughes' place. As he recovers, Mickey seems to be genuinely grateful. In spite of being pressured by Mickey's parents and her own mother, Francine refuses to remarry Mickey. However, he still considers himself to be her husband. When she tries to leave, he takes custody of the children. She contacts a number of social agencies to assert her rights, but none are able to help her. She realizes that in order to be with her children she has to return to the house adjacent to the Hughes' home. Mickey's abusiveness continues to get worse. At one point, she has to flee and locks herself in the closet at the home of her in-laws. The police come to get her out and take a statement, but they would not charge Mickey because they did not witness his assault. Francine decides to complete her education and wins a special scholarship. Mickey decides to undercut her new independence by beating her and ordering her to burn her books. He then forces her to have sex with him. After he falls asleep, Francine takes the gasoline he made her use to burn her books and pours it around the bed in which he is sleeping. She ignites it, driving off with her three children. At this point the flashback ends, and Greydanus begins to research her case. The law does not provide any loophole for battered women to claim self-defense in their state (Michigan), so he decides to take the risky course of claiming temporary insanity. Mickey's parents are witnesses for the prosecution, claiming that they never witnessed any abuse. Christy, the eldest daughter, however, provides devastating testimony about her father's relentless abuse. Francine herself makes a credible witness, and she wins acquittal.

Critique

The Burning Bed has been credited with inspiring legal reforms regarding women's rights in many states. The telefilm, in fact, caused a minor uproar. It is a remarkable effort on many levels. The brutality is very difficult to watch, quite different from the stylized violence that flavors so many films. The performances are remarkable and believable, particularly Farrah Fawcett's as Francine. The choices she makes throughout are frequently wrong, although her intentions are correct and honest. Her biggest mistake is her sympathy for Mickey after his accident and her decision to help in his rehabilitation. She had escaped the trap, and then foolishly stepped back in, even without her firm decision not to remarry. This essential point is misunderstood by some viewers, who do not realize that Francine and Mickey are divorced during the last half of the flashback. Technically, Mickey's attacks are not spouse abuse, but straightforward assault and battery. The consideration of rape, another obvious situation in the case, is never addressed. When Francine seeks help from various social agencies, they let her down, advising her to get a lawyer. For some reason, she is unable or unwilling to take this step, and she even shows a reticence at first to deal with her own court-appointed attorney. Her fears are that the law might turn against her, declare her an unfit mother, or otherwise destroy her life.

The picture, however, is not flawless. The story is presented in a haphazard fashion, which sometimes dilutes its clarity and impact. The courtroom scenes are flat and unrealistic. For example, there never appears to be any cross-examination. The story could have been further enriched by examining the district attorney's attitude in prosecuting the case. The audience is never aware if he even acknowledges the horrendous abuse. Interestingly, the jury is largely female, one that could more readily understand Francine's desperate plight. Besides women's rights, abuse, and divorce, the screenplay also addresses other factors affecting Francine: her poverty and lack of psychological support. Her main breakthrough, her decision to return to school, is in many ways a triumph. She only snaps after Mickey destroys this dream, her lifeline to a better future. One of the best areas for discussion after viewing *The Burning Bed* might be an examination of Francine's possible options and the prospect of success for each alternative. Conversely, it is important to decipher Mickey's character. Was he a hopeless case, a monster with no redeeming features? Did he have such an inferiority complex due to his lack of education that he panicked when Francine began to improve herself? At what point in the storyline could an intervention with him have been successful? What about Mickey's parents? To what extent are they responsible since they were on the premises during all the main events of the story? Finally, what was the impact of these experiences on the three children? Did they suffer any guilt for the events after they unfolded? Could they ever have a normal relationship with their grandparents? *The Burning Bed*, in any case, addresses a large number of social concerns worth exploring.

Cell 2455 Death Row
(1955)

Principal social theme: capital punishment

Columbia. No MPAA rating. Featuring: William Campbell, Vince Edwards, Marian Carr, Robert Campbell, Kathryn Grant, Harvey Stephens, Allen Nourse, Diane DeLaire, Paul Dubov, Tyler MacDuff, Eleanor Audley, Buck Kartlian, Bart Braverman, Howard Wright, Joe Forte, Jonathan Haze, John Zaremba. Written by Jack DeWitt based on the book *Cell 2455 Death Row* by Caryl Chessman. Cinematography by Fred Jackman Jr. Edited by Henry Batista. Produced by Wallace MacDonald. Directed by Fred F. Sears. B&W. 77 minutes.

Overview

Caryl Chessman was a small-time criminal who was convicted in 1948 as the notorious "Red Light Bandit." He was sentenced to death under a loophole of the law that allowed capital punishment in robberies involving instances of personal assault. Serving as his own lawyer, Chessman pleaded his case and wrote a series of appeals. In 1954, he published a book, *Cell 2455 Death Row*, which told of his life and his battle to overcome the death penalty. In 1955, Columbia made a film based on Chessman's memoirs. Chessman continued his lengthy legal battle for many years, winning stays of execution at the last minute. On May 2, 1960, however, he exhausted all possible legal maneuvers, and the death penalty was finally carried out. At the time, Chessman set the record for the longest wait on death row, eleven years and ten months.

Synopsis

The Columbia film opens at San Quentin prison on the evening of July 29, 1954, where a prisoner is awaiting execution in the gas chamber. The warden visits the man, known only as "Whittier" or "Whit" and offers him any reasonable last request, but the man has none. He chooses to wait in his cell and review the course of the life that had brought him to his present state. A series of flashbacks reviews Whit's life. His parents moved to California when he was a young boy, and soon his father was able to afford his first automobile. A car accident, however, crippled his mother and threw the family into poverty. In an effort to help, Whit began to shoplift and steal food. He soon fell in with a bad crowd, and after stealing a car, he was placed in reform school. Whit rebelled against authority, and his years in the reformatory were hard. By the time he was released, Whit had become a hardened criminal, committing a series of armed robberies and earning a sentence in San Quentin. He decides to become a model prisoner and is transferred to a work farm, from which he escapes. Returning to a life of crime, Whit is soon picked up again, drawing a stiffer sentence at Folsom Prison. When he is released, Whit is no wiser and again returns to his criminal ways. The next time he is arrested, however, he is accused of being the Red Light Bandit, the perpetrator of a series of brutal thefts. Whit thinks he can beat the rap because his physical appearance differs markedly from the eyewitness descriptions of the Red Light Bandit. While in the custody of the sheriff, he is informed that his mother has died and he is allowed to attend her wake. His lawyer drops his case, however, and rather than rely on the public defender, he attempts to represent himself. Whit is convicted and sentenced to the gas chamber due to the application of a legal technicality. While on death row, Whit studies the law to handle the appeal process. Through brilliant legal maneuvers, he manages to postpone his execution for six years. He even publishes his autobiography, *Cell 2455 Death Row*, which becomes a best seller. But his battle seems at an end in July 1954, and the flashbacks conclude. As he prepares for his trip to the gas chamber, the warden appears and tells him that he has been granted a last-minute stay. The film ends as Whit begins work on another legal brief, resuming his battle against capital punishment.

Critique

Although the character in this film is never identified as Caryl Chessman, the situation is made clearer if one realizes that Whittier is Chessman's middle name. William Campbell delivers a serious, low-key performance as the condemned man, making him more sympathetic than the real-life Chessman, who was far more arrogant and cocky than Campbell's depiction. In the film, Whit is clearly not the Red Light Bandit, but in real life the issue is still hotly debated. In any case, Chessman was condemned to death not for murder but for robbery, and the issue of the justness of this sentence is paramount. Undoubtedly, if Chessman was not such an unsavory character with such a tarnished record, the death penalty would never have been applied. The script treats the issue of capital punishment with ambivalence, trying to avoid the critical interpretation that the film is too soft on crime. The dramatic highlight of the film is Chessman's self-examination, at which point he finally condemns himself not for being the Red Light Bandit but for being addicted to deceit: "I know now what brings a man to death row. Not society, not heredity, not environment, only the man himself. I alone am to blame." An analysis of this statement would make a worthwhile thesis. Another element of the film worth studying is how a man may change while imprisoned. Campbell portrays Chessman as a changed man, altered not only by his ordeal but by the education he attains while writing and studying law. His statement to the warden that he is now more valuable to society "alive rather than dead" is one of the most poignant moments in the film, and this is another aspect worth investigating. On the whole, *Cell 2455 Death Row* is a laudable B film, certainly mixed with some elements from exploitation films, but nevertheless a serious study. Chessman is well played by William Campbell, an actor best remembered for two colorful guest appearances on *Star Trek* in the episodes "The Squire of Gothos" and "The Trouble with Tribbles." Campbell's younger brother plays the teenage Chessman, and Bart Braverman (billed as Bart Bradley) plays Chessman as a child. Braverman is best remembered as Binzer from *VEGA$*. Later, the story of Chessman was retold in a 1977 telefilm, *Kill Me While You Can*, featuring a miscast Alan Alda in the title role.

Chicago Calling
(1951)

Principal social themes: suicide/depression, addiction (alcohol), homelessness/poverty

United Artists. No MPAA rating. Featuring: Dan Duryea, Mary Anderson, Gordon Gebert, Ross Elliott, Melinda Plowman, Judy Brubaker, Marsha Jones, Roy Engel, Dick Curtis, Gene Roth. Written by Peter Berneis and John Reinhardt. Cinematography by Robert De Grasse. Edited by Arthur H. Nadel. Music by Heinz Roemheld. Produced by Peter Berneis. Directed by John Reinhardt. B&W. 74 minutes.

Overview

Chicago Calling is an atypical little production, influenced by European trends such as the postwar rubble films in Germany and the neo-realist cinema of Italy. Shot in the run down, lower-class areas of Los Angeles, the picture is filled with a social consciousness quite unusual in American films. Critics were strongly divided about *Chicago Calling*, a few seeing it as a minor masterpiece but many others were turned off by the rather contrived denouement of the story.

Synopsis

Dan Duryea plays Bill Cannon, an alcoholic, out-of-work photographer who is unable to provide adequately for his wife, Mary, and his young daughter, Nancy. After Bill's all-night bender, Mary decides to leave the squalor of their dingy apartment and return to her mother's home in Baltimore. Bill is heartbroken, but pawns his last valuable so Mary can pay $30 to ride with an elderly couple driving to Maryland. His daughter's last request before she leaves is for her father to care for her dog Smitty. Bill gets drunk after their departure, and only comes out of his haze days later when he receives a stunning telegram from Mary. There was an auto accident, and Nancy is critically injured and will undergo surgery. Mary tells him to expect her phone call the following morning between 9 and 10 o'clock to give him an update. The telephone repairman arrives with a disconnect order, and Bill begs him to leave the telephone for one more day. He agrees, but explains that Bill will have to settle his unpaid account of $53 to activate the line. Bill visits the phone company to ask for an extension, and then turns to his closest drinking buddy to ask for a loan. He becomes desperate when he is turned down, and next tries a finance company and finally a charity agency. They sympathize with him, but explain that he has to register to receive funds and that takes time. Downcast, he stops at an outdoor lunch counter to spend his remaining money on soup and a hamburger patty for Smitty. The waitress asks him his troubles, and she slips him $5, claiming it came from a sympathetic bystander. Smitty is run over by a youngster on a bicycle. The dog is slightly injured and the boy, Bobby Kimball (Gordon Gebert), befriends Bill. He offers him the loan of his piggybank savings, which comes to $50. Bill learns that Bobby is an orphan, who is being raised by Babs, his older sister. She complains that she is sick and tired of being saddled with the boy. When Bobby learns that his sister has confiscated his bank, he steals a roll of bills that had fallen out of the pocket of Art, Babs's boyfriend, who is napping in Bobby's bed. Bobby offers this money to Bill, but when he returns to the phone company, their office has already closed. Bill passes the evening with Bobby, who loses and later recovers the roll of money. Bill decides to return the money to Art, who is outraged by the theft and threatens to file charges with the police. Bill works all night at a construction site to earn a few bucks. Early in the morning, he spends all these funds using a pay phone to call the Chicago police, but they are unable to find information about his daughter before his money runs out. Dejected, Bill returns to his flat. To his surprise, the phone rings, and he learns that the telephone repairman, on his own volition, has just reattached his line for one hour so that he can receive his emergency call. Two police detectives show up, however, to arrest Bill due to Art's complaint. As they are taking him away, the phone rings and they allow him to answer it. He learns from his wife that Nancy died during her operation. One of the officers, understanding the situation, calls the station and manages to void the order for Bill's arrest. They release him, but Bill has sunk into a deep depression. Bobby tries to follow him as he walks down the street. Bill walks deliberately into traffic, attempting to get hit, but the cars and trucks either stop or swerve so that he is unharmed. Bill heads to the rail yard and plans to stand in front of a moving train. Bobby enlists the aid of an elderly railroad engineer, but they lose sight of Bill who disappears behind a second train traveling in the other direction. Bobby screams, but as the last of the boxcars pass, sees that Bill is unharmed and runs into his arms. They embrace, and Bill assures the boy that he will be all right. The engineer asks if he is related to Bobby. Bill replies "He's my son," and the music swells as the closing credits appear.

Critique

The Hollywood ending, as Bill replaces his lost daughter with Bobby, seems contrived, particularly when you consider the two had met less than twenty-four hours earlier. Given Bill's circumstances, there would seem to be no way he would be allowed to gain custody of the Kimball boy, in spite of Babs' comment, "Let me know whenever you want him and he is yours for keeps." There is also something aberrant that Bill so easily replaces his daughter with a son. True, he loved his daughter, but psychologically he seems to wish she were a boy instead. He tries to instruct her to act with male aggressiveness, for example, by physically confronting bullies. Yet despite this jarring and synthetic conclusion, *Chicago Calling* is memorable for a number of reasons. The uncompromising and stark portrayal of poverty is unforgettable. The gritty cinematography, almost entirely filmed on location, is impressive. Dan Duryea gives an honest and deeply felt performance. His numbing despair and impulse to commit suicide are totally convincing. The script carefully weaves many social issues throughout the story, particularly depression, alcoholism, and poverty. Throughout the story, Bill Cannon is handed one psychological blow after another until suicide seems the only path to end his ordeal. In behavioral terms, what is Bill's breaking point? Is it greater or less than the average individual? What motivates him, and in what way does he fit into society? *Chicago Calling* can be seen on different levels, such as a study in human endurance or even as a black comedy, in which "Murphy's law" is played out. Students of this film might find it useful to project Bill's future course. Will his wife ever rejoin him? Will he revert back to alcoholism and his suicidal tendencies?

The Choice
(1981)

Principal social theme: abortion

Greene Productions. No MPAA rating. Featuring: Susan Clark, Mitchell Ryan, Largo Woodruff, Paul Regina, Jennifer Warren, Kathleen Lloyd, Lisa Jane Persky, John Chappell, Joanne Naile, Justin Lord, Cheryl Smith. Written by Dennis Nemec. Cinematography by Stevan Larner. Edited by Parkie Singh. Music by Johann Sebastian Bach and Leopold Stokowski. Produced by Joseph M. Taritero and David Greene. Directed by David Greene. Color. 97 minutes.

Overview

The Choice is a motion picture that focuses on a wide range of viewpoints about abortion and the difficulty of the decision, as both a mother and daughter confront the issue with their own unexpected pregnancies. Susan Clark and Largo Woodruff are excellent in this telefilm, which premiered on CBS on February 10, 1981.

Synopsis

Twenty-year-old Lisa Clements (Largo Woodruff) discovers she is pregnant. She keeps her discovery secret from Michael (Paul Regina), her live-in boyfriend who has just graduated from college. He is offered a job at a new company in Idaho, and he asks Lisa to accompany him. She asks Michael to drive her to her parent's home in southern California for the weekend. When they are alone, Lisa tells Kay (Susan Clark), her mother, about her problem. Kay reveals that she also had an unwanted pregnancy the previous year. She tells Lisa about the ordeal of coming to a decision about whether to have an abortion. At first, she wanted to confide in her husband, Jerry (Mitchell Ryan), but he was depressed and angry about losing a promotion at work. Kay seeks advice from an abortion counseling service, but is upset when she learns that the group has a hidden agenda, to frighten women about abortion. She visits an abortion clinic, but seems repelled by their casual attitude about the process. Kay tries to visit Lisa at college, but returns home after learning her daughter had plans for the weekend. She catches Jerry planning a weekend getaway with his secretary. She decides to have an abortion, but only under general anesthesia. She is referred to a hospital and is placed in a ward with three other women, who all have rather different reactions to their intended abortions. Kay undergoes the abortion with ease, but she decides to stay at the bedside of one of the other women who is undergoing a late-term abortion through induced labor. After her ordeal is over, Kay returns home to find her husband believing she had been out overnight with another man. Jerry admits his error with his unsuccessful weekend fling, but demands to know the details of Kay's affair. He is stunned to learn she had an abortion and realizes he had pushed Kay away when she tried to tell him that she had a problem. They reconcile and Kay's flashback ends. She tells her daughter only one essential piece of advice, to make her decision quickly. The film ends as Lisa decides to tell Michael and involve him in making her choice.

Critique

One of the major strengths of *The Choice* is its honest exploration of the variety of opinions, problems, and attitudes surrounding the issue of abortion by the woman involved, her loved ones, and those whose advice she seeks. The four women in Kay's ward form a small microcosm. Kay is the oldest, having her abortion in secret. The second woman is also married, accompanied by her concerned husband. This is the woman who wants to have a child but learns her baby has Down's Syndrome and would probably not live if carried to full term. The third woman is in her early twenties and is casual about the procedure but disappointed that her boyfriend offers her only token support. The fourth woman, in her late teens, is delighted with her abortion. She had relations with six different men just before her pregnancy, and each one paid her the full cost of the operation. She plans to take her windfall and spend it on a vacation in Hawaii. So the reasons for these abortions are due to necessity, to convenience, to fear, and for profit. Kay does not believe her marriage would survive if she has the child. At thirty-eight, she believes she does not have the strength or desire to rear another child. She has also just taken a job as a home decorator, an experience that she finds completely fulfilling. She also has many doubts, including moral concerns about taking a life and whether her fetus would feel any pain. She talks with a great many people about her reservations and encounters a wide range of reactions, from her personal doctor who disapproves of abortion to a teen who says her parents prefer abortion to the concept of birth control. Kay's situation is largely determined by the crisis in Jerry's life. It is only in the end, after he learns of Kay's pregnancy, that her husband realizes the misery he caused by not being supportive when his wife most needed him. Finally, Kay's ordeal makes it possible for her daughter to make her decision with the support of those around her.

A Civil Action
(1998)

Principal social theme: environmental issues

Touchstone/Paramount. PG-13 rating. Featuring: John Travolta, Robert Duvall, Tony Shalhoub, William H. Macy, John Lithgow, Kathleen Quinlan, Zeljko Ivanek, Bruce Norris, Peter Jacobson, Sydney Pollack, Dan Hedaya, James Gandolfini, Kathy Bates, Howie Carr. Written by Steven Zaillian based on the book by Jonathan Harr. Cinematography by Conrad L. Hall. Edited by Wayne Wahrman. Music by Danny Elfman. Produced by Scott Rudin, Robert Redford, and Rachel Pfeiffer. Directed by Steven Zaillian. Color. 115 minutes.

Overview

A Civil Action is a dramatization of a famous lengthy legal case involving water pollution with toxic chemicals and a nearby cluster of leukemia deaths in Woburn, Massachusetts. Based on the book by Jonathan Harr, a journalist who closely followed the actual events, the film portrays how a lawyer sacrificed his thriving practice and career to concentrate on this one particular case. The legal process ended in a technical stalemate with a relatively unimpressive settlement, and the lawyer went bankrupt. Later, he turned his records over to the Environmental Protection Agency, and they eventually undertook the largest environmental cleanup in the history of New England.

Synopsis

The story opens in the early 1980s as flamboyant Boston attorney Jan Schlichtmann (John Travolta), a personal injury specialist, appears on the Howie Carr radio show to talk about his successful law practice. He receives an on-air phone call from Anne Anderson (Kathleen Quinlan) imploring the lawyer to look at her case. She and eight other families believe that a cluster of leukemia cases that affected their families was the result of the polluted water of their community of Woburn. Schlichtmann meets with them, advising that they do not have a plausible case. After receiving a speeding ticket near the Aberjona River, the lawyer notices that two factories bordering the river are owned by major conglomerates: The John J. Riley Tannery by Beatrice Foods and Cryovac Manufacturing by the W. R. Grace Company.

He and his five-man law firm decide to take the case and file a major lawsuit claiming the dumping of hazardous waste resulted in wrongful deaths. The two companies are represented by two high-power attorneys, Grace by Arthur Cheeseman and Beatrice by Jerry Facher (Robert Duvall), a colorful eccentric who specializes in dragging things out. Years pass as Schlichtmann prepares the case, taking depositions and gathering the scientific evidence to prove that the two companies, by dumping toxic waste, were responsible for the pollution of the wells used as the town's water supply. His law firm spends millions of dollars preparing the case, and most of the staff mortgage their own homes to fund the lawsuit. Judge Skinner (John Lithgow) seems hostile to Schlichtmann. Before the trial begins, the two companies meet to discuss a possible settlement with Schlichtmann, but the financial sum he demands is so exorbitant that they walk out of the meeting without making a counteroffer. In court, Facher makes a proposal to divide the case into two parts, first requiring the plaintiffs to prove the companies were responsible for the pollution. Skinner agrees over Schlichtmann's objections. When this part of the case goes to the jury, Facher, on behalf of Beatrice, offers Schlichtmann a twenty-million dollar settlement on the spot, but Schlichtmann turns him down. The jury then returns finding the Grace Company liable for illegal dumping, but not Beatrice Foods. Facher is delighted as the case against Beatrice is dropped. Time again passes, and the other members of the law firm are becoming desperate. When Schlichtmann is summoned to the headquarters of the Grace Company in New York City, they make a settlement offer of eight million dollars. With this amount, each of the families would receive about four hundred thousand, and the law firm would come close to breaking even. Over Schlichtmann's objections, the other members of his firm insist he accept the offer. After settling, they decide to break up the firm, leaving Schlichtmann on his own. He opens a small one-room office. Facing personal bankruptcy, Schlichtmann files an appeal on the verdict that released Beatrice from liability because they withheld a report that bolstered the plaintiff's argument. Unable to pursue the case further, Schlichtmann turns his files over to the Environmental Protection Agency. Closing title cards reveals that the EPA eventually ordered a massive cleanup of the polluted area, and Beatrice Foods and the Grace Company were required to pay for most of the cleanup. Schlichtmann moved to New Jersey, where he becomes involved in another controversial water pollution case in Toms River, New Jersey.

Critique

A Civil Action is a well-made and insightful film dealing not only with environmental pollution, but also the archaic legal system in which justice seems to take a backseat to judicial wrangling and one-upmanship. Like the original best-selling book, the screenplay stresses the "David vs. Goliath" aspects of the legal battle of a small law firm against the resources of two huge corporations. Although based closely on facts, there are two significant differences from actual events. There was a third company involved in Schlichtmann's lawsuit, the Unifirst Corporation, which settled with the plaintiff before the case began. Second, the picture makes it appear that the EPA was not involved until late in the process when Schlichtmann turned over his records to them. In fact, the EPA was involved in the case well before Schlichtmann. They had identified Grace, Beatrice, and Unifirst as being responsible for the pollution. EPA officials believed that Schlichtmann actually delayed the cleanup effort because of his lawsuit, since the companies did not want to cooperate with them while the lawsuit hung over their heads. This certainly undercuts the lawyer's hero status as depicted in the film. Even sticking to the screen story, however, Schlichtmann also loses luster because of his arrogant self-confidence. He becomes so personally committed to the case that he loses his professional detachment, obvious in his refusal of Facher's impressive settlement offer of twenty million dollars. *A Civil Action* must be commended for covering the issue of industrial pollution in an intelligent and coherent way while still remaining entertaining. The cast of characters is colorful, such as the curmudgeon Facher, brilliant played by Robert Duvall, or the slimy tannery operator John J. Riley, played by the talented Dan Hedaya. William H. Macy and Tony Shalhoub are also outstanding as Schlichtmann's partners, and James Gandolfini shines as Anne Anderson's neighbor who testifies about the illegal toxic chemical dumping by his employer. John Travolta, of course, holds the film together as the crusading lawyer in a credible reading. *A Civil Action* manages to include considerable environmental facts in its presentation, how drinking water can be contaminated by trichloroethylene, tetrachloroethylene, and other industrial solvents. Viewers might also note that Robert Redford was one of the film's producers.

Colors
(1988)

Principal social theme: violence/gangs

Orion. R rating. Featuring: Robert Duvall, Sean Penn, Maria Conchita Alonso, Randy Brooks, Grand Bush, Don Cheadle, Rudy Ramos, Trinidad Silva, Damon Wayans, Glenn Plummer, Sy Richardson, Geraldo Mejia, Bruce Beatty, Charles

Walker, Sherman Augustus, Fred Asparagus; Written by Michael Schiffer and
Richard Dilello. Cinematography by Haskell Wexler. Edited by Robert Estrin.
Music by Herbie Hancock. Song "Colors" written and performed by Ice-T.
Produced by Robert H. Solo and Paul Lewis. Directed by Dennis Hopper. Color.
127 minutes (original version); 120 minutes (revised version).

Overview

When initially released to theaters, this 1988 portrait of Los Angeles street
gangs provoked riots in a number of West Coast urban theaters, not so much
because of the film itself, but because rival gangs turned out to see it and
their rivalry spilled over. Nevertheless, Orion studio edited out about six and
a half minutes of violent footage (and some sex scenes) before its general
release. This footage was later restored on video. *Colors* gained a reputation as
one of the most realistic portraits of youth gangs, although some critics
regarded it as an updated variation of *Dragnet* with a rap score.

Synopsis

An opening scrawl describes how the Los Angeles police force has formed a
special division to deal with the problem of youth gangs. The unit is called
CRASH, for "Community Resources Against Street Hoodlums," and it
contains 250 men. The total membership of the street gangs, however,
exceeds 70,000. Danny McGavin (Sean Penn), a cocky young rookie added to
CRASH is paired with Bob Hodges (Robert Duvall), a wily veteran one year
away from retirement. Danny is a gung-ho dynamo, and Hodges tries to slow
him down to focus on the big picture and to gain the respect of the youth on
the street. A bloody turf war in the barrios of East L.A. has developed between the two most active gangs, who fly their rival colors, red and blue. A
series of night-time drive-by shootings sets the community on edge. After a
scuffle, Danny makes his first collar, a young thug nicknamed "High Top,"
and he is furious when Hodges lets him go after a warning. It later turns out
that High Top is identified as a top drug courier. When their police car is hit
with a rock, Hodges demonstrates his style in identifying the culprit. They
also meet Philipe, a young Hispanic they hope to prevent from becoming a
gang member. When another drive-by shooting occurs, Danny pursues the
culprits in a wild chase through the back alleys of East L.A. The killer's car
finally crashes and burns, but though Danny loses control and also crashes,
he and Hodges are unhurt. Hodges invites his new partner to dinner. Danny
invites a local waitress, Louisa, to come as his date. Hodges comes to believe
that he and his new partner are not making a good team after Danny gets
out of control and roughs up a handcuffed suspect. Louisa also breaks off
with Danny after he spray paints the face of a kid he is arresting. When
Danny asks her for the reason, she tells him the kid is her cousin. The

confrontations between the gangs become increasingly more violent. Rocket, one of the gang leaders, organizes a major hit. Philipe joins a rival gang just before they launch a revenge strike against Rocket's headquarters. Rocket and his top henchmen are wiped out, but the police ambush the rival gang while they celebrate their victory. Bob Hodges is hit in the raid, and he dies as Danny tries to comfort him. The story ends a few months later. Danny has a new partner, a boisterous rookie. A more serious Danny has adopted the ways of Hodges and tries to break in his new partner using the same advise and anecdotes that Hodges told him. Meanwhile, life on the streets continues with the same pattern of pointless violence.

Critique

In order to film in the heart of gang territory in East L.A., director Dennis Hopper employed actual gang members to serve as advisors, protectors, and extras. In fact, two of these hired hands were killed in gang violence during the film's shooting schedule. Authentic gang hangouts were also used in the filming. So *Colors* comes very close to documenting the lifestyle, language, and nihilistic philosophy of these gangs. The dialogue of the street toughs is sometimes hard to follow, as well as being reliant on the use of obscenity. The cinematography is gritty, dark, and claustrophobic, even the scenes in Griffith Park. One of the major goals of *Colors* was to call attention to the growing gang phenomenon, largely ignored by middle America. It succeeded in this even if it did not suggest any solutions. So the picture focuses totally on the problem. The rap song, "Colors" by Ice-T, succinctly sums up the gang philosophy, living only for revenge and for their colors. The drug trade is only a means to an end. Each time one gang's leadership is exterminated, others quickly take their place. The character of Philipe serves as a metaphor for how each successive generation is drawn into gangs. Since CRASH proved unable to guide, frighten, or inspire the boy not to fall in with the street thugs, how can they stem the flow? The police seem to be fighting an endless holding action, with the phrase "Operation Safe Streets" expressing only a faint hope. The ending of *Colors* is somewhat predictable, following the pattern set by *Sands of Iwo Jima* (1949), in which the younger John Agar takes over for the fallen John Wayne. It is also not entirely convincing, since Sean Penn's Danny still has a considerable way to go to match the streetwise instincts and experience that Robert Duvall's Hodges had developed. One wonders if Danny could ever possibly match his rapport with the youth in the streets.

Compulsion
(1959)

Principal social theme: capital punishment

20th Century Fox. No MPAA rating. Featuring: Bradford Dillman, Dean Stockwell, Orson Welles, E. G. Marshall, Martin Milner, Diane Varsi, Richard Anderson, Robert Simon, Edward Binns, Voltaire Perkins, Wilton Graff, Louise Lorimer, Gavin MacLeod, Russ Bender, Gerry Lock, Harry Carter, Terry Becker. Written by Richard Murphy based on a novel by Meyer Levin. Cinematography by William C. Mellor. Edited by William Reynolds. Music by Lionel Newman. Produced by Richard D. Zanuck and Darryl F. Zanuck (executive). Directed by Richard Fleischer. B&W. 103 minutes.

Overview

Meyer Levin attended college with the notorious Nathan Leopold and Richard Loeb, the brilliant teenage pair who conceived the thrill killing of a child in Chicago in 1924. The two young murderers were given life sentences after one of the most publicized trials of the twentieth century, which hinged almost exclusively on the issue of capital punishment. Years later Levin wrote both a novel and a play about the famous crime, only altering the names of the characters but not the events. After Leopold was paroled from prison in 1958, he attempted to sue Meyer over his work, but his case failed. (Loeb died in prison). *Compulsion*, the screen version of the story, was both an artistic and financial success. More importantly, *Compulsion* served as the clearest and most intellectually disciplined examination of the topic of capital punishment on film.

Synopsis

For all intents and purposes, *Compulsion* is the authentic story of the famous murder case that rocked Chicago in the 1920s, but with the actual names altered: the arrogant Nathan Leopold, played by Bradford Dillman, is called Artie Straus; the hypersensitive Richard Loeb, played by Dean Stockwell, is now Judd Steiner; the famous attorney Clarence Darrow, played by Orson Welles, is transformed into Jonathan Wilk, and the young victim, Bobby Franks, is called Paulie Kessler. In structure, the drama is divided into two halves, somewhat in the format of various noted television series such as

Arrest and Trial or *Law and Order*. The first half shows the conception of the crime as the two brilliant students decide to prove their natural superiority by executing a perfect crime, the heinous murder of a local child. Soon, however, their scheme unravels as they blunder and are caught due to Steiner's dropping his glasses (with a frame featuring a distinctive hinge) at the scene of the crime. Under questioning, the two boys are trapped by their inconsistent stories, which lead to their arrest. Their families hire Jonathan Wilk, considered to be the country's leading defense attorney and opponent of capital punishment.

The second half of the film concentrates on the trial and legal maneuverings. The prosecuting attorney, excellently played by E. G. Marshall, fears that Wilk will use an insanity defense and builds his case to withstand that ploy. Instead, Wilk switches his plea to guilty after a jury is seated, since he concludes that there is no way he could persuade the men selected to vote otherwise. He chooses to plead before the judge alone to determine the punishment. After calling a few witnesses to detail possible mitigating circumstances, Wilk's main thrust is his final appeal to the bench, a calm, sincere plea examining the issue of capital punishment. He also stresses the age of the defendants, legally minors when they committed the terrible crime. At the conclusion of his lengthy address, the prosecutor stands in tribute to the eloquence of Wilk's presentation. The judge gives Straus and Steiner life imprisonment. Unrepentant, Strauss mocks Wilk, a known agnostic, for his mention of God in his plea to the judge. In reply, Wilk asks who Artie believed was responsible for the key piece of evidence, the glasses, being dropped at the scene of the crime.

Critique

Orson Welles was uniquely qualified to deliver the spellbinding address on capital punishment that provides the climax of the film. In his youth, Welles met and knew Clarence Darrow, and he was able to draw on that experience to craft his performance in *Compulsion*. The actual Darrow address lasted two days, and it was distilled into a fourteen-minute speech, one of the longest speeches in cinema history; Welles' oratory was also issued as a long-playing record at the time of the film's release. It is interesting to note that Darrow's original speech, perhaps the most influential airing of the issue in the twentieth century, and the trimmed down version delivered by Welles, owe much to the famous speech by Maximilien Robespierre before the Constituent Assembly of France on May 30, 1791, in which he proposed the abolition of the death penalty.

When shooting this crucial scene, Welles knew the production was behind schedule, so he agreed to do the scene not in sequential order, but in order of the camera setups. This saved tremendous time, and it was only possible because Welles knew the speech so thoroughly. Nevertheless, Welles' perfect delivery, including the proper flow of the speech, is considered a remarkable achievement. Jonathan Wilk's address to the court is very basic and down-to-earth, without histrionics. It is straightforward, heartfelt, low-key, and logical, and Welles presents the arguments in a most effective manner. Students could analyze this speech on a number of different levels. Which of the arguments of the address apply exclusively to the case at hand and which to the issue at large? Why do the points raised by Robespierre and Darrow have such a universal appeal? Why is the speech delivered by Welles so persuasive and memorable in comparison to other screen presentations of social issues that seem stuffy or preachy? Would Welles' speech carry a lesser impact if the case were fictitious? Finally, does the fact that the murder is so heinous either help or hurt the arguments in the final address?

Compulsion received a unique honor at the 1959 Cannes Film Festival when Orson Welles, Bradford Dillman, and Dean Stockwell received a three-way award as best actor in a feature film.

Conrack
(1974)

Principal social themes: education/literacy, homelessness/poverty, racism/civil rights

20th Century Fox. PG rating. Featuring: Jon Voight, Paul Winfield, Hume Cronyn, Madge Sinclair, Tina Andrews, Antonio Fargas, Ruth Attaway, James O'Reare, Gracia Lee, C. P. MacDonald, Jane Moreland, Thomas Horton, Nancy Butler, Robert W. Page, John Kennedy. Written by Irving Ravetch and Harriet Frank Jr. based on the novel *The Water Is Wide* by Pat Conroy. Cinematography by John A. Alonzo. Edited by Frank Bracht. Music by John Williams. Produced by Martin Ritt and Harriet Frank Jr. Directed by Martin Ritt. Color. 107 minutes.

Overview

Pat Conroy, the popular author of *The Prince of Tides* and *The Lords of Discipline,* was originally a teacher, and his experiences instructing a group of poor black children on a small island off the coast of South Carolina in 1969 provided the basis for his autobiographical novel *The Water Is Wide.* The book was quickly picked up for major film treatment starring Jon Voight as

Conroy. The picture was principally filmed on St. Simons Island, Georgia. When released, *Conrack* became a modest hit domestically, but a blockbuster in many international markets. *Conrack* also received a number of critical awards.

Synopsis

In March 1969, Pat Conroy is appointed the new teacher of Yamacraw, a small, impoverished island off the coast of South Carolina. The residents are exclusively black, except for the owner of the general store. Pat is startled at the very low education level of the two dozen children at the one-room school. The students cannot even pronounce his name correctly, and he lets them call him "Conrack." The principal, Mrs. Scott (Madge Sinclair), calls the students her "babies," and she warns Pat that the children are lazy and need discipline. Pat believes that traditional educational methods have left these kids behind, so he instigates a free-wheeling, stream of consciousness style, jumping from one topic to another, hoping to stimulate their interest. At random, he switches topics, asking questions about history, baseball, poetry, pop culture, astronomy, and geography. Slowly, the children begin to respond. When he takes them on a field trip around the island, identifying wild flowers, Pat is attacked by a hermit named Mad Billy (Paul Winfield). Later, Mad Billy apologizes and offers to trade moonshine, his only viable commodity, to Pat if he would teach him to read and write. Pat also hires Mary, a teenage local, as a cook and tries to persuade her to attend school. Mr. Skeffington (Hume Cronyn), the district school superintendent, visits the island to observe Pat's methods. Skeffington is amiable but very old-fashioned. When they go to the general store for a drink, Skeffington rails against the Vietnam War protesters they see on television. The super-intendent becomes upset when he sees that one of the marchers is Ralphie, his own estranged son. Since Pat wears long hair and also opposes the war, Skeffington is not impressed with him either. A few weeks later, he pays a sur-prise return visit to the island to warn Pat that he has complaints about his teaching methods and about being late to class. Pat suspects Mrs. Scott as the source of the bad reports, but the response of the students convinces Pat that his methods are succeeding. When one of the locals drowns, Pat learns that most of the islanders cannot swim. He takes his class to the beach and teaches them to swim. He plays classical music for them, such as Rimsky-Korsakov's *Flight of the Bumble Bee* and Beethoven's *Fifth Symphony*. All the students agree to attend summer school, and Pat arranges more field trips around the island. He finds a projector and screens *The Black Swan*, an old pirate movie with Tyrone Power for them, the first film ever seen by most of the class, who have never been off the island. In the fall, Pat wants to take the class to Beaufort on the mainland so the kids could go trick-or-treating on Halloween. Skeffington disapproves of this outing and orders Pat to keep his kids "on the other side." Pat carries through with his plans, which go very well. Skeffington treats the kids kindly when they come to his door on Halloween, however he fires Pat a few days later. Mrs. Scott urges Pat to fight for his job, saying she will back him because she knows he loves the "babies." The teacher appeals to Skeffington to reconsider. The superintendent listens to him patiently, but does not change his mind. Pat rents a sound truck in Beaufort, saying that the old South will have to make way for a new South where racial prejudice will no longer be tolerated. When Pat packs and leaves the island, his students see him off at the dock. As his boat pulls off, they play the recording of Beethoven's *Fifth Symphony* to demonstrate that his influence will not be forgotten.

Critique

Conrack is an unusual film noted for its vital and energetic approach to education and its overall lyrical and inspirational tone. The picture is unusually rich with topics for discussion. Why was Pat's approach with the children successful? Why did they respond? Would he have been as successful in an urban school? Consider the pessimistic rationale behind Mrs. Scott's attitude, being tough on the kids because the world (and "the man") will be tough on them. Pat, on the other, is an idealist, trying to get his students to reach out and attempt the impossible. The long-term impact of Pat's approach is not apparent in the film, but the change in Mary is a modest indication of his influence, when she rejects the offer to move in with a man named Quickfellow. Also note how Pat himself changes. At first, he largely talks over the heads of his students, but by the time he introduces them to Beethoven ("Beetcloven") and prepares them to listen to the composer's *Fifth Symphony*, he speaks in terms that the students can grasp. The consequences of poverty are also stressed in the film, and although it is never directly addressed, *Conrack* rather clearly spells out that education is the only forceful and effective solution to overwhelming poverty. Racism is another major social issue considered in *Conrack*. Is the racism portrayed in the film primarily fueled by hatred or simply habit? Could Skeffington be seen as a passive racist? Pat encounters three reactions when he seeks to board the black children in Beaufort: Some slam the door in his face; Some say they need to check with their spouse, and others simply say "OK." How convincing are Pat's criticisms when he rents the sound truck? Why does this scene fall flat? In contrast, the final episode, when the children gather on the dock and play the Beethoven *Fifth Symphony*, is extraordinarily moving and effective, closing the film at a very high point.

Cradle Will Rock
(1999)

Principal social themes: censorship, homelessness/ poverty, homosexuality

Touchstone. R rating. Featuring: Hank Azaria, Ruben Blades, Joan Cusack, John Cusack, Cary Elwes, Philip Baker Hall, Cherry Jones, Angus MacFadyen, Bill Murray, Vanessa Redgrave, Susan Sarandon, Jamey Sheridan, John Turturro, Emily Watson, Bob Balaban, Barnard Hughes, John Carpenter, Gretchen Moll, Harris Yulin, Steven Skybell, Susan Heimbeinder, Corina Katt Ayala. Written by Tim Robbins based on a story by Orson Welles. Cinematography by Jean Yves Escoffier. Edited by Geraldine Peroni. Music by Marc Blitzstein and David Robbins. Produced by Jon Kilik, Lydia Dean Pilcher, and Tim Robbins. Directed by Tim Robbins. Color. 134 minutes.

Overview

Cradle Will Rock is based on the controversial 1937 debut of the Marc Blitzstein opera, which was initially sponsored by the Federal Theater Project, but then shut down by the government. Locked out of their theater, Welles took a gamble and moved the premiere to another theater where the composer presented the work alone at the piano on an empty stage. Unexpectedly, the original cast members joined in the singing from their seats in the audience. This sensational debut became one of the most memorable events in the history of New York theater. To this main story, Tim Robbins added the 1933 episode, in which a mural painted by the Mexican artist Diego Rivera was ordered destroyed by Nelson Rockefeller, who had originally commissioned it. Other subplots, some fictional, were added, highlighting the issues of artistic freedom, competing political ideologies, and most importantly, censorship.

Synopsis

Cradle Will Rock opens with a lengthy scrawl, describing the atmosphere of the Great Depression during the 1930s, including the influence of events in European countries such as Fascist Italy, Nazi Germany, and Communist Russia. The Works Progress Administration (WPA) was one American program designed to relieve unemployment. The Federal Theater Project (FTP), a division of the WPA, intended to provide jobs for out-of-work actors and relatively inexpensive entertainment for the public at large. The Federal theater was headed by Hallie Flanagan (Cherry Jones), who had run Vassar's experimental theater project. She turned to the young genius Orson Welles (Angus MacFadyen), who operated the classical unit of the FTP out of the Maxine Elliott Theater on 39th Street in New York City. His administrative partner at the Elliott was John Houseman (Cary Elwes). The story proper opens as homeless actress Olive Stanton (Emily Watson) awakens in her makeshift bed in the backstage of a motion picture theater. She is chased out of the theater when an usher spots her. Olive tries to earn money singing for nickels on Broadway. She overhears piano music coming from an apartment where composer Marc Blitzstein (Hank Azaria) is working on his opera *The Cradle Will Rock*. Olive goes to the employment line at the FTP to look for work. She does not have enough experience to qualify as an actress or singer, but she accepts work as a stagehand and is assigned to the Maxine Elliott Theater. She observes Orson Welles preparing his production of *Faustus* by Christopher Marlowe. Welles is upset that many of the performers are sticklers for union rules instead of the production. John Adair (Jamey Sheridan), an actor and the union representative for the FTP, befriends Olive. Another popular actor is Aldo Silvano (John Turturro), who is having considerable difficulty providing for his large family. Welles becomes interested in doing *The Cradle Will Rock* as his next production. Adair pushes Olive to audition in his place, and Welles hires her as the leading female character, a prostitute, for the opera. Aldo Silvano gets the male lead, a union organizer.

Other storylines intercut with the events at the Maxine Elliott Theater. One of them involves Nelson Rockefeller (John Cusack), who is passionately interested in modern art. He wants to hire a famous artist to paint a huge mural to be called *Man at the Crossroads* for Rockefeller Center. He decides to hire Diego Rivera (Ruben Blades), the fiery Mexican master. As Riviera works on the mural, Rockefeller is excited, but also concerned by the socialist tone of the work, which seems to include a May Day celebration. He asks an old friend of Rivera, Margherita Sarfatti (Susan Sarandon), to intercede and suggest making the mural more cheerful. Rivera, however, argues with Sarfatti, whom he now considers to be a lapdog for Italian dictator Benito Mussolini. Another plot follows Sarfatti's attempts to sell art to wealthy American industrialists in exchange for steel contracts for the Italian government. The industrialists are upset by attempts to unionize the steel industry, which is rumored to be the storyline of *The Cradle Will Rock*. FTP clerk Hazel Huffman (Joan Cusack) is upset by the socialist leanings of many FTP projects. She runs a meeting to discuss the issue, where she meets ventriloquist Tommy Crickshaw (Bill Murray), who is actually more interested in Hazel than in politics. They decide to testify before the House UnAmerican Activities Committee, chaired by conservative Democrat Martin Dies (Harris Yulin), to denounce the hidden leftist agenda of the FTP. The film jumps back and forth among these various plots. Things become serious when the federal government decides to pull the plug on *The Cradle Will Rock*. The WPA first institutes a twenty percent cutback to the project. When this does not force Welles to cancel the Blitzstein premiere, they send troops to barricade the theater. Welles is outraged by this attempt at censorship. He, Blitzstein, and Houseman confer in an attempt to save the project. Nelson Rockefeller is outraged when Rivera's mural includes a large portrait of Lenin. Rivera offers to also include a portrait of Lincoln, but Rockefeller insists that he remove Lenin. When Rivera refuses, Rockefeller pays him off and orders work halted on the mural. He later has the work destroyed. Hallie Flanagan goes to Washington to testify before the Committee on UnAmerican Activities, where she is treated very rudely. One of the representatives asks if Christopher Marlowe is a Communist playwright, and Flanagan replies that he was a contemporary of Shakespeare. Tommy Crickshaw accuses his two FTP students studying ventriloquism, of being Communists. They deny it, saying they are homosexuals instead. Crickshaw has a change of heart, and in his next performance, he has his dummy sing the Communist anthem, *The International*. When Welles decides to move *The Cradle Will Rock* to a theater he rented himself, Actors Equity rules that none of their actors may appear on stage. On the night of the performance, Welles leads the audience who show up outside the locked Maxine Elliott theater on a thirty-block walk to their new location just rented for the evening. As Blitzstein sings the opening number, a song by the prostitute who finds a nickel under her foot, Olive Stanton starts to sing from the audience. Other cast members join in at their proper entrances, except for Jerry Adair who stomps out of the theater. The evening performance is a dramatic sensation and a legendary hit. In the last shot of the film, a present-day image of Times Square and the theater district fills the screen.

Critique

Cradle Will Rock (note the film title drops the opening "The" of the opera title) is a sensational film, but very difficult to follow unless the viewer is familiar with the background of the June 18, 1937, debut of Blitzstein's opera. After the dramatic success of the opening, Actor's Equity reversed their decision and agreed to allow the actors to appear on stage, but Welles, aware of the dramatic impact, continued to do the show with the cast performing from the audience. In the wake of his defiance, Welles was finished at the FTP, but he and Houseman then formed their own privately financed group, The Mercury Theater. They successfully launched their project with a version of Shakespeare's *Julius Caesar* reset in Fascist Italy. They also continued with their production of *The Cradle Will Rock* under the Mercury Theater. The idea for a film version about these events came from Welles himself in the early 1980s. Welles intended to play himself, but he would largely be off screen, a voice in the shadows or on the telephone, since he was so much older. Unfortunately, Welles was unable to finance the film, but the idea eventually inspired Tim Robbins to tackle the project. His film magnificently captures the kinetic energy of New York in the 1930s, as well as the various passions from that era concerning Socialism, Fascism, and Communism. The performances of Blitzstein's songs in the picture are simply brilliant. The events of his version about the production of the opera are largely accurate, with a few exceptions. Olive Stanton, for example, was a real individual, but Aldo Silvano is fictitious. (In real life, Howard da Silva played the role of the union organizer in the opera.) The portrayals of Orson Welles and John Houseman are intriguing, but at times they seem like caricatures, too far over the top. The same could be said for the depiction of William Randolph Hearst. On the other hand, John Cusack successfully underplays Nelson Rockefeller.

The subplots Robbins added, however, are a mixed bag. The Rockefeller Center mural by Rivera is authentic, but this event actually occurred in 1933, and Rockefeller had the mural destroyed in February 1934. The mural as seen in the film, however, conforms exactly to Rivera's original. Hallie Flanagan's appearance before the House Committee happened a year after the debut of *The Cradle Will Rock*, but the Committee's question about Christopher Marlowe was authentic. The other subplots are largely fabricated. Tommy Crickshaw, for example, is a fictional character. Robbins' screenplay is dazzling, but somewhat confusing, as real-life figures appear and vanish without being properly introduced to the viewers. The various social issues are well integrated into the storyline. The opening sequence about Stanton's homelessness is very poignantly depicted. The film tones down Blitzstein's personal radicalism somewhat, but has him boast about his homosexuality. Hank Azaria plays Blitzstein with a surreal touch, having imaginary conversations with his late wife and playwright Bertolt Brecht. The best moments of the film are about censorship—by the government in the case of the opera and by private sources in the case of the mural. The film attempts to accurately portray the reasons for the censorship. There had been deaths in the riots for the unionization of the steel industry, and there was fear (totally unfounded) that the opera would foster fresh violence. Diego Rivera withheld his intention from Rockefeller about including the figure of Lenin in the mural. Since Rockefeller paid for the artwork, he was within his legal rights to destroy it. Both these cases can provide lively discussions for teachers, students, as well as the general public on the topic of censorship.

Cruising
(1980)

Principal social theme: homosexuality

United Artists. R rating. Featuring: Al Pacino, Paul Sorvino, Karen Allen, Richard Cox, Don Scardino, Joe Spinell, Jay Acovone, Gene Davis, Ed O'Neil, Randy Jurgensen, Larry Atlas, Allan Miller, James Remar, Linda Gray, William Russ, Powers Boothe. Written by William Friedkin based on the novel by Gerald Walker. Cinematography by James Contner. Edited by Bud Smith. Music by Jack Nitzsche. Produced by Jerry Weintraub. Directed by William Friedkin. Color. 106 minutes.

Overview

Cruising was one of the most controversial movies ever made about homosexuality, a mainstream film that was initially denounced by the gay community and ignored by the general moviegoing public. Years later, numerous adherents of the film appeared among homosexual and straight critics, who regarded the picture as a misunderstood masterpiece. In 1998, the film had a major revival in theaters. It is a haunting film, one not easily forgotten and that still is able to fascinate viewers.

Synopsis

At night, a tugboat crewman finds an arm floating in the Hudson River. Members of New York City's gay community are being murdered by a knife-wielding serial killer. Captain Edelson (Paul Sorvino) assigns a rookie cop, Steve Burns (Al Pacino), to pose as a homosexual and infiltrate the world of the sadomasochistic (S & M) underground. He chooses Burns because he is the same physical type as most of the victims. It is an awkward transition for Burns, a straight man who decides not to tell his girlfriend, Nancy (Karen Allen), the details of his new assignment. Steve moves into an apartment in Greenwich Village using the name John Forbes. The undercover cop meets Ted Bayley, a personable man who lives in the same building. Bayley lives with Greg, a dancer who is currently working out of town. Steve associates with Bayley, an aspiring writer, to gain familiarity with the gay lifestyle. Bayley tells Steve about the first victim of the serial killer, a professor from Columbia University. Steve tentatively starts to go "cruising," visiting a number of S & M clubs and raunchy gay bars. At first, he is asked to leave by the bouncers because he does not seem to fit in, but soon Steve learns the proper dress, walk, and attitude to pose as a member of the gay community. He begins to have suspicions about a man who tries to pick him up. A brutal killing takes place in a booth that shows gay movies. The cops discover a clue when they identify a coin that has the victim's blood and a fingerprint of the killer. Based on Steve's tip, the cops set up a trap for his suspect and give him a brutal interrogation, but he turns out to be innocent. When Steve visits Nancy, he tells her that his new assignment is troubling him, changing him. She suggests that they temporarily split up. Edelson gives Steve pages from a Columbia yearbook with students of the professor who was the first victim. Steve recognizes one of the photos as someone who frequents the S & M clubs. He begins to stake out the student, Stu Richards, but does not tell Captain Edelson about the new suspect. Steve sneaks into Stu's room, finds his knife and a box full of incriminating letters that Stu wrote to his father but never mailed. When Steve meets Greg, Bayley's lover, he is insulting and Steve gets into a fight with him. Later, when Stu goes cruising at night, Steve manages to accidentally bump into him in the park. They head to an isolated tunnel to be alone together, get into a scuffle, and Stu is stabbed. At the hospital, Captain Edelson arrests Stu, whose fingerprint matches the coin from the murder scene. Steve is released from his assignment and gets a promotion to the detective division. He returns to Nancy's apartment. Ted Bayley's body is found murdered in his apartment, stabbed to death. Greg is the main suspect in this new crime. Steve shaves while Nancy dresses up in the leather coat and dark glasses that Steve just discarded. Steve looks wearily into the mirror and the picture dissolves to show the same tugboat in the Hudson River from the film's opening scene, except this time in daylight.

Critique

Many viewers and critics were puzzled by *Cruising*'s ambiguous ending, which could be interpreted that Steve is returning to normal or that he might have been responsible for Bayley's death, killing the man to whom he felt attracted in order to shed his gay persona. This latter assessment seems unlikely, but one element has led to this sense of perplexity about Steve. When he confronted Stu in the park, Steve sang the little chant, "Who's here, I'm here, You're here," that Stu sang to each of his victims. The script never explains how Steve knew the killer's trademark tune. In an earlier scene, a gay cross-dresser told a detective that the killer's song was overheard when he committed one of his crimes. One can only assume that this information somehow got back to Steve. Since this point is never clarified in the story, it led to confusion for many viewers. In an interview, writer/director Friedkin suggested that he did this to create apprehension in the mind of the audience, so that Steve would become somewhat of an enigma by the end of the picture. It all becomes a matter of audience interpretation. This is also true of the issue of homosexuality in the entire film. After the film's previews, Friedkin added a written prologue and stated that the segment of the homosexual community depicted in the film was only one component and not representative of the whole. This was the raunchy, in-your-face S & M crowd, repellent perhaps to many members of the audience, but the point of view of the film is neutral toward the activities in these hardcore clubs. Critics looking at the film in revivals have noted a new possible interpretation, that the gay killer preying on this community could now be seen as an allegory of the AIDS epidemic. Of course, nothing like this was intended in the original film since the crisis was just emerging, but the metaphor seems perfect. Other elements of the film can also be studied. How does Steve's attitude toward homosexuality change? At the start of the film, two police officers are observed harassing homosexuals and ridiculing them. What does their loutish depiction suggest in terms of the attitude of the police? Do the detectives ever take the complaints against these two cops seriously? If so, at what point? Is Ted Bayley the most likable character in the picture? Does he represent a positive portrayal of a homosexual? If so, what is the implication of his murder? Multiple viewings reveal *Cruising* to be a far more complex film than it may initially seem.

Dangerous Child
(2002)

Principal social themes: child abuse/spouse abuse, divorce

Hearst Entertainment. PG-13 rating. Featuring: Delta Burke, Ryan Merriman, Vyto Ruginis, Marc Donato, Barclay Hope, Rosemary Dunsmore, Deborah Odell, Jonathan Payne, Asia Viera, Richard Zeppieri. Written by Karen Stillman and Alan Hines; Cinematography by Nikos Evdemon. Edited by Michael Schweitzer. Music by Peter Manning Robinson. Produced by Terry Gould. Directed by Graeme Campbell. Color. 90 minutes.

Overview

Dangerous Child is the poignant story of a divorced mother facing a crisis: increasing violence and abuse at the hands of her teenage son. When she finally overcomes her tendency to ignore the problem, she is unable to find help for her particular situation from any social agency. Her former husband intervenes, making matters worse since it was his initial abuse of her that is the root of this problem. *Dangerous Child* is an extremely potent telefilm that portrays spouse abuse as a generational problem. It also highlights a flaw in the management of social service agencies through their inability to help with a problem outside their main area of concern.

Synopsis

As the film opens, Sally Cambridge (Delta Burke) is being arrested as her ten-year-old son, Leo (Marc Donato), is carried on a stretcher to an ambulance. At the police station, Sally sits in an interrogation room with Detective Mike Green and Virginia Malloy, a state social worker. The mother tries to explain what happened. A lengthy flashback follows, dating back to the sixteenth birthday of Jack (Ryan Merriman), her elder son. Sally, a single parent, finds it increasingly difficult to cope with Jack's temper. When she tries to talk with him, Jack blasts rap music and paces the room like a caged tiger, finally pushing his mother out. Brad (Vyto Ruginis), her former husband, is abrupt when Sally brings the issue up to him, saying she merely needs to set peri-meters for Jack's behavior and he will conform. Jack is picked up for sho-plifting candles at the mall, trying to impress a girl. The police drop the charges, but Jack is banned from the mall. Sally is asked out to dinner by Frank, her first date since the breakup of her marriage. Jack is supposed to stay home and babysit his brother, Leo. Instead, he slips off to a party, where he gets into a fight after seeing his girlfriend kissing another boy. Sally rebukes Jack for sneaking out, and he takes a punch at her, missing and ramming his fist through the window. At the hospital, Jack and Sally pretend it was an accident. Brad shows up and confronts Jack, who insinuates that Frank is responsible. His father explodes and forces Leo and Jack into his car, taking them to his home. Brad actually wants to get permanent custody of his children, but Marcia, his current wife, opposes the idea. Brad relents, bringing Leo and Jack back to their mother the following day, but threatening her he will sue for custody if there is another incident. Leo's cat is found myster-iously injured, and later Sally overhears Jack crying, apologizing to the cat for hurting her. She decides to seek help through the library. They refer her to various abuse hotlines, but each one passes the buck when she calls, saying they do not deal with parental abuse by children. She visits a shelter, where she is advised to get a court order against her son, a step she considers im-possible to take. Jack tries to reform and suggests that his mother invite Frank home for dinner. Later, Jack has another temper fit and attacks his mother. Leo tries to intervene, but Jack shoves him aside, and his brother hits his head on the table as he falls. Sally calls an ambulance and this leads to a reprise of the film's opening scene. The detective is largely convinced by her statement. He and the social worker take Sally to the hospital, where they intend to question Jack. At first, the boy hesitates, saying his mother was at fault. When

Brad confronts him, Jack breaks down and confesses. The boy is arrested and locked up. The next day, a state attorney explains that the assault case will not be dropped. Legally, if one offspring hurts another, the parents can be charged with child abuse. There is one alternative, however. Jack could be registered in a special program. If he follows the program and shows marked improvement, the charges would be set aside. Unfortunately, the program is only offered in another county, and Jack would have to be placed in foster care to attend. Sally and Brad would also need to undergo separate counseling. Sally and Brad agree to set aside their differences and work with the program. Later, in group therapy, it is apparent that Jack has learned to use his anger to get his way by watching his father's actions. In the final scene, Sally visits Jack, who seems to be responding well to therapy.

Critique

Dangerous Child takes the conventional issue of familial abuse and turns it on its head, demonstrating both the root cause of the problem and how it can expand and worsen. It does this with an extremely literate and plausible script, one that avoids sermonizing. In addition, the picture manages to address an important number of side issues, such as parental authority, the traumatic impact of divorce on children, and the controversy of being wrongly accused of child abuse. The script is basically fair, casting equal share of blame for the crisis resulting from Jack's lack of self-control. Sally is a weak parent, always backing off and allowing Jack to get away with inappropriate behavior. Brad is overbearing, domineering, and a bad example to his children. Although he loves his mother, he has no respect for her or for her authority, which he challenges at every opportunity. Granted, he does show genuine remorse, but he remains a slave to his volcanic temper. Only Leo seems blameless in this scenario, meekly trying to be a mediator whenever possible. Even he has one outburst at the dinner table with Brad and Marcia, an incident that even surprises Jack. One of the most disturbing sequences in the film is the bureaucratic nightmare Sally finds when she tries to get help and is rejected by a series of social agencies who just seem uninterested in her problem. Ironically, the legal route that Sally considered too extreme provides the only viable solution and enables Jack to get the help he needed. *Dangerous Child* could serve as an excellent sounding board for discussing the issues of both child abuse and divorce.

Dead Man Walking
(1995)

Principal social theme: capital punishment

Polygram. R rating. Featuring: Susan Sarandon, Sean Penn, Robert Prosky, Raymond J. Barry, R. Lee Ermey, Celia Weston, Lois Smith, Roberta Maxwell, Margo Martindale, Barton Heyman, Peter Sarsgaard, Larry Pine, Scott Wilson. Written by Tim Robbins based on the book by Sister Helen Prejean. Cinematography by Roger A Deakins. Edited by Lisa Zeno Churgin. Music by David Robbins. Produced by Jon Kirk, Tim Robbins, and Rudd Simmons. Directed by Tim Robbins. Color. 122 minutes.

Overview

Sister Helen Prejean has become one of the leading advocates for the abolition of the death penalty over the past twenty years. Her 1993 book *Dead Man Walking: An Eyewitness Account of the Death Penalty in the United States* portrays the development of her prison ministry when she became the spiritual advisor for Elmo Patrick Sonnier, who was sentenced to die in Louisiana's Angola State Prison. The book became an international best seller and was developed into a motion picture. The film version fictionalizes her account to a considerable degree. For example, Sonnier went to the electric chair whereas Matthew Poncelet, his alter ego in the film, was given a lethal injection. Poncelet, in other words, became a composite of a number of death row inmates that Sister Helen met instead of Sonnier alone. Additional changes were done for dramatic purposes and for the protection of the victims' family members, who are given prominent roles in the film. Sister Helen served as technical advisor for the production, appearing briefly in one scene at a candlelight vigil. *Dead Man Walking* was well received and one of the major contenders for Best Picture at the Academy Awards. Susan Sarandon won the award for Best Actress for her portrayal of Sister Helen.

Synopsis

The plot outline for *Dead Man Walking* is rather straightforward. After corresponding with death row inmate Matthew Poncelet, Sister Helen Prejean visits the prisoner, who asks her for legal help in filing a brief. Poncelet is an unrepentant, bitter man, who claims he was not responsible for the murders of a teenage couple parked in a lover's lane, blaming his cousin, Carl. Sister

Helen agrees to help him, persuading a lawyer to help handle his appeal. A hearing is held, after which Sister Helen is approached by the family members of the victims who ask why she never tried to contact them. Poncelet's appeal is denied, and when an execution date is set, Sister Helen agrees to serve as his spiritual advisor. She also meets with the victims' family members and tries to counsel them. But one set of parents rejects her and asks her to leave when they learn she still intends to minister to Poncelet. As the time for the execution nears, Sister Helen helps Poncelet come to terms with the crime he committed, and the inmate finally accepts responsibility. A flashback reveals the cruel and senseless murders. He had intended to taunt the families of his victims with his last words, but instead he offers an apology and dies with a sense of dignity.

Critique

Unlike a number of other pictures dealing with capital punishment, *Dead Man Walking* attempts to balance the presentation of the issue by showing the feelings and opinions of the parents of the victims, albeit briefly. The film plays slowly, methodically, more like a series of character portraits than a linear plot. Susan Sarandon plays Sister Helen like the calm in the eye of a storm, revealing her emotions only when she is alone or with another member of her order. She reaches out during the excruciating execution process to everyone involved, from the condemned man's family, the prison staff, and the loved ones of the murdered teenagers. The film does play on the emotions of the audience, yet it does not seem artificial or forced, except for one moment toward the end of the execution scene when Poncelet is raised after he is strapped to a table (in a Christ-like pose) to address the witnesses with his last words. Sean Penn has to be credited with the honesty and conviction of his performance. His character is most definitely unsympathetic, an arrogant racist and brutal man. He undergoes a change in his last scenes, but it is a believable transformation, neither maudlin nor phony but a forthright acceptance of his situation. Viewers studying this film could approach it in various ways, such as determining the attitude toward capital punishment and which, if any, their opinion changed as the film progresses. In what ways does the violent flashback of the murders, intercut with the execution scene, affect the attitude of the audience on the issue, either by making the death penalty seem justified or by demonstrating that taking a life under any circumstances is abhorrent? Is the hostility of the angry set of parents well handled or too strident? Although critical opinion about *Dead Man Walking* had a wide range of interpretation, almost reviewers agree that the film avoided offering any easy answers. If this picture intended to make audience members rethink their own convictions, then it certainly achieved its purpose.

Divorce His
(1973)

Divorce Hers
(1973)

Principal social theme: divorce

World Film. No MPAA rating. Featuring: Richard Burton, Elizabeth Taylor, Barry Foster, Carrie Nye, Gabriele Ferzetti, Daniela Surina, Rudolph Walker, Mark Colleano, Eva Griffith, Rosalyn Lander, Ronald Radd. Written by John Hopkins. Cinematography by Ernst Wild and Gabor Pogany. Edited by John Bloom. Music by Stanley Meyers. Produced by Terence Baker and Gareth Wigan. Directed by Waris Hussein. Color. 76 minutes (*Divorce His*); 73 minutes (*Divorce Hers*).

Overview

A most unusual format distinguishes this film, or pair of films, to be more accurate. The premise is that each film portrays the breakdown of a marriage through the point of view of one of the spouses. The two stories cover the same time period, and certain scenes, with both spouses present, appear in both films but with different camera angles. These films were initially run on successive nights on CBS, February 6 and 7, 1973. Reviewers were intrigued, but critical that the storylines were too demanding, particularly since both pictures included numerous flashbacks. Missing even one brief scene could force a viewer to lose the thread of the plot. Nevertheless, this experimental approach well suited the theme of the film, the traumatic events that lead to a divorce.

Synopsis

Divorce His concentrates on the thoughts, reflections, and events of a three-day period in the life of Martin Reynolds (Richard Burton). An influential economic advisor to an African government, Martin arrives in Rome to handle the negotiations with AWI, a firm that has a thriving industry in Africa. He once served as a top executive with AWI. The advisor is separated from his wife, Jane (Elizabeth Taylor), who lives with their three children in an elegant villa in Rome. As Martin prepares for his negotiations, his mind is drawn back to when he first took his job in Africa and his wife refused to accompany him, choosing to remain in Rome instead. He also recalls other troublesome aspects of his marriage, fights in which he struck Jane and her attempted suicide. He accidentally runs into Jane at a cocktail party hosted by Diana Proctor, a mutual friend. Jane was unaware that Martin was back in Rome. They leave the party and talk over old times. Their son, Tommy, visits him at his hotel the next day, both to introduce his girlfriend and to borrow money. Martin takes his youngest daughter, Judith, for an afternoon outing. Later, Martin learns that the prime minister of the country he represents has undercut his negotiations with AWI, striking his own deal with the company, which Martin feels is inadequate. He quits his job and goes to his villa to see Jane and his children. She is not home, and Peggy, his older daughter, yells at him angrily and tells him to leave. Martin heads to the airport and is about to board a plane when he hears his name being paged over the loudspeaker to answer an urgent phone call. It is from Jane, imploring him to come back to the villa at once so they can talk. *Divorce His* ends here. *Divorce Hers* returns the story back to Diane Proctor's cocktail party a few days earlier. This time, the camera follows Jane Reynolds, exploring her thoughts and memories. She is having an affair with a married man, and she decides to withdraw from this relationship. Jane is filled with mixed feeling about her estranged husband. Diane visits her, and confesses that she had an affair with Martin several years earlier. Outraged, Jane asks her to leave. She is out when her husband visits, and is upset to hear that Peggy threw him out. Judith is furious with Peggy and refuses to speak with her. Jane desperately tries to locate Martin before he leaves Rome and has him paged at the airport. (This is the point at which *Divorce His* concluded.) Martin and Jane have a long discussion. Martin wants a reconciliation, which stuns Jane who believed that Martin no longer loved her. Unfortunately, Jane feels it is too late. Their talk is interrupted by a representative from the African country who asks him to resume his job. He says that the cabinet will not support the deal the prime minister had made and that it is essential for Martin to return to Africa at once. Jane urges Martin to take back the job, and they clear up a few of their differences. She insists, however, that it is time that they get a divorce. As Martin prepares to leave, Jane tells him that Peggy will get over her hostility, and that the children would be free to visit him in Africa whenever they wish. As the film ends, Jane and Martin each decide to get on with their lives.

Critique

There is much to commend in this unusual dramatic pair of films, but there are a few drawbacks as well. Some viewers might find it hard to relate to the

Reynolds family, given their status, wealth, and lifestyle. The dynamics of their marriage as it spirals inevitably toward divorce, however, are universal. Martin's reticence and apparent boredom contrast magnificently with Jane's unending scheming and grasping. Neither of them wants to hurt the other, but it seems that is all they can do whenever they come into contact. Several inconsistencies undercut the film. Although Jane is an American, all three of the children seem British, like their father, although his presence in their development seems minimal. Details are never spelled out. When a flashback begins, it is sometimes hard to place the event in the context of their eighteen-year story. Another problem is the poor sound. Largely shot at a German studio in Munich, the soundtrack is recorded at too low of a level, so many conversations come across as mumblings. The structure of the films is brilliant, but can only be appreciated after several viewings, as both pictures overlap, have common scenes, yet contradict each other in the flashbacks. It can be viewed as a mini-*Rashomon* (1950), the famous Japanese film in which the same event is seen quite differently by the participants. This brilliantly conveys the common problem in marriage when husband and wife recall the same event in vastly different ways. Other moments of the story require a good memory on the part of the audience. For example, in one scene of *Divorce His*, we hear Martin's side of a telephone conversation. The other side of the same phone call is only revealed halfway through *Divorce Hers*. These films can provide discussion about the nature of divorce. At times, one spouse or the other appears to want to save the marriage, but never both at the same time. Both have been unfaithful. Both have ignored or exploited the other. Yet neither has attempted to use the children as pawns in their struggle, even though the three children are wildly divided in their attitudes about Martin's possible return. Tommy is in favor, but only mildly since his father bores him. Peggy appears to hate her father when she sees him, yet in private she cries over his loss, blaming herself for his abandonment. Judith adores her father, and despises her sister for the hostility she shows him. This film is at its strongest when it shows the effect of marital troubles on the children. Finally, *Divorce His* and *Divorce Hers* are unique in that the script does not appear to take sides. It shows Martin and Jane both at fault for their problems. The psychology of the film goes somewhat deep at times. Jane in fact wants Martin to hit her, because that event would give her a hold over him. It prevents him from leaving her, forces him to respond to her by his very sense of shame and decency. Despite the abuse scene, Martin seems much of the time to be a victim. Only at the end, after Jane asks for the divorce, does he seem to be on the mend, to becoming a whole man again. Jane, on the other hand, portrays herself as a victim, but much of the time it is she who is in control, managing events and anticipating their outcome. On the whole, these films form a rather rich tapestry of marriage, and some of this might be that Richard Burton and Elizabeth Taylor were themselves modern icons, larger than life, and noted for their two stormy marriages in real life. Watching their arguments and embraces on screen, one wonders to what extent life is following art or art is following life.

The Divorcee
(1930)

Principal social theme: divorce

MGM. No MPAA rating. Featuring: Norma Shearer, Chester Morris, Robert Montgomery, Conrad Nagel, Florence Eldridge, Helene Millard, Robert Elliott, Mary Doran, Tyler Brooke, Zelda Sears, George Irving, Helen Johnson, Carl Stockdale, Theodore von Eltz. Written by John Meehan, Nick Grinde, and Zelda Sears based on the novel *Ex-Wife* by Ursula Parrott. Cinematography by Norbert Brodine. Edited by Hugh Winn. Produced by Robert Z. Leonard and Irving J. Thalberg (executive). Directed by Robert Z. Leonard. B&W. 83 minutes.

Overview

Considered one of the most daring films of the early talkie era, the plot hinges on the concept of complete sexual equality in marriage. A husband, having a brief affair, asks his wife for forgiveness. Later, however, he refuses to forgive her for a similar transgression. *The Divorcee* is considered a prime example of cinema before the enforcement of the production code, which was basically a form of self-censorship by the film industry. Norma Shearer won the Academy Award as Best Actress for her role in *The Divorcee*.

Synopsis

The Divorcee opens at a raunchy party in upstate New York with a handful of the social elite. Jerry Bernard (Norma Shearer), informal leader of the group, surprises them by announcing her engagement to newsman Ted Martin (Chester Morris). This deflates Paul (Conrad Nagel), who is in love with Jerry himself. He gets drunk and on the way home to New York City, gets into an automobile accident that disfigures Dorothy (Helen Johnson), a passenger in the car. Remorseful, Paul decides to marry her in a hospital bedside ceremony on the same day Jerry and Ted have their lavish wedding. Several years pass happily for the Martins. On their third anniversary, Ted is called out of town to a meeting in Chicago. Their friends gather to celebrate and take them out to a party. They bring along Janice Meredith (Mary Doran), which upsets Ted. The woman corners him in the kitchen, and we learn that she had a brief affair with Ted a short time earlier. Jerry enters the kitchen to find Janice's arms around her husband. Before leaving on his trip, Ted admits the affair to his wife. He dismisses it, saying he had been drunk and that it was just an unfortunate incident. After he leaves for Chicago, Jerry becomes depressed, and Ted's best friend, Don (Robert Montgomery), takes her out to cheer her up. Don flirts with her and Jerry responds. A week later, Ted returns, filled with remorse. He begs Jerry's forgiveness, saying the affair meant nothing and should be overlooked. They appear on the verge of reconciliation when Jerry admits that she "had balanced their accounts" during his absence. She likewise admitted her fling meant nothing to her. Ted, however, is shocked and demands to know the man's name. She refuses to betray Don, who warned her not to confess their dalliance to Ted. Jerry feels she should be honest, however, and is outraged when Ted becomes unreasonable and refuses to forgive her. After arguing, they decide to divorce. Angrily, Jerry proclaims that her bedroom door will be open to every man, except for Ted. Apart, they regret the breakup, but both are too stubborn to reconcile. Jerry has a series of affairs, but is serious about none of them. Years pass. Embittered and not wanting to be in the same city with his former wife, Ted loves his job and moves to Paris. Paul, traveling by train, encounters Jerry in the company of Ivan, a continental gigolo. Paul knocks him out when he insults Jerry. Wanting to marry Jerry, Paul decides to dump his wife. The disfigured Dorothy visits Jerry to plead with her so she could save her marriage. Jerry renounces Paul and heads to Paris, hoping to find Ted. She visits various nightclubs on New Year's Eve, finally locating Ted and "accidentally" bumping into him. Stunned at first, he thinks she is on her honeymoon with Paul, but she says that he is her only real husband. They reconcile just as the New Year begins.

Critique

Attitudes have changed greatly since *The Divorcee* first appeared. Some of the film seems antiquated, displaying the frivolousness of the flapper era, in which everyone is affluent, without any hint of the Great Depression. In spite of this, much of the dialogue between Jerry (Norma Shearer) and Ted (Chester Morris) still seem relevant. Jerry is a more modern woman, and at one point Ted says he admires her because she reasons like a man. In the central scene of the film, when Ted returns from his Chicago trip, he is contrite as he seeks his wife's forgiveness. He presents logical reasons about how a spouse might have an unintended sexual encounter that has no bearing on his love for his wife. It is nothing but a foolish mistake. He did not expect his wife's reasoning when she admits that she made the same mistake. His male ego is unable to deal with the same situation in reverse. The idea of sexual equality is beyond him. At this point in the film, Jerry expects to have a grand reconciliation, since she actually has reaffirmed her love for Ted, but his mind is on a completely different track, unable to provide the forgiveness he had been seeking moments earlier. To the modern viewer, Ted is obviously in the wrong, but to the audience in 1930, it is Jerry's actions that are more reprehensible. By the end of the film, Jerry also tends to blame herself; after seeing Dorothy fight for her marriage, she realizes she did not fight for hers. Her tactical retreat leads to the film's traditional happy ending. *The Divorcee* is still able to provide ample grounds for discussion.

Dolores Claiborne
(1995)

Principal social themes: women's rights, addiction, aging, child abuse/spouse abuse, suicide/depression, end-of-life issues, homelessness/poverty

Columbia. R rating. Featuring: Kathy Bates, Jennifer Jason Leigh, Christopher Plummer, Judy Parfitt, David Strathairn, Eric Bogosian, John C. Riley, Ellen Muth, Bob Gunton. Written by Tony Gilroy based on the novel by Stephen King. Cinematography by Gabriel Beristain. Edited by Mark Warner. Music by Danny Elfman. Produced by Taylor Hackford and Charles Mulvehill. Directed by Taylor Hackford. Color. 131 minutes.

Overview

Based on Stephen King's most powerful nonhorror novel, *Dolores Claiborne* focuses on an investigation by the Maine State Police of the death of wealthy Vera Donovan on a small, offshore island. Detective John Mackey wants to build a case against her employee, Dolores Claiborne (Kathy Bates), whom he believes murdered her husband twenty years earlier. Dolores' estranged daughter arrives on the island to assist her mother, and the two of them sort out their differences in their troubled lives.

Synopsis

The format of *Dolores Claiborne* is somewhat complex, with a great number of flashbacks, some lengthy and some only lasting a few seconds, mostly

Dolores' memories. This summary, therefore, concentrates on the highlights in a more linear fashion. Selena St. George (Jennifer Jason Leigh) is a successful young magazine writer in New York in a career rut. She pleads with her editor (Eric Bogosian), a former lover, to be assigned a hot new assignment in Arizona. She receives an anonymous fax of an article from the *Bangor Daily News* reporting that her mother, Dolores Claiborne (her maiden name), is being investigated in the suspicious death of her employer, Vera Donovan (Judy Parfitt). Selena travels to remote Little Tall Island off the coast of Jonesport, Maine, her first visit home in fifteen years. Dolores is being held at the town hall, not yet under arrest. John Mackey (Christopher Plummer), from the Maine State Police, reminds Selena that they met in 1975 when he investigated the death of her father, Joe St. George (David Strathairn). He concluded that Dolores was responsible, but the prosecutors refused to indict her. Mackey claims he solved eighty-two of the eighty-three homicide cases in his career, with the Joe St. George case being the exception. Selena reminds him that her father's death was ruled an accident. Dolores is released into her daughter's custody, and they return to the small, neglected house owned by Dolores. For the past several years, her mother had lived in the Donovan mansion, nursing the semi-invalid matriarch of the island. Memories haunt Dolores as she lights the stove and tries to make the house livable. She tells Selena that she did not kill Vera, who actually attempted suicide by throwing herself downstairs. Badly hurt, Vera pleaded with Dolores to finish the job, and she grabbed a rolling pin out of the kitchen, but was unable to strike. The letter carrier arrived at the exact moment that Vera died from her injuries, and he assumed that Dolores was responsible. Selena leaves her mother at home to get some groceries from the only store on the island. After she leaves, Dolores looks through Selena's purse and, finding a large number of pills, concludes that her daughter is addicted to prescription drugs. When her daughter returns from the store, she also brings a bottle of liquor and becomes drunk. Both Dolores and Selena talk out their troubles during the next few days. Mackey shows up and asks for a sample of Dolores's hair for testing. He advises her to hire an attorney, but she refuses. Dolores is allowed to return to Vera's house to collect her belongings, but discovers that Mackey has impounded most of them. She insists, however, in taking her scrapbook, a collection of Selena's magazine articles, including her famous interview with Richard Nixon. When they leave the Donovan mansion, Mackey drops a bombshell, revealing that Vera left her entire fortune, over a million dollars, to Dolores. This, he declares, establishes a motive, but Dolores claims to know nothing about Vera's will. Later, Mackey drops off a copy of his report on Vera's death at the Claiborne house. Selena is alarmed, but her mother refuses to look at it. A hearing at the town hall is scheduled for the following morning. As they discuss the past, Dolores is stunned to learn that Selena has no memory of being sexually abused by her father. Selena is astonished by her mother's revelation.

She decides to leave and take the report to a lawyer in New York. As she leaves, Selena advises her mother to accept his call.

On the ferry to the mainland, Selena discovers a cassette tape her mother had secretly recorded for her. On it, she tells the full story of Joe's death fifteen years earlier. At age thirteen, Selena's school grades had fallen dramatically, arousing her mother's suspicions. The girl had become moody and secretive. Her mother suspected drug use, but instead discovered that Joe had been molesting her. He had been an abusive husband, but Dolores never realized he was molesting their daughter. She travels to the bank on the mainland where she had deposited her earnings as Vera's maid in a passbook account in trust for Selena. She is stunned to learn that Joe had closed the account, and the bank had never checked with her. Accusing the bank manager with sex discrimination, she persuades them to transfer the money back. Vera plans a party to celebrate the upcoming total solar eclipse. Dolores breaks down while doing her chores and tells Vera about her troubles with Joe. Vera advises that there is only one solution, to arrange for Joe's death. Desperate, Dolores follows Vera's advice, and comes her home early. She gets Joe drunk, and as the eclipse begins, she tells him that she got her money back from the bank. Enraged, Joe chases her, and she lures him to a deep, hidden dry well. He falls in and hangs onto the rim, begging her to help him. Instead, she turns to watch the eclipse as he drops to his death. As Selena finishes listening to the tape, she suddenly starts to recall her father's sexual abuse, memories she had repressed all these years. She now realizes her mother's sacrifice, as well as the cause of her own addiction problems. She returns to the island, interceding before the judge who is considering Mackey's report. She persuades him to clear Dolores, with whom she is now totally reconciled.

Critique

Dolores Claiborne is a poignant, haunting cinema effort, magnificently filmed with a memorable, lyrical score by Danny Elfman. The plot is a virtual compendium of social issues including poverty, addiction, child abuse, depression, aging, and suicide. Perhaps the category "women's issues" is most apt, given that the key phrase in the movie, "sometimes being a bitch is all a woman has to hold on to," is repeated at three key moments in the story by Vera, Dolores, and Selena. Vera was a demanding, finicky woman, obsessive in her rules about cleanliness. We later learn that her philandering husband subjected her to mental cruelty by. When discussing Dolores' troubles with Joe, Vera reveals to her maid that she arranged her husband's automobile accident. After becoming a widow, she more or less imprisoned herself in her mansion on Little Tall Island, frustrated by life and growing older with only the companionship of Dolores, to whom she was usually distant. Vera never told Dolores that she would be her sole heir. In the film, she grew to hate the infirmities inflicted on her by old age and decided to end it on her own terms in her own home, not in a hospital. The movie differs at this point from the book, in which she throws herself down the stairs trying to escape from a hallucination. The film version actually improves and enriches the scene, making Vera's decision a genuine choice, not an accident. It also makes the earlier scene in which Vera asks for Dolores to wind her porcelain pig music box, which plays "Happy Days Are Here Again," far more touching and meaningful. It grants Vera one last moment of contentment, reflecting on a pleasant memory. The issue of mercy killing is also introduced during the death scene, in which Vera pleads with Dolores to help her die.

Dolores herself is a hard, ornery woman who has both suffered and sacrificed much. She was a stubborn fighter, standing up to various men in the film. She confronts her brutal, abusive husband, hitting him with a milk pitcher and holding him at bay with an axe in a vibrant flashback. After his death, she asserts her independence by dropping his surname. Likewise, she defied the vindictive Mackey as well as the local island teenagers who call her names. Her most successful confrontation, however, is exemplified in the bank scene, in which she exclaims, with indignation, that the bank overlooked her rights because she is a woman. The bank manager, arguing with her at first, becomes convinced that she has a point and takes action to remedy it. In dealing with women, however, Dolores is more tolerant, putting up with Vera's excesses and her own daughter's unruliness.

Of the three women, Selena seems both the strongest and the weakest. Brilliant and creative, she has is a writer of renown, an international success. At the same time, her private life is a mess, she is completely reliant on drugs and alcohol to function, and she is haunted by demons she neither understands nor attempts to confront. After her father's death, she completely suppresses all memories of his abuse, blaming her mother as his killer. The truth only becomes apparent to her after hearing her mother's confession on tape. Selena's strength as an advocate really shines through in the hearing, using both common sense and the rights of women in her arguments.

The three lead actresses, Kathy Bates, Jennifer Jason Leigh, and Judy Parfitt, turn in performances of extraordinary depth, intensity, and subtly. The intricate script handles all the various themes, especially the social issues, with honesty and intelligence. *Dolores Claiborne* has many unforgettable moments, including the magnificent staging of the eclipse sequence, which is of an extraordinary beauty and dramatic impact.

Domestic Disturbance
(2001)

Principal social themes: divorce, women's rights,
child abuse/spouse abuse

Paramount. PG-13 rating. Featuring: John Travolta, Vince Vaughn, Steve Buscemi, Teri Polo, Matt O'Leary, Ruben Santiago-Hudson, Angelica Torn, Susan Floyd, Steve Roberts. Written by Lewis Colick based on a story by Lewis Colick, William Comanor, and Gary Drucker. Cinematography by Michael Seresin. Edited by Peter Honess. Music by Mark Mancina. Produced by Donald DeLine and Jonathan Krane. Directed by Harold Becker. Color. 89 minutes.

Overview

Domestic Disturbance is a straightforward thriller largely based on a realistic consideration of social issues, principally on the question of parental responsibility after divorce.

Synopsis

Frank Morrison (John Travolta) is a divorced boat builder in Maryland whose twelve-year-old son, Danny, is becoming an increasing problem with local authorities due to truancy and vandalism. Sergeant Edgar Stevens of the local police summons Frank and his former wife, Susan, to discuss what is setting Danny off. Susan reveals that she is getting remarried. Frank has a long talk with his son, explaining that he and his mother tried hard to make their marriage work, but they failed. His mother now has the right to get on with her life and that includes a new husband. Danny says he loathes Rick Barnes (Vince Vaughn), his mother's fiancé, an entrepreneur who recently moved to town. Susan suggests that Frank take Rick along on his next sailing outing with Danny. Frank reluctantly agrees, and they have a pleasant voyage. Rick offers Frank a large boat-building contract. When Danny refuses to attend the wedding ceremony, Frank agrees to come to the ceremony as well, something he was not planning to do. At the reception, Frank encounters Ray Coleman (Steve Buscemi), a sleazy individual who claims to be an old friend of Rick's. When Coleman talks to the groom in private, he calls Rick by his real name, Jack Parnell. They were both thieves who were involved in a large robbery, and Rick got away with the loot. Coleman now demands his cut. Rick tells him that he will arrange payment later, but he needs time since he just got married. Coleman tells him he will take up residence at a motel just outside of town. A few days later, Frank sees Coleman at a local diner and stops to chat with him, questioning him about Rick. Passing by the restaurant, Rick becomes alarmed when he sees the two of them sitting together. He visits Coleman to make arrangements. The former convict tells Rick that he located him by stumbling across his photo when his wedding was announced. Rick warns him to stay away from Frank.

Several weeks pass, and Danny's relationship with his stepfather remains awkward. He panics, however, when he learns his mother is pregnant. He hides in Rick's SUV, planning to sneak a lift into town so he could run away. Instead, Rick drives to pick up Coleman, supposedly to pay him off. The hidden Danny is stunned when Rick stabs Coleman, killing him and throwing his body into a flaming superheated kiln at the brickworks factory. The boy remains quiet, awaiting his chance to sneak out of the vehicle. He runs to his father's place and tells him that he witnessed the murder. Frank calls the police, and Sergeant Stevens investigates. When no blood is found in the SUV, he dismisses the boy's story as a fabrication in light of his mother's pregnancy. Frank is not convinced, and he refuses Rick's boat contract. Although Danny had lied in the past to his teachers, the police, and his mother, Frank could not think of an occasion when the boy lied to him. He takes Danny away after school the next day, and the police pick him up for abduction. He then hires a lawyer to claim custody of Danny. Frank's girlfriend breaks with him, not wanting to get involved in a custody battle. Susan tells Rick that she intends to fight to keep Danny. In private, Rick threatens Danny that he will kill his father if he asks the court to leave his mother's custody. The boy is called to the stand and says he made up the story about Rick killing someone. He then asks to remain with Susan and Rick. Frank is thunderstruck by the admission, and Danny refuses to go with Frank on their regular Sunday outing. Frank, a recovering alcoholic, starts drinking again. He shows up when Rick is honored with a community service award and demands to talk with his son. When Frank is turned away, Danny pretends he dropped his wallet and whispers to his father not to oppose Rick or he might kill him. Assuming his son told him the truth originally, Frank tries to locate Coleman, the only man who could have been his target. He locates a prostitute frequented by Coleman, and she sells Frank a lighter with a horseshoe that Coleman gave her. He asks the police to dust the lighter for fingerprints, but too many people had handled the lighter. Working on a tip that Coleman came from Chicago, Frank discovers a police file on the Internet showing that Rick is actually Jack Parnell, a wanted fugitive. He e-mails the file to Sergeant Stevens. Meanwhile, Rick breaks into Frank's boathouse and knocks him out. He sets fire to the place, burning his arm in the process, but Frank manages to slip out of the burning building. Danny and Susan see a news bulletin about the fire on TV.

Danny tells her that Rick must have started it, that he threatened to hurt Frank before his appearance before the judge. Susan does not believe him, until she comes across Rick nursing his burnt arm in the bathroom. She starts to flee with Danny, but Rick strikes her, causing a miscarriage. Frank shows up and battles with Rick, who gets electrocuted when he accidentally strikes the fuse box with a crowbar. The police finally show up, and Stevens apologizes to Danny for not believing him. Susan and Frank appear reconciled before she is taken by ambulance to the hospital.

Critique

While the synopsis of *Domestic Disturbance* may sound wildly melodramatic, the story itself is depicted in a low-key and credible fashion. Much of it is centered on Danny's problems such as his inability to accept his parents' divorce, a traditional screen plot for years in such films as Walt Disney's *The Parent Trap* (1961) and others. Matt O'Leary is very believable as Danny, a very difficult role, and his quiet reading keeps the melodrama from getting out of hand. For the first half, the realistic tone of the film highlights the social issues, the continuing residue of the problems of divorce. In this case, Frank and Susan have largely settled the personal issues between themselves, sharing the responsibilities of raising Danny and attending counseling sessions to help their son cope with the reality of their split. Custody never appears to be a problem, and Susan never tries to interfere with Frank's weekly visitations. This naturally falls apart after Danny accuses his stepfather of murder. Susan is blinded and does not accept her son's word for an instant. Like "the boy who cried wolf," Danny has lied to her once too often, although he never deceived his father. In many divorce cases, the children may try to pit their warring parents against each other to get their way. In Danny's case, he acted wild merely to get his parents to function together in dealing with him.

Other social concerns are also reflected in the plot. The court scene is very poignant, as Susan asserts her maternal rights, and the judge tries to allow Danny's own preferences to weigh in his judgment on custody. This becomes moot, however, when Danny unexpectedly sides with his mother. This tears his father apart, however, and Danny is no longer able to face him, both because he wounded him and because of Rick's threat. The abuse Danny suffers from his mother is unintentional. He lost her trust, and her love for him is unable to bridge the gap. The abuse from his stepfather, Rick, is on several levels. It is evident that Rick dislikes Danny long before the murder scene. When they are playing ball, for example, their hostility and inability to relate make a very potent scene. Oddly enough, when Danny tells the police about the murder, he seems equally insistent to stress that he overheard Rick admit that he hates him. It is this personal wound, perhaps, that Sergeant

Stevens misread in his decision to ignore Danny's accusation. *Domestic Disturbance* is a surprisingly rich and intelligent film, apart from the stereotypical climax after Susan sees Rick's burned arm.

Driving Miss Daisy
(1989)

Principal social themes: aging, education/literacy,
racism/civil rights

United Artists. PG rating. Featuring: Morgan Freeman, Jessica Tandy, Dan Aykroyd, Patti LuPone, Esther Rolle, Joann Havrilla, Alvin M. Sugarman, Clarice F. Geigerman, Muriel Moore, Sylvia Kaler, Carolyn Gold, Crystal R. Fox, Bob Hannah, William Hall Jr. Written by Alfred Uhry based on his play. Cinematography by Peter James. Edited by Mark Warner. Music by Hans Zimmer. Produced by Lili Fini Zanuck and Richard D. Zanuck. Directed by Bruce Beresford. Color. 99 minutes.

Overview

Driving Miss Daisy depicts the relationship between an elderly Jewish lady and her chauffeur, a black man who is a retired milk truck driver, over a twenty-year period from the late 1940s through the late 1960s. Based on a Pulitzer Prize–winning play, *Driving Miss Daisy* won the Academy Award as the best film of 1989. In addition, Jessica Tandy won the Oscar as Best Actress, and writer Alfred Uhry won for Best Adapted Screenplay.

Synopsis

In 1948, in suburban Atlanta, Daisy Werthan (Jessica Tandy) has an accident backing her car out of her driveway. Her son, mill operator Boolie Werthan (Dan Aykroyd), hires a chauffeur to drive her around. At first, the feisty woman is resentful, but her son explains that with her driving record at age seventy-two, no insurance company will issue her a policy. When Hoke Colburn (Morgan Freeman) reports for work, Daisy ignores him, and her housekeeper Idella (Esther Rolle) tells him he will face a difficult time fitting in. Short on groceries, Daisy plans to take a bus to the local supermarket.

Hoke follows her in the new car, a Hudson, until Daisy relents and climbs into the backseat. When they arrive at the store, Hoke calls Boolie to tell him of his success. Daisy is still very crotchety about the situation and asks Boolie to dismiss the chauffeur for stealing a can of salmon. When Hoke arrives at work in the morning, he brings a can of salmon as a replacement since he was unable to eat the meal left for him the previous evening. Daisy is impressed by his honesty.

The first sign of friendship occurs when Daisy is driven to the cemetery to visit her husband's grave. She asks Hoke to locate another grave, but he admits he is unable to read. A former teacher, Daisy decides to teach him, finding him an intelligent student. She gives him a book as a Christmas gift, even though she claims she never follows the Christmas custom. As the years pass, the film becomes episodic, highlighting different incidents in their relationship. When Boolie buys a new Cadillac for his mother, Hoke buys the Hudson for himself. Later, when Daisy's brother turns ninety, she asks Hoke to drive her to his home in Alabama. At one point, a policeman stops them to check Hoke's license and the car registration. As they leaves, the cop remarks to his partner that nothing is more depressing than watching an old Negro driving an old Jewess. Years later, Idella passes away while preparing supper, and Daisy and Hoke attend her funeral in the Baptist church. With some difficulty, Daisy takes over the cooking. The most upsetting incident is when Hoke drives her one Saturday to her synagogue, but becomes ensnared in traffic. Leaving the car, Hoke learns that an arsonist had torched the synagogue. Daisy becomes interested in the civil rights movement and attends a dinner in honor of Martin Luther King Jr. Boolie suggests that she ask Hoke to accompany her. She hems and haws and only asks him while he is driving her to the event. Feeling somewhat slighted, Hoke declines, but he listens to King's dinner speech on the radio. Daisy comments how pleased she is that relations seem to be changing between the races, but Hoke replies ironically that they have not changed all that much.

Eventually, Daisy begins to show signs of dementia, and she is placed in a nursing home. No longer able to drive, the elderly Hoke is unable to visit her, so Boolie brings him along when he pays a visit. In the last scene, Daisy is having one of her better days, and she chats warmly with Hoke, whom she now regards as her best friend.

Critique

Driving Miss Daisy manages to be profound, subtle, and insightful while on the surface seeming only a simple and amusing story. The events of the changing times of the 1950s and 1960s are seen obliquely through the prism of the two main characters, Hoke and Daisy. The foremost issue is aging, as both of them are approaching their twilight years, with Hoke about a decade younger. The ravages of time take their toll in a slow but inevitable process on them both. The signals of the passing years are marked by the almost imperceptible decline in their interests and abilities from scene to scene. The only rude shock in this process is Daisy's dementia, for which Hoke is unprepared when the elderly woman imagines she is still a schoolteacher who has lost the homework assignments of her students. His gentle attempt to bring her out of it is one of the most poignant moments of the entire picture. The adult literacy issue is also skillfully handled by the performers and the script. In watching the film, viewers should carefully observe the scenes with Hoke paging through the newspaper to note the almost hidden signs that he cannot read. As a milk truck driver and later chauffeur, Hoke had to be familiar with the meaning of road signs. It is also clear he has no trouble with numbers, for example memorizing Boolie's phone number so he could call him to report his success the first time Daisy permits him to drive her. Another interesting point is the enthusiasm Daisy feels when she teaches Hoke and observes his progress. Watching her joy and enrichment as she passes on these basic skills to the receptive student is another of the film's special moments. The issue of civil rights, however, is more bluntly portrayed as an issue that separates Daisy and Hoke, as typified by her inability to invite Hoke to accompany her to the Martin Luther King Jr. dinner. The earlier scene in which her son Boolie explains why he should not attend the dinner is very well handled, particularly by Dan Aykroyd in his finest scene in the film. Another important moment occurs when the synagogue is destroyed, and Daisy rejects Hoke's comparison of the incident to the targeting of black churches in the South. Hoke's wistful comment about the slow change in race relation is another exceptional instance.

Director Bruce Beresford and the two major stars, Morgan Freeman and Jessica Tandy, deserve the critical praise they earned for this remarkable film.

An Early Frost
(1985)

Principal social themes: AIDS, suicide/depression, homosexuality

NBC Productions. No MPAA rating. Featuring: Aidan Quinn, Gena Rowlands, Ben Gazzara, Sylvia Sidney, John Glover, Terry O'Quinn, D. W. Moffett, Sydney Walsh, Bill Paxton, Cheryl Anderson, Christopher Bradley, Sue Ann Gilfillan, Don Hood, Barbara Iley, Scott Jacek, John Lafayette. Written by Ron Cowen and Daniel Lipman based on a story by Sherman Yellen. Cinematography by Woody Omens. Edited by Jerold L. Ludwig. Music by John Kander. Produced by Perry Lafferty. Directed by John Erman. Color. 97 minutes.

Overview

An Early Frost was the first motion picture ever to deal with AIDS, It proved to be an artistic triumph, debuting on November 11, 1985, on NBC. The storyline focused on a young lawyer who developed AIDS, returning home to visit his parents and revealing both his condition and his homosexuality. Their varying reactions form the heart of the story, as well as the lawyer's encounter with others who had contracted the disease. *An Early Frost* was one of the most acclaimed telefilms, receiving fourteen Emmy nominations that included five members of the cast. It also won a Director's Guild Award.

Synopsis

An Early Frost opens as young Chicago lawyer Michael Pierson (Aidan Quinn) visits his family in Pennsylvania. Michael is fearful about telling his loved ones that he is a homosexual, only revealing his secret to his sister. When he returns to Chicago, he tells his live-in lover, Peter Hilton (D. W. Moffett), that he was unable to tell his family he is gay. Feeling ill, Michael consults a doctor who informs him he has tuberculosis. Dr. Redding (Terry O'Quinn) does further testing and concludes that Michael has AIDS. The doctor probes the sexual histories of both Michael and Peter. He conjectures that Peter might be a carrier who does not have the disease himself. Peter and Michael argue and break up. Michael returns home to stay with his family. When he tells them the situation, his mother, Katherine (Gena Rowlands), is desperately worried, but Nick, his father (Ben Gazzara), is hostile and angry, almost striking his son. The reaction of other family members is unpredictable. His sister panics and refuses to see him again. His grandmother (Sylvia Sydney) is warm and loving, giving Michael his first whole-hearted embrace since he revealed his condition. Michael visits his father at his office, but finds him cold and unresponsive. That night, Michael has a seizure and passes out. The ambulance drivers refuse to transport him after they learns he has AIDS. His father is outraged and carries his son to his car, driving him to the emergency room. At the hospital, Katherine questions a flustered Dr. Gilbert (Don Hood), who says that the prognosis for surviving AIDS at the present time is remote, almost hopeless. But the patient must be encouraged to hope, since it is the only weapon he has. In an attempt to be supportive, Katherine invites Peter to visit them. Nick is distant, but as they discuss Michael's character, he grows warmer. At the hospital, Michael starts to recover from his infectious episode. He meets with an AIDS support group, but walks out, unable to relate to them. One patient, Victor DiMato (John Glover), is very ill, but he tries his best to be humorous and upbeat. He talks with Michael, getting him to accept his condition. They become friends. When he is about to leave the hospital, Michael is surprised by his father, who comes to bring him home. Nick is becoming more tolerant and sympathetic to the difficulties facing his son. Michael and Peter reconcile, and when his lover leaves for Chicago, Michael promises to follow in another week. Visiting the hospital, Michael prepares a last will for Victor. When he returns with the will drawn up, he learns he is too late, that Victor passed away during the night. Katherine is horrified when she learns that Victor's entire family had rejected him and he had died alone. She vows that their family will stand by Michael under any circumstances. She finally persuades Michael's sister to reconcile with him. As he prepares to return to Chicago, Michael feels strengthened by the support of his family.

Critique

The topic of AIDS was still largely unfamiliar to the public at large, except for those immediately touched by the condition, when this telefilm aired. Considering this, it is amazing how much information writers Cowen and Lipman were able to include in the script without making it seem pedantic or forced. They did this by skillfully peppering the information throughout the course of the story, correcting one character's misconception or answering another one's question. Terry O'Quinn, for example, is sensitive and reassuring as he breaks the news of Michael's condition to Michael and Peter, assuring them he is not being judgmental when he asks about their sexual history. Don Hood, as Dr. Gilbert, is brutally honest when he describes AIDS to Katherine, and it may be the most powerful scene in the film. Much can be learned from the crusty attitude of Nick, well played by Ben Gazzara. His attitude goes through many changes, from outright disgust and hostility, perhaps feeling it to be a personal insult that his son is a homosexual, to slow understanding and finally to compassion. Undoubtedly, the writers felt that attitudes of viewers might develop as Nick's do, step by step. Gena Rowlands's performance as Katherine is a less-compelling portrayal, but her honesty in learning about AIDS and bringing that knowledge to those in her family denying the condition is admirable. Of course, *An Early Frost* has to touch many bases, but it does so honestly, without seeming forced. Michael is still in the early stages of the disease, but this is counterbalanced by Victor, John Glover's wacky but poignant character, who depicts the latter stages of AIDS. Finally, *An Early Frost* avoids being maudlin or sentimental, a very delicate balancing act. It carefully manages to avoid portraying Michael as having a "golden parachute" due to his family's wealth and overall understanding. The film clearly suggests that Michael will face a terrible and ultimately losing battle. There is another AIDS film made for cable, *In the Gloaming* (2000), featuring Glenn Close and directed by Christopher

Reeve. This film is very elegiac, focusing on a young man who returns to his parents' home to die. This worthwhile production would make a splendid companion volume to *An Early Frost*, even if it covers some similar ground in the storytelling.

Environment *(AKA Trial of Earth)*
(1971)

Principal social theme: environmental issues

BFA. No MPAA rating. Featuring: Robert Cornthwaite, John A. Dean, William Brandt, Theodore Fisher, Dixie Becker, Daniel Williams, Nick Torre, Larry Ruschetski. Written by Bernard Wilets. Cinematography by Frank Stokes. Edited by Bernard Wilets. Music by John Biggs. Produced and directed by Bernard Wilets. Color. 48 minutes.

Overview

Inspired in part by the Irwin Allen film *The Story of Mankind* (1957), *Environment* is a featurette that is a cross between a Pirandello play, a science fiction film by Edward D. Wood Jr., and a mundane scientific documentary. The premise is that five individuals from one community, Eagle Valley, are abducted by aliens who then put them on trail for environmental crimes as typical representatives of the human race. *Environment* was primarily shown in high schools to stimulate discussion on the balance of nature, pollution, and human consumption.

Synopsis

In the middle of the night, a heavy-set individual wearing dark glasses supervises the apprehension of five individuals from their homes. They are taken to the balcony of an abandoned theater where they witness duplicate images of themselves on a stage arranged as a courtroom set. A tall, lanky judge with a black patch over one eye takes his place on the bench. He speaks to an invisible jury seated in the main floor of the auditorium. The prosecutor is the bulky man with dark glasses, who announces that all mankind should be exterminated in order to save the environment of Earth. The defense council is a balding man with a kindly face. During his opening statement, the prosecutor describes Eagle Valley, a sixty-mile stretch of land, which is the subject of his case study of man's impact on the environment. The first man, a farmer who lives in the upper valley, is then called to take the stand. The prosecutor questions him about his increasing use of chemicals and pesticides. The farmer replies that they are necessary for him to grow food and make a living. The prosecutor berates him for not considering the damage caused by his use of chemicals, particularly on the water supply. The defense council asks about the productivity of his land, which has increased steadily over the past ten years. He also asks the farmer about his respect and love of his land, which he intends to leave to his children. Watching from the balcony, the farmer seems satisfied by the answers that his doppelgänger gives on the witness stand.

The next witness is the manager of the six power plants operating in Eagle Valley. The prosecutor grills him about the pollution, soot, and smog that belches forth from the smokestacks of the plants. The defense attorney, conversely, asks him about the power needs that his plant fulfills and about efficiently reducing the overall levels of pollution. The third witness is a real estate developer. The prosecutor questions him about the rape of the land, the reduction of forests and nature in his quest to build more and more houses. He cites the worldwide figures about the land robbed from wildlife for human housing and development. The defense attorney asks him to tell about meeting the needs of the growing population of Eagle Valley, meeting the dreams of individual families to own their own property. The fourth defendant, a housewife, is called to the stand. She gives sarcastic answers to each of the queries posed by the prosecutor. She claims that her neighbor does her shopping for her while she stays at home writing symphonies. In the balcony, the woman laughs at the cleverness of her double's testimony. When she admits she has four children, the prosecutor grills her about how much she and her family consume. He then speaks about the Malthusian theory, how the population of Earth is growing at an increasing rate devouring the planet's resources. The defense attorney declines to cross-examine her, instead calling the fifth individual as his witness, a black man who lives in the city at the lower end of Eagle Valley. The man denounces all the talk about the biosphere and the environment. He insists that first man should solve the issues of racism and poverty, and only then turn their attention to managing and correcting any harm to the environment. The prosecutor, in his turn, observes that when the meek inherit the Earth, it will do them no good if it is already ruined and depleted.

In his closing statement, the prosecutor says that while each individual may not appear guilty in their own field of endeavors, collectively they are all guilty. He points out that the other species on Earth, such as whales, have a high level of intelligence but face extinction at the hands of mankind. He demands that man be eradicated so the rest of the planet can survive. The defense attorney gently mocks the doom and gloom of the prosecutor, observing that there is a growing awareness in mankind that they are a part of nature and that they are in the process of becoming good stewards of the land, air, and water. He finds hope in their intelligence and their capacity for learning to solve the problems of maintaining the environment. The defendants are dismissed as the judge tells them they will learn the decision of the jury in good time. The defense council consoles them, saying that the trial went well according to his expectations. In the balcony, the actual five individuals seem less reassured, and they return to their lives with a new concern for their surroundings.

Critique

Although very low budget and somewhat corny, *Environment* is nevertheless successful in its efforts to engage and stimulate a juvenile audience who would have ignored or ridiculed a straightforward presentation of environmental issues. The only name star in the production is Robert Cornthwaite, who played the defense attorney, a talented character actor whose best screen moments were as the misguided scientist Dr. Carrington in *The Thing* (1950), as well as the hip "film within a film" mad scientist in Joe Dante's brilliant *Matinee* (1993). The other performers all have a satirical "edge" to their readings, which also makes the film more interesting to young viewers. The prosecutor is based on the part played by Paul Birch in *Not of This Earth* (1957) as the dark bespectacled and emotionless alien. The judge, with the black patch over his eye, is suggestive of the imperious god Wotan from German mythology. Cornthwaite, as the defense counsel, seems the most human and ordinary of the characters (although he, too, is an alien). His presentation of the environmental issues is straightforward but unexaggerated, unlike the speeches of the prosecutor. All of the arguments about earthly ecology are presented in a clear and unambiguous manner, although the accompanying stock footage, showing sludge or smoking chimneys, is somewhat dry and tedious. The device of having the five human abductees appear twice, both onstage and in the balcony, is a trifle confusing at first. It appears that the characters on the stage are facsimiles, whereas those in the balcony are the actual individuals. The reason for this device is somewhat subtle and never really driven home by the script. There really is no unseen jury on the main floor of the theater. The jury is the five people themselves, and they will render their verdict by how they live their lives after becoming enlightened about the basic issues concerning the environment. By extension, the jury can also be regarded as the students watching the film in their school auditoriums, undoubtedly seated in orchestra seats as the unseen jury of the film. In conclusion, *Environment* is a rather ingenious pedagogical effort that succeeds by being campy, maintaining the student's attention and making the topics seem relevant. An interesting side issue would be modern students' perception of the film, as well as their opinions as to the film's original success as a learning tool.

Focus
(2001)

Principal social themes: racism/civil rights, hate groups

Paramount. PG-13 rating. Featuring: William H. Macy, Laura Dern, David Paymer, Meat Loaf, Kay Hawtrey, Michael Copeman, Kenneth Welsh, Joseph Ziegler, Arlene Meadows, Peter Oldring, Robert McCarrol, Shaun Austin-Olsen, Kevin Jubinville, B. J. McQueen, Pat Patterson. Written by Kendrew Laselles based on the novel *Focus* by Arthur Miller. Cinematography by Juan Ruiz Anchia. Edited by Tariq Anwar. Music by Mark Adler. Produced by Robert A. Miller and Neal Slavin. Directed by Neal Slavin. Color. 106 minutes.

Overview

Noted playwright Arthur Miller experimented with novel writing in 1945 with *Focus*, which depicts a meek, middle-aged man, Lawrence Newman, whose life changes dramatically after he starts to wear glasses. People now see him as "looking Jewish," and he becomes a target of anti-Semitism. Miller's book was dramatized on television in 1966. In 2001, the project was developed as a feature film with a solid cast and strong production values. It debuted at the Toronto Film Festival, received largely positive reviews, and had a limited but distinguished theatrical run.

Synopsis

Focus is set in a residential area of Queens during World War II. Lawrence Newman (William H. Macy) is a finicky bachelor living with his elderly mother. One night he hears a woman being attacked in the street. Going to the window, he sees that one of his neighbors is the attacker, but he refuses to get involved. He later learns that the woman was hospitalized with serious injuries, but he still says nothing to the police. He has worked as a personnel officer in a stolid New York firm for twenty years. Criticized for accepting a Jewish applicant, Newman claims he made a mistake because he is no longer able to read the application forms. He is ordered to get glasses, and that is when his troubles begin. As his own mother initially observes, wearing glasses gives Newman a Jewish appearance. At work, he refuses to hire an applicant, Gertrude Hart (Laura Dern), because he fears she might be Jewish. Leaving his office, she denounces him for his prejudice. However, Newman is soon told that his firm no longer wants him in a high-visibility job, and he resigns instead of accepting a demotion. However, he now finds himself mysteriously unable to find a new job, slowly realizing that it is because of his appearance.

His neighbor, Fred (Meat Loaf), is a member of a populist hate group, the Union Crusaders, who have targeted the Finkelsteins, the Jewish proprietors of the corner candy store. Newman himself is somewhat anti-Semitic, and he joins in the boycott. Soon, however, he finds himself the victim of the group's attacks, when his garbage is scattered across his front lawn. He complains to Fred, saying they should know he is not Jewish. Eventually, Newman applies at a Jewish-owned firm in New Jersey, surprised to find a friend in Gertrude Hart, who is now an employee there. They date, fall in love, and get married. At this point, harassment increases against the Newmans, because the neighbors believe Gertrude is Jewish. When the newlyweds go on vacation to the Jersey shore, they are refused lodgings at resorts that are restricted. Gertrude is familiar with the Union Crusaders, since she had once dated a leading member of the group. She encourages her husband to talk to Fred and join the organization, but Newman cannot bring himself to do it. He reluctantly attends a meeting sponsored by a local church, but is thrown out because he refuses to applaud during a racist speech. Newman visits Finkelstein and tells him that it would be best for him to move, but the shopkeeper refuses. One night, a group of thugs attacks Newman as he and his wife are returning from the movies. Swinging a baseball bat, Finkelstein comes to his aid and together they fight off their enemies. Gertrude runs to Fred for help, but Newman has had enough. He decides to go to the police and file a formal complaint against the Union Crusaders. His wife follows him, telling the police that she can provide the names of the attackers. The desk sergeant assumes the Newmans are Jewish, but Lawrence and Gertrude no longer bother to correct the error. They now completely sympathize and identify with the victims of anti-Semitism.

Critique

Focus is one of the most impressive films examining American anti-Semitism since *Gentleman's Agreement* (1947). It is particularly effective on two levels, first as a historical portrait of America when radio demagogues such as Father Coughlin (represented in the film by Kenneth Welsh as Father Crighton) had considerable influence, and second, as a portrait of a man who personally experiences the poisonous results of attitudes that he himself has believed. At times, Miller's allegory seems to overreach. For example, while racism might flourish in Newman's Queens neighborhood, the setting of the Manhattan business world is more cosmopolitan. There was a shortage of manpower due to the war, and an experienced worker such as Newman should have had little trouble securing employment. Also, Newman never considers exchanging his glasses for a different pair. Nevertheless, the racist attitudes, the hostility, and the prejudice that Newman encounters are brilliantly conveyed. William H. Macy is an ideal actor to portray Newman, endowing the role with intelligence, sensitivity, and unending frustration. Former rocker Meat Loaf (Marvin Lee Aday) is exceptional as Macy's bigoted neighbor, showing an impressive acting range. David Paymer is equally good as the long-suffering Finkelstein, who continually tries to reach out to Newman whom he recognizes as a decent man. Laura Dern may be a little too highly charged as Gertrude, but she carries her part well.

The film could serve as a rich focal point for studying racism and the psychology of hate groups such as the Union Crusaders. For instance, since this group has a large Catholic component, how would they feel about the strong anti-Catholic fervor of other hate groups such as the Ku Klux Klan? What events feed or reduce racism? Will the revelation of the European Holocaust defuse their anti-Semitism? Why is the key achievement in this film, its victory, an internal one, specifically the changes of attitude within Newman and his wife? Such a resolution is usually a very difficult thing to portray onscreen, but *Focus* manages to bring it off quite well, and the audience is able to share in their new resolve.

Fourteen Hours
(1951)

Principal social themes: suicide/depression, homosexuality, divorce

Twentieth Century Fox. No MPAA rating. Featuring: Richard Basehart, Paul Douglas, Barbara Bel Geddes, Debra Paget, Agnes Moorehead, Robert Keith, Howard da Silva, Jeffrey Hunter, Martin Gabel, Grace Kelly, Frank Faylen, Jeff Corey, Ossie Davis, Harvey Lembeck, Russell Hicks, Leif Erickson, Joyce Van Patten. Written by John Paxton based on an article by Joel Sayre. Cinematography by Joe MacDonald. Edited by Dorothy Spencer. Music by Alfred Newman. Produced by Sol Siegel. Directed by Henry Hathaway. B&W. 92 minutes.

Overview

Fourteen Hours is a well-made suspense film about a man who steps onto the ledge outside his New York hotel room and threatens to jump. All events in the film rotate around this key event, including the police efforts to talk the man out of suicide, the media coverage, and the reaction of people watching the occurrence. The end credits encourage the work of emergency rescue squads in dealing with troubled individuals threatening suicide.

Synopsis

A young man named Robert Cosick (Richard Basehart), registered in an upper-story room of the Hotel Rodney in lower Manhattan, climbs out onto the ledge while a bellhop wheels in and sets up his breakfast. Noticing the open window, the bellhop pokes his head out, and Cosick warns him to stay away or he will jump. A woman below sees Cosick on the ledge and screams, alerting Dunnigan (Paul Douglas), a traffic cop patrolling Broadway. He phones in a report and races upstairs. A crowd begins to gather on the street. Dunnigan tries to talk to the nervous man on the ledge, and his easygoing manner starts to win Cosick's confidence. A police squad under Deputy Chief Moskar (Howard da Silva) arrives and relieves Dunnigan. Cosick clams up when other people try to talk with him. Ruth, a young woman on her way to work, decides to watch the unfolding drama instead. She makes the acquaintance of Danny, a young businessman who also stops to watch. Newsmen and television cameras are set up to cover the event. Mrs. Fuller (Grace Kelly) visits her lawyer to sign divorce papers, but her husband is delayed due to the traffic tie-up in the streets. She starts to concentrate her attention on observing Cosick from the office window. Dr. Strauss (Martin Gabel), a psychiatrist assisting the squad, advises Moskar to bring Dunnigan back to converse with Cosick. The more he talks, the better the chance the man will abandon his suicide attempt. Cosick starts to open up with Dunnigan, saying that he has to think things through before he makes a decision. He trusts Dunnigan enough to accept a cigarette and a glass of water from him. Alerted by the media publicity, Cosick's divorced parents come to the scene. Christine (Agnes Moorehead), his mother, only upsets Cosick when she tries to talk to him. Dr. Strauss considers her a manipulative woman who likely provoked many of her son's problems. Cosick responds better with his father, a nervous but mild-mannered man whom Cosick had not seen for many years. Finally, the police locate Virginia Foster (Barbara Bel Geddes), Cosick's girlfriend, and she arrives to talk with him as the stand-off continues into the night. Dunnigan slowly makes progress with Cosick, until he agrees to come in off the ledge. Suddenly, a spotlight is turned on from the street below, which startles Cosick and he falls. He is caught, however, in a net that the police set up several floors beneath the ledge. Cosick is brought in and Dr. Strauss begins to treat him. The psychiatrist tells Dunnigan that Cosick will be all right, that the crisis has passed largely due to Dunnigan's efforts. The policeman's wife meets him in the street below as he finally gets to head home. Other people have also been brought together by the fourteen-hour ordeal. Ruth and Danny, the observers, have fallen in love. The Fosters have reconciled, due in part to their concern for the man on the ledge.

Critique

Fourteen Hours provides an excellent focus on the issue of suicide. Richard Basehart is convincing and excellent in his portrayal of a person on the verge of self-destruction. Incidentally, Basehart faced a personal crisis during the making of this film when his wife, Stephanie, passed away due to a brain tumor. Production shut down briefly until Basehart was able to resume work. Paul Douglas is equally good as the cop who talks him through his crisis, with advice from the psychiatrist. The script is not flawless. Setting the critical events in mid-March (St. Patrick's Day) is a mistake because the drama is depicted as taking place in summer-like temperatures instead of the end of winter. The subsidiary stories with the divorce drama of the Fosters and the emerging romance of Ruth and Danny are not bad, but they are somewhat intrusive. The other subplots, such as the cabbies who bet on the hour when Cosick will jump, are far better integrated into the story. The best moments of the script are the ones that deal with the psychology of suicide and the roots of Cosick's depression. What factors drove him to consider suicide? How did his relationships with his mother, father, and girlfriend set up his crisis. Was his parents' divorce a delayed catalyst to his attempt? How did Dunnigan, with minimal training in crisis intervention, fulfill Cosick's needs? Are the psychiatrist's comments really intended for Dunnigan or the audience as a whole? Is Chief Moskar an asset or an obstacle to the attempt to prevent Cosick's suicide? How would a suicide rescue squad have operated in his place? Considering that Cosick began his experience on the ledge in the middle of his encounter with the bellhop, can this suicide attempt be seen as a cry for help? Can this be true of most unsuccessful suicide attempts? One suggested theory was that Cosick was a homosexual and unable to come to terms with his orientation. The script, it is insinuated, tried to suggest this possibility without bringing it out into the open. Since *Fourteen Hours* was one of Twentieth Century Fox's major productions of 1951, the studio did not want to confront this controversial issue head on, but still wanted this to be left open as a plausible interpretation. How does the dialogue and facts we learn about Cosick support or undercut this possibility? *Fourteen Hours* set the model for later, derivative films. Another telefilm, *Man on the Ledge* (1955), is actually a remake with Cameron Mitchell assuming the part played by Richard Basehart.

The Glass Wall
(1953)

Principal social themes: immigration, homelessness/
poverty

Columbia. No MPAA rating. Featuring: Vittorio Gassman, Gloria Grahame, Ann Robinson, Douglas Spencer, Robin Raymond, Jerry Paris, Elizabeth Slifer, Kathleen Freeman, Richard Reeves, Joe Turkel, Ned Booth, Michael Fox, Else Neft, Jack Teagarden. Written by Ivan Tors and Maxwell Shane. Cinematography by Joseph F. Biroc. Edited by Herbert L. Strock. Music by Leith Stevens. Produced by Ivan Tors. Directed by Maxwell Shane. B&W. 80 minutes.

Overview

This minor film noir effort centers on a sensitive issue, the horde of refugees known as displaced persons or "DPs" resulting initially from the upheaval of World War II and further propelled by the Communist takeover of Eastern Europe. In this story, a Hungarian stowaway jumps ship in New York City in a desperate attempt to locate the American soldier whose life he saved during World War II, an action that would give him priority status for immigration to the United States.

Synopsis

The Glass Wall opens in semidocumentary fashion as the plight of "displaced persons" is described. A shipload of immigrants enters New York harbor. As the new arrivals joyfully disembark, one man, however, remains on board, a stowaway named Peter Kuban (Vittorio Gassman), who speaks fluent English. Inspector Bailey (Douglas Spencer) of the American Immigration Bureau interrogates him, learning that he has been imprisoned since he was fifteen and his family was murdered in a Nazi death camp. Since the war, Peter has lived in one refugee camp after another. He escaped from Hungary and walked hundreds of miles to Triste to hide on the America-bound ship. Peter believes he should be entitled to immigrate to America because of Statute Six of the Displaced Persons law passed by the U.S. Congress. Since he took up arms against the Nazis and rescued an American soldier, he has the right to enter America without a quota number. As Bailey continues his questioning, he learns that all Peter knows of this American is his first name, Tom, and that he is a professional clarinet player, who usually works in the area of Times Square. With such sketchy information, Bailey has no choice but to refuse entrance to Peter, who then jumps ship, hurting his ribs in the fall. Despite his injuries, he gets to his feet and runs off, pursued by the immigration authorities. The newspapers soon get word of his plight, and his story and photograph appear on the headlines of the evening edition. Bailey concludes that if Peter is telling the truth, he would probably go to the Times Square area to search for his American friend. He advises that the search for Peter be concentrated there.

That evening, Peter searches every nightspot and bar in the area, anyplace with musicians, hoping to find Tom. He has only eight dollars, and he stops in a cafeteria to eat a small meal. He notices a young woman, Maggie (Gloria Grahame, who steals the coat of another customer. He follows her outside into Central Park. He helps her elude the police and she takes him back to her apartment. When her landlady starts pestering her for her past-due rent, Peter gives her his remaining few dollars. He tells her about his ordeal, and she has an idea to help. They could visit the musician's union the next day to track down all clarinetists named Tom. The landlady's grown son, however, comes to her room and starts to pester Maggie. Peter defends her, and they both run off. The landlady calls the police, and Peter is now wanted by the police on an assault charge. Maggie steals some coins from kids raising money by street dancing, and gives the money to Peter to hide in the subway. The police spot them. Peter escapes, but Maggie is captured. She asks to be taken to the immigration authorities to explain Peter's plight.

Meanwhile, Tom (Jerry Paris) recognizes Peter's picture in the paper. He is auditioning for a spot in Jack Teagarden's jazz band, but leaves early. He also goes to the immigration authorities to back up Peter's story and act as his sponsor. Bailey now believes Peter, but insists that he must be captured or surrender by 7 A.M. (the hour the boat leaves) or he will be classified as a fugitive, forfeiting his right to immigrate. Peter is picked up by a Hungarian stripper who feels sorry for him. She wants to offer him shelter for the night, but her brother wants to throw him out. Not wanting to make trouble between them, Peter slips out the window and runs off. Following the stripper's advice, he decides to head for the United Nations building and appeal to the office for displaced persons. He is spotted entering the building, and Bailey, Tom, and Maggie head there at once. Peter slips into the completely deserted office of the Human Rights Commission and starts to plead his case to the empty chamber. He then observes police entering the building and he flees to the roof. He almost falls over the side when he hears Tom's voice calling him. He is rescued, and Bailey tells him that he will be able to stay in America because he was located before the legal deadline when the ship was due to depart New York harbor.

Critique

The various difficulties faced by immigrants, particularly those classified as displaced persons, are well illustrated in *The Glass Wall*. Using actual footage of refugees disembarking and being greeted by their sponsors and relatives, the promise of liberty and a new beginning is dramatically portrayed in the film's opening minutes. The script shifts from this background to the individual case of Peter Kuban smoothly, cataloging his years of misery at the hands of the Nazis, including the gassing of his family at Auschwitz, to years of stagnation at one refugee camp or another. Kuban, of course, represents "Everyman" in this scenario, skimming over many horrific details of his past, only to be stymied by red tape and legal technicalities on the doorstep of his goal. Inspector Bailey represents both the best and the worst of the immigration system. In spirit he may be with immigrants such as Kuban, but he is an absolute stickler for the letter of the law. Viewers might wonder if he would have actually rejected Kuban if he were apprehended one minute past 7 A.M., as the plot suggests. Bailey is also a skeptical man, having heard his share of lies by immigrants hoping to skirt the law. Yet when he receives confirmation of Kuban's story, Bailey does go all out in the search to locate him. Of course, in Kuban's case, his potential sponsor Tom is on hand. If Tom had moved to another city or had been on tour, the results of the case would have been different, as Kuban was prepared to die rather than be returned to Communist hands. Of course, the script does contain some far-flung exaggerations. For example, it had to have been an incredibly slow news day for Kuban's story to make the headlines of the *New York Daily News*. Likewise, it is ridiculous to see the city police call out a dragnet of dozens of men to block off all the entrances to Central Park to apprehend a woman who snatched (and dropped) a plain cloth overcoat. On the other hand, the film provides magnificent location footage of New York City, particularly Times Square, the subway system, and the United Nations building. The scene of Kuban pleading to the empty chamber of the Human Rights Commission is a memorable one. In addition, the film has some powerful observations about homelessness and poverty. Maggie, a decent girl, is at the end of her rope, her savings wiped out when she had an appendectomy. She now has to resort to stealing to try to make ends meet. The scene in which Gloria Grahame places her foot over two coins among the money tossed in the street for the dancing boy and his companion is a poignant one, an unexpected episode in a basic "man on the run" thriller. The conversation between Maggie and Peter about the various degrees of poverty is another unusual, and enlightening, touch. In addition to being a good film covering the issue of immigration, *The Glass Wall* is a very well-structured production, making the most of a modest budget. One special highlight is the wonderful audition interlude featuring jazz great Jack Teagarden in one of his rare screen appearances, the perfect touch to balance the intense search scenes.

Gods and Monsters
(1998)

Principal social themes: homosexuality, end-of-life
issues, suicide/depression

BBC. R rating. Featuring: Ian McKellen, Brendan Fraser, Lynn Redgrave, Lolita
Davidovich, David Dukes, Kevin J. O'Connor, Mark Kiely, Jack Plotnick, Jack
Betts, Rosalind Ayres, Matt McKenzie, Arthur Dignam, Todd Babcock, Martin
Ferrero, Cornelia Hayes O'Herlihy, Amir Aboulela, David Millbern, Brandon
Kleyla, Pamela Salem, Michael O'Hagen, Kent George, Jesse Long, Jesse James,
Lisa Darr; Written by Bill Condon based on the novel *Father of Frankenstein* by
Christopher Bram. Cinematography by Stephen M. Katz. Edited by Virginia Katz.
Music by Carter Burwell and Franz Waxman. Produced by Paul Colichman,
Greg Feinberg, Mark R. Harris, and Clive Barker. Directed by Bill Condon.
Color. 106 minutes.

Overview

Gods and Monsters is an obsessive and bittersweet portrayal of the last weeks
in the life of director James Whale in 1957, during which time he suffered a
series of small stokes that conjured up mental images from his past. It
concentrates on the friendship of Whale, a flamboyant homosexual, with
Clayton Boone, a heterosexual gardener who agrees to pose as a model for
the elderly director. Scenes from Whale's most famous film, *The Bride of
Frankenstein*, permeate the story, as do reminiscences of World War I. Bill
Condon won the Academy Award for Best Adapted Screenplay for this film.

Synopsis

Returning from the hospital after a stroke, director James Whale (Ian
McKellen) is deeply depressed and dislikes having to rely on medication. His
housekeeper, Hanna (Lynn Redgrave), tries her best to care for him. A university student, Edmund Kay (Jack Plotnick), arrives to interview the director, but he seems disinterested when Whale starts to discuss his past. Kay is
only interested in Whale's four famous horror films: *Frankenstein, The Old
Dark House, The Invisible Man*, and *The Bride of Frankenstein*. Becoming bored
with the interview, Whale offers to answer each question truthfully only if
Kay removes an article of clothing. The director admits his homosexuality
and also reveals the sexual proclivities of other Hollywood personalities such

as director George Cukor. Whale suffers a seizure before he finishes the interview, and Hanna sends Kay home. Later, Whale becomes interested in the muscular young gardener, Clayton Boone (Brendan Fraser), who is mowing his lawn. He strikes up a conversation with the young man, who is unaware of Whale's past. His interest grows when he hears that Whale directed *Frankenstein*. Whale shows Boone some of his paintings and asks if he would pose for him. Hesitant at first, Boone eventually agrees. When *The Bride of Frankenstein* is broadcast one evening on television, Boone persuades his friends at the local bar to watch the film. They find it funny. At the same time, Whale watches the film at home with Hanna, and his memories of the cast and crew sweep over him. Boone becomes uncomfortable after learning that Whale is a homosexual, and he storms off when the director boasts about the naked, all-male pool parties that he threw back in the 1930s. Boone returns, however, making Whale promise to avoid any locker-room talk, letting the director know unequivocally that he himself is straight. When Whale questions why the gardener returned to pose for him, Boone admits that he finds his stories fascinating, unlike any he had ever heard before. The director becomes increasingly disturbed by his memories of World War I, particularly about a young soldier he befriended in the trenches. Later, his companion was killed, and his body was unable to be retrieved since it was in "No Man's Land."

Whale receives an invitation to attend a fancy outdoor reception in honor of Princess Margaret's visit to Hollywood. He asks Boone to drive him and accompany him to the party. Whale learns that his invitation was arranged by Edmund Kay, now working for George Cukor. Kay wanted to reunite Whale with Elsa Lanchester and Boris Karloff, who played the monsters in *The Bride of Frankenstein*. They have a brief gracious meeting and pose for photographs. When a rain shower develops, Whale asks Boone to take him home, commenting that he no longer is able to blend with the Hollywood crowd. The gardener agrees to model for Whale semi-nude. At one point, Whale asks Boone what he thinks of mercy killing, but the gardener gives a noncommittal reply. He reacts furiously, however, when the director embraces him, until he realizes that Whale was hoping to be struck and possibly killed. Whale apologizes, and Boone helps put him to bed. The gardener himself falls asleep on the sofa in the living room. When he is awakened in the morning by Hanna, Boone finds an envelope with his name on it containing Whale's original sketch of the Frankenstein monster with a handwritten dedication to "Clayton ... Friend?" (a reference to the monster's question to the blind man in *The Bride of Frankenstein*). Hanna comes screaming down from the director's room on finding his suicide note. They find his body floating in the pool. Hanna suggests that Boone leave to avoid any awkward questions from the police.

The scene switches to many years later. Boone is watching *The Bride of Frankenstein* on TV with his ten-year-old son, who loves the movie. His father shows him the sketch of the monster given him by Whale, and he is impressed that his dad knew him. Boone's wife asks him to take out the garbage before coming to bed. A thundershower develops, and as he walks in the rain, Boone imitates the lumbering gait of the monster as the end credits roll.

Critique

Gods and Monsters is a truly remarkable effort. Ian McKellen's interpretation of Whale has been described as fairly accurate. Even the paintings shown in the film are authentic works by Whale. The character of Clayton Boone, however, is largely fictionalized, more of a composite of different true-life personages. The title *Gods and Monsters* is, of course, a reference to the famous toast delivered by Ernest Thesiger in *The Bride of Frankenstein*. The Oscar-winning screenplay of the film provides ample material for discussion, particularly on the issue of homosexuality. Actor Ian McKellen, himself a homosexual, avoids clichés in his portrayal of James Whale, who was known for his flamboyance and black humor. The relationship between Whale and Clayton Boone is filled with tension and genuine affection. Whale sees Boone as many things, a sounding board to whom he can confide and perhaps a living counterpart to his famous screen creation, the Frankenstein Monster. Whale respects Boone and finds him attractive, even though he knows his friend is not a homosexual. When Whale meets Edmund Kay (a possible homosexual), he feels no genuine interest in him at all. While Whale enjoys teasing and even shocking Boone, he responds to him and becomes fascinated by the man's honesty and openness. On his own part, Boone is touched by the aging director, although he has a personal revulsion to homosexuality, and he became more tolerant due to Whale's friendship. Brendan Fraser brings considerable depth to Boone, not as a person who may be corrupted by Whale but one who develops a genuine understanding of him. Hannah, magnificently played by Lynn Redgrave, loves her employer as well, although she feels repugnance for what she calls his vice "of which no man may speak." The parallel attitudes of both Hanna and Clayton respond to the warm, sensitive, and tormented personality of Whale despite their rejection of homosexuality. One tenuous message of the film is that homophobia can be breached by coming to know homosexuals as individuals.

The flashbacks to the making of *The Bride of Frankenstein* are the most fascinating parts of the film, highlighting the homosexuality of the major players, the highly strung Colin Clive as Dr. Henry Frankenstein and the cordial but prissy Ernest Thesiger as Dr. Praetorius. Whale pokes subtle fun at both characters in his famous film, but never at the monster, whom he considers a noble savage (as he does Boone). The complex script of *Gods and Monsters* can be open to various differing interpretations, particularly in the dream sequences when images of World War I and the monster become entwined. Other important themes in the film include the dignity Whale tries to maintain while he is entering his frightening final days, troubled by visions from his past that he cannot control. His most horrendous moment is when he tries to provoke Boone into killing him, an instant of desperation that he regrets. In this light, his suicide is almost an act of redemption for the burden he almost inflicted on Boone. In real life, Whale's death, although probably a suicide, was never clearly identified as such.

The technical credits of *Gods and Monsters*, cinematography, editing, make-up, and so forth, are uniformly excellent. The score by Carter Burwell is brilliant. It both uses and adapts Franz Waxman's memorable music for *The Bride of Frankenstein*. The depictions of noted actors such as Colin Clive, Elsa Lanchester, Boris Karloff, and Ernest Thesiger are both credible and entertaining.

Good Morning, Vietnam
(1987)

Principal social theme: censorship

Touchstone. R rating. Featuring: Robin Williams, Forest Whitaker, Bruno Kirby, Robert Wuhl, Noble Willingham, J. T. Walsh, Richard Edson, Juney Smith, Tung Thanh Tran, Chintara Sukapatana, Richard Portnow, Floyd Vivino, Dan Stanton, Don Stanton, Cu Ba Nguyen. Written by Mitch Markowitz. Cinematography by Peter Sova. Edited by Stu Linder. Music by Alex North. Produced by Mark Johnson and Larry Brezner. Directed by Barry Levinson. Color. 121 minutes.

Overview

Good Morning, Vietnam was comedian Robin Williams's breakthrough film that transformed him into a major star. Loosely based on the true-life experiences of Adrian Cronauer as a broadcaster for Armed Forces radio during the Vietnam War, the film not only portrays Cronauer's battle with the military censors, but also shows the deadly consequences when censorship is applied in an arbitrary fashion.

Synopsis

Adrian Cronauer (Robin Williams), a member of the Air Forces, is a talented radio disk jockey. In 1965, General Taylor overhears one of Cronauer's shows over Armed Forces radio in the island of Crete, and he requests his transfer to his command in Vietnam. Sergeant Major Dickerson (J. T. Walsh), nominal head of the operation of the radio station, is upset that this new man is assigned as a DJ without his consent, but Taylor insists that Cronauer is hilarious and will be great for morale. The general personally greets Cronauer when he arrives at the station, but Dickerson treats him with disdain. He is ordered to report the news only after it has been edited by the censors. Cronauer is puzzled by this since these news items are already public knowledge, having been issued by the news wire services. As he begins his first broadcast shift at 6 A.M., Cronauer makes a dramatically different impression, shouting, "Good morning, Vietnam!" and doing a wild, fast-paced monologue including impressions of a wide range of voices from Elvis Presley and Rod Serling to characters from *The Wizard of Oz.* He also plays rock and soul music. Lieutenant Hauk, his immediate supervisor, is outraged, upset by Cronauer's irreverent and satirical tone as well as his musical selections. He tells him to only program old standards by performers such as Lawrence Welk, Perry Como, and Percy Faith. Cronauer is an immediate hit, however, with listeners as well as the other broadcasters. Private Garlick, the station's clerk, takes the new DJ to Jimmy Wahs, a Saigon bar and hangout favored by GIs. Cronauer spots Trinh, a beautiful Vietnamese girl passing by the bar and follows her to a classroom where the military provides English language lessons. Cronauer volunteers as a teacher and takes over instruction of the class. The girl remains aloof, but Cronauer makes friends with Tuan, her younger brother, who is in the class. When he brings Tuan to Wahs' bar, a few roughneck soldiers object, and Cronauer gets into a fight for his new friend's rights.

Cronauer continues to gain in popularity as the leading DJ, and he continues his own freewheeling style despite Hauk's continued badgering. Dickerson and Hauk appeal to Taylor to take Cronauer off the air, but the general dismisses their complaints, saying the DJ gives a real lift to the men in the field who listen to him. After leaving the general's office, Dickerson tells Hauk he will find a way to get rid of the popular announcer. While Cronauer is relaxing at Wahs' bar, Tuan shows up and tells him that his sister has agreed to meet him. Just as they leave, a bomb explodes in the bar, killing and wounding a number of men. Cronauer is stunned, and when his next radio shift starts, he talks about the blast even though the censors have not cleared the story. Dickerson cuts him off the air. Taylor reluctantly agrees to suspend the announcer, and Dickerson appoints Hauk to fill the slot. He is a complete disaster on the air, however, and soon phone calls and letters start to pour in from soldiers demanding that Cronauer's show be brought back. Within a short time, Taylor orders his reinstatement. When Private Garlick informs Cronauer about this, the DJ remains discouraged, tired by his battles with the censors. Garlick introduces the announcer to a number of soldiers en route to various bases, and they respond so vigorously to Cronauer that he is filled with a new resolve when he returns to the airways. Later, he gets the idea to visit An-loc and tape a group of interviews with soldiers in the field. When Dickerson learns that route IA, the road to An-loc, has fallen under enemy control, he urges Hauk to approve the trip. Garlick and Cronauer take a jeep to make their journey. They continue to listen to the radio, but the censors eliminate the news that their road is unsafe. They fall under Vietcong attack, and their jeep is destroyed. They try to reach safety on foot. To their surprise, Tuan shows up with a car to rescue them, but it breaks down. Fortunately, a helicopter shows up and flies them to safety. When Dickerson hears of the escape, he discovers that Tuan is suspected of being a member of the Vietcong by the South Vietnamese police. He threatens Cronauer to resign or he will expose his friendship with Tuan to the authorities. General Taylor tells Cronauer that he is unable to intervene. After the DJ leaves the station, Taylor berates Dickerson and orders him transferred to a backwater post in Guam. Cronauer seeks out Tuan and learns that his friend was behind the bombing of Wahs' bar, but he risked his life to make sure Cronauer was safe. The DJ is confused and troubled by this revelation. He says farewell to the members of his class for new English speakers and stages an impromptu softball game for them. Trinh also shows up to see him one last time, voicing her regrets that her culture would not allow them to become friends. As he boards his flight home, Cronauer gives Garlick a tape to play over the air, a final show saying goodbye to his audience in his usual freewheeling style.

Critique

Good Morning, Vietnam proved to be a very popular film and one that deals with the issue of censorship in a special way. It clearly recognizes the need for secrecy in terms of security and military necessity. At the same time, if this censorship becomes arbitrary, it can prove to be dangerous. By deleting the radio news that Route IA was unsafe, the censors put at risk the lives of any military personnel traveling on the road who would have benefited from the report. The censorship had gotten out of hand, mindlessly blanking out all information that the war was even in progress. Viewers can analyze how the treatment of censorship in the film can apply to the issue on a wider scale, as well as the demarcation line between the necessary and the capricious use of censorship. To Dickerson, the control of the programs had to be complete, premeasured for content in both terms of music and information. In contrast, General Taylor saw the station as just radio, a morale booster to give the troops a lift while they are undergoing their hazardous duty. He enjoyed Cronauer's irreverence, saw his humor and musical tastes as a safety valve for the pressure cooker of the military involved in guerrilla warfare. Cronauer himself is an innocent as the film opens, but he is changed by the carnage he witnesses after the bombing. His encounter with the soldiers brings him a greater maturity. He is finally stunned that the friend he fought for to be allowed to enter Wahs' bar would use the opening to plant a bomb. His instincts about censorship, however, are proven sound, and as the film ends, the other DJs at the station have started to follow his lead, in both their on-air banter and musical selections. Incidentally, the real-life Cronauer was far less a performing dynamo than the character as portrayed by Robin Williams, whose rapid-fire monologues included a large portion of improvisation. The actor even admitted a few of his wilder ad-libs were quite reasonably censored by the film's editor. Years later, Williams became a regular on USO tours, even reprising some of his routines from *Good Morning, Vietnam* for the troops in Iraq.

Good Will Hunting
(1997)

Principal social themes: education/literacy,
homelessness/poverty, child abuse,
violence/gangs

Miramax. R rating. Featuring: Matt Damon, Robin Williams, Ben Affleck, Casey Affleck, Minnie Driver, Stellan Skarsgård, Cole Hauser, Brian Ricci, Richard Fitzpatrick, Rachel Marjorowski, George Plimpton. Written by Matt Damon and Ben Affleck. Cinematography by Jean Yves Escoffier. Edited by Pietro Scalia. Music by Danny Elfman. Produced by Lawrence Bender. Directed by Gus Van Sant. Color. 126 minutes.

Overview

Good Will Hunting is an unusual character portrait of a self-taught genius named Will Hunting, who grew up as an impoverished orphan in South Boston, suffered abuse at the hands of his foster father, and engaged in gang violence. When Gooding is on trial, a professor, one of the world's leading mathematicians, learns about his predicament and intervenes with the judge. The boy is released into the professor's custody on condition that he receive therapy. The crux of the film concerns the Pygmalion-like efforts to mold Gooding into a responsible individual who can properly utilize his potential. *Good Will Hunting* received an Academy Award for Best Original Screenplay, and Robin Williams received an award for Best Supporting Actor.

Synopsis

The film opens at an advanced mathematics class at M.I.T. (Massachusetts Institute of Technology) taught by Dr. Gerald Lambeau (Stellan Skarsgård), who challenges his class with a theorem he places on a chalkboard outside the classroom, saying any student who proves it will gain special school recognition. A young school janitor, Will Hunting (Matt Damon), glances at the problem as he cleans up in the hallway. At his small rundown flat, Will solves the problem effortlessly, writing on his bathroom mirror. The next night, mopping up the corridors, Will writes out his solution on the chalkboard. Lambeau is stunned when he sees the answer the following day. At his next class, he asks for the student to step forward, but nobody does. He replies by announcing the posting of a new problem, one that took Lambeau himself two years to prove, for the mysterious math wizard to tackle. Later, Lambeau and Bob, his assistant, catch a janitor writing on the board. He yells at him not to place graffiti on his problem board. The professor chases him, but Will disappears after slipping around a corner. Bob alerts the professor to read what Will had written. Apparently, he had solved the difficult problem on the spot. He tries to track down the identity of the janitor, assuming he is a student with a temporary job. Meanwhile, Will, hanging out with his tough young friends, gets involved in a street brawl and he is arrested for striking a cop. After he is released, Will heads to a fancy tavern favored by college students. Chuckie Sullivan (Ben Affleck), Will's best friend, tries to pick up a girl. Spotting Sullivan as an ordinary working stiff, a brash intellectual cuts in hoping to impress the girls. He shows up Sullivan, questioning his knowledge of history by dropping the names of a few prominent historians. Will intervenes, however, and puts the intellectual to shame with his own knowledge of these historians and their theories. One of the girls, Skylar (Minnie Driver), a premed student from England, gives Will her phone number as she leaves for the evening. Lambeau learns Will's identity and that he gained his job through the parole board. He attends Will's trial, where the judge intends to throw the book at him because of his lengthy rap sheet. Lambeau talks to the judge, who decides to release him into the professor's custody under condition that he is treated by a therapist.

Will agrees to meet weekly with Lambeau to study advanced mathematics, but is reluctant to undergo therapy. He manages to outfox each therapist that he is assigned to see, either by reading their books or other-wise learning their weak points and challenging them. Lambeau finally decides to turn to his old college roommate, Shawn Maguire (Robin Williams), a psychology teacher and counselor, who grew up in South Boston just like Will. Their first session becomes an intellectual battle. When Will analyzes a painting by Shawn, he suggests that he married the wrong woman. For a moment, Shawn becomes violent, grabbing Will by the neck and warning him to never cast aspersions against his wife. Later, Shawn tells Lambeau that he will accept Will's case. When they next meet, Shawn takes Will to the park. He explains about his late wife, Nancy, who had been the center of his life. For a moment, he forgot that Will was just a child trying to be provocative. Being self-taught, Will's experience is only through books, nothing first hand. In fact, he has never left the Boston area. He was an orphan who had suffered abuse at three foster homes. Shawn states, even through he has read *Oliver Twist*, he would not presume to know the difficulties Will has faced in his short life. He asks that Will show him the same respect, and not to pass judgment because he has a vast background in book knowledge. Touched by Shawn's honesty, Will tenta-tively agrees to give the therapy sessions a try.

He calls Skylar and they go on a date, but Will is too nervous to call her back. Lambeau is continually impressed by Will's natural ability. Shawn makes progress only when Will starts to talk about Skylar. Shawn urges him to call her again and give their relationship a chance. Will pursues her, and they fall for each other. But Will is not completely honest with her, saying, for example, that he comes from a large family with twelve brothers instead of admitting he is an orphan. Skylar is brilliant in her own way, and she is independently wealthy due to a large inheritance left her by her father. She tells Will that she would have given up the money if she could have had her father a few months longer. Months pass, and Lambeau asks Shawn if he could help channel Will's future plans. Lambeau wants to set up Will with a job with a think tank or with the National Security Agency. Shawn, however, wants Will to make up his own mind (even though he is disturbed by his lack of ambition). Will seems content to hang out with his South Boston friends. He tells them he does not care if he remains a manual laborer for the rest of his life. This upsets Chuckie Sullivan, who wants Will to make something of himself. Every time Sullivan appears at his pal's small flat, he secretly hopes that Will is no longer there, that he has decided to step out into the world and start a new life.

When Skylar has to move out to California to start medical school, she asks Will to join her. Will backs off, unable to respond when Skylar pro-claims her love for him. Lambeau and Shawn get into a heated discussion over Will's future, just as the boy arrives for his weekly session. Will is ap-proaching his twenty-first birthday and will soon be free of Lambeau's guardianship. Shawn feels he has to make a breakthrough and talks about how he himself was abused as a child. He explains that Will is now held back because he will not face up to his own history of being abused. It is this that makes him unable to trust anyone, to reject someone like Skylar before she can reject him. Shawn simply keeps repeating, "It is not your fault," until Will breaks down his reserve. Chuckie Sullivan and his South Boston pals buy and restore a car to present to Will on his birthday. At this juncture, Will first agrees to take a high-paying job with a think tank, but then he changes his mind and decides to drive to California to seek his future together with Skylar. He leaves a note with Shawn, who is delighted with his decision. The next time Sullivan comes to Will's door, he is pleased to find the place is empty. He knows his friend has finally moved on. The end credits run as Will is out on the road driving westward.

Critique

Good Will Hunting is a fascinating, if wayward, film that touches on many issues such as education, the nature of intelligence, ambition, self-awareness, class consciousness, poverty, street violence, and abusive foster homes. The premise is that a poor orphan raised in foster homes in the tough surroundings of South Boston is an extraordinarily gifted genius, whose talents in mathematics are equivalent to that of Wolfgang Amadeus Mozart in the field of music. Due to his environment and background, he developed an arrogant, cocky attitude that masks his basic insecurity. He only trusts his roughneck friends, with whom he feels comfortable because of their uncompromising loyalty. When he notices Dr. Lambeau's challenge, it piques his interest. On the other hand, although he has a great affinity for mathematics, he has no love for it. It is just something he can do, but it is too easy. In one remarkable scene, he puts a match to a mathematical report that he wrote, and Lambeau dives to the floor to put out the flames and rescue the pages that Will believes are meaningless. On the whole, Will sees little value in education. When he confronts the in-tellectual in the bar, he mocks him for spending a hundred and fifty thousand dollars for an education that he could have obtained at the library for just a few dollars in overdue fees. Yet, Will's own friends have a respect for the education they lack. Skylar struggles with her studies, but admires the ease with which Will can handle any subject. When she discusses this with Will, he admits there are many areas where his intellectual prowess does not apply, such as his inability to play a musical instrument.

Good Will Hunting provides a unique framework for scrutinizing the con-cept of education in terms of its inherent value and the respect it is accorded by different individuals. In this regard, the film is similar to *The Corn Is Green* (1945), except that the young miner-turned-scholar in that film had to struggle to gain his education. Lambeau wants to draw Will out of the cocoon of his mean streets niche. But Lambeau is too in awe of Will's abilities to make any headway. Shawn Maguire, on the other hand, is himself stuck in his own cocoon, which he protects as tenaciously as Will does his own. By drawing Will out, however, he is in turn drawn out by Will, who sees his counselor's own limitations in withdrawing from life after the death of his wife. Their weekly meetings become symbiotic after Will comes to trust him. This is due in part to Shawn's own past, growing up in South Boston in an abusive household. Another interesting idea in *Good Will Hunting* is the debate between Lambeau and Maguire on the individual's responsibility to society. Lambeau feels if one has the ability he must utilize it in a way that would advance human knowledge, with Einstein as his model. Shawn Maguire, alternately, believes that an individual must seek his own personal fulfillment first, since that is the essence of life. They are both right, from their own respective viewpoints. Will Hunting has to make his own choice, and both Lambeau and Shawn have provided him with the means to do so. One final note is the film's ability to faithfully reproduce various cultures, from the refined world of academia and the pretentiousness of psychology to the rough and tumble world of the "Southies." Viewers should be aware of the raw and vulgar language used to illustrate the latter.

The Grapes of Wrath
(1940)

Principal social theme: homelessness/poverty

Twentieth Century Fox. No MPAA rating. Featuring: Henry Fonda, Jane Darwell, John Carradine, Charley Grapewin, Dorris Bowdon, Russell Simpson, O. Z. Whitehead, John Qualen, Eddie Quillan, Zeffie Tilbury, Frank Sully, Frank Darien, Darryl Hickman, Shirley Mills, Roger Imhof, Grant Mitchell, Charles D. Brown, John Arledge, Ward Bond, Harry Tyler, Charles Tannen, Selmer Jackson, Charles Middleton, Mae Marsh, Frank Faylen, Eddy Waller, Robert Homans, Trevor Bardette, Walter Miller, Max Wagner, Tom Tyler, Irving Bacon, Paul Guilfoyle, Hollis Jewell, Kitty McHugh, William Pawley; Written by Nunnally Johnson based on the novel by John Steinbeck. Cinematography by Gregg Toland. Edited by Robert Simpson. Music by Alfred Newman. Produced by Nunnally Johnson and Darryl F. Zanuck (executive). Directed by John Ford. B&W. 129 minutes.

Overview

One of the most acclaimed pictures of all time, *The Grapes of Wrath* focuses on the plight of Oklahoma tenant farmers who were driven out of their homes during the Great Depression and migrated with their families to California, only to find work scarce and most farmworkers exploited. Based on John Steinbeck's famous novel, *The Grapes of Wrath* was the highest grossing feature of 1940. John Ford won the Academy Award as Best Director for his work on this film.

Synopsis

The film opens as Tom Joad (Henry Fonda), recently paroled from prison, is traveling home to his family's farm. He tells a truck driver who gives him a lift that he killed a man in a fight. Hiking along the road he comes across Jim Casy (John Carradine), a former preacher who "lost the callin'." He joins Tom on his journey home, but they encounter a dust storm and find the homestead abandoned. Neighbor Muley Graves passes by, explaining that the company that owned the land has displaced all the sharecroppers. The drought has rendered the traditional method of tenant farming obsolete, and the company now uses tractors and large-scale irrigation to operate the farms. Tom's family is at his uncle's house, and they all are planning to drive to California, inspired by brochures offering work picking fruit. Ma Joad (Jane Darwell) is overjoyed to see her son, happy that his four years in prison did not embitter him. Tom joins his parents, grandparents, aunt and uncle, and his brothers and sisters in the overloaded truck. His pregnant sister, Rosasharn, and her husband also join the throng. They even invite Casy to come along as well. The trek proves to be a real nightmare, considering the age of the truck, their frequent flats, and meager funds to pay for food and gas. Grandpa Joad dies, and they bury him along the side of the road with a note explaining that he died of natural causes in case his body is ever dug up. Several days later, as they reach the California border, Grandma Joad dies as well. When they reach Barstow, they are told that all the jobs have been taken, and they are directed to stay at a squatter's camp. Poor as they are, Ma offers to share some of her stew with the starving kids in camp who watch her while she cooks. Rosasharn's husband, disgusted with conditions, abandons her and runs off. Deeply depressed, Rosasharn gives birth several days later.

A man passes through camp offering work, but one of the campers says that they trick you with the price they pay, cutting their rate in half when the growers settle up. Tom protests when they try to arrest the man who had spoken up. He runs away, and a deputy fires a shot, missing the man but hitting an innocent woman bystander. Tom tackles the deputy and runs off as well. When the deputy comes to, Casy takes the blame for the entire incident, and he willingly leaves in the custody of the lawmen. Tom returns after hearing a warning that the townspeople are planning to burn out the camp that evening. They drive off, and wander about for some time, eventually hearing of a ranch that is offering five cents a bucket for unbruised pickings. The place, however, is run like a military camp, with armed guards and a tent city of workers outside the gate. Eventually Tom sneaks out to visit these workers and learns they were displaced after complaining when their wagers were arbitrarily cut in half. Casy is now with these workers, and he urges Tom to join them. Their tent is raided by guards, searching for Casy whom they believe is an agitator. After escaping under a bridge, they are spotted. One guard strikes Casy with a pick handle, killing him. Tom responds by killing the attacker. He escapes after being scarred on his left cheek. The next day the camp is searched for a man with a scar, and Ma Joad hides her son. The family leaves the camp in the night, saying they have another job offer. They are searched, but Tom is well hidden in the truck. They run out of gas the next day in front of a different migrant camp, this one operated by the Department of Agriculture. They are offered a decent campsite and shelter for one dollar a week, which they can work off with chores if they are short of cash. There is also occasional work offered by nearby farms. Tom is surprised by the respectable living conditions. The camp has a weekly dance, and some agitators plan to cause a disturbance so the local lawmen can legally raid the camp without a warrant. The campers learn of the plan and remove the agitators before trouble can start. Tom learns that the local authorities are planning to get a warrant to enter the camp and arrest him as the scarred man wanted for murder. He says goodbye to his ma, saying he will be out in the world fighting for poor people who are oppressed. A few days later, the Joad family leave the camp undaunted, hearing of a decent four-week job offer in the northern part of the state.

Critique

The Grapes of Wrath had been a sensation in its day, although the script had to filter out most of the vulgar language as well as some of the earthy situations from Steinbeck's Pulitzer Prize–winning novel of social consciousness. The film's visual impact has remained undiminished for the past sixty-five years, although the dialogue sounds far too broad with overtones of the original *Li'l Abner*, filmed the same year. No film ever conveyed the tragic circumstance of homelessness or poverty better than *The Grapes of Wrath*. Some of the visual images, such as the tractor that topples Muley's farmhouse or the faces of the hungry children in the migrant camp, are indelible for anyone who has seen the film. The closeups of the many faces in the film are similarly unforgettable, conveying the loss of people who have spent their entire lives on one farm only to have it snatched away from them. The Joad family, for example, struggle through one loss after another with stoic dignity, yet their characters are permanently wounded by their ordeal. Muley, for example, asks his friends if he seems "tetched" to them, and Casy (who is a bit "tetched" himself) replies that he does not. The scars on their personalities, however, are plainer than the scar on Tom's face, which marks him as the killer of the brutal deputy.

There is abundant imagery in the film. John Carradine's preacher is a Christ-like figure, sharing the same initials in addition to his spirit of self-sacrifice and helpfulness. Tom appears to carry on inspired by Casy's example, as best reflected in his famous farewell speech to his mother, with its pantheistic fervor and social concerns. The twin themes of homelessness and poverty naturally lead to a consideration of the results of these problems. *The Grapes of Wrath* provides ample area for discussion on this topic. One charge leveled against *The Grapes of Wrath* is that it is socialist in spirit. Other reviewers reflected, however, that these people are too concerned with day-to-day survival to consider politics. At one point, Tom exclaims, "Reds, what are these Reds anyway?" Are these displaced workers to be considered the breeding ground for social radicals, or are they simply individuals who just want to get along. The government camp, for example, seems like paradise compared to the other migrant camps, either filthy or run like a prison. What is the message behind this comparison? Finally, *The Grapes of Wrath* has often appeared on noteworthy lists of the greatest films ever made. To what extent is this due to its handling of the social issues that permeate the film? Why have other social issue films lacked the enduring impact of John Ford's masterpiece?

Green Card
(1990)

Principal social themes: immigration, environmental issues

Touchstone. PG-13 rating. Featuring: Gerard Depardieu, Andie MacDowell, Bebe Neuwirth, Gregg Edelman, Robert Prosky, Ann Wedgeworth, Ethan Philips, Jessie Keosian, Mary Louise Wilson, Ronald Guttman, Lois Smith, Simon Jones. Written by Peter Weir. Cinematography by Geoffrey Simpson. Edited by William Anderson. Music by Hans Zimmer. Produced and directed by Peter Weir. Color. 108 minutes.

Overview

Green Card is a romantic comedy based on the rules and regulations of the Immigration and Naturalization Service (now the U.S. Citizenship and Immigration Service). An American woman agrees to a marriage of convenience to a French visitor so he can obtain a green card enabling him to remain in the United States. Government agents, conducting a spot check, suspect their marriage is spurious, forcing them to live together to prepare for a formal investigation. Unable to tolerate each other at first, the couple eventually fall in love. The film marked the American film debut of French megastar Gerard Depardieu.

Synopsis

Brontë Mitchell (Andie MacDowell) is a horticulturalist, a passionate member of the Green Guerrillas, a group of environmentalists dedicated to creating gardens and parks in vacant lots of the inner city. When she hears about the availability of an apartment with a greenhouse, she is determined to secure it. She learns, however, that the apartment board of trustees wants to rent the place to a married couple. Antoine, a mutual friend, persuades her to marry a French immigrant named Georges Fauré, who is described to her as being a composer. It is to be just a technical wedding so that he may legally obtain residency status in America. Later, they can secure a divorce. She meets Georges at Afrika, a cafe in downtown Manhattan, and they chat for a few moments before going through a quick ceremony at the nearby courthouse. Later, Brontë is able to convince the board to rent her the apartment, and she is ecstatic. When her neighbors and the doorman inquire about her husband, she tells them he is away in Africa doing musical research. One evening, she and her friends visit a fancy French restaurant, and she is surprised to see that Georges is a waiter, After several weeks, Brontë is contacted by the Immigration Service saying they want to visit her to conduct a routine interview. They are cracking down on cases of counterfeit marriages undertaken merely to get around the immigration laws. She tracks down Georges to inform him. He arrives at her apartment late, just a few minutes before the authorities, so they do not have time to concoct a convincing story. The two agents seem satisfied with the brief interview. However, when Brontë answers the telephone, one agent asks to use the bathroom, and Georges directs him to a closet instead. Their suspicions aroused, the agents summon them for a full and formal interview in two weeks at the immigration office. Brontë speaks with her lawyer, who informs her that she could be charged with a crime if the authorities learn of the circumstances of the marriage. She invites Georges to move in so they can become familiar with each other, learn about their past, and fabricate a plausible story about their relationship. They reveal details of their lives, such as the fact that Brontë's father named each of his children after famous writers, so her siblings are Colette, Austen, Elliott, and Lawrence. During this time, they discover that they can barely tolerate each other. For example, Georges smokes, loves to cook fatty foods, and is somewhat of a slob. Brontë is an uptight house-keeper devoted more to her plants than anything else. Lauren, Brontë's closest friend, learns about Georges, making it awkward to keep his existence secret so Phil, her regular boyfriend, another Green Guerrilla, does not find out about him.

Lauren's parents are planning to leave New York and are considering giv-ing their large collection of trees and plants to the Green Guerrillas. Brontë is invited to their dinner party to discuss the issue. Lauren intervenes, bringing Georges along to the gathering. When the guests learn that he is a composer, they ask him to play. At first, he bangs and hammers at the piano, and Brontë assumes the story that he is a composer is a mere fabrication. Then, however, he plays an impressionistic piece set to a poem about children and trees, which greatly impresses Lauren's folks, who agree to donate the trees. Brontë is touched by Georges' considerate gesture. On another occasion, Brontë's parents make an unexpected appearance, and Georges poses as her handyman. However, when Phil returns from his trip and takes Brontë out, Georges spoils their outing when they return to the apartment, by revealing himself as being her husband. After that, Brontë tosses him out, but they reconcile and complete their preparations for the interviews. They are questioned sepa-rately, and Brontë is completely convincing. Georges, however, falters when asked about Brontë's cold cream. He confesses that the marriage was a ruse simply for him to get a green card. He agrees to his deportation, as long as Brontë is not charged with a crime. Leaving the office, Georges pretends that the officers were satisfied, and they part. A few days later, she receives a note to meet him at Afrika. When she notices one of the immigration officials nearby, she realizes that he is being deported. She finally realizes that she loves Georges, and she tells him she will follow him to France where they will live as man and wife.

Critique

Green Card is a delightful and entertaining romance, cleverly using the immi-gration scenario as backdrop to the proceedings. The issue of the U.S. Citi-zenship and Immigration Service investigating marriages between American citizens and foreigners is both legitimate and timely. A marriage that has been arranged solely to circumvent immigration law is considered a criminal act, although the principal focus of the authorities in their investigations has been to break up criminal groups that exploit foreigners by providing such mar-riages for exorbitant cash sums. Marriages of convenience have also been subject to periodic review, however, as depicted in this film. Numerous visi-tors have gone to great lengths to stay in America, the "land of opportunity," avoiding the sometimes lengthy red tape of the quota list. Marriages performed abroad between Americans and foreigners have also been closely examined, and there have been cases in which the spouse has been denied entry as an undesirable alien. Immigration laws in other countries vary considerably, and in many cases the alien spouse is automatically granted citizenship. One drawback to *Green Card* is that the last scene is somewhat confusing and unresolved. It appears that Brontë will emigrate and follow her husband abroad. Presumably, sometime in the future, Georges can apply for readmission to the United States. It is unclear if this will be allowed or not because of the initial deceit. It would probably be in the hands of the agents who would oversee the case, since by that time the legitimacy of his marriage to Brontë would be clear.

Green Dragon
(2002)

**Principal social themes: immigration,
suicide/depression**

Franchise Pictures. PG-13 rating. Featuring: Patrick Swayze, Forest Whitaker, Don Duong, Trung Nguyen, Hiep Thi Le, Kathleen Luong, Billinjer Tran, Phuoc Quan Nguyen, Long Nguyen, Catherine Ai, Phu Cuong, Jennifer Tran, Khu Chinh. Written by Timothy Linh Bui. Cinematography by Kramer Morgenthau. Edited by Leo Trombetta. Music by Jeff and Michael Danna. Produced by Tony Bui, Tajamika Paxton, Elie Samaha, and Andrew Stevens. Directed by Timothy Linh Bui. Color. 113 minutes.

Overview

Green Dragon is a detailed portrait of several months at an internment center for Vietnamese refugees on the grounds of the Marine base of Camp Pendleton, California, during 1975. Most of the people have lost everything in leaving their homeland, and they look forward with both trepidation and hope to their future in their new country, the United States. *Green Dragon* provides an excellent overview on the topic of immigration, concentrating on the treatment of a mass influx of more than 120,000 individuals during a brief span of time. The many problems they face—from language difficulties, cultural shock, and the separation and loss of family members—is examined through the experiences of a small number of people who are the central focus of the story. The political and religious differences of the refugees themselves are covered, as well as the efforts of the Americans who care for them and try to make their transition from the camp to American society as smooth as possible. On the whole, *Green Dragon* has been critically acclaimed as one of the finest efforts ever dealing with the issue.

Synopsis

Green Dragon opens in April 1975, as Vietnamese refugees arrive at Camp Pendleton. The main focus is a seven-year-old boy named Minh, who keeps hoping his parents will show up at the camp. Meanwhile, he and his young sister, Anh, are looked after by their Uncle Tai. Gunnery Sergeant Jim Lance, in command of the camp, asks Tai to serve as his camp manager since he is fluent in English. His duties have him act as liaison to the various groups in camp, expedite requests, settle problems and keep Lance informed of any unusual situations. Meanwhile, Minh becomes friendly with Addie, a volunteer working in the camp kitchen. Addie draws sketches for the youngster, including one of the boy in a Mighty Mouse costume, his favorite comic book. For relaxation, Addie is painting a large mural in the back of the mess hall, and he invites Minh to paint the right half of the mural while he concentrates on the left.

Tai proves to be very useful to Lance, helping to separate out individuals who have decided to return to Vietnam, for example. When a Vietnamese general arrives in camp, Tai questions him and learns that his brother, Minh's father, died in battle. The general is depressed, and some of the other refugees berate him as a failure. After the news reports the fall of Saigon to the Communists, the general commits suicide. Sergeant Lance tries to comfort the general's daughter, but she assaults him, blaming him and the other Americans for abandoning their country to the Vietcong. Lance is troubled by her outburst, and he later reads to Tai the last letter written by his own brother, whom Lance encouraged to volunteer for duty in Vietnam. Tai concludes that the people of both America and Vietnam have lost much in the war that just ended.

Among the various people Tai encounters is a beautiful young woman who claims she is the second wife of another refugee. In fact, she is little more than a servant to the first wife and her husband, who keeps her around for his own carnal desires. Tai tells her she is not legally wed and offers to marry her himself. Lance puts together a wonderful ceremony for their wedding, and another of Tai's brothers shows up. He brings the sad news that their sister, Minh's mother, died trying to escape Vietnam by boat. Minh suffers another loss when his friend Addie dies. Unknown to anyone, the volunteer had a terminal illness. Lance gives all of Addie's sketches to Minh, but their wall mural is painted over. Many of the refugees begin to feel too attached to the camp. Lance and Tai have an argument when the sergeant explains that they need to encourage the refugees to move on with their lives once a sponsor is found for them. The sergeant takes Tai on a tour outside the camp so he can get a feel for the American lifestyle and demonstrates how various immigrants cope with employment, handle their own money, and so on. He explains about minimum wage, for example, and other lifestyle factors. Tai becomes filled with a fresh enthusiasm, and he gives informal talks to spark the interest of the other camp residents about their future. Finally, Tai, Minh, and Anh leave the camp, given a fond send-off by Sergeant Lance. End titles explain that the refugee camp was closed in October 1975, and more than a million and a half Vietnamese were assimilated into American society.

Critique

Green Dragon would be an especially useful film to recommend to students to illustrate various aspects of the issue of immigration. The individual reasons for immigration, the search for economic security, the desire for freedom, and flight from oppression are represented by various characters in the story. All of the refugees appear to be treated equally, but it is also clear that they will face different hurdles in blending intro their new country. The various educational levels among them, for instance, will be a prime factor. Many of these refugees are of middle-class background, doctors, professionals, officers, and so forth. Some are also tied to their past, such as the general who saw himself as an uprooted old tree that could not be replanted. Other individuals in the camp, missing relatives left behind in Vietnam, want to return to their homeland no matter who is in political control. Other refugees sometimes denounce them as Communists, and this infighting and rivalry are realistically portrayed. Many in the camp are just too weary to plan for their future and suffer from a debilitating inertia. On the other hand, a large number will face both poverty and racism. One entrepreneur in the camp is already making inroads as a merchant operating on a bicycle. He boasts that there will soon be a "Little Saigon" in America, with a thriving economy of shops, restaurants, and curio dealers. The real heart of the film is Addie's relationship with the young Minh. The contrast of Forest Whitaker, a large, beefy black man, with the somewhat melancholy Minh is remarkable, as when Addie shows the youngster sketches of his father, who abandoned him in his youth, or his mother who died when he was young. Patrick Swayze is excellent as the well-meaning Sergeant Lance, who endeavors to treat the refugees as fellow human beings, although his military demeanor and attitude sometimes undermine his efforts. As Tai tells him, he needs to quit relying on his megaphone when trying to talk to people. On the whole, the point of view of *Green Dragon* is very positive, and a benevolent portrayal of the old American dream symbolized by the Statue of Liberty (which appears in Addie's mural). The message is that the American dream is still alive, but it must be embraced and pursued to come to complete fruition.

Guess Who's Coming to Dinner?
(1967)

Principal social theme: racism/civil rights

Columbia. No MPAA rating. Featuring: Spencer Tracy, Sidney Poitier, Katharine Hepburn, Katharine Houghton, Cecil Kellaway, Beah Richards, Roy Glenn, Isabel Sanford, Virginia Christine, Barbara Randolph. Written by William Rose. Cinematography by Sam Leavitt. Edited by Robert C. Jones. Music by Frank De Vol. Produced and directed by Stanley Kramer. Color. 108 minutes.

Overview

When the milestone *Guess Who's Coming to Dinner* was first released, it was criticized from both ends of the cultural spectrum as being either too controversial (for simply exploring the subject of mixed marriage) or too lightweight (since its approach seemed too fluffy and lacked seriousness). Thirty-five years later, the film remains a remarkable one, perhaps a bit of a balancing act, but nevertheless a comedy that managed to take on the issue of racism with a laser-like clarity. It was also Spencer Tracy's last film. Tracy turned in an exceptional performance, along with his longtime friend, Katharine Hepburn, who won an Academy Award for her portrayal. *Guess Who's Coming to Dinner* probably provided a stronger sounding board for discussion of racial issues in the mid-1960s America than any two more serious films combined.

Synopsis

Matt Drayton (Spencer Tracy) is a wealthy, liberal newspaper publisher in San Francisco. His twenty-three-year-old daughter, Joy (Katharine Houghton), returns home from a holiday in Hawaii with surprising news: She is engaged. Her fiancé, Dr. John Prentice (Sidney Poitier), a specialist in tropical medicine, however, is a black man. Privately, Dr. Prentice tells Matt that there will be no marriage if he does not approve. The publisher only has a few hours to make his decision, because Dr. Prentice has to be on a flight to Switzerland that evening. After her initial amazement, Matt's wife, Christina (Katharine Hepburn), accepts the concept rather quickly. Her husband is stunned that she does not see any problems, particularly the hostility any grandchildren would face. Matt's best friend, Monsignor Ryan (Cecil Kellaway), also approves. Matters become more complicated when Joy invites the parents of Dr. Prentice to fly up from Los Angeles and join the Draytons for dinner. His parents are unaware that Joy is white. When they finally meet, John's father is stunned and displeased. Joy makes up her mind to leave on the plane with John that evening. As the two families meet at the Drayton house for dinner, everyone divides into groups of two for private discussion, with the two fathers opposing and the two mothers approving. Finally, Dr. Prentice's mother tells Matt that he is a dried up old man who has no memory of what it felt like to be in love. This troubles Matt, who spends a long time on the patio thinking the matter over. He then makes his decision and gathers everyone together before the meal. He discusses the events of the day in a long monologue, finally concluding that if his daughter and John love each other as much as he loved Christina when they married, nothing will spoil their marriage. He gives them his blessing, and everyone sits down to the long-delayed dinner.

Critique

In this production, Stanley Kramer clearly demonstrates how the familiar framework of a film can be extended to embrace new concepts. The model for *Guess Who's Coming to Dinner?* is undoubtedly *Father of the Bride* (1950), another Spencer Tracy classic, but in this case race consciousness and the entire background of the civil rights movement substitute for the relatively banal concerns of the earlier film. A lot of this is etched into the screenplay in shorthand. When Spencer Tracy talks about the problems his daughter and new son-in-law would face, he never spells them out. He does not have to; he lets the audience do that for him in their own minds. With that one suggestion, the issue of bigotry, racial prejudice, and human dignity is brought front and center without belaboring the obvious. Yet this same technique is used in many other circumstances, such as when Sidney Poitier tells his father, "You think of yourself as a colored man. I think of myself as a man." The implications of that line are also considerable, embracing not only self-awareness and racial pride, but also a larger sense of community.

Guess *Who's Coming to Dinner?* is also extraordinary for its use of stock characters to remarkable effect. First, there is the black maid played by Isabel Sanford, who at first seems drawn out of a line of racial stereotypes leading back to the early days of silent movies. At first, she opposes Joy's marriage, thinking Dr. Prentice to be an uppity black who does not know his place. The postponed supper becomes her main concern, until Spencer Tracy's big speech, which he interrupts to bring her out from the kitchen since she is "a member of the family." This last bit looks at first to be a throwaway, but it helps to establish her as a person of importance in the Drayton household, moreover a person whose opinion matters. The second stock character is the fashionable but catty Hillary St. Joseph, played by sceen veteran Virginia Christine, who manages Katharine Hepburn's art gallery. (Some viewers tend to forget that her character, Christina, is a businesswoman in her own right.) When she offers her snide condolences to Christina over Joy's forthcoming marriage, it provides the opportunity for Hepburn to execute the classiest dismissal of an employee in screen history, snuffing out rather than tolerating her "holier than thou" prejudice. The final stock character is Cecil Kellaway as Monsignor Ryan, a delightful parody of the old busybody Irish priest. When he delivers his line about being a dispenser of religious platitudes, it is one of the highlights of the picture. His presence also seems to briefly un-cover an anti-Catholic attitude on the part of Dr. Prentice's father, another example of the various ripples of prejudice that can exist among individuals. The use of these stock characters helps to focus the emphasis on the subtext of the picture, which is the attitude of society about race. Although Tracy's character gripes about the slowness of the changes in society, he ironically epitomizes it as his own attitude evolves in the course of the film.

In essence, a lot more appears to be going on just under the surface of the screenplay than is apparent during a first, or even second, viewing. The film, however, is undermined by a number of flaws. First is the dreadful music score by Frank De Vol, which endlessly grinds out the popular song "The Glory of Love." Next is the awkward editing, which makes a muddle of the middle third of the film. Finally, it is somewhat disturbing at times to watch Spencer Tracy, who looks so unwell during most of his scenes. In fact, he was dying as he made the film and passed away two weeks after completing his work on *Guess Who's Coming to Dinner*? Tracy's magic is still there, undoubt-edly, but his obvious frailty can detract from viewer's enjoyment of the story. The rest of the cast is magnificent. Katharine Hougton, Hepburn's real-life niece, is perfect in her role, and Sidney Poitier delivers an understated but powerful reading that would have stolen the show if the other leads were not Spencer Tracy and Katharine Hepburn.

I Want to Live!
(1958)

Principal social theme: capital punishment

United Artists. No MPAA rating. Featuring: Susan Hayward, Simon Oakland, Virginia Vincent, Theodore Bikel, Wesley Lau, Philip Coolidge, Lou Krugmar, John Marley, Dabbs Greer, Gavin MacLeod, Raymond Bailey, Rusty Lane, Jack Weston. Written by Nelson Gidding and Don M. Mankiewicz based on a series of newspaper articles by Ed Montgomery and selected letters by Barbara Graham. Cinematography by Lionel Lindon. Edited by William Hornbeck. Music by Johnny Mandel. Produced by Walter Wanger. Directed by Robert Wise. B&W. 120 minutes.

Overview

This film was based on the true life story of convicted killer Barbara Graham, one of the most controversial cases in which a woman received the death penalty. The screenplay and production made an extra effort to strive for authenticity, although it did portray Graham as a completely innocent party, a contention that has few adherents among criminologists and crime historians. The strength of the film is its powerful depiction of the details of the process of execution, an emotionally draining experience for the viewer. *I Want to Live!* was a considerable success, and Susan Hayward won an Academy Award as Best Actress for her portrayal of Graham. Two other films were inspired by the case, *Why Must I Die?* (1960) starring Terry Moore and a 1983 telefilm remake with Lindsay Wagner in the title role. Although good, neither film had the power or impact of the original production.

Synopsis

The film opens with a printed testimony by journalist Ed Montgomery attesting that the film is a dramatization of the factual story of Barbara Graham. The story then unfolds; in an almost haphazard fashion, showing Barbara's background as a gutsy "good-time girl," who gets into trouble by perjuring herself to help two hoods whom she likes. She does jail time and eventually weds a bartender named Hank Graham, her fourth marriage. She becomes a mother, but the marriage is soon on the rocks when Hank develops a drug habit. In real life, Barbara also had a drug habit, but the film presents her as free of drugs. Barbara is forced to resort to crime to earn a living. Finally, she is arrested with her crime partners Emmett Perkins, Bruce

King, and Jack Santo. Barbara is stunned when she learns that she is charged with the murder of a crippled woman named Mabel Monahan, who was brutally pistol-whipped to death during a robbery. (The film never portrays the killing, so the audience assumes that Barbara knows nothing about it.) King becomes a state witness, claiming that Barbara committed the murder. Barbara has no alibi, but a girlfriend offers to provide her with a witness, Ben Miranda, who will claim Barbara was with him the night of the crime. At the trial, however, Miranda turns out to be an undercover cop who claimed Barbara confessed to him that she is guilty. She is convicted and sentenced to death.

One reporter who covered the trial, Ed Montgomery, comes to believe that the trial and conviction were irregular and unjust. Carl Palmberg, a noted criminologist, also takes up Barbara's cause. He strongly believes he can win an appeal. She is crushed, however, when Palmberg dies unexpectedly. The rest of the picture covers the execution process in minute detail, including legal maneuvers, last-minute stays, and the death watch. The process becomes agony for Barbara, who slowly breaks down. She leaves a letter for Ed Montgomery to be opened after her execution in which she expresses her appreciation for his support.

Critique

Much of the impact of *I Want to Live!* is based on the charismatic performance of Susan Hayward in the title role. Students of the case contend that Hayward makes Graham a far more sympathetic character than the actual Graham, who was a hardened criminal. For example, when she was originally charged with the Monahan murder, Graham did not protest her innocence, as Hayward does, but instead boasted, "You will never prove it." At each turn, Graham is presented in the best possible light, emphasizing that she was nothing but a fun, party girl at heart. Hayward also endows her character with a number of colorful gestures, such as always rattling a pair of imaginary dice to demonstrate that she is a carefree gambler in the hands of fate. The last half hour of the film is shattering, as the audience witnesses the torment experienced by a condemned prisoner trying to maintain her composure and dignity as she faces her final moments. The screenplay also depicts the effect of an execution on those who carry it out as well, the warden, prison guards, clergy, witnesses, doctors, and nurses who are involved in this process. Whether or not these people believe Graham is guilty seems immaterial; they are largely repelled by the process. The decorum and quiet compassion of the warden, excellently played by Raymond Bailey, speaks more eloquently about the issue of capital punishment than the wordy diatribes that are present in other similar productions. This aspect of the film could serve as an excellent discussion point for students in analyzing the issue. How does witnessing an execution affect the viewer's attitude toward capital punishment? What would be the impact of televised executions? *I Want to Live!* is able to serve as an excellent sounding board for a number of aspects regarding the death penalty.

If These Walls Could Talk
(1996)

Principal social theme: abortion

HBO. PG-13 rating. Featuring: (Part 1) Demi Moore, Shirley Knight, Catherine Keefer, Jason London, Kevin Cooney, Robin Gammell, Phyllis Lyons, Aaron Lustig, C. C. H. Pounder; (Part 2) Sissy Spacek, Xander Berkeley, Hedy Burress, Jana Michaels, Joanna Gleason, Jordana Spiro, Harris Yulin; (Part 3) Anne Heche, Cher, Diana Scharwid, Lindsay Crouse, Eileen Brennan, Lorraine Toussaint, Jada Pinkett, Rita Wilson, Georganne La Pierre, Brendan Ford, Aaron Cash, Craig T. Nelson. Written by Nancy Savoca (1, 2, 3), Susan Nanus (2), and I. Marlene King (3). Cinematography by Ellen Kuras (1), Bobby Bukowski (2), and John Stanler (3). Edited by Elena Maganini (1, 2) Peter Honess (3). Music by Cliff Eidelman. Produced by Laura Greenlee. Directed by Nancy Savoca (1, 2) and Cher (3). Color. 100 minutes.

Overview

This cable telefilm was both highly acclaimed and somewhat controversial. It highlights the story of three women who lived in the same house in three different time periods who faced an unwanted pregnancy and wrestled over the question of having an abortion. *If These Walls Could Talk* provoked considerable discussion, particularly on radio talk shows. It was followed four years later by a semi-sequel, *If These Walls Could Talk II*, which adopted the same format to provide a trio of stories about lesbianism.

Synopsis

The film opens with a montage of pro-life and pro-choice demonstrators from the mid-1990s. These images fade away, replaced by a new selection of images from the early 1970s, followed by those from the early 1950s. The camera then focuses on a house, and the year 1952 is displayed. The first story concentrates on Claire Donnelly (Demi Moore), a young widowed nurse living alone in the house. Her husband died in the Korean War, and she is more or less without any friends except her late husband's family. She is stunned to learn that she is pregnant, the result of a one-time liaison with her brother-in-law to whom she turned in her loneliness. She becomes desperate and cannot envision any possibility of allowing her pregnancy to become known. The news would devastate her husband's family. When her doctor refuses to help with an illegal abortion, Claire tries taking pills to cause a miscarriage. The attempt fails. She then tries to abort the fetus using a knitting needle, another painful and unsuccessful effort. For guidance, Claire turns to an older nurse at the hospital where she works, but is rebuffed. Later, the nurse slips her a phone number. Claire calls, but learns the process is too expensive. She is later put in contact with a "kitchen abortionist," who would do the operation at her home for $400. She agrees and undergoes the procedure. The man leaves, saying if she has a hemorrhage to go to the hospital at once. Claire goes to bed in great pain, not wanting to call the hospital since she fears the news would get back to her husband's family. She starts to bleed profusely, and by the time she telephones the hospital, she is too weak to complete the call.

The house is shown again from the outside, and the decor changes as the year 1974 is displayed. Barbara Barrows (Sissy Spacek) is a harried mother of four. She has just resumed her college education with plans to become a teacher. She suddenly discovers she is pregnant. Her husband, John, a policeman, says that she should have the baby, and the family will make sacrifices to accommodate the newborn. Her eldest daughter, Linda, an avid women's libber, learns about the pregnancy and starts pressuring Barbara to have an abortion. Linda fears that her mother's pregnancy might prevent her from going to college. Barbara calls the local women's clinic to learn about the procedure. In the end, she decides against an abortion, and she assures Linda that this decision will not affect her college plans.

The outside of the house changes again, becoming shabbier. The year is now 1996, and the house has become a college dorm. One student, Christine Cullen (Anne Heche) is having an affair with one of her teachers. When she becomes pregnant, the professor breaks off the relationship and gives her money to have an abortion. Chris's roommate tries to talk her out of it, saying that if she decides to go that route, their friendship would be over. Nevertheless, Chris visits the local abortion clinic run by Dr. Beth Thompson (Cher). She discusses her options, such as adoption, with a counselor at the clinic. Chris chooses to wait. Several women picketers from a religious group pester Chris as she enters and leaves the clinic. She talks with her roommate, who offers to accompany her to the clinic even though she opposes abortion. The next day, a pro-life rally is held outside the clinic, and it slowly gets out of control. This time Chris decides to go through with the abortion, and Dr. Thompson gently prepares her and talks to her while the abortion is performed. When the process is finished, a young man bursts into the operating room and shoots Dr. Thompson, calling her a murderer. He apologizes to Chris if the shooting frightened her, and the man leaves. Chris slides off the table and embraces Dr. Thompson on the floor. The counselor sounds an emergency alarm as the doctor dies.

Critique

If These Walls Could Talk is dramatic, well written, and well performed. The production values are excellent, and the issue of abortion is examined carefully through three case studies, mainly from a pro-choice viewpoint. The first story, 1952, is the best, showing the harrowing ordeal faced by a woman who wanted an abortion at that time. The film pulls no punches, and the squeamish might find Claire's attempt to end her pregnancy with a knitting needle too grisly to watch. There is very little decision making in this story. Circumstances trap Claire into the need for an abortion; her agony is simply her inability to obtain a safe one. The channels that she is forced to go through are demeaning and terrifying, and eventually cost her her life. The second story, 1974, finds Barbara in a genuine dilemma. Abortions are now safe and legal. It is her right to choose, but others, particularly her daughter, try to make her decision for her. Her husband is more supportive, but he assumes that Barbara will choose to have the baby. Barbara weighs the problem, the loss of her chance to become a teacher, and the financial burden. She may also have moral objections, but they are unexpressed. She finally decides that abortion is not the right answer for her. The third story, 1996, has incredible impact, even if its premise seems more artificial than the earlier two tales. Unlike the other stories, the house seems no longer to be the axis of the story, which has now shifted to Dr. Thompson's clinic. The film at this point seems to concentrate on the demonstrators as much as on Chris. They are all strange people, either religious fanatics or glassy-eyed zombies. Chris' roommate is the only antiabortion character in the film who appears rational. The message of the third story is that the choice available to Barbara in 1974 is imperiled in 1996 due to intimidation and violence. *If These Walls Could Talk* is brilliantly conceived, and viewers would find much to debate in its presentation. Which story is the most effective? What could Claire have done to avoid her terrible fate? Why exactly did Barbara choose not to have an abortion? Is the third story too strident? Is the portrayal of the pro-life forces honest or not? Can the third story be regarded as antireligious in tone? Certainly, abortion clinics have been bombed and abortion practitioners have been murdered. To what extent can this violence be attributed to the pro-life movement? Is the film strengthened or weakened by not addressing any moral concerns? Perhaps the greatest attribute of the film is the stark contrast between the botched abortion in the first story to the safe, clinical procedure in the third story.

In Cold Blood
(1967)

Principal social theme: capital punishment

Columbia. No MPAA rating. Featuring: Robert Blake, Scott Wilson, John Forsythe, Paul Stewart, Jeff Corey, Gerald S. O'Laughlin, John Gallaudet, James Flavin, Charles McGraw, John McLiam, Ruth Storey, Will Geer, Vaughn Taylor, Duke Hobbie, Sheldon Allman, Sammy Thurman, Raymond Hatton, Paul Hough. Written by Richard Brooks based on the book by Truman Capote. Cinematography by Conrad Hall. Edited by Peter Zinner. Music by Quincy Jones. Produced and directed by Richard Brooks. B&W. 134 minutes.

Overview

Author Truman Capote spent years researching the case of killers Perry Smith and Dick Hickock, who brutally killed four people during a bungled robbery in rural Kansas in November 1959. Capote got to know the killers quite well during their long wait on death row, and they opened up to him, revealing intimate details of their lives and their terrible crime. In the film, Capote's role is assumed by Paul Stewart, playing a low-key magazine reporter who closely follows the case. When Capote published his book, he called it a "nonfiction novel," an attempt to portray the events as close to reality as possible while maintaining a literary framework atypical of true crime stories. *In Cold Blood* was a literary sensation, and Richard Brooks's 1967 film brilliantly translated the book to the screen while maintaining most of the power of Capote's original. It was undoubtedly the most effective cinematic presentation of the issue of capital punishment of the 1960s. In 1996, a telefilm remake was undertaken, but it was merely a stagnant run-through compared with the original.

Synopsis

The film opens with credits, but without any title card. Former convict Perry Smith is traveling by bus to Kansas City, Missouri, to meet Dick Hickock, who claims to have targeted a perfect score with a big payoff. While in prison, Hickock made friends with Floyd Wells, who once worked for a family named Clutter, and he claimed they kept more than ten thousand dollars in a safe in their Kansas home. Dick goads Perry into pulling off the theft, and the two make an unusual team. Perry is a frustrated musician and Korean war veteran, quiet, moody, but with a hair-trigger temper. His dream is to go to Mexico and hunt for the lost gold of Cortes with treasure maps that he found. Dick is more polished and self-assured, a smooth and folksy talker who can become a persuasive confidence man. The next day, the two criminals undertake the four-hundred mile drive to the Clutter ranch in Holcomb, Kansas. The story does not proceed with a linear plot, as the troubled Smith has numerous flashbacks to his youth intercut with scenes of the Clutter family as they go about their normal everyday routine. Stopping en route, Perry and Dick pick up supplies for their intended burglary. Perry wants to include black stockings, but Dick insists that they will not leave any living witnesses. The screen blacks out as the two pull up to the Clutter ranch late at night.

The story resumes the next day with the grizzly discovery of the bodies of Mr. and Mrs. Clutter and their two teenage children. The story then divides its attention between the two killers and the police as they try to solve the crime. Back in Missouri, Perry and Dick are desperate since their "big score" only netted them $43, and they embark on a series of petty crimes as Dick starts to pass bad checks. The police find their investigation stalled until they decide to post a reward. At the penitentiary, Floyd Wells claims the reward and informs the police that Dick had pumped him for information about the Clutters when they were cellmates. A manhunt for Hickcock is launched. Finally, Perry and Dick are picked up in Las Vegas for car theft, and Dick eventually breaks down during questioning. Through a flashback, the audience learns that Perry alone executed the four members of the Clutter family, largely to impress his overconfident partner. They are tried, convicted, and sentenced to be hanged, and Perry and Dick spend five years in adjoining cells on death row.

Journalist Jenson gains their trust and interviews them. Hickcock discusses the death penalty, which he supports, as do the other prisoners on death row, with the exception of Perry. As the hour of his execution nears, Perry tries to come to terms with his bitter memories of childhood and his brutal father. The death sentence is carried out during a dark, rainy night. Dick is executed first. For his last words, Perry wants to apologize, but he does not know to whom he should direct his comments. After Perry is hanged, the missing title card finally appears on screen: *In Cold Blood*.

Critique

Many factors, including the taut direction, the magnificent cinematography, and a strong sense of authenticity, combined in making this one of the most compelling of true-crime films. *In Cold Blood* was filmed, whenever possible, on the actual locations, such as the actual courtroom where the trial took place and the Clutter farm. Several jury members from the real-life trial appeared as jurors in the film. The most compelling factor, however, is the mesmerizing performances of the two leads, Robert Blake and Scott Wilson, as the amoral killers with a strange symbiotic relationship. Ironically, Blake was arrested and charged years later with the murder of his wife. The film also has a personal reference for Blake, whose character, Perry Smith, expressed admiration for *Treasure of the Sierra Madre* (1948) with Humphrey Bogart. Blake himself played a scene in that film with Bogie.

In the book, Capote took a detached, almost clinical approach to the developments in the story, leaving the reader to form his own opinions about capital punishment. Director Brooks takes a decided stand against capital punishment, although with an unusual emphasis. His viewpoint is that the death penalty is totally ineffective as a deterrent and therefore should be discarded. Other observations made by various characters during the film conclude that capital punishment never seems to be carried out against wealthy defendants and that most death row prisoners are psychologically unfit, so killing them is merely a convenient solution for a society that does not want to deal with these individuals. Brooks makes his point by skewing events at certain moments. For example, we hear Will Geer as the prosecuting attorney deliver a vindictive closing argument that is somewhat weakened by the reading of two contradictory biblical passages. His presentation jars the audience. The closing argument by the defense, however, is never heard. Students of this film could be challenged to debate to what extent the concepts highlighted by Brooks might offset the heinous nature of the crime committed by Perry Smith and Dick Hickock.

Indictment
(1995)

Principal social theme: child abuse

HBO. PG-13 rating. Featuring: James Woods, Mercedes Ruehl, Sada Thompson, Henry Thomas, Shirley Knight, Mark Blum, Alison Elliott, Chelsea Field, Joe Urla, Scott Waara, Valerie Wildman, Roberta Bassin, Dennis Burkley, Richard Bradford, Miriam Flynn, James Cromwell, Gabrielle Boni, Lolita Davidovich. Written by Abby Mann and Myra Mann. Cinematography by Rodrigo Garcia. Edited by Richard A. Harris. Music by Peter Rodgers Melnick. Produced by Diana Pokorny and Oliver Stone (executive). Directed by Mick Jackson. Color. 129 minutes.

Overview

Indictment is a meticulous and passionate docudrama based on the controversial McMartin case, a ten-year ordeal focusing on the issue of child abuse. The prosecution has been called the twentieth-century equivalent of the Salem witch trials and had wide-ranging ramifications on society and law enforcement. A family who operated a preschool were imprisoned and popularly denounced in the media on the flimsiest evidence extracted from young children by a social worker with an agenda. *Indictment* was one of the most successful television films of the 1990s, winning numerous awards from the Director's Guild, the Golden Globes, as well as the Emmy as the best television film of 1995.

Synopsis

A single complaint of child abuse is made on August 12, 1983, by Judy Johnson (Roberta Bassin) against the operators of the McMartin Preschool in Manhattan Beach, California. In February of the following year, the owners and teachers of the schools are arrested, including seventy-six-year-old Virginia McMartin (Sada Thompson). The main targets are Virginia's daughter Peggy Buckey (Shirley Knight) and her children, Ray (Henry Thomas) and Peggy Ann (Alison Elliott), all teachers at the school. Three other teachers, elderly women, were also indicted. Many children were questioned and all denied any abuse. The district attorney then referred them to child therapist Kee McFarlane (Lolita Davidovich), who claimed they all revealed gross sexual misconduct under her intense examination using puppets and unclothed, anatomically correct dolls. Danny Davis is assigned to defend the accused molesters. The prosecutor in the case, Leal Rubin (Mercedes Ruehl), is passionately committed to pushing this case to the limit. In an unprecedented move, she files more than four hundred separate charges against the accused, and bail is denied to Peggy, Ray, and Peggy Ann. As the prosecutors prepare their case, Rubin's co-counsels, Glenn Stevens (Joe Urla) and Christine Johnson (Chelsea Field), become increasingly doubtful of the main evidence, the tapes of McFarlane interviewing the children. It becomes increasingly apparent to them that she is putting words in the children's mouths, rewarding them when they say they have been molested, but calling them stupid if they deny it. No independent doctor will testify that there is medical evidence of abuse. No pornographic photos, a key element from McFarlane's tapes, were ever discovered. Finally, some of the children's stories become too fantastical, referring to horses decapitated by Ray and trips on airplanes or visits to the local church where Satanists forced them to drink blood. Meanwhile, a mood of general hysteria starts to break out in southern California, and cases start appearing at virtually every daycare center and preschool. Serious investigation discovers that almost all these cases are without merit, and the children recant.

Many months pass and DA Rubin continues to block attempts by Davis to get more information. He finally is allowed to view McFarlane's tapes, but only in the courtroom under supervision. He is astonished by the degree to which the children are manipulated by the unscrupulous therapist. The preliminary hearing is a fiasco. Finally, Stevens is called by Judy Johnson, who now claims someone is sexually molesting her dog. The lawyer learns that she is mentally unstable. The attorney has had enough, leaks his reservations to the press, and resigns. In reaction to this, in January 1986, head DA Ira Reiner (Richard Bradford) decides to drop the charges against most of the defendants, except for Ray Buckey and his mother. Public reaction, however, is furious that these five defendants were set free. It is then discovered that Wayne Satz (Mark Blum), the TV reporter leading the media vendetta against the McMartins is actually the live-in boyfriend of therapist Kee McFarlane. This conflict of interest is pummeled by the rest of the media. When Davis learns about Judy Johnson's mental instability, he moves for a mistrial because the information was never passed on to him. The judge criticizes the prosecution, but allows the trial to continue. Johnson dies of an alcohol overdose shortly afterward. Prosecutor Rubin then decides to rely on the testimony of George Freeman (Dennis Burkley), a perjurer and convicted child molester, who claims that Ray Buckey confessed to him while in prison. Davis discredits Freeman in his cross-examination. Davis also manages to discredit much of McFarlane's testimony by playing her tapes interrogating the children. The judge finally decides to grant Ray Buckey bail, and he is released to Davis's custody after five years in prison. Ray has to undergo a grueling cross-examination by Rubin when he takes the stand to proclaim his innocence. She fails to shake his story. The trial concludes, and the jury announces its verdict in January 1990. Peggy Buckey is cleared of all charges. Ray is cleared of more than forty charges, but the jury remains deadlocked on thirteen other counts. The prosecution decides to retry him on these counts, although DA Ira Reiner dismisses Rubin from the case. Martinez, her replacement, offers Ray a deal, no jail time if he pleads "no contest" to a single charge, but he refuses. The prosecution again fails to obtain a conviction, and the case is dropped. Now free, the McMartins struggle to salvage their lives, upset that they can never fully escape the taint of the charges. Ray Buckey decides to pursue the study of law.

Critique

The McMartin trial remains one of the most inflammatory and controversial cases in American history. *Indictment* tells the story in spellbinding fashion, due in large part to the literate script (based largely on the actual court transcripts) and the use of authentic television clips of news luminaries such as as Geraldo Rivera, Dan Rather, Tom Brokaw, Ted Koppel, and Peter Jennings, featuring their actual on-air comments about the case. This provides a striking air of verisimilitude. It also is an indictment of the rush to judgment by the media. The entire cast, particularly Shirley Knight and Henry Thomas, deliver unforgettable performances. James Woods walks a fine line in his part, gradually transforming the personality of Danny Davis from a heartless sleazeball to a fervent advocate of justice. Joe Urla, as Glenn Stevens, is likewise memorable as the state attorney who puts his career at risk rather than continue an unjust prosecution.

Indictment is one of the most important films on the topic of child abuse, revealing much about the psychological damage that can be inflicted on the innocent. It would have been valuable to contrast how young children who were actually abused would have reacted in contrast to those who were coerced into making untrue accusations. In this case, it was actually the therapist who abused the children, intimidating them and molding them into supporting her own agenda of self-aggrandizement. The script also contained an important reference that independent psychiatrists rejected both McFarlane's techniques and conclusions. Without doubt, *Indictment* would provide abundant material for discussing the actual trauma of child abuse and how it can be accurately detected.

The Intruder (AKA I Hate Your Guts and Shame!)
(1962)

Principal social themes: racism/civil rights, hate groups

Pathé American. No MPAA rating. Featuring: William Shatner, Frank Maxwell, Beverly Lundsford, Robert Emhardt, Jeanne Cooper, Leo Gordon, Charles Barnes, Charles Beaumont, Katherine Smith, George Clayton Johnson, William F. Nolan, Phoebe Rowe, Bo Dodd, Walter Kurtz, Ocee Ritch. Written by Charles Beaumont based on his novel *The Intruder*. Cinematography by Taylor Byars. Edited by Ronald Sinclair. Music by Herman Stein. Produced and directed by Roger Corman. B&W. 80 minutes.

Overview

This unique film was the first to portray the issue of school integration in the South. It was the first and only social issue film by Roger Corman, who previously had specialized in westerns, science fiction, horror, and juvenile delinquent films. After failing to obtain studio funding, Corman self-financed this effort with his brother Gene Corman for $80,000, and shot it entirely on location in and around Sikeston, Missouri. *The Intruder* was a critical success, garnering enthusiastic reviews from the *New York Times*, the *Saturday Review*, and the *New York Herald Tribune*. The picture, however, was a box office failure, which received very few bookings in the South. It led Corman to avoid social issues in his future films.

Synopsis

The credits are shown as the camera follows Californian Adam Cramer (William Shatner), a member of a northern segregationist movement known as The Patrick Henry Society, as he arrives by bus in the small, fictitious town of Caxton, Missouri. Cramer moves into the local hotel, making friends with traveling salesman Sam Griffin (Leo Gordon) and his wife, the only other regular residents of the hotel. He also flirts with Ella McDaniels, a high school student and daughter of the editor of the town paper. School integration is due to start that week in Caxton, and Cramer sounds out the feelings of the local residents about the issue. Many oppose the idea, but accept it as the law. Cramer urges organized resistance and starts working with Vern Shipman (Robert Emhardt), the town's leading citizen. After a series of racist speeches, Cramer riles up the general populace. He joins the local Ku Klux Klan when they drive through the black section of town to burn a cross. When Sam Griffin is out of town, Cramer seduces his wife.

Events spiral out of Cramer's control when a black church is bombed and the minister is killed. Accused of provoking the incident, Cramer is jailed, but the locals rally to his defense and he is released. Editor Tom McDaniels (Frank Maxwell) is incensed. When the local black students decide to pull out of the high school, McDaniels goes to them and urges them to continue. He personally escorts them to the school. Later, the editor is beaten by outraged citizens and hospitalized. Cramer knows that violence will hurt his cause, but he concocts a scheme that might help him to achieve his goal. He persuades Ella that her father will be killed unless she accuses one of the black students of trying to molest her. She fakes an attack in the supply room of the high school, and the accused young man is brought before the principal. A mob gathers when news of the incident spreads. Cramer urges that the accused student be escorted to the police station, but the mob, led by Shipman, intends to lynch him instead. Griffin turns up with Ella McDaniels, who reveals her false accusation to be one invented by Cramer. Shocked at the crime they were about to commit, the crowd disperses, and Shipman strikes Cramer, knocking him down. Griffin helps the racist up, telling him that he is through in Caxton and offers to drive him to the bus depot.

Critique

This film is one of the most effective and compelling portraits of the South in the late 1950s and early 1960s as it reeled under the impact of integration and the civil rights movement. One of its strongest assets is its feeling of *cinema verité*. The location footage is both magnificent and convincing, since most of the cast, except for the leads, are locals hired by Corman. When Shatner delivered his white supremacist speech from the courthouse steps, many townspeople, appearing as extras, cheered him on, believing he was the hero of the film. Ironically, the extras recruited by Corman for the klan scenes, it turns out, were actual klan members. When the locals finally tracked down Charles Beaumont's novel and learned it was not prose-gregation, all cooperation ceased, and the local police harassed Corman and his crew continually as they wrapped up the film.

The flavor and atmosphere of the film remain impressive more than forty years later. The casual nature of the racism, from the manner in which even elderly women refer to blacks as "niggers" to the scenes of the cross-burning, are powerful, indelible images that seem completely authentic. This film can serve as an excellent vehicle for students to grasp both the authentic ambience of the period and the progress made over the past decades. The acting, directing, and writing are exceptional. Interestingly, the screenwriter and novelist Charles Beaumont appears in the role of the high school principal. Shatner reports that this film garnered him his most positive reviews up until his appearance on *Star Trek* six years later.

Iris
(2001)

Principal social themes: aging, end-of-life issues

Miramax. R rating. Featuring: Judi Dench, Jim Broadbent, Kate Winslett, Hugh Bonneville, Penelope Wilton, Juliet Aubrey, Kris Marshall, Pauline McGlynn, Sam West, and Timothy West. Written by Richard Eyre and Charles Wood based on the books *Iris: A Memoir* and *Elegy for Iris* by John Bailey. Cinematography by Roger Pratt. Edited by Martin Walsh. Music by James Horner. Produced by Robert Fox and Scott Rudin. Directed by Richard Eyre. Color. 90 minutes.

Overview

Iris is a poignant and reflective film on the life of famed British novelist Dame Iris Murdoch (1919–1999), concentrating on her final years when she fell victim to Alzheimer's disease, and the efforts of her husband, college professor John Bailey, to care for her and to cope with her condition. This film received enthusiastic praise and numerous awards, including the Best Supporting Actor Oscar for Jim Broadbent as the elder John Bailey.

Synopsis

This film unfolds on two interrelated tracks, cutting back and forth frequently from scene to scene. The first storyline takes place in the 1950s as literary critic John Bailey (Hugh Bonneville) pursues his courtship of the brilliant writer and free-thinker Iris Murdoch (Kate Winslett); the second follows Dame Iris Murdoch (Judi Dench) as she completes her last novel in the mid-1990s and begins to suffer the effects of Alzheimer's disease, and the efforts of her husband (Jim Broadbent) to care for her. At first, the effects of her condition are hardly noticeable. She continues to lecture brilliantly, but she starts to have difficulty finding the right words in her writing. Her mind begins to wander occasionally, but it is only when she draws a complete blank in the middle of a taped interview that she is alarmed enough to have some tests. Her physician comes to her home and asks a series of questions. She is upset when she cannot remember the name of the British prime minister. John tries to reassure her as the diagnosis suggests Alzheimer's disease. She takes another series of tests, this time in the hospital, and starts to exhibit dyslexia with a number of simple words. The doctors inform them that the progress of the disease will be inexorable.

Iris completes her novel, but by the time the book is published, she has lost all interest in it. She becomes increasingly disoriented. When John takes her swimming, one of her favorite pastimes, she panics, having forgotten how to swim. (This scene, like most others, is interedited with an earlier scene in the 1950s when the nude Iris takes John swimming in the same location.) Iris starts to lose all contact with reality. She wanders off one day while John is busy typing, and he desperately tries to find her, calling the police and driving around the village. Finally, Iris is brought home by an elderly gentleman whom John fails to recognize as one of Iris' lovers from the 1950s. Another crisis occurs when Iris panics in the car and opens her door while the vehicle is still in motion. John pulls over and searches the wooded embankment, finding Iris lying in a pile of leaves. While checking to see if she is hurt, Iris tells John that she loves him, one of her last coherent thoughts. The time has come when John is no longer able to care for her, and she is placed in a nursing home. She has completely retreated into her own dream world. John visits her frequently, and when she passes away, he is sitting by her bedside holding her hand. As John starts to pack away her clothes at home, he thinks back on his wife, both in her vibrant days of the 1950s and her radiant lectures of the early 1990s.

Critique

Iris manages to be tender, compelling, funny, yet almost painful to watch as the elder John Bailey observes his beloved wife transform from an extraordinary scholar to a helpless shut-in devoid of personality. The film shows the happy couple aging in almost gracious terms at first. As her condition worsens, Iris becomes irritable, frightened, and restless as she loses her personality a bit at a time. This process is most difficult for John, who tries in vain to stem the tide of her condition. If any audience member has suffered the trauma of losing a loved one to Alzheimer's disease, this picture might be too heartbreaking, as it accurately charts the stages of the condition. *Iris* shines a clear light on the issue of aging, such as the inability to no longer care for a loved one, and touches on end-of-life concerns as well in a most understanding presentation.

Judge Horton and the Scottsboro Boys
(1976)

Principal social themes: racism/civil rights,
hate groups

Tomorrow Entertainment. No MPAA rating. Featuring: Arthur Hill, Vera Miles, Lewis J. Stadlen, Ken Kercheval, Ellen Barber, Suzanne Lederer, Tom Ligon, David Harris, Ronny Clanton, Gregory Wyatt, Wallace Thomas, Larry Butts, Bruce Watson. Written by John McGreevey based on the book *Scottsboro: A Tragedy of the American South* by Dan T. Carter. Cinematography by Mario Tosi. Edited by Eric Albertson. Produced by Paul Leaf. Directed by Fiedler Cook. Color. 98 minutes.

Overview

In 1931, nine black men were accused of raping two white women in Scottsboro, Alabama, while hitching a ride on a freight train. On the flimsiest evidence, they were tried and sentenced to death in one of the most controversial legal cases in America since the trial of Sacco and Vanzetti.

When the Alabama Supreme Court threw out the convictions, the "Scottsboro Boys," as they were called, were retried in 1933 in Decatur, Alabama, in the court of Circuit Judge James Edwin Horton. This telefilm concentrates on this unusual trial, which eventually led to greater protection of the civil rights of minority defendants in the American justice system. This telefilm received critical acclaim and recognition by the Emmy Awards.

Synopsis

This film largely presents the story of the trial from the viewpoint of Judge Horton (Arthur Hill) and his wife, who alternately serve as narrators for the unfolding events. Horton and his legal friends regard the Scottsboro case with suspicion and open hostility to the outsiders, such as the National Association for the Advancement of Colored People (NAACP), who are providing the defense with legal council. They regard them and other northern groups as Communist inspired. They do agree that the first trail was a mockery, forcing the state supreme court to step in because the defendants did not have adequate legal council. When the new trial was shifted to Horton's court, his friends observed that he was being groomed for a seat on the state's supreme court.

Due to state law, each of the defendants was scheduled to receive a separate trial. The first defendant to be prosecuted was Haywood Patterson (David Harris), a brash, angry, black man who is older and more hostile than the other accused prisoners, who are as young as thirteen years old. When the trial begins, Horton tries to operate his court in a proper, impartial manner. Patterson is defended by Sam Liebowitz (Lewis J. Stadlen), a Jewish attorney from New York. The prosecutor is DA Tom Knight, one of the most popular lawyers in the state. The prosecution's case is based solely on the testimony of Victoria Price (Ellen Barber), who claims the nine men raped her. The second woman has vanished. Horton first realizes something is wrong when one of the two doctors scheduled to testify asks to be excused. In private, the doctor tells Horton that no rape took place, but that he was afraid to testify because the Ku Klux Klan would ruin his career. The defense calls a white hobo as a witness, and he contradicts much of Victoria's story. Later, the defense has a breakthrough. They locate the second woman, Ruby Bates (Suzanne Lederer), who claims she lied at the first trial due to pressure from Victoria. She testifies that no rape occurred, that she made up the story to avoid arrest when lawmen pulled off all the freeloaders who were riding on the freight train. The courtroom erupts with hostility at Ruby's testimony, and they pelt her with eggs as she leaves the courtroom.

At the end of the trial, the DA whips up the courtroom with anti-Semitic and racist slurs. Horton warns him twice. When Horton hands the case over to the jury, he insists that they ignore race and concentrate solely on the evidence. Instead, they bring in a guilty verdict and impose the death sentence.

The defense appeals to Judge Horton to set the jury's verdict aside. This is a routine motion that is almost always dismissed. Instead, Horton stuns the courtroom by ordering a new trial, declaring that the prosecution's case was clearly insufficient. The courtroom audience, including many KKK adherents, erupts in anger, and Liebowitz looks at the judge in total surprise. The DA tells Horton that he has just ruined his career. A closing narration confirms that Horton was defeated for reelection as judge and never again served in a public office. All of the Scottsboro Boys were retried, convicted, and sentenced to death, but the U.S. Supreme Court overturned these convictions, imparting new guidelines for the civil rights of defendants. All of them were eventually pardoned and released. The fate of all the principals in the case was also revealed in the closing narration. James Edwin Horton was widely hailed as a courageous advocate of justice. He lived until 1967.

Critique

The Scottsboro case was a mockery of the justice system as practiced in the Deep South, where racism and the influence of the KKK was enormous. The case also inspired the courtroom drama in Harper Lee's novel *To Kill a Mockingbird*, in which a black defendant accused of rape is found guilty despite proof that he was physically incapable of the attack. Likewise, one of the Scottsboro defendants was legally blind. *Judge Horton and the Scottsboro Boys* is a stunning portrait of the culture of racism, in which decent men of law abandon all sense of right and wrong. All of the evidence proved that Victoria Price was a perjurer, yet her word was taken without doubt. If the defendants were white, this case never would have been brought to trial. Students of the film can explore other factors involved in the case, such as regional xenophobia and mob rule. Much of the film is presented in a low-key fashion, allowing the facts to stand for themselves without exaggeration. Arthur Hill is magnificent as the conscientious Judge Horton, who truly believes justice is blind. There are few other sympathetic characters. Even Lewis J. Stadlen's Sam Liebowitz seems to grandstand too much at first, weakening his client's slim chances. One of the film's finest moments is when Liebowitz gradually realizes the depth of Horton's dedication to objectivity and truth.

Kate's Secret
(1986)

Principal social themes: disabilities, women's rights

Columbia. No MPAA rating. Featuring: Meredith Baxter Birney, Ed Asner, Ben Masters, Georgann Johnson, Tracy Nelson, Shari Belafonte, Leslie Bevis, Mackenzie Phillips, Sharon Spelman, Liz Torres, Mindy Seeger, Duke Moosekian, Summer Phoenix, Liberty Phoenix. Written by Denise DeGarmo and Susan Seeger. Cinematography by Dennis Dalzell. Edited by Millie Moore. Music by J. Peter Robinson. Produced by Stephanie Austin. Directed by Arthur Allen Seidelman. Color. 98 minutes.

Overview

Perhaps the most important and inclusive film about eating disorders, *Kate's Secret* manages to encapsulate public misconceptions and accurate facts within a relatively brief time frame. It also delves into the psychological and cultural pressures that nurture the condition, which can even be classified as a disability. *Kate's Secret* debuted on NBC on November 17, 1986. Several later television movies imitated it, but without this film's impact.

Synopsis

Kate Stark (Meredith Baxter Birney) is the wife of Jack, an up-and-coming attorney in southern California. She is obsessive about her appearance, even forgoing her husband's amorous advances to go jogging. She is equally hard on Becky, her young daughter, forcing her to eat as if she were dieting. When Kate's mother arrives for a visit, we see the first chink in Kate's image as the "perfect housewife," when she stops at a supermarket and shoplifts a package of cookies that she wolfs down, then heads to the alley behind the store and forces herself to vomit. Kate's secret is that she is a bulimic. Several additional episodes of Kate's binging and purging occur, particularly after she hosts a party for members of Jack's law firm. Kate starts to have dizzy spells and collapses during an exercise class. She passes out while driving Becky home from a Girl Scout meeting. When she awakens in a hospital, she is questioned about her "condition," which she refuses to acknowledge. When Jack arrives, he is told that Kate is a bulimic, and her tests show that her health is at serious risk. Dr. Resnick (Ed Asner), a specialist in eating disorders, recommends that she be hospitalized until her condition becomes stable.

The hospital has a ward that treats conditions such as anorexia and bulimia. The patients are strictly monitored as to their diet and use of the bathroom. Kate feels imprisoned and learns what is expected of her from Patch Reed (Tracy Nelson), her roommate, who is a fashion model and another bulimic. During group therapy, Kate's denial of her problem is overcome. Dr. Resnick believes Kate's problem comes from her mother, who stresses the idea that she must be a perfect wife or she will lose her husband. Patch helps Kate sneak out of the hospital to attend another office party with her husband (who thinks Kate was given permission by Resnick to attend). When attempting to binge and purge, she suffers a stomach hemorrhage and is rushed to the emergency room. She recovers and is returned to her ward where she learns that Patch died of a heart attack when she overdosed on diet pills. This event shocks Kate, who then seriously struggles to come to terms with her condition. She is finally released from the hospital, secure that her husband loves her and that their marriage is not in any danger. Kate reconciles with her mother, and she and Jack see her mother off at the airport.

Critique

Kate's Secret goes through various phases in its attempt to portray the problem of eating disorders. First, the condition is made to appear trivial, even humorous, as Kate gobbles down handfuls of food with her fingers, be it cake, meatloaf, or ice cream. It is only when the scene shifts to the hospital that the implications of the condition take on a serious tone. Kate's system has become weakened by lack of balanced nutrients; her potassium level is dangerously low. She learns how her repeated enforced vomiting has increased the risk of a deadly stomach rupture. Finally, the psychological pressures that promulgate these disabilities are examined. The cultural pressures of our time play on many women's fears that they must be thin, so much so that many slender women see themselves as fat even when they are not. These ideas are reinforced from many sources, including advertising, fashion, and peer pressure. In Kate's case, her mother stressed that she must be thin to keep her husband, a prejudice that Kate was passing on to her own daughter. In other cases, this pressure may come from a woman's spouse, her friends, or role models. An eating disorder is primarily a condition facing women. The script portrays a clandestine rivalry in the ward between patients with anorexia and bulimia. At times, Ed Asner seems to be an odd choice as the specialist in eating disorders. In one scene, he lectures a patient on the need for sensible eating, but at the same time the camera angle seems to concentrate on Asner's own rather bulky waist.

Another subsidiary issue is Kate's rights as a patient. For example, her husband is told the complete details of her medical condition without her consent. She almost appears to be coerced into the ward. True, her husband gives his approval, but how would this have been handled if Kate were single.

In this case, would an eating disorder be considered the equivalent of insanity so a patient would have no rights? Inadvertently, the film suggests a husband can arrange for the incarceration of his wife. This is a troubling factor in the overall issue of coercive treatment. Until the death of Patch Reed, it seems that Kate is merely pretending to be a responsive patient. She can only come to terms with her condition until the death of her friend to the disability. Eating disorders is then clearly portrayed as a life-threatening condition equivalent to alcoholism or drug addiction.

Key Witness
(1960)

Principal social theme: violence/gangs

MGM. No MPAA rating. Featuring: Jeffrey Hunter, Dennis Hopper, Pat Crowley, Joby Baker, Susan Harrison, Johnny Nash, Corey Allen, Frank Silvera, Bruce Gordon, Terry Burnham, Dennis Holmes, Ted Knight, and John Zaremba. Written by Alfred Brenner and Sidney Michaels based on the novel by Frank Kane. Cinematography by Harold E. Wellman. Edited by Ferris Webster. Music by Charles Wolcott. Produced by Kathryn Hereford. Directed by Phil Karlson. B&W. 82 minutes.

Overview

Although somewhat overdone, *Key Witness* is basically a dramatic parable about the influence of gangs and the intimidation of the public by them and their violent culture. The production stressed its social concerns by commissioning the attorney general of California to write a preamble highlighting the issue with which the film opens. Dennis Hopper, who played the gang leader, was so motivated by the theme that twenty-eight years later he directed another film, *Colors*, dedicated to the same issue, also set in the streets of East Los Angeles.

Synopsis

Jeff Morrow (Jeffrey Hunter) is a realtor who stops at a phone booth in East Los Angeles to make a business call. He watches the teenagers dance to music from a jukebox in the nearby diner, when a motorcyclist (Dennis Hopper) drives into the restaurant. He and his gang surround Emilio, a Hispanic boy in the street. Jeff telephones the police. The youth is stabbed with a switchblade and his attackers drive off. Jeff rushes to the aid of Emilio, who says, "Cowboy did it!" By the time the police arrive, the boy is dead. No one in the crowd who watched the scene admits seeing anything. Jeff agrees to come to the station, and he identifies the gang leader from a mug shot. He signs a statement and agrees to testify when the case is brought to trial. Meanwhile the gang, consisting of Cowboy, Muggles, Magician, Ruby, and Apple, hear that a witness has been found who will identify Cowboy. He is outraged that anyone on his turf would dare squeal on him. The gang ambushes one of the cops who had recorded Jeff's name and address in his notebook. They telephone Jeff and threaten to kill his wife and two kids unless he recants his testimony. Jeff telephones the cops for help, but the gang slashes his tires and throws a rock through his window. Cowboy is picked up after a chase. At his arraignment the next day, however, Jeff refuses to testify after his wife is attacked in the corridor right outside the court-room. Jeff tells Lieutenant Turno (Frank Silvera), the detective in charge of the case, that if they could not protect his wife from violence inside the courthouse, how could they guarantee the safety of his kids. Later, two of the gang members confront Morrow's son on the playground. Apple, the only black member of the gang, knocks Muggles's arm when he attempts to shoot the boy, wounding him in the leg. Apple goes to Jeff and asks his help to turn himself over to the police, but Jeff, filled with anger, refuses. The rest of the gang invade Jeff's home, and he and Apple have to fight for their lives until the police turn up and arrest the entire gang. This time, Jeff tells Turno that there is no doubt he will testify.

Critique

In many ways, *Key Witness* provides a foreshadowing of the growing problem of youth gang violence. Of course, Cowboy's gang is meant to be taken only on a symbolic level, since this small gang (five members) seems to have the influence of a much larger group of thugs. Also, Cowboy's gang seems a little too old for the characters they are meant to portray. In allegorical terms, however, the issue is clearly laid out: Much of the power of these gangs stems from the code of silence they can enforce on any innocent bystanders who live in their home neighborhood. When Jeff looks over the witnesses of Emilio's murder, they all seemed elderly, frightened, and submissive. It also seems clear that the police at this point are largely incapable of dealing with these young offenders. The entire film is seen from Jeff's viewpoint. How does his attitude change as the film develops? Would an audience member, watching Jeff's ordeal, be more likely in real life to identify a killer in a street crime or remain silent? Would the concept of a neighborhood watch orga-nization have been useful in this situation? What other methods could have been used to help? Was Lt. Turno's attitude realistic or fatalistic? Why did Jeff change his opinion about Turno by the end of the film? How did the gang situation in East Los Angeles evolve between the making of *Key Witness* and *Colors*? In what ways are the problems similar or different in both films? In what ways does the attitude of the police and the general public differ in these films? A close study would be helpful to determine which elements of *Key Witness* remain relevant today.

Kissing Jessica Stein
(2001)

Principal social theme: homosexuality

Fox Searchlight. R rating. Featuring: Jennifer Westfeldt, Heather Juergensen, Scott Cohen, Esther Wurmfeld, Hillel Friedman, Robert Ari, David Aaron Baker, Jennifer Carta, Ben Webber, Brian Stepanek, Nick Corley, Jackie Hoffman, John Cariani, Michael Mastro, Michael Showalter, Jon Hamm, Tovah Feldshuh; Written by Jennifer Westfeldt and Heather Juergensen. Cinematography by Lawrence Sher. Edited by Kristy Jacobs Maslin and Greg Tillman. Produced by Eden H. Wurmfeld and Brad Zions. Directed by Charles Hermann-Wurmfeld. Color. 96 minutes.

Overview

Kissing Jessica Stein was an engaging attempt to portray lesbianism in a fresh fashion. The result is a light romance reminiscent of the popular romantic comedies from the 1950s and 1960s, but peppered with a dash of hip Woody Allen humor. The story depicts the romance of a bisexual art gallery manager and a straight but high-strung journalist weary of dating unsuitable nerdy men. Beneath the froth, the film provides an honest and serious consideration of human sexuality. *Kissing Jessica Stein* won numerous awards as best picture at independent film festivals.

Synopsis

Jessica Stein (Jennifer Westfeldt) is an intense journalist in her late twenties who is becoming increasingly frustrated in her love life. Her mother, Judy (Tovah Feldshuh), and her grandmother, Esther, continually try to set her up with new suitors, hoping to find Mr. Right. They even size up possible candidates while attending services at the synagogue. She has a series of dates, finding each of them unsatisfying. Josh (Scott Cohen), Jessica's boss, is her old college flame, and he makes a cruel observation that Jessica is far too fussy and will never find a man who will meet her standards. Helen Cooper (Heather Juergensen) is a sexually active woman who manages an art galley. In spite of her many boyfriends, she finds herself more attracted to women. With the help of Sebastian and Martin, two homosexual friends with whom she runs the gallery, Helen writes a heartfelt personal column ad in the paper seeking a new relationship. Jessica is moved by the ad, even though it appears in the section of "Women Seeking Women." Feeling depressed after learning that her brother, Dan, had become engaged, Jessica calls Helen and they agree to meet. Jessica is very nervous and uncertain about this move, and after meeting Helen in a coffee shop, tries to back out. Helen deliberately dumps the contents of her purse in the street, and Jessica stops to help her as they begin to chat. Eventually, they wind up at a restaurant and talk all night.

Walking home, Jessica states that she could not consider a lesbian relationship. In response, Helen kisses her and walks away. Jessica is both stunned and intrigued, finally deciding to contact Helen again, telling her she is willing to give the relationship a try, but she wants to keep their liaison a secret. Jessica insists on taking things slow, but Helen wants to seduce her as quickly as possible. When she finally sparks a response from Jessica, one of Helen's boyfriends shows up at her apartment, and Jessica makes an excuse to leave. Finally, Judy Stein invites Helen to the Stein home for Shabbat dinner and to meet Jessica's brother Dan. When the weather turns bad, she is invited to stay over, sharing Jessica's bed at last. Helen becomes hurt, however, when she learns that Jessica was not planning to bring her to Dan's wedding. Being very perceptive, Judy figures out the situation and tells her daughter that Helen is a very fine person. Jessica invites Helen as her guest to Dan's wedding, bringing their relationship out into the open. She decides to move in with her. Jessica also decides to quit her job and become an artist. Months pass, and Jessica is completely happy with the relationship, but Helen is frustrated because she feels that Jessica never wants to make love. Helen finally decides to dump her. More months pass, and Josh runs into Jessica in a bookstore. When he learns that she is no longer with Helen, he asks her out. Later, Jessica meets Helen at a cafe. They have become best friends now that they are no longer lovers, and Helen advises Jessica in her renewed romance with Josh. So at the conclusion, Jessica has returned to the straight world and Helen has chosen to continue wholeheartedly as a lesbian.

Critique

Written and occasionally improvised by its two co-stars, *Kissing Jessica Stein* owes its success to the believability of the main characters and their changing attitudes. Although influenced by such television series as *Friends* and *Sex and the City, Kissing Jessica Stein* has its own unique vitality. Jessica is a "type A" personality in the extreme—hypercritical yet totally lacking in self-confidence. She chatters on and on, covering her insecurity as best she can. She became so frustrated with her love life that she wanted to try something different, as long as it was genuine. Once she entered the relationship with Helen, she remained tentative until she received her mother's approval. At that point, she reached her own comfort level, relaxed, and became herself. Unfortunately for Helen, Jessica was not a lesbian at heart. She just basked in the glow of the "sisterhood" of her relationship with Helen, which lacked any true passion. Helen, on the other hand, wanted to be desired more than anything. This was perhaps the reason she had so many boyfriends. She wanted to find that same intensity level with a woman, something Jessica could never provide. It is fascinating to listen to Helen's uninhibited conversations with her two gay artist friends. At one point she refers to Jessica as "a Jewish Sandra Dee," reinforcing the 1960s film undercurrent.

Jennifer Westfeldt is a wonderful actress who really brings Jessica alive. Her voice has the same mellifluous tones as Helen Hunt, but often accelerated to a crescendo that is simply amazing. Jessica becomes more appealing as the film wears on, losing the high tension level that is so abrasive in the opening scenes. Heather Juergensen is far more sensual as Helen, more down to earth and honest. She is the more interesting of the two main characters. *Kissing Jessica Stein* can provoke lively discussion about the nature of friendship, romance, and the actual nature of lesbianism. It is also an extremely amusing film, shot almost entirely on location in New York City. One interesting point, much of the footage was reedited before the film's release to cut out the many visual references to the World Trade Center contained in the original print.

The Lady Gambles
(1949)

Principal social themes: addiction (gambling), suicide/depression

Universal. No MPAA rating. Featuring: Barbara Stanwyck, Robert Preston, Stephen McNally, Edith Barrett, John Hoyt, Elliott Sullivan, John Harmon, Phil Van Zandt, Leif Erickson, Curt Conway, Housely Stevenson, Don Beddoe, Nana

Bryant, Frank Moran, Tony Curtis. Written by Roy Huggins. Cinematography by Russell Metty. Edited by Milton Carruth. Music by Frank Skinner. Produced by Michel Kraike. Directed by Michael Gordon. B&W. 98 minutes.

Overview

This film patterned its approach to the issue of gambling addiction along the same lines as *The Lost Weekend* tackled alcoholism, perhaps with an added dash of *A Rake's Progress*. With legalized gambling recently established in Nevada, it is noteworthy how this film ties the Vegas casinos to organized crime, corruption, and the seductive lure of gambling. Moreover, the addiction is treated not as a moral failing but as a genuine illness.

Synopsis

The Lady Gambles opens with a startling and violent "attention getter" as a man is caught using loaded dice in a back-alley crap shoot. He runs off, but his partner, a woman played by Barbara Stanwyck, is caught by the outraged players, and they beat her until she is unconscious. When she is brought to the hospital, a Chicago reporter named David Booth (Robert Preston) shows up asking about the case. The doctor in charge tells Booth that he may not be able to release her into his custody as there may be some police charges against her. Booth reveals that the woman is his wife, Joan, whom he has not seen in over a year. Intrigued, the doctor asks about her background. A lengthy flashback begins as Booth explains that she is a warm, intelligent woman and that they had a happy marriage, until Joan's sister moved in with them. Since Ruth raised Joan, his wife felt very beholden to her.

Booth brought Joan with him on a trip to Las Vegas so he could write a series of articles about the Hoover Dam. Joan decided to do a photo essay about people who gamble at the casinos. When she is caught with her hidden camera, the casino owner, Horace Corrigan (Stephen McNally), agrees to cooperate and provides her with worthless "house chips" so she could blend in with the other gamblers. Soon however, the gambling bug bites Joan, and she starts playing with real money, losing $600 she sneaks out of her husband's business expense envelope. Desperate, Joan pawns her camera and manages to win back her losses. When Booth finishes his assignment, Ruth shows up in Vegas. Booth decides to drive back to Chicago, leaving his wife to stay with her sister. Then Joan goes on a serious gambling binge. She only makes money when Corrigan stakes her in a private poker game. When Booth calls, he is surprised when Ruth tells him that Joan spends all night at the casino. He returns to Vegas and discovers that Joan has become a gambling addict. He decides to quit his job, take all their savings, and rent an oceanfront cottage in Mexico where he intends to write a book and devote his time to Joan. When he takes a short trip to do library research, Joan is again bitten by the gambling bug, takes all of their savings, and loses it. Booth is crushed when he finds out. He splits the remaining funds he has left with Joan and decides to drive back to Chicago. He tells Joan she can either use her share of the money to return home or go elsewhere. Joan decides to go to Las Vegas and work for Corrigan.

Corrigan uses Joan as a front for a gambling syndicate that intends to make a fortune at the racetrack. They buy an outstanding horse, but deliberately run it "slow" when they enter it in a race. Joan continues to gamble on the side and always loses. The syndicate decides to make their move when the odds against their horse make it a long shot. They plan to place huge wagers at the last minute with bookies around the country and then run their horse to win. Joan is warned to stay away from the track on that day, but she gets a letter from Booth asking her to sign divorce papers. She decides to return to him and goes to the track to bet on the horse. Sharp-eyed track regulars spot her placing the huge wager, and they decide to place large bets on the horse. Rumors spread through the stands, and soon the 30-to-1 odds drop to 8-to-5, and the payoffs on the syndicate's winnings are meager. The gambling racketeers are outraged. They catch Joan calling her husband, and threaten to hurt her. Corrigan tells them to back off and drives Joan into a small town in the middle of nowhere and dumps her.

Booth begins an intensive search for her, but is never able to locate her before she moves on. He discovers that she is living a vicarious existence taking, odd jobs and gambling away her earnings. The lengthy flashback concludes. Joan is barely conscious when Ruth arrives at the hospital and tries to persuade her sister to send Booth away. Deeply depressed, Joan steps out onto the ledge of her hospital room and threatens to jump. Booth saves her, and she finally tells Ruth to leave her alone. The doctor is convinced that the crisis has passed and that Joan will be able to recover under her husband's care.

Critique

The Lady Gambles is a powerful, effective film, although viewed today some of the plot points appear rather perverse, such as the nebulous police charges pending against Joan who is found beaten in an alley. Also, after David Booth urges the doctor to tend to Joan's treatment, he spends a long time distracting him with his story. John Hoyt delivers a stunning performance as the cynical, rather cold-hearted doctor, who only develops a trace of compassion when he sees how Ruth tries to manipulate the battered Joan. Stephen McNally is also quite good as the rather sardonic and world-weary mobster who takes an interest in Joan. Robert Preston is not fully believable as David Booth, who is too easily deceived too often by his wife. Barbara Stanwyck, of course, dominates the entire film with her compelling portrayal.

She develops a genuine fire in her eyes when she rolls the dice, and she depicts the gambling compulsion as an uncontrollable physical need. The major weakness in the film is the subplot of the rivalry between Ruth and David in their attempts to influence Joan, which leads to her suicidal state. The reason behind this conflict is never clearly explained in the plot. The gambling becomes a form of self-punishment for Joan, and even her gangster employer detects that she really wants to lose. An examination of Joan's psychology would be useful as one of the keys to her gambling addiction. Can self-loathing be the major reason behind any addiction? Naturally, the turn of events in the story also highlights the issue of legalized gambling as the state enables gangsters to control and ruin the lives of average citizens.

Lean on Me
(1989)

Principal social themes: education/literacy, racism/civil rights

Warner Brothers. PG-13 rating. Featuring: Morgan Freeman, Beverly Todd, Robert Guillaume, Alan North, Lynne Thigpen, Robin Bartlett, Michael Beach, Ethan Phillips, Sandra Reaves-Phillips, Ivonne Coll, Karina Arroyave, Jermaine Hopkins, Karen Malina White, Sloane Shelton. Written by Michael Schiffer. Cinematography by Victor Hammer. Edited by John Carter and John G. Avildsen. Music by Bill Conti. Produced by Norman Twain. Directed by John G. Avildsen. Color. 109 minutes.

Overview

Joe Clark became one of the most famous educators in America during the 1980s, best known for revitalizing the rundown Eastside High School in Paterson, New Jersey, and raising it to the standard of a model school just two years after his appointment as principal. He was later voted among the top ten principals in the country. The screen version of how Clark transformed Eastside High was quite influential, and numerous college education programs included it in their curriculum. When Clark himself is questioned about the film, he comments, "I think they toned me down."

Synopsis

The film opens with a portrayal of a young, colorfully dressed black teacher, Joe Clark (Morgan Freeman) at Eastside High in 1967. He ruffles some feathers with his kinetic style, so he is transferred to a grammar school. Twenty years later, the mayor of Paterson faces a crisis when the state of New Jersey threatens to take control of any high school that continually fails the basic skills test. Only 38 percent of Eastside High students passed this exam, the lowest score in the state. The school superintendent recommends that Joe Clark be installed as principal, the only educator in the city with the grit to turn things around. Eastside High is shown to be in chaos. The corridors are lined with graffiti. Students are hassled by various cliques. Drug dealers enter and leave the school at will peddling their goods.

When Joe Clark assumes his post as principal, he ignores the pleasantries from the staff and starts to issue orders in a semimilitary fashion. He directs the maintenance department to repaint the school's interiors, with a standing order to paint over any new graffiti within twenty-four hours. He asks the teachers to prepare lists of any drug dealers or incorrigible troublemakers in the student body. Clark reviews the lists and selects three hundred for expulsion. He challenges the students to concentrate on basic skills, particularly reading. It is the essential goal of the school that 70 percent pass the next state exam testing these skills. To build morale, Clark insists that every student also learn the school song. He later fires the music teacher, one of the most highly regarded members of the staff, because he believes she is resisting his efforts. He suspends the most popular black teacher for a minor infraction. One of the expelled students implores Clark to reinstate him. Clark questions him sharply before finally relenting and giving the youngster another chance. The school superintendent warns Clark that he is alienating people who could be his allies. At a parent's meeting, Clark runs afoul of Leona Barrett, a local black activist, for expelling so many students. Barrett vows to remove Clark as principal and tries to enlist the mayor in her efforts. He tries to placate her with an appointment to the school board, but her main goal remains Clark's dismissal.

Clark has an open door policy so that any student may visit him and discuss any problems. In private, the principal becomes understanding and helpful. If trouble at home interferes with the student, he visits the parents and offers practical solutions to assist them. Slowly, the school's spirit begins to change. One real challenge happens when drug dealers continue to barge into the school, let in by their clients. Clark responds by chaining the school doors while classes are in session. This gives Leona Barrett an opening to catch Clark in a fire code violation. The city attorney, however, tips off Clark about this plan. Clark prepares an emergency announcement, Code Ten, to alert teachers to remove the chains whenever the fire chief shows up. Just before the state exam, Clark holds an assembly in which he addresses all students, the black majority and the white and Hispanic minorities, telling them that they all are in same boat. He fires their enthusiasm, and the entire staff and student body sing "Lean on Me." When the exam is given, each student puts forth his or her best effort.

The fire chief eventually catches Clark with the chains on the doors, and he is arrested. Barrett holds a school board meeting calling for Clark's dismissal. The entire student body holds a rally outside City Hall, shouting "Free Joe Clark!" The mayor visits Clark in jail and asks him to tell the students to disperse. Barrett tries to address the students, saying they will get a better principal. They shout her down, but one of the teachers shows up with the test results: Eastside students passed with flying colors. The confrontation turns into a celebration, as this announcement assures that the school board will retain Clark in his position and that the legal case against him will be dismissed.

Critique

The screen treatment of Joe Clark's struggle at Eastside is partially fictionalized, particularly with the personalities portrayed on screen such as the mayor and the members of the staff. There is also a time discrepancy, since Clark was actually appointed principal in 1983, not 1987 as in the film. However, most of the incidents and Clark's hardnosed approach to education are factual. He did indeed expel three hundred students shortly after taking over as principal. He did chain the exit doors during the school day to keep out drug dealers, and this procedure did lead to conflicts with the fire department and elements of the community. Without a doubt *Lean on Me* presents a controversial approach to education. Students viewing the film could debate many aspects of it. What are the advantages and disadvantages of Clark's methods? What is his philosophy of education? Is it worth the price to expel 10 percent of the student body if it allows the remaining 90 percent to receive a proper education? What happens to those he expels? The film itself shows one student petitioning Clark to be allowed to return. In actuality, several dozen did return to school to become successful students. The controversy over the locked school doors was resolved; with the installation of new doors that would sound an alarm if opened during school hours. Is Clark fair to his teaching staff? To what extent is Clark a role model? If not, why not? Could a white principal have instituted Clark's get-tough policy? The film mentions in passing Eastside's literacy outreach program to the community. How important are efforts of this kind in the overall mandate of an inner city high school? The title *Lean on Me* suggests a team effort, yet testing by its nature is competitive. Does Clark effectively inspire the students to be mentally prepared to compete? After serving seven years at Eastside High, Clark went on to other challenges, becoming one of the leading motivational speakers on the topic of education.

Lenny
(1974)

Principal social themes: censorship, addiction (drugs)

United Artists. R rating. Featuring: Dustin Hoffman, Valerie Perrine, Jan Miner, Stanley Beck, Gary Morton, Lee Sandman, Frankie Man, Rashel Novikoff, Guy Rennie, Susan Malnick, Phil Philbin, Clarence Thomas, Mark Harris; Written by Julian Barry based on his play *Lenny*. Cinematography by Bruce Sertees. Edited by Alan Heim. Music by Ralph Burns. Produced by Marvin Worth. Directed by Bob Fosse. B&W. 112 minutes.

Overview

Lenny Bruce (1926–1966) was a controversial nightclub comic noted for his acerbic wit and colorful use of obscenity. Because of foul language in his act, Bruce became a target for local officials who tried to censor him by applying archaic laws to have him arrested. His trials became landmark studies of First Amendment rights, and when convicted, he often won on appeal to higher courts. Due to his frequent arrests, he found fewer and fewer clubs willing to hire him, and he went into debt trying to cover his legal fees. Eventually Bruce died of a drug overdose. The film *Lenny* was an adaptation of a play by Julian Barry who obtained permission to incorporate many of Bruce's routines into his script. *Lenny* was critically acclaimed and received a large number of nominations for the 1974 Academy Awards, but lost to *Godfather II* in most categories.

Synopsis

Lenny has a rather freewheeling structure, centering on interviews about Bruce by his wife, his mother, and his agent. Each individual is shown as they respond to questions, and their comments are recorded on an open-reel tape recorder. Sometimes their reflections overlap, and frequent flashbacks are inserted to portray Lenny's career, not always in chronological order, although the usual emphasis is on his nightclub routines. In the early clips, Bruce is clean-shaven; he is bearded in his later performances. Some of the earliest scenes trace Bruce's work at resorts in the Catskills, where his occasional off-color remarks get him into trouble until the comic, feeling too confined by this barrier, throws a tantrum and curses out his audience. Bruce then starts working at strip clubs, where he meets his wife, Honey. They have some small success working together, but Honey is injured in an automobile accident and becomes addicted to drugs due to her medical treatment. Later Honey is arrested because of her drug habit and imprisoned for eighteen months. Bruce's career starts to take off while she is in jail, and he visits her frequently, bringing his record albums as examples of his success.

Lenny's first arrest actually works in his favor. He is acquitted at a jury trial, and the publicity makes it "hip" to catch his routines. His gigs start drawing large crowds. Bruce starts to read up on laws about free speech as his arrests continue, and he starts reading transcripts of his cases during his performances. The tide turns, however, when the pressure drives Lenny to develop his own drug habit. Some of his performances become incoherent. He starts to get fewer engagements as the nightclub owners are threatened with loss of their liquor licenses if they hire Bruce. His debts mount up, and he dismisses his lawyers and tries unsuccessfully to defend himself. He is also arrested for possession of narcotics and fears going to prison. Finally, his body is discovered in his bathroom, dead of a drug overdose. His agent observes that Lenny's use of language in nightclubs is now considered routine, and that Lenny was the target of an unjust vendetta. His wife and mother continue speak of him with affection as the interviews conclude.

Critique

Some critics of *Lenny* claim that the film tries inflate his significance. Nevertheless, the script is basically very honest in its approach, using the comic's actual dialogue and text from his court appearances. In one of his monologues, Bruce states that he does not have a social agenda; he simply wants to make a buck as an entertainer. It is his political comments, however, that seem to be behind the move to censor him, not his dirty language. A number of the court cases present very rational arguments about the issue of censorship. When a policeman who arrests Bruce claims that he never used the obscene word spoken by the comic, he seems unbelievable and dishonest. He has to finally admit that he hears the language on a daily basis at the police station. Bruce also attacks the concept of "community standards" in defining obscenity. In the later cases, Bruce is denied the right to perform his act to illustrate the context of his remarks, to demonstrate that they are not obscene.

Individuals interested in learning more about Bruce might find it useful to see the authentic Bruce perform in a low-budget film he wrote and starred in together with his wife, titled *Dance Hall Racket* (1953). More important is *The Lenny Bruce Performance Film*, an unedited record of one of his last nightclub appearances. This film reveals the embittered, angry Bruce as magnificently captured by Dustin Hoffman in *Lenny*. If, on the other hand, you want to hear Bruce at his satirical best, you would have to track down his recordings, particularly his 1963 Carnegie Hall one-man show recorded shortly after the assassination of President Kennedy. It seems odd that this concert, in which Bruce performs before the largest crowd of his career, is not depicted in *Lenny*, but then it was not a controversial performance, and the film was basically concerned with the controversial aspects of his career.

The Lost Weekend
(1945)

Principal social themes: addiction (alcohol), depression/suicide

Paramount. No MPAA rating. Featuring: Ray Milland, Jane Wyman, Phillip Terry, Howard da Silva, Frank Faylen, Doris Dowling, Mary Young, Anita Bolster, Lilian Fontaine, Lewis L. Russell, Frank Orth. Written by Charles Brackett and Billy Wilder based on the novel by Charles R. Jackson. Cinematography by John F. Seitz. Edited by Doane Harrison. Music by Miklos Rozsa. Produced by Charles Brackett. Directed by Billy Wilder. B&W. 101 minutes.

Overview

When Paramount executives first previewed *The Lost Weekend*, they concluded it was a well-made example of social conscience filmmaking but with rather poor market potential. They were quite surprised when the film opened in New York not only to rave reviews, but with sizable box-office returns as well. When the West Coast premiere proved equally successful, they realized that director Billy Wilder and his film had tapped a problem that had been simmering in the American subconscious. *The Lost Weekend* touched many people who responded strongly to the film's presentation and message. It went on to become a cinematic milestone, the most popular social issue film up to that time, spawning a number of other cinematic projects focusing on social problems, such as *The Snake Pit* (1948), dealing with mental illness, and *The Well* (1951), focusing on racism. *The Lost Weekend* won Academy Awards for Best Picture, Best Actor, Best Director, and Best Adapted Screenplay.

Synopsis

The premise of *The Lost Weekend* is simple—an unflinching examination of four days in the life of Don Birnam (Ray Milland), an alcoholic writer living with his brother in New York City. As the story begins, Don and Wick (Phillip Terry), his brother, are preparing for a weekend holiday in the country, but Don's mind is not on his packing. It is on a bottle of rye whisky suspended on a rope hanging outside their apartment window. When Don's girlfriend, Helen (Jane Wyman), an editor at *Time* magazine, shows up to wish them well, Don hatches a scheme to persuade them to go to the afternoon symphony concert. By then, Don explains, he would be ready to take the evening train to the country. Reluctantly, Wick agrees. Before he and Helen leave, they find Don's bottle hidden outside the window. Don asks them to have faith in him and promises to be ready for their trip. After they leave, he searches desperately through the apartment, but Wick has already found all his hidden stashes of liquor. When their housekeeper turns up for her wages, she tells Don where the money is usually placed for her. Don finds it, but pretends the money is not there, telling the woman to come back next week for her pay. He then heads to the local liquor store and the bar, and his downward journey begins.

Don never makes it back to the apartment in time to leave for the trip. Disgusted, Wick tells Helen he has decided to go on the trip anyway. He is tired of caring for his brother through his many binges and he leaves, telling Helen to let Don fend for himself. She will not, but since she is working the entire weekend, she is unable to look after him. Don's downward spiral continues. Returning to the bar the following morning, he tells Nat the bartender (Howard da Silva), how he met and fell in love with Helen. Don vows to write his novel about alcoholism, to be titled *The Bottle*, but finds himself unable to get past the title page. He ends up at a nightclub unable to pay his bar tab. After stealing some money from a lady's purse, he is caught and tossed out into the street. The next day, Don becomes desperate for a drink and tries to pawn his typewriter, but finds himself stymied when all the pawnshops are closed due to Yom Kippur. He begs a drink from Nat at the bar, and then goes to borrow money from Gloria, a prostitute who likes Don's courtly manners. He collapses and is taken to the drunk-tank ward at Bellevue. Bim Nolan (Frank Faylen), a male nurse, warns Don that he is an "alkie" and will soon suffer other symptoms, such as seeing visions during spells of delirium. Later that night, one of the patients in the ward has a violent spell. As the nurses and guards take him down to the elevator, Don sneaks out of the usually locked ward, steals a doctor's coat, and escapes into the night. He waits outside a liquor store, and as the proprietor opens up, he bullies him into handing over a bottle of rye whisky.

Don goes back to his apartment and starts to scream when he imagines he sees a bloody encounter between a bat and a tiny mouse. The landlady calls Helen, who comes over immediately, and tends to the groggy, frightened Don. The next morning, Don has regained his composure and makes a decision to end his life. He swipes Helen's fur coat, taking it to the pawnshop. Helen follows him and is stunned when she learns from the pawnbroker that Don had purchased a gun. When she returns to the apartment, Don seems calm and resolved. She offers him a drink, but he refuses. Helen tries to talk him out of suicide, but Don says it is the only way out. At the climatic moment, Nat shows up at the door with an unexpected gift, Don's typewriter, which Gloria had retrieved when Don was taken to the hospital. Gloria had brought it to Nat for safe-keeping. Don and Helen are moved by this gesture, interpreting it as a sign that Don can overcome his problem. Don begins his novel again, this time in earnest, in which he intends to detail the experience of his "lost weekend."

Critique

Ray Milland wrote honestly about his work on *The Lost Weekend* in his autobiography *Wide-Eyed in Babylon*. When he was given the book to read, he found it repellent. He also had doubts that he would be convincing in the drunk scenes. In real life, he was a very light drinker, and his drunk scenes in earlier films were done mostly for laughs. As the film was shot, he relied heavily on Billy Wilder for direction. The novel's author, Charles Jackson, also spent much time with the actor, explaining his personal ordeal with liquor, which led to his writing of the book.

The Lost Weekend was largely shot in inverse order, with Milland's most haggard scenes done first. Location work was added in New York City, including the hospital ward scene actually shot in the drunk-tank ward at Bellevue. A hidden camera filmed the scenes of Milland staggering up Third Avenue. He was recognized, and sidebars appeared in gossip columns saying that the actor was actually on a bender in New York City. When the picture was completed, his publicist was able to correct these stories with fact.

When watching the film today, it is hard to realize the original impact, when such stark, unrelenting melodrama was largely limited to over-the-top exploitation films such as *Reefer Madness*. *The Lost Weekend* is successful on many levels. Milland's acting seems natural and unforced, and he is completely convincing. The supporting players, particularly Howard da Silva, Frank Faylen, and Jane Wyman, deliver masterful performances as well. Wyman's part as written is a thankless role, but she is able to fill it with a special, quiet pathos. The editing and continuity of the film is disturbing. If you follow the story closely, Don seems to experience Saturday twice. This confusion is deliberate, as Don stresses in his dialogue about the loss of time—not knowing if it is dawn or dusk, Sunday or a weekday—which is one of the most disturbing aspects of being on an alcoholic binge. Miklos Rozsa's music score, with its use of the theremin, is superb. The shrill, electronic whining of the instrument became one of the most distinctive elements of the film. The cinematography is exceptional and straightforward. Wilder considered using a greater number of expressionistic shots, but then decided that it might prove distracting. In fact, the bat attack scene is one of the weakest in the film, with special effects below that of the typical vampire film. The bat, however, was supposed to be an alcoholic hallucination, so the cheesy effect was not entirely out of place. Milland's frantic screaming managed to save the scene in any case. The other special effects scene, however, worked perfectly. This is the flashback where Don goes to see *La Traviata*, and during the drinking song, he imagines the cast dissolving into floating raincoats, reminding him that he has a bottle of rye whisky in the pocket of his coat. The only facet of the film that seems artificial is Don's redemption at the end, which seems a trifle quick. The return of the typewriter, although well handled, just does not seem persuasive enough to reawaken Don's will to live. Milland's final narration, looping back to the opening scene of the film, is a remarkable and powerful screen moment and wraps the film up magnificently. One powerful testament to *The Lost Weekend* is that many problem drinkers have cited the film as one that personally influenced them in getting help for their alcoholism.

Mad at the World
(1955)

Principal social theme: violence/gangs

The Filmakers. No MPAA rating. Featuring: Frank Lovejoy, Keefe Braselle, Cathy O'Donnell, Karen Sharpe, Stanley Clements, Joe Turkel, Paul Dubov, Aaron Spelling, Paul Bryar, James Delgado, Joe Besser. Written by Harry Essex. Cinematography by William Snyder. Edited by Stanford Tischler. Music by Leith Stevens. Produced by Collier Young. Directed by Harry Essex. B&W. 76 minutes.

Overview

Mad at the World is one of the first films to attempt to identify the causes of random violence by youth gangs. Writer/director Harry Essex adapted several true-life cases to develop this scenario, which so impressed U.S. Senator Estes Kefauver of Tennesee, head of a special Senate subcommittee investigating juvenile crime, that he agreed to appear in a prologue discussing the epidemic of teenage violence in America and how it can spill over to the entire community. He suggests that a few useful answers have been found. He cites *Mad at the World* as a case study showing how one police department handled the problem.

Synopsis

After Kefauver's preface, the credits roll followed by a short narration in documentary style by Frank Lovejoy, who plays Captain Tom Lynn. He discusses how the problem of gang violence develops among the youth of Chicago. An elderly pedestrian is assaulted by four youths in an alley. Released from the hospital, the man is escorted by Lynn through the holding pen, where various teenage felons are held following their arrest. Lynn describes each offender, including Hispanics, blacks, as well as white kids, all with lengthy rap sheets. The man also examines the mugshot books, but does not come across any of his four attackers. The focus then shifts back to the four young thugs, Marty, Jamie, Frank, and Pete, who decide to borrow a car to seek some thrills. They bully the elderly parking lot attendant to loan them a car that would not be missed for the evening. They hot rod about and then decide to find some victims to hassle. They observe Sam and Anne Bennett, out walking with their baby. Jamie throws a liquor bottle at them, which strikes the baby on the head. They speed off and later hear a radio broadcast saying the baby is in critical condition.

The police make an intensive effort to identify and arrest the gang members. When they believe that they have located the car used in the crime, they arrest the owner, a young man named Willie Hansen. Further investigation clears Hansen, however, who was sick with a high fever during the night of the crime, a fact verified by a doctor. Bennett is outraged when the police release Hansen, and he waylays the youth in the police parking lot. Lynn rescues the boy and warns Bennett that he is out of line. Bennett, however, has decided to start his own investigation. Using the name Bill Holland, he rents a space in the parking garage used by Hansen. After nosing around, he suspects that the thugs might be members of the Hijackers, a tough neighborhood club. He befriends Tess, a local waitress and a member of the club. He asks her about finding a place to stay, and she recommends the rooming house where she lives. Returning home, he receives news from the hospital that his son has died. He tells his wife that he is going away for a few days. When Captain Lynn arrives to offer his condolences, Bennett slugs him, afraid he would interfere with his scheme to do his own undercover investigation. The police lab finally identifies a fingerprint from the smashed liquor bottle as belonging to Pete Johnson, a juvenile formerly booked on assault. They arrest him, and after questioning, he finally tells the police the names of the other gang members, identifying Jamie Ellison as the one who threw the bottle.

Meanwhile, Tess takes her new friend "Bill" to a dance at the Hijackers. She introduces him to Jamie and Marty. He offers to buy them a drink, and they decide to crash a college frat party. Once they leave the Hijackers, Jamie slugs "Bill," recognizing him as Bennett, the father of the dead baby. They plan to dump his body in the furnace at the nearby lumber mill. When Marty refuses to go along with Jamie's plan, his friend shoots him. In the commotion, Bennett escapes, heading to the upper floors of the building. The police raid the Hijackers Club and when they learn their suspects have left, they initiate an all-points search. They head to the lumberyard after hearing reports of a shooting. Jamie follows Bennett, firing at him, but missing his target. Bennett knocks the gun out of his hand, and they fight until Jamie is badly injured in a fall. The police arrive, and Bennett hands them Jamie's gun. Captain Lynn questions Jamie as he is dying. He asks him why he kills for kicks. He replies, "You gotta find your kicks or go without. . . . Dames like a guy who is tough. I was tough." Lynn shakes his head in disbelief as the thug expires.

Critique

Mad at the World makes a number of strong points in its presentation. Casting, however, works against the story as Stanley Clements, Joe Turkel, Paul Dubov, and James Delgado are simply too old to play teenage gang members realistically. Ironically, Aaron Spelling, cast as the slightly older Willie Hansen, is the only one who could reasonably pass as a teenager. (Spelling, incidentally, quit acting to become one of the leading producers in television history.) The most effective acting in the film is provided by Keefe Braselle, as the tormented Sam Bennett out to avenge his child's murder. He also has a number of powerful speeches, first to Captain Lynn complaining about the easy treatment accorded teenage criminals, and later to Tess, when he apologizes for using her to gain entrance to the Hijackers. Usually dismissed as a weak actor, Braselle fills his performance here with convincing fire and passion. Frank Lovejoy is also effective as Captain Lynn. His comments on the nature of youth violence provide a solid basis on the issue of delinquency that makes the film worth watching and studying for the treatment of the issue. The authentic street footage is very well utilized, giving the film a gritty, realistic air that disappears only when the over-age thugs enter the scene. The script seems to stray off course in the last third of the picture, when Lynn's attention seems to switch from salvaging the youths to saving Bennett. The death scene of Dubov as Jamie seems to bring things back into focus. Lynn pleads with Jamie in an attempt to understand his motivations. He encounters a sense of nihilism that eerily foreshadows a major segment of the youth culture over the next fifty years. This remarkable scene makes it a unique one for study and analysis.

The Man Who Played God
(1932)

Principal social themes: disabilities, suicide/depression

Warner Brothers. No MPAA rating. Featuring: George Arliss, Bette Davis, Violet Heming, Oscar Apfel, Andre Luguet, Louise Closser Hale, Ivan Simpson, Donald Cook, Charles Evans, Murray Kinnell, Hedda Hopper, Ray Milland. Written by Julien Josephson and Maude T. Howell based on the play *The Silent Voice* by Jules Eckert Goodman and the original short story by Gouverneur Morris. Cinematography by James Van Trees. Edited by William Holmes. Music by Leo Forbstein. Produced by Jack Warner and Darryl F. Zanuck. Directed by John G. Adolfi. B&W. 81 minutes.

Overview

George Arliss (1868–1946) was a well-known actor from the Victorian era who managed to transfer his popularity to motion pictures. One of his most popular stage vehicles was the role of Montgomery Royle, a piano virtuoso who goes deaf. Arliss made a silent version of the story in 1922 and undertook this sound remake ten years later. *The Man Who Played God* was one of the first screen treatments to deal realistically with the development of a disability and the efforts of rehabilitation.

Synopsis

Montgomery Royle is one of the world's leading classical pianists. He is loved by two women, his young protégée Grace Adair (Bette Davis) and by the attractive widow Mildred Miller (Violet Heming). When Grace proposes to Monty, he says he is too old for her, but agrees to marry her if she feels the same way in six months. After a concert in Paris, Monty gives a private recital for a visiting king. Terrorists set off a bomb hoping to kill the monarch, but he is unharmed. Monty, however, becomes deaf because of the blast.

Monty returns to his New York penthouse overlooking Central Park and becomes a hermit, brooding over his lost hearing. His only human contact is with his sister, his manservant Battle, and Grace, who visits him daily. He becomes even more despondent when Grace reminds him that Beethoven also became deaf. His doctor suggests that Monty learn lip reading, and in time he becomes very proficient at it. His mood, however, continues to worsen, and he even loses his belief in God. Grace continues to insist that Monty marry her, and he agrees. But when she leaves for a holiday in California, Monty decides to commit suicide by leaping from the window. Battle confronts him and talks him off the ledge. He hands Monty binoculars and implores him to look at the beauty of nature in the park. Quite by accident, Monty begins to lip read the conversations of people sitting on a park bench. He becomes intrigued by their problems, and tries to find ways to help them. A sick young man tells his girlfriend that he has been told he will die unless he takes a rest cure in a warm, dry climate, a treatment he cannot afford. The couple start to pray. Monty sends Battle down to them with a note offering to pay for the cure, but keeping his name secret. Monty gets a new lease on life by eavesdropping on others and "playing God" to help solve their problems. When Mildred visits Monty, she is surprised by how happy he has become.

A strange turn of events happens when he spots Grace in the park with a young man. He learns that they are in love, but Grace feels obligated to marry Monty. When she arrives for a visit, Monty releases her from their engagement. He then fulfills an old promise to donate a new organ in memory of his mother at the church she used to attend. Mildred, now free to express her love to Monty, meets him at the church and he plays a hymn on the organ.

Critique

Arliss is an actor of the old school, with every gesture and every tremor of his voice closely regulated, reflecting his years of experience on the stage. However, he is very entertaining to watch. Arliss reportedly did months of study on deafness for his portrayal of Montgomery Royle, and his careful preparation is apparent in his reading. A close study reflects how the script follows the traditional pattern of an individual's reaction to a traumatic disability—from denial, withdrawal, and despair to gradual acceptance. Arliss was known to "chew the scenery" on occasion, yet his anguish and attempt to commit suicide is very convincing.

The Man Who Played God emphasizes another issue concerning disabilities, how it affects the people around the handicapped individual. Grace is prepared to sacrifice her own happiness for him. Mildred and Monty's sister are always walking on eggs in their relations with him. Only Battle attempts to treat Monty in a normal fashion. *The Man Who Played God* was updated in 1955 as a vehicle for Liberace in *Sincerely Yours*, an unsuccessful and critically panned effort. Two years later, Boris Karloff starred in a far more successful treatment for television on *Lux Video Theater*.

The Man With the Golden Arm
(1956)

Principal social theme: addiction (heroin)

United Artists. No MPAA rating. Featuring: Frank Sinatra, Eleanor Parker, Kim Novak, Arnold Stang, Darren McGavin, Robert Strauss, John Conte, Doro Merande, George E. Stone, George Matthews, Leonid Kinskey, and Emile Meyer. Written by Walter Newman and Lewis Meltzer based on the novel by Nelson Algren. Cinematography by Sam Leavitt. Edited by Louis R. Loeffler. Music by Elmer Bernstein. Produced and directed by Otto Preminger. B&W. 119 minutes.

Overview

The Man With the Golden Arm is noted as the first mainstream American feature film to focus on the issue of drug addition as the central theme. Otto Preminger, whose father was attorney general of the Austrian Empire, was a lawyer who turned to dramatics, working with the legendary director Max Reinhardt. He built a reputation as a brilliant iconoclast who liked to tackle controversial issues, which led to this milestone film. *The Man With the Golden Arm* pulled no punches, portraying heroin addiction in stark, dramatic terms and setting the standard against which most later films about drugs were compared. Frank Sinatra, his singing career temporarily in eclipse, delivers a masterful performance, which earned him an Academy Award nomination for Best Actor of 1955.

Synopsis

Frankie Machine (Frank Sinatra) returns to his skid row neighborhood after a six-month jail sentence. Frankie is upbeat and enthusiastic to be home, since he has been cured of his drug habit and learned a new trade as a drummer while he was imprisoned. His wife (Eleanor Parker), nicknamed "Zosch," is crippled due to an auto accident three years ago when her husband was driving drunk. In truth, she has recovered, but continues to use a wheelchair because she fears Frankie would leave her for their neighbor Molly (Kim Novak), a nightclub cashier who is in love with him (and Frankie is in love with her). Zosch tries to discourage her husband's new career, wishing he would return to his old trade as a house dealer for Schwiefka, who bankrolls a floating neighborhood poker game. Frankie is well regarded as an honest dealer, and is called "The Man with the Golden Arm." He was originally arrested when Schwiefka's game was raided, and Frankie is angry that the gambler did not give Zosch a monthly payoff as he promised. Frankie's best pal is Sparrow (Arnold Stang), a street hustler who steals dogs, bathes them, and returns them to their owners claiming a finder's fee. The neighborhood drug pusher, Louie (Darren McGavin), tries to offer Frankie a free "hit," but he rejects it.

Schwiefka arranges to have Frankie arrested on a theft charge (for wearing a jacket shoplifted by Sparrow). The gambler bails him out when Frankie agrees to resume his old job. The pressures of the gambling scene weaken Frankie's resolve to stay off drugs, and he again becomes addicted. Frankie finally is called for an audition with a professional band. Louie pressures him to operate one last game for Schwiefka after two gamblers with big bankrolls are persuaded to sit in. After winning for the gambler, Frankie tries to quit early. Schwiefka takes over the dealer's slot himself, but loses. Louie refuses to give Frankie drugs unless he returns to the game, which he does, but he loses and is finally caught cheating. He tries to run away, and Louie bursts into his apartment and discovers that Zosch is able to walk. She shoves Louie down the stairs when he attempts to blackmail her. The police assume Frankie killed the pusher. He hides out with Molly. She helps him kick the drug habit cold turkey. After his cure, Frankie heads back to confront Zosch, telling her he plans to leave. He is stunned to learn she is able to walk. The police show up, and conclude that Zosch is the killer. She runs off when they try to arrest her, falling to her death from the back porch. Frankie, Molly, and Sparrow watch in silence as her body is driven away.

Critique

As written, Frank Sinatra's role as Frankie Machine is not a sympathetic one. He is likable, but with a weak personality very atypical of a Hollywood production. Even the name "Machine" has connotations that undermine his humanity. Frankie is also a bit of a lush, a hustler, and a ladies' man. Sinatra makes his character seem authentic, not contrived. He is persuasive in portraying the cravings of a heroin addict. The sequence in which he goes cold turkey to kick his addiction is one of the most brutal, intense, and graphic moments of any film of the 1950s. The script also is significant in that it avoids being preachy. Frankie claims he became a junkie "for kicks," however, the actual reason is more likely to bury his feelings of guilt for having crippled his wife in a car accident. The audience learns early on that his wife is faking to manipulate him, so Frankie's attachment to Molly is not only tolerated but encouraged by viewers. Like a traditional film noir, Frankie appears trapped by circumstances very early in the plot by the triangle of gambling, alcohol, and heroin. Frankie is also the target of endless manipulations, by his wife, by Louie the pusher, by Schwiefka, by the police, and even by his only pal Sparrow. Only Molly does not seek to pull his strings. The script also shows Frankie troubled by his lack of confidence as a musician. He knows he is only an adequate drummer. His real talent is dealing and overseeing a poker game, but his only avenue is the backroom dive, as any legitimate casino is beyond his scope.

The Man With the Golden Arm can be examined from various angles, as a character study, as an inquiry into the consequences of a poor environment or as a case study of the trap of drug addiction. The production qualities are excellent. The grimy, claustrophobic sets, the stark lighting, and the perceptive editing provide the perfect backdrop for the story. The acting of the supporting cast is first rate and compliments Sinatra in every scene— particularly the performances by Emile Meyer, Kim Novak, and Darren McGavin (whose Louie is one of the great unsung screen villains). Eleanor Parker perhaps steps over the edge in her performance, but she also provides an excellent counterpoint in her scenes with Sinatra. The hard-hitting jazz score by Elmer Bernstein also reinforces each scene. The conclusion is somewhat open ended and could provide opportunity for discussion of whether Frankie and Molly can escape their troubled past. Louie's assessment that the addict can never completely free himself from the monkey on his back is a sober and memorable line that sticks with the viewer long after the end of the picture.

Mask
(1985)

Principal social themes: disabilities, addiction, end-of-life issues

Universal. PG-13 rating. Featuring: Eric Stoltz, Cher, Sam Elliott, Estelle Getty, Richard Dysart, Laura Dern, Dennis Burkley, Ben Piazza, Lawrence Monoson, Marsha Warfield, Barry Tubb, Kelly Mintner, Micole Mercurio, Harry Carey Jr. and Andrew Robinson. Written by Anna Hamilton Phelan. Cinematography by Laszlo Kovacs. Edited by Eva Gardos. Produced by Martin Starger. Directed by Peter Bogdanovich. Color. 120 minutes.

Overview

Based on the true story of Rocky Dennis, *Mask* is a character portrait of a teenager afflicted with craniodiaphyseal dysplasia (lionitis), a rare disease in which calcium is deposited on the cranium at an advanced rate, continually thickening the skull and distorting the features of the head, which becomes greatly enlarged. The condition is incurable and eventually fatal. Despite the poor prognosis, his mother tries to enable Rocky to enjoy as normal and happy a life as possible.

Synopsis

In a basically linear fashion, the plot of *Mask* covers the last year in the life of teenager Rocky Dennis (Eric Stoltz), afflicted with a terrible disease that distorts his features. Rocky is raised by his mother, Rusty (Cher), a free spirit who pals around with a motorcycle gang, whose members also help look after her son. Rocky has various hobbies, such as collecting baseball cards (his main goal is to gather a complete set of the 1955 Brooklyn Dodgers) and to save money to tour Europe by motorcycle with his friend Ben. When Rusty tries to register Rocky in the ninth grade at his new school in Azuza, California, the principal tries to dissuade her, suggesting Rocky would find his needs better met at a special school. She hands over Rocky's grades from his old school, where he finished in the top 5 percent. She insists she knows her rights and would take legal action if necessary. This is a bluff, as the lawyer she cites is Dozer, a brawny, semi-mute member of the motorcycle gang. Next, Rocky attends his regular medical clinic appointment. A new doctor (Andrew Robinson) consults with Rocky and his mother, explaining that the pressure on his spinal cord is becoming greater due to the increasing size of his skull. His life expectancy is only three to six months. Rusty acts unconcerned, saying the same prognosis has been repeated to her for the past twelve years. The doctor is astounded by her attitude, as Rusty and her son breeze out of the office. When Rocky starts school, he at first has difficulty being accepted by his new classmates, who stare at him in amazement. When someone, first seeing him, asks Rocky to remove his mask, the deformed teenager playfully tears at his face, saying he just cannot take it off. Rocky's wit and good humor soon win over the other students, particularly when he offers to tutor some of the slower students.

Gar (Sam Elliott), one of Rusty's favorite boyfriends, a wandering biker, turns up and soon they resume their friendship. When her son suffers from his regular bad headaches, she manages to relieve the symptoms through autosuggestion, talking the headache into vanishing. One weekend, the biker gang takes Rocky and his mother to an amusement park. At the fun house, Rocky is astonished when he looks at himself in one of the trick mirrors, which makes him appear normal.

Although Rocky is usually upbeat, he sometimes gets the blues, such as when he realizes his deformity will prevent him from ever having a girlfriend. When he mentions this to his mother, she leaves the house for several hours, finally returning with a teenage prostitute who stays with Rocky for the evening (even though they just talk). Rocky has mixed feelings about his mother's actions, partly insulted but somewhat pleased as well. Rusty sometimes has difficulty maintaining her positive front, and she often turns to pills or alcohol to drown her fears. Rocky urges her to kick the habit, but she simply ignores his nagging. Ben and Rocky continue to earn money for their trip. As the school year winds down, the principal approaches Rocky with a suggestion. He might earn some good money as an aide at a summer camp for the blind. Initially, he turns down the offer, although he agrees to think it over. At the end of the school year, Rocky wins top honors in almost every subject. Dozer speaks for the only time in the film, telling Rocky that he is proud of him. His grandparents visit one weekend, although they do not get along well with Rusty. They take the boy to a Dodgers baseball game. When they get home, Rusty has become stoned. Angered, Rocky tells his mother that he intends to take the summer camp job and maybe she can kick the habit while he is gone.

At the camp, Rocky meets a beautiful girl named Diana (Laura Dern), another aide who has been blind since birth. They spend all their free time together, falling in love. Rocky finds an innovative way to explain color to Diana, using a heated stone to depict red and a frozen stone to depict blue. At the end of camp, Diana wants to continue their friendship, but when her parents see Rocky, they are horrified by his appearance. Returning home, Rocky is delighted to find his mother has kicked her drug habit. He is also delighted when he learns that Gar has moved in. As he prepares for his next year of school, Rocky begins to feel depressed. He is thunderstruck when Ben tells him that he is moving away. When Ben suggests that their planned trip was just a daydream, Rocky throws a temper tantrum. He is also frustrated when attempting to telephone Diana, who never seems to be home. Actually, her parents are keeping them apart, destroying each tape he sends to her. Finally, Rocky takes a bus to visit her hometown, surprising her at the stable where she boards her horse. Diana suspected her parents were keeping them apart. Diana is being sent for one semester to an exclusive boarding school that has a special program for the blind. They kiss and agree to remain true to each other.

Rusty throws a party to cheer up Rocky up, but he goes to his room early, claiming he has a bad headache. He removes all the pins from his map of Europe that marked places he intended to visit. He straightens up his room carefully before going to bed. The next morning, Rusty is awakened by someone from the school calling to ask why Rocky has not shown up. She goes to his room and finds that he has died in his sleep. After Rocky is buried, Dozer arranges his baseball cards on Rocky's tombstone.

Critique

Mask is an unforgettable character portrait brought to life by the credible performances of Eric Stoltz and Cher as Rocky and his mother. The film is magnificently directed by Peter Bogdanovich. Although largely uneventful, the picture is a remarkable case study that can provoke discussion. Since Rocky was essentially doomed from the outset, was there any better way for him to spend his last year? In what ways was Rusty's approach successful or harmful to Rocky's well-being? Did Rocky cope better with the situation than his mother, who became drug dependent? By befriending the bikers, she managed to form her own support group of outcasts. How did this benefit them? Was she correct in rejecting the doctors? Were Diana's parents too protective of her, or were they just prejudiced against Rocky because of his deformity? Rocky managed to maintain his positive outlook by ignoring his condition and winning friends by mocking his own disabilities. He also relied on a technique to avoid sadness by concentrating on a single happy thought. Did this fail him toward the end? Rocky chose one day at camp, the "New Years in July" dance, to serve as his perfect memory. But this appeared to fail when he lost his dream of someday touring Europe. What really caused him to give up at the end? To what extent did Rocky's disability mold his character? Finally, it is interesting to note that many of the intimate touches that appeared in the film were due to the real Rusty Dennis, who served as technical advisor in this project honoring her son.

The Men (AKA *Battle Stripe*)
(1950)

Principal social theme: disabilities

National. No MPAA rating. Featuring: Marlon Brando, Teresa Wright, Jack Webb, Everett Sloane, Richard Erdman, Dorothy Tree, Howard St. John, Arthur Jurado, Virginia Farmer, Nita Hunter, Cliff Clark, Ray Teal, John Hamilton, Jim Backus, Virginia Christine, DeForest Kelley. Written by Carl Foreman. Cinematography by Robert de Grasse. Edited by Harry Gerstad. Music by Dimitri Tiomkin. Produced by Stanley Kramer. Directed by Fred Zinnemann. B&W. 85 minutes.

Overview

The Men is an intense film focusing on the rehabilitation of soldiers suffering from spinal injuries during World War II and the Korean conflict. In terms of authenticity, the production was filmed at the Veteran's Hospital in Birmingham, Alabama, and forty-five members of the cast were actual paraplegic patients at the facility. The script focuses on the treatment and recovery of a single patient, played by Marlon Brando in his screen debut.

Synopsis

The Men opens with a battlefield sequence showing the wounding of a soldier, Ken "Bud" Wilchek (Marlon Brando). After he is shot, the scene cuts to his bedroom in the VA hospital in Birmingham. It is night and Bud cannot sleep. The scene shifts again to the next day, as Dr. Gene Brock (Everett Sloane) delivers a lecture to about twenty-four women relatives, wives and friends of soldiers undergoing treatment for paraplegia. It is a blunt presentation, stressing the importance of accepting the condition. In almost all cases, walking will never be possible and neither willpower nor medical science is capable of repairing spinal cord injuries. The doctor discusses bladder control and sexual function, which can differ from patient to patient based on the location of the injury. Finally, he discusses the psychological impact on the patients, who often suffer from depression and other problems in adjusting to life in a wheelchair. After the meeting, Ellen (Teresa Wright) asks his help because Bud, her fiancé has refused to see her since his injury.

Later that day, Brock leads a team of physicians on a round of the paraplegic ward. (One of the doctors is played by DeForest Kelley, who later played Dr. Leonard "Bones" McCoy in *Star Trek.*) Brock questions the patients about their various physical problems. The beds are usually laid out in groups of four. Brock spends a lot of time with one particular group, which includes Leo Doogin (Richard Erdman), a sharp wit who acts as a bookie, Norm Butler (Jack Webb), an intellectual who acts as local head of the PVA (Paralyzed Veterans of America), and Angel Lopez (Arthur Jurado), nicknamed "Tarzan" due to his devotion to exercise. The fourth bed is empty as the previous patient was recently discharged. Brock plans to move Bud from his private room to this bed, figuring the feisty example of the others might do his embittered patient some good. Bud is very hostile at first to the others. Leo, a classical music buff, plays his radio louder and louder until Bud throws a glass of water at it. Norm responds by throwing his water at Bud, telling him to "cool off." Later that evening, when the other patients attend a wedding reception for one of the patients, Brock slips Ellen into the empty ward to confront Bud. Angry at first, Bud sinks into a fit of self-pity. He mellows, however, when Ellen explains how much she needs him. Touched by her openness, Bud agrees to let her visit him regularly. Soon, Bud becomes motivated to work out and build up his strength so he can become more self-sufficient.

Each of the men in the group suffers a setback. Leo is disappointed that his father only visits when he desires a cut from his son's gambling receipts. Norm, who had previously proclaimed that it is impossible for a paraplegic to have a successful marriage, falls in love with Laverne, a girl working at the local drive-in. After borrowing nine hundred dollars, she dumps Norm and heads off to

Canada. Bud thinks he has some feeling returning to his legs, but Dr. Brock conducts a test that demonstrates that it was only a phantom sensation. He tells Bud he must accept the fact that he will never walk again. Angel suddenly becomes seriously ill. A shell fragment lodged near his spine has become infected, leading to meningitis. His unexpectedly quick death demoralizes the others, who considered Angel the healthiest man in the ward. Seeing their depression, Brock becomes enraged, saying they must never stop fighting.

Bud learns to drive a specially modified car, and frequently leaves the hospital on dates with Ellen. She sincerely wishes that they get married, and Bud finally consents. When Ellen's parents learn of her plans, they try to discourage her, saying they want grandchildren. Dr. Brock counsels her that some paraplegics are capable of having children while others are not. In Bud's case, the doctor is simply not sure. Nevertheless, Ellen decides to go ahead with the wedding, which is held in the hospital chapel. Bud insists on standing for the ceremony, but he starts to collapse when he lets go of the altar railing. That evening, when the couple move to the small apartment Ellen prepared, they both become tense and argumentative. When Bud asks if she is sorry that she went through with the marriage, she says she is. Angry, Bud leaves and returns to the hospital. The next day Ellen visits to apologize, saying that she is sure they belong together. That evening, Bud gets into a car accident after he and Leo visit a bar. The local PVA board meets and recommends that Bud be discharged from the hospital. Bud appeals to Brock, who refuses to intercede on his behalf. He tells him that medically, he no longer belongs in the hospital. The doctor tells him about his own wife, a paraplegic who died many years ago, and how every day he wishes she were still alive. He believes that Ellen feels the same way about Bud. Hearing this revelation convinces Bud to give his own marriage a real chance. He drives back to see Ellen, who is waiting for him and greets him warmly.

Critique

Although part soap opera, *The Men* provides a serious and accurate portrayal of the challenges facing a paraplegic, particularly in recovering his own sense of identity, dignity, and worth. The case of Bud and his three ward companions, Leo, Norm, and Angel, provide a solid cross-section of different attitudes and results. Ironically, Angel, who had the most positive attitude, is the one who failed to survive. In a sense, this demonstrates that willpower and conviction can take one only so far. Blind luck is also an important factor in the struggle. Norm and Leo represent alternate concerns. They both prefers to kibitz and sit on the sidelines, but Norm becomes involved in the Veterans association and even takes a chance dating Laverne. Leo prefers to gamble on everything—except on his own emotions.

It is basically the strong cast that makes the film successful. Most of the attention centers on Bud, an excellent performance by Brando, who conveys the angst and torment of his situation quite credibly, never seeming forced. Jack Webb is equally excellent as Norm, who manages to see Bud's problems quite clearly but knows that lecturing his friend will do no good. His deciding vote when the PVA board recommends that Bud be kicked out of the hospital is in many ways the climax of the film. Richard Erdman and Arthur Jurado are superb in their supporting roles. Everett Sloane, as Dr. Brock, is both brittle and crotchety, yet his final session with Bud is extraordinary. Teresa Wright, however, is less persuasive as Ellen, particularly in the awkward and artificial scene in which she seems to reject her husband on their wedding night. In regard to the medical and psychological aspects of paraplegia, the script is fine, even brilliant, especially by highlighting Brock's frank lecture at the very opening of the picture. The screenplay excels by showing how other individuals are either skilled or insensitive in dealing with the paraplegics. Character actor Jim Backus, for example, is magnificent in the scene in which he approaches Leo and Bud in a restaurant, attempting to be gracious while actually demeaning the men with his superficial bluster. Bud, drunk and hostile himself, is unable to let the unintended insult go and slugs the man. Later, he and Leo get into a car accident driving back to the hospital. This scene is well thought out by demonstrating the degree of accountability that handicapped individuals must bear for their own actions, a crucial point since rights and responsibilities are intertwined. The handicapped cannot hide behind their condition if they wish to merit the respect to which they are entitled. Overall, *The Men* is both daring and very perceptive in presenting this case study.

Modern Times
(1936)

Principal social themes: homelessness/poverty

United Artists. No MPAA rating. Featuring: Charlie Chaplin, Paulette Goddard, Henry Bergman, Stanley Sanford, Hank Mann, Chester Conklin, Richard Alexander, Stanley Blystone, Louis Natheaux, Allan Garcia, Lloyd Ingraham, Edward Kimball, Wilfred Lucas, Mira McKinney, Cecil Reynolds, Murdoch McQuarrie, Ed Le Sainte, Fred Malatesta, Juana Sutton, Sam Stein, John Rand, Walter James, Ted Oliver, Gloria DeHaven. Written by Charlie Chaplin. Cinematography by Rollie Totheroh and Ira Morgan. Music by Charlie Chaplin. Produced and directed by Charlie Chaplin. B&W. 87 minutes.

Overview

Modern Times is a truly unique motion picture, basically a silent film released seven years after the demise of the form. In this picture, Charlie Chaplin added a backdrop of social issues, homelessness, poverty, and unemployment, which although subservient to the comic routines, broadened the canvas of his presentation.

Synopsis

Modern Times is essentially a hybrid talking film, as voices are heard on television monitors and over the radio, but when people speak on screen, they are silent and their words appear in title cards. This changes at the finale of the film, when the tramp is required to sing a song in a cafe but misplaces the words. He improvises nonsense words in fragments of various languages (thus preserving his international appeal), but his character returns to silence after finishing his number. *Modern Times* is constructed as a series of loose episodes. Charlie's character first appears in a factory production line, tightening bolts on products as they pass by on a conveyer belt. He eventually "cracks up" from the tedium of the work and is taken away to a mental hospital. Released when he is cured, the tramp saunters down the street and notices a red warning flag that falls off an overloaded truck. He picks up the flag and waves it to catch the driver's attention. He does not realize, however, that a Communist rally had just turned the corner behind his back. When the police arrive to break it up, the tramp is arrested since they assume he is their leader. In jail, the tramp accidentally ingests cocaine, which was hidden in a sugar jar in the mess hall. Feeling fearless, he intervenes when the other prisoners riot and helps restore order. The grateful guards then treat the tramp more like a guest than a prisoner.

Outside, the camera starts to follow another character in the poor waterfront district, a teenage girl stealing bananas for her two little sisters. Title cards identify her as 'the gamin," although later in the film her name, Ellen Peterson, appears in a document shown on screen. Her father is unemployed and desperate to feed his children. Later, he is shot during a bread riot, and the authorities take away the three orphans, but Ellen escapes. The tramp is pardoned from jail, and the sheriff provides him with a testimonial letter to help him find work. His job attempts, however, all end in disaster, and the tramp resolves to go back to jail. The gamin steals a loaf of bread from a baker, and the tramp intercedes when she is arrested, claiming he stole the bread. The girl is arrested nevertheless, so the tramp buys a huge meal at a cafeteria. When presented with the check, he waves a cop passing by into the restaurant to arrest him. He meets the girl in the paddy wagon, but they fall out when the vehicle turns a corner. As they pass by a residential community, the tramp fantasizes with the girl about living in a real home. Becoming inspired, the tramp pledges he will work hard to make this dream a reality. He obtains a job as a night watchman in a department store. He lets the girl into the empty store so she can spend the night sleeping in one of the model beds. Some homeless men break into the store and recognize the tramp; they had also worked in the factory before it closed. They get drunk on the liquor they steal from the store. The next day, the tramp is discovered drunk when the store opens, and he is arrested. The girl, however, awakens early and escapes. She finds an abandoned shack in a marsh area and tries to fix it up. When the tramp is released from prison, she takes him to the rundown shanty, which he describes as "paradise." Learning the factory is going to reopen, Charlie rushes to apply for the start-up crew. He is assigned to be the apprentice to the master mechanic testing the long-idle machines. However, due to low wages, the other workers call a strike, and they are forced to leave the building. When the cops think the tramp deliberately tosses a brick at them, he is again arrested. While in jail, the gamin manages to get a job dancing at a cafe. When the tramp is released from jail, the cafe owner promises him an audition to be a singing waiter. Meanwhile, the juvenile authorities receive a tip that Ellen is working at the cafe. The tramp keeps forgetting the words to his song, but the girl writes them down on his cuffs. As he dances around before starting his number, the tramp accidentally tosses away his cuffs. He then sings his nonsense song and is a hit. The owner hires him, but at this moment of triumph, the juvenile officers step in to take custody of Ellen. She and the tramp escape. By dawn, they prepare to set off down the road to another town. Tired by their struggle against homelessness and poverty, the gamin sees no point in going on. The tramp tells her to "buck up" and smile, and they head down the road together at the fade out, accompanied by Chaplin's tune "Smile" on the soundtrack.

Critique

Chaplin's earliest comedies, such as *The Vagabond* (1916), *The Immigrant* (1917), *Easy Street* (1917), and *A Dog's Life* (1918), all touched on such themes as poverty, immigration, and crime. The usual approach of many critics, however, has been to ignore or downplay the social issues aspects of *Modern Times*, which are considerable. Charlie's tramp character had been homeless in many of his earlier films, but that aspect was never really highlighted. With the addition of his companion, the gamin, homelessness and poverty become paramount in the character's concerns. No other comedy of the era even mentioned the Great Depression or touched on such issues as poverty, homelessness, drug addiction, unemployment, rioting and civil unrest, unjust imprisonment, or juvenile delinquency. To classify all this as mere window dressing for Chaplin's routines is both myopic and specious. Let us examine one of the most intricate routines, that of the Communist rally. Even though the film is in black and white, Chaplin establishes the red flag by its function, a warning signal indicating the overhang from the rear of the truck. The tramp picks it up to do a good deed by alerting the driver that his flag had fallen. Yet, as the Communist agitators flock around the corner, it would certainly appear that the tramp is leading the march. In seconds, Chaplin created a perfect sight gag to illustrate both Red-baiting and jumping to mistaken conclusions. Years before the actual McCarthy era, Chaplin had created the ideal visual metaphor satirizing it. This gag, however, only works because of its social context, that the audience recognizes that reputations have been ruined by charges of being a Communist. It is also ironic that Chaplin, who was one of the biggest capitalists of his era, was so often branded a Communist by political commentators.

Another remarkable episode is the shanty. When the tramp exclaims, "It's paradise," the line drew only a modest reaction from middle-class audiences but absolute howls in poorer neighborhoods. Again, the gag only works if the viewer understands the joke's context. *Modern Times* should provide ample material for students to analyze and study the social framework of the film's plot and humor.

Monkey on My Back
(1957)

Principal social themes: addiction (morphine and gambling)

United Artists. No MPAA rating. Featuring: Cameron Mitchell, Paul Richards, Dianne Foster, Jack Albertson, Kathy Garver, Lisa Golm, Barry Kelley, Lewis Charles, Dayton Lummis, Raymond Greenleaf. Written by Crane Wilbur, Anthony Veiller, Brad Harris, Richard Benedict, and Paul Dudley based in part on the book *No Man Stands Alone* by Barney Ross. Cinematography by Maury Gertsman. Edited by Grant Whytock. Music by Paul Sawtell and Bert Shefter. Produced by Edward Small. Directed by Andre de Toth. B&W. 93 minutes.

Overview

Monkey on My Back is based on the true story of Barney Ross (1909–1967), an outstanding prizefighter who won titles in three different weight divisions and was never knocked out in eighty-one professional fights. During World

War II, he distinguished himself in the Marine Corps, winning the Silver Star for his valor during the campaign at Guadalcanal. Seriously wounded in action, Ross was treated with morphine to which he became addicted. *Monkey on My Back* largely focuses on his battle against the addition.

Synopsis

The film opens as Barney Ross (Cameron Mitchell) voluntarily admits himself into the drug treatment program at a federal hospital. Dr. Sullivan, in charge of the withdrawal ward, informs Ross he will be given injections in decreasing doses until he no longer needs them. Alone in his hospital room, Ross reflects back on the earlier battles he fought. A flashback picks up his story at his second fight with Jimmy McLarnin, when he regained the title as welterweight champion. Sam, his trainer, however, seems more concerned with Ross' out-of-control betting with the bookies than with winning the fight. He wins the bout easily, but refuses to give up his gambling or free-spending lifestyle. He meets and falls in love with showgirl Cathy Howard (Dianne Foster), a single mother with a young daughter. She loves him, but is troubled by his inability to refuse a bet. When he proposes, she puts him off, saying she cannot afford to gamble. He gives her the ring anyway, telling her to put it on when she decides to accept.

When Ross losses his title to Henry Armstrong in 1938, he decides to retire, believing he no longer has enough speed to compete. He becomes a partner in a restaurant called Ringside, but his gambling becomes even more extravagant, and he is dumped from the business. When Cathy is offered the opportunity to tour with a show, she accepts. Barney decides to enlist in the Marines when the World War II breaks out, and Cathy finally agrees to marry him before he is shipped out. Stationed at Guadalcanal, Barney is trapped behind enemy lines, and his unit is almost wiped out. He refuses to surrender, killing dozens of the enemy before succumbing to malaria. When rescued, he is delirious and treated with morphine. By the time he is shipped home, he has become addicted to the narcotic. Awarded the Silver Star, Barney becomes a popular celebrity, a goodwill ambassador for the war effort on the home front. The father of one of the soldiers whose life he saved hires Barney as a public relations expert. His reliance on morphine, however, becomes unrelenting, despite his attempts to wean himself from the drug. He tells his wife that his health problems are just recurring bouts of malaria. When a drug pusher named Rico starts pressuring him for larger payoffs, Barney becomes desperate for money. Cathy finally figures out Barney's problem and offers him her support, urging him to seek professional help. The flashback ends, and the story continues as Barney faces terrible withdrawal spells at the hospital. He tries to accelerate the treatment, even refusing his low-dosage shots. Once his drug dependence is gone, Barney has to face the psychological fear that the craving will return. After four months, Barney is discharged from the hospital as cured, and Cathy is waiting for him as he leaves the hospital grounds.

Critique

Cameron Mitchell delivers probably the best performance of his career as Barney Ross, playing his part with particular fervor and commitment. His reading is entirely convincing, from the boxing ring footage and the wartime scenes to the internal struggles of his addiction. Mitchell goes through a number of subtle changes without relying on any acting gimmicks. At first, the character of Barney Ross is not particularly likable, filled with arrogance and a stubborn pride that mellows slowly as the plot unfolds.

The screenplay makes a rather subtle distinction between his two addictions. Barney always feels he can manage his gambling addiction, even when it practically ruins him. When he decides to join the Marines, he simply discards his gambling persona like a worn suit. The drug addiction, however, is one he feels he can never control. He was never ashamed of his gambling (he even bragged about it), but he was paranoid about hiding his reliance on morphine, especially from his wife, who at first thought he had lost interest in her and was involved with another woman. Ironically, Cathy seemed relieved once she learned Barney was addicted, because it was a problem she could comprehend, unlike his gambling fever, which she could never understand. Of course, Barney chose to indulge his gambling passion, craving the excitement and the sense that he was a winner. The drug addiction, on the other hand, was one imposed on him, bringing no emotional thrills like the gambling, only shame, self-loathing, and despair. Viewers of *Monkey on My Back* can find many other similarities and differences between the two addictions. The withdrawal scenes in the hospital are extraordinarily effective, and recall the power of similar scenes of Ray Milland's alcoholic visions in *The Lost Weekend.*

There are a number of flaws in *Monkey on My Back.* Noreen, Cathy's daughter, never gets any older despite the fact that ten years pass in the course of the story. Ample screen time is spent on Barney's dark moments, his wartime battle in the jungle and its counterpart in the urban jungle, with his stalking the streets at night, encountering prostitutes and other junkies, while trying to work off his drug craving. However, one wishes that his initial contact with the authorities, confessing his addiction and desire to be helped, had also been filmed. This was indeed a heroic moment that seems particularly lacking because of its omission. Some of the events of the plot are fictionalized for dramatic purposes, although it is accurate in regards to the major events of the story.

My Name Is Bill W.
(1989)

Principal social theme: addiction (alcohol)

Warner Brothers. No MPAA rating. Featuring: James Woods, James Garner, JoBeth Williams, Gary Sinese, George Coe, Fritz Weaver, Norman Max, Rick Warner, Ray Reinhardt, Robert Harper, Jack Garner, Meredith Strange Boston. Written by William Borchert. Cinematography by Neil Roach. Edited by Paul Rubell and John Wright. Music by Laurence Rosenthal. Produced by Paul Rubell and James Garner. Directed by Daniel Petrie. Color. 99 minutes.

Overview

My Name Is Bill W. is based on the true-life story of Bill Wilson and how he came to form Alcoholics Anonymous (AA) in the 1930s, one of the most effective organizations in helping people cope with their alcoholism. The film is a balanced, impressive treatment of the issue, which by example is also useful in dealing with other addictive problems such as drug abuse, eating disorders, or gambling (including companion groups such as Gamblers Anonymous).

Synopsis

My Name Is Bill W. opens in the early 1950s, as Bill Wilson (James Woods) and his wife, Lois, visit their friend Dr. Bob Smith (James Garner) on his deathbed. As they talk, a flashback displays the story of Bill Wilson, starting in 1919 when he returns from World War I as a hero. Bill turns down a job with Thomas Edison and attempts to launch his own operation as a stockbroker and investigator of developing companies. Bill is very successful in his endeavors, but his wife Lois becomes concerned with his increased drinking. After the stock market crash in 1929, Bill's alcoholism goes out of control. Lois moves in with her father, Dr. Burnham, and asks him to care for Bill. His drinking continues nevertheless, and she considers placing him in a sanitarium. Bill is hospitalized after stumbling into traffic. After reforming, he feels a need to reach out and try to help other drunks, but he finds he is unable to get their attention by preaching at them. In 1935, he gets an assignment to investigate a stock proxy fight in Akron Ohio. Bill finds himself with much time on his hands, and he is tempted to begin drinking again. He calls a local minister and asks if he could be introduced to another alcoholic with whom he could discuss his problems. He is introduced to Dr. Bob Smith, a chronic alcoholic who is suffering from a hangover. Bob is cool at first because he thinks Bill intends to lecture him. Instead, Bill says he actually needs Bob's support. They strike up a friendship, share stories, and form a pact that they will help each other avoid drinking. After several weeks, they decide that the concept of mutual support may be the most effective means of dealing with alcoholism. They try reaching out to other alcoholics, who begin to respond to their honest approach. When Bill returns home to New York, Lois is upset that he spent four months in Akron, but supports his plans to form a new organization to be called Alcoholics Anonymous. Bill writes a book to set out the basic principles, and soon national magazines start to publicize the group. The flashback ends as Bob tells Bill to remember to "keep it simple" when reaching out to help other alcoholics. Bill and Lois tour the country, visiting AA groups wherever they go. Bill does not inform the groups that he is the AA founder, but individually he helps others whenever possible. The end title informs the audience that Bill Wilson continued with his work until his death in 1971.

Critique

My Name Is Bill W. is an exceptional film that explores the different approaches to dealing with alcoholism. Different characters in the film regard the condition in various ways, such as a moral failing, a crutch, or a refuge from disappointments. Dr. Silkworth, who specializes in treating alcoholism, proclaims that it needs to be regarded and treated as a disease. The scene in the Elmswood Sanitarium is remarkable, not overdramatized yet tremendously effective. Wisely, the film spends little time focusing on the guidelines of Alcoholics Anonymous. Instead, it shows the effect of the organization by illustration. The film avoids any outright preaching on the issue, implying that this approach is rarely successful. One character, Ebby (Gary Sinese) is Bill's best friend. He overcomes his alcoholism because of his religious faith, but he later relapses, because he feels jealous that Bill struck up a closer relationship with Dr. Smith instead of himself. All the principal actors, James Woods, James Garner, JoBeth Williams, Fritz Weaver, and Gary Sinese are excellent and convincing, never overplaying their roles.

Night Unto Night
(1947/1949)

Principal social themes: end-of-life issues,
suicide/depression

Warner Brothers. No MPAA rating. Featuring: Ronald Reagan, Viveca Lindfors, Broderick Crawford, Rosemary DeCamp, Osa Massen, Art Baker, Craig Stevens, Erskine Sanford, Ross Ford, Lillian Yarbo, and Joe Devlin. Written by Kathryn Scola based on the novel *Night Unto Night* by Philip Wylie. Cinematography by Peverell Marley. Edited by Thomas Riley. Music by Franz Waxman. Produced by Owen Crump. Directed by Don Siegel. B&W. 85 minutes.

Overview

This legendary Ronald Reagan portrayal of a dying scientist was the most unusual role of his career. When the offbeat film was considered too depressing in its original 1947 version, it was shelved for two years while the editors recut the picture with some of the details about the terminal condition of Reagan's character deleted. The film lost money when it was released in 1949, yet *Night Unto Night* has a haunting and somber quality that makes it unique among the mainstream films of the 1940s, an unsentimental meditation on loss, suicide, and the end of life.

Synopsis

Research scientist John Galen (Ronald Reagan) inquires about renting a mansion along an isolated stretch of the Florida coast. Ann Gracey (Viveca Lindfors), the widow who owns the house, is obsessed about her late husband and believes her husband's spirit haunts the place. While giving Galen a tour, she suddenly bolts and leaves the building. Galen drops her off at a home of a friend, the artist C. L. Shawn (Broderick Crawford) and his family. Later, Ann telephones Galen at his hotel room and tells him that she has decided to let him rent the mansion. Galen is seriously ill and while writing a letter to his friend in Chicago, Dr. Poole, who had first diagnosed his condition, he falls into a trance-like state. He takes some medicine and then collapses. He consults Dr. Altheim, the nation's top specialist in epilepsy. In fact, one of the reasons Galen moved to Florida was to be treated by him. Altheim informs his patient that he is allergic to the only medicine that could be used to treat his condition, and there is nothing that can be done for him medically. Either his disease will go into remission or his symptoms will continue to worsen, eventually leading to death. Resigned to his fate, Galen decides to move into the mansion and to continue his biochemical research studying the properties of mold spores.

He soon discovers that many visitors drop by the mansion besides the maid he hired to do his cooking and cleaning, including Lisa, Ann's impudent sister and the Shawn family. When Ann visits the house again, she hears the voice of her husband's ghost, asking that she accept life and saying that he will not visit her again. She tells Galen, who does not believe in the afterlife. Ann and Galen develop a closer relationship, and she falls in love with him after they kiss. Soon afterward, John has a serious seizure and passes out on the beach in front of the mansion. When he recovers the next day, he skips his meeting with Ann, brushing her off when she calls. He is surprised when Dr. Poole arrives on his doorstep. His friend explains that Galen called and asked him to come. The ill man realizes that he made the call during his blackout spell. They discuss his relationship with Ann and the fact that she knows nothing about his condition. They plan to tell her the next evening, when Galen plans to host a dinner for his friends. A tropical storm strikes during the meal. Dr. Poole takes Ann aside and tells her about Galen. Lisa, slightly drunk, overhears their conversation and then makes fun of Galen and her sister to the other guests. Galen retreats to an upstairs room, planning to shoot himself. Ann interrupts his attempt, saying she is in love with him and does not care if they may have only a year or two together. Galen embraces her, deciding to make the most of the short time he has left.

Critique

Night Unto Night is perhaps the most death-obsessed film made by a major studio during the 1940s. The topic seems to consume each character, even the artist Shawn, a happy family man, but one who paints oversized canvases with allegories of death. They all try to come to terms with their own mortality, and John Galen's attempted suicide is not to relieve his own suffering but as a form of self-sacrifice to save Ann from the trauma of losing another loved one. But whereas Ann and Shawn romanticize death, Galen regards it in cool scientific terms, the mere finish of a biochemical process. He accepts it with dispassionate resignation. The script perhaps makes a mistake by portraying Ann's supernatural episodes. At first, Ann's experiences come across as figments of her troubled mind. However, during the second visitation, the audience also hears the voice of the ghost as it speaks to her. This alters the dynamics, since that makes it seem that the ghost is real instead of in her imagination. When the ghost bids her farewell, this element of the story disappears completely and is not even referenced during the second half of the film. Another problem with *Night Unto Night* is the casting. Broderick Crawford is simply not convincing as the intellectual artist. Viveca Lindfors is also not right for her part, but only when one understands that she was having an affair with the director Don Siegel, whom she married in 1949, does her presence in the film make any sense. Ronald Reagan, despite being panned by some critics, delivers an exceptional reading in a quiet, understated manner far unlike his usual screen persona. For the only time in his career, Reagan rewrote some of the screenplay, correcting, for example, an unlikely riding accident that was written into the original script. Reagan's performance in the film can only be appreciated after several viewings, demonstrating a dignified and realistic consideration of his approaching death after reviewing his options. It is a most unusual screen representation, a man without any religious convictions who comes to terms with his shortened lifespan without fanfare or agitation, choosing instead to go "gently" into that good night.

No Blade of Grass
(1970)

Principal social theme: environmental issues

MGM. R rating. Featuring: Nigel Davenport, Jean Wallace, Nigel Rathbone, Lynne Frederick, John Hamill, Patrick Holt, Wendy Richard, Christopher Lofthouse, George Coulouris, Tex Fuller, Anthony May, Geoffrey Hooper, Mervyn Patrick, Ross Allan, Joan Ward, Karen Terry, Bruce Miners, Margaret Chapman, Brian Crabtree, Christopher Neame, Surgit Soon, John Buckley, Malcolm Toes, Cornel Wilde. Written by Sean Forestal and Jefferson Pascal based on the novel *The Death of Grass* by John Christopher. Cinematography by H.A.R. Thomson. Edited by Eric Boyd-Perkins and Frank Clarke. Music arranged by Burnell Whibley. Produced and directed by Cornel Wilde. Color. 97 minutes.

Overview

No Blade of Grass is a bleak and unsettling film that portrays a world crippled by global pollution and complete environmental catastrophe. In addition, the film explores the darkest regions of human nature, as civilization begins to disintegrate. The script also managed to do this while avoiding a preachy tone. The powerful message of *No Blade of Grass* was too dark and disturbing for most audiences, failing at the box office. Nevertheless, it also achieved cult status as the most unrelenting screen depiction of an environmental holocaust.

Synopsis

The picture opens with a montage of global pollution while Cornel Wilde, as narrator, describes how the ecosystem of the planet was abused during the decade of the 1970s until a worldwide famine began. Because of the pollution, a lethal virus has appeared, which destroys all plant life, leading to the complete breakdown of agriculture. The title song, resembling a folk tune, describes this green blight where no blade of grass can survive. The proper story begins in 1979, as Roger Burnham (John Hamill) calls his friend John Custance (Nigel Davenport) with a warning that martial law is about to be declared and the city of London will be closed. John, a distinguished-looking man who wears a patch over one eye, alerts his wife, Ann (Jean Wallace), and teenage daughter, Mary (Lynne Frederick), to prepare to escape to his brother's sizable farm in the remote hill country. Roger joins them, and as they set off in two cars, they hear increasingly ominous news over the radio. The Chinese are bombing their own cities, killing 300 million people, in an attempt to stretch their meager food supplies. Other organized governments are collapsing, and there are reports of cannibalism. Each of the characters has a flashback of events leading up to the current crisis. The travelers find their way blocked by a street riot as looters pillage the remaining stores. After the police quell the riot with firearms, John decides that they will need to obtain guns if they are going to survive. They stop at the home of Sturdevant (George Coulouris), who runs a firearms store for hunters. His shop is closed, but he opens up for his old customers. He refuses to sell them guns when they do not have the proper permits. They try to explain that their need is desperate and that they are going to a safe refuge in the country. Custance invites the shopkeeper to join them, but he refuses. Sturdevant is then shot and killed by his own clerk, Pirrie (Anthony May), who asks the Custances to allow him and his wife to join them. Now with three cars, the caravan encounters a military blockade, and they get into a gunfight provoked by a belligerent officer who threatens to shoot Roger, and a few soldiers are killed in the battle.

The Custances pick up their young son, Davy, at his boarding school. When Ann learns that Davy's friend Spooks is now an orphan, she invites him along. While on their way, the boys are warned by Ann never to speak with Pirrie or his wife. Bulletins on the radio report that the country is falling into anarchy and the prime minister has proclaimed martial law. Pirrie and his wife had originally planned to rob and abandon the others but now think it is wiser to stay with them, finding safety in numbers. One car gets separated from the others by the barricades at a railroad crossing, which turns out to be an ambush. After overpowering John, a gang of bikers kidnaps Ann and Mary, dragging them off and raping them. Burnham and Pirrie revive Custance and rescue the women. One of the thugs is wounded in the scuffle and begs for his life. Ann Custance grabs the rifle out of Pirrie's hands and kills the rapist with one shot. Continuing on their way, the group monitors the latest developments on the radio. A citizens' committee topples the British government when it learns of plans to use nerve gas on the populace of London. The prime minister flees the country, and the revolutionary committee attempts to restore order. At another roadblock, a citizens' militia commandeers their vehicles and rations, leaving them with only their clothes, but Pirrie manages to conceal a pistol. They set off on foot and decide to raid a local farmhouse, killing the owners. Custance has difficulty explaining the violence to his son, but after Spooks compares the situation to a western, the boys seem to take it in stride. They tune in America on a shortwave radio in the house and learn that almost all governments have ceased to exist except in North America. The U.S. president starts to speak, but the signal fades away.

After resting, the group sets out again, walking through a rainstorm. They pass the night in an abandoned barn. While there, Pirrie catches his wife trying to seduce Custance, and he shoots her. Custance asks him not to let the boys know of this episode. The landscape gets more rugged as they continue on their way. Mary begins spending more time talking with Pirrie, and her father tries to stop her. A confrontation is avoided between Custance and Pirrie only when Mary says she feels safer being with Pirrie and that it is her own choice. In her eyes, he has become a more preferable partner than Roger. Near a picturesque aqueduct, they chance upon an armed band of stragglers. Custance approaches them, saying that if they band together, they will have a better chance of survival. He says his brother's farm can serve as a sanctuary they can share and help defend as civilization disintegrates. Joe Ashton, their leader, is hostile and tries to start an argument; he is shot by Pirrie. Custance tries to make peace with the others, stating his that proposal is still open. First one family and then another decides to join with Custance until the group swells to a sizable band. The large group pushes forward relentlessly until the women are too exhausted to continue. John is concerned when he sees that the green blight has already progressed so far north, and the countryside is covered with dead animals who have eaten the diseased grass. A woman goes into labor, and Pirrie sets up an armed perimeter with a handful of men to protect their makeshift camp. Custance helps the mother deliver the new infant, but the baby dies moments after its birth. Weary after avoiding a rebellious army unit, the survivors finally reach the outskirts of the farm of David Custance. The boundary of the farm is very well fortified, and several sniper shots are fired as they approach. A voice shouts out for them to move on. John Custance proceeds with a white handkerchief on a stick, proclaiming his identity. David appears out of the scrub, and the brothers embrace. David is shocked that his brother has so many people with him. He will make room for John's family and Roger, but no others. David himself has a large assembly billeted on his land and fears they may already exceed the capacity of the farm to support them. John pleads for his associates, but his brother remains adamant. Returning to his followers, John notifies them that they will either have to move on or fight their way in. That night, they try to sneak onto the land through the woods. David's men are on the alert, and another onslaught occurs. Pirrie and David Custance kill each other in the fracas. After a number of deaths, a truce is declared, and John is recognized by all survivors as the new leader. The victims of this last fight are buried, and John leads a forlorn prayer at their graves, asking God's forgiveness for everyone. As the survivors return to their compound, the scene is inverted like a photographic negative, suggesting their that days are numbered. The film ends with a reprise of the folk tune reiterating that no blade of grass will survive.

Critique

No Blade of Grass is remarkable, a genuine masterpiece on various levels. Cornel Wilde's direction is exceptionally hard-edged and brilliant, but the film is so unrelentingly dark that it is difficult to watch. Many viewers are unable to handle such a pessimistic vision. One must commend Wilde for the picture's unflinching integrity. There is no compromise, and Wilde allows no sentimentality to intrude on his black depiction. At one point, in the childbirth sequence, there seems to be a hint of redemption—of a future—but this comes crashing down when the baby perishes. The style of the picture is very sophisticated, and to a certain extent, *No Blade of Grass* is really an art film. The editing is both clever and innovative. The techniques include not only flashbacks, but flashforwards as well. Early in the film, Mary suggests to Roger that they begin a sexual relationship, that she wishes to lose her virginity and become a woman. At this point, a quick cut reveals her future rape. These flashforwards occur regularly throughout the film. The script of the film is compelling. The radio bulletins are particularly colorful and interesting as humankind slips further and further down the vortex. The last message on shortwave from the United States describes how all European royalty and heads of government have sought asylum in North America. The president then begins a cliché-filled speech about the lofty ideals of civilization, and he is soon drowned out by static. When his voice resumes, no one remains to hear his empty words. This is a subtle and effective moment.

The characters in the film are unconventional and richly portrayed. John Custance reminds one at times of Wotan, the weary head of the Germanic gods in Richard Wagner's opera cycle, *Der Ring des Nibelungen*. Like Wotan, he is silver-haired, wears an eye patch, and is forced into making devastating choices. Nigel Davenport plays Custance with flawless precision, as his character violates his moral code again and again in the name of survival. He has one remaining dream, an idyllic fantasy of his brother's farm, where the green virus will never spread and where people may live in harmony and dignity as human beings. Of course, he then winds up inviting so many people to come with him that his proposal becomes only another cruel illusion. By the end of the film, John is only an empty shell of a man, and his prayer at the graveside of the victims is hollow and lifeless. Cornel Wilde's wife, Jean Wallace, delivers a powerful performance as Ann. In another film, her performance might have garnered an Academy Award nomination. Lynne Frederick, who was later married to both David Frost and Peter Sellers, is splendidly convincing as the daughter. She is coquettish and playful at first, but after she is attacked she becomes morose and hardened. Like her father, she is forced to make painful choices, such as when she betrays Roger and selects Pirrie as her future mate because she feels he can protect her. Pirrie is probably the most remarkable character of all. In any other movie, he would be seen as a psychopath and a monster, but in this film, the gun-crazy rake is practically the hero. With the downfall of civilization, Pirrie's cunning and ruthlessness has made him the most valuable individual traveling with Custance. He saves the situation time and again, and he and Custance develop a grudging respect for each other. When they openly quarrel over Ann, Pirrie restrains his natural "shoot-first" instinct for the only time in the picture. He always refers to John as "Mr. Custance" with a sense of esteem, even when he is shot and dying in the guerrilla attack on the farm. Pirrie is the only one who seems to fit into the savage world, and at times he seems like a modern version of Doc Holiday, brutal and calculating but with a certain code of honor. Anthony May is brilliant as Pirrie, and he pushes the envelope in a marvelous reading. Again, if this were a more popular film, May would have been a contender for an Academy Award for best supporting actor. Another worthwhile cameo is turned in by veteran George Coulouris, perfectly cast as the crusty gun shop owner, a stickler for details and a traditionalist with total confidence in the government.

Despite the high quality of the production on many levels, this remains an uncomfortable film to watch. The brutal procession of events is too unrelenting, and there is no nobility or unselfishness to be found in any of the characters. Religion is not invoked to provide any consolation until the vapid prayer at the film's conclusion. In some ways, *No Blade of Grass* resembles Alexander Solzhenitsyn's towering work, *The Gulag Archipelago*, the three-volume chronicle of the Soviet slave labor camps. Both works challenge their audience to chart out unblinkingly the lowest depths of humanity. Finally, no other film can rival this one in showing the consequences of environmental disaster.

No Way Out
(1950)

Principal social themes: racism/civil rights, hate
groups, disabilities

20th Century Fox. No MPAA rating. Featuring: Richard Widmark, Sidney Poitier, Stephen McNally, Linda Darnell, Ruby Dee, Ossie Davis, Mildred Joanne Smith, Harry Bellayer, Stanley Ridges, Dots Johnson, Rudolph Anders, Ian Wolfe, Amanda Randolph, Will Wright, Ruth Warren, Fred Graham. Written by Joseph L. Mankiewicz and Lesser Samuels. Cinematography by Milton Krasner. Edited by Barbara Melkan. Music by Alfred Newman. Produced by Darryl F. Zanuck. Directed by Joseph L. Mankiewicz. B&W. 106 minutes.

Overview

At one time, *No Way Out* was considered a highly provocative and controversial examination of racial hatred. More than fifty years later, the production still holds up very well, and it still can impress viewers as being both audacious and well balanced. The production marked the screen debut of several major black film stars such as Sidney Poitier, Ruby Dee, and Ossie Davis.

Synopsis

No Way Out opens as Ray and Johnny Biddle are brought to County General Hospital with gunshot wounds after a failed gas station holdup. Dr. Dan Wharton (Stephen McNally), chief medical officer, assigns a talented and newly certified black doctor, Luther Brooks (Sidney Poitier), to oversee the prison ward. Ray (Richard Widmark), a loudmouth racist, demands a white doctor and starts to insult Brooks. The doctor is alarmed by Johnny's symptoms, which seem more serious than a bullet wound in the leg. He suspects a brain tumor, but Johnny dies as Brooks administers a spinal tap. Ray claims that Brooks murdered his brother. Upset, Brooks turns to Wharton to discuss if he might have done anything wrong. George, a third Biddle brother (who is a deaf-mute), reads the lips of the two doctors as they have their private conversation and learns that Brooks wants to have an autopsy to determine the cause of Johnny's death. George passes this information on to Ray, who refuses to permit an autopsy. When Wharton learns that Johnny had been married, he takes Dr. Brooks to visit Edie, the wife, to ask her permission for the autopsy, but they learn that she and Johnny were divorced. She agrees to visit Ray in the prison ward to persuade him to give his permission. It turns out, however, that she and Ray were former lovers, and he convinces her that Johnny was murdered and that the doctors want the autopsy to cover up the crime.

Ray comes from a tough district, Beaver Creek, and he and local thugs have in the past raided the adjacent black neighborhood to cause mayhem. Ray tells Edie to pass the word that it is time for an all-out raid, using Johnny's death as an excuse. However, a rival black gang, headed by Lefty, a hospital orderly, learns about their plan. They recruit a large number of black men and attack the junkyard at Beaver Creek where the white thugs are meeting to prepare for their attack. A major race riot breaks out; this time it is Biddle's gang who are defeated. The hospital is overwhelmed with a large number of injured. Dr. Brooks storms out of the hospital when the mother of one of the battered white men starts ranting at him. Edie seeks refuge with Dr. Wharton to confess her part in launching the violence. Wharton is later visited by Mrs. Brooks, who explains that her husband has taken a drastic step. He has gone to the police claiming that he murdered Johnny Biddle. This tactic forces the police to order an autopsy. Ray Biddle, under police escort, is taken to the coroner's office to await the results. The procedure determines that Johnny died of a brain tumor and that Dr. Brooks' treatment had been correct. Ray, outraged by the coroner's verdict, escapes from police custody with George's help. They kidnap Edie and force her to call Brooks so that he walks into a trap at Wharton's home, where Ray is hiding. He captures the black doctor and beats him while yelling racial slurs. Meanwhile, Edie escapes from George, summons the police, and breaks in on Ray just as he is about to kill Brooks. She shuts off the lights as Ray shoots, wounding Brooks in his shoulder before the doctor knocks the gun away from him. Ray's wounded leg starts to bleed after the scuffle. Edie tells Brooks that he should let him die, but Brooks tends to the racist's wound until the police arrive.

Critique

A number of factors make *No Way Out* a milestone among social issues films. The acting is excellent across the board. Poitier's poise and charisma are both readily apparent. His interpretation of Luther Brooks is complex, with alternating moments of self-doubt and professional competence, yet never secure in terms of his acceptance by the white world. Like Jackie Robinson when he broke the racial barrier in baseball, Brooks tries to maintain a cool exterior in the face of racist insults, but he is not always successful. Richard Widmark captures the virulent demeanor of an uneducated hatemonger to perfection. Reportedly, Widmark often apologized to Poitier after shooting scenes in which he shouted "nigger" or other racist remarks. Poitier had to keep reassuring Widmark that he knew he was only acting. Yet, Widmark's performance as Ray Biddle also has a pathetic quality, especially toward the end, when his racism starts to come across as mental illness. Stephen McNally is adept as Dr. Wharton, a man who seems truly color blind. He supports Brooks to the hilt not because he is a black man but because he thinks he is a good doctor. Harry Bellayer's conception of George Biddle is also surprising. The character of George is often overlooked due to his disabilities (one of the guards at the hospital refers to George as "the dummy"), yet he can be as sneaky and loathsome in his own way as his more belligerent brother.

The numerous scenes of violence and racial hatred in the film can be disturbing. One of the men at the junkyard keeps smashing a heavy chain at the wreck of a black car, urging Edie to join him in hitting the "nigger." Somehow this is even more upsetting than the actual race riot with the black gang. The camera pulls away before any real beating can be seen, yet the overall impact is probably greater than if the scene were shot graphically. In addition, *No Way Out* shows that racism is not a one-way street, particularly with the character of Lefty, who can be regarded as Ray's black counterpart in terms of racial hatred. The script uses Edie as an example of someone whose attitude changes during the film, yet this is one area that seems a bit artificial. The audience can identify with Dr. Brooks and his efforts to be professional and maintain control, yet Edie is somewhat of a cipher. She treats Brooks with dignity in the opening scene, then picks up a portion of Ray's bigotry after talking with him, but seems to come out right again after talking with Wharton's black cook and meeting Mrs. Brooks. *No Way Out* can be viewed as a virtual compendium of racial attitudes, pro, con and indifferent. A study can be made simply by the way in which all of the characters, including the minor ones, interact with Dr. Brooks. In the hospital, for example, some staff respond to him with hesitation while others treat him as they would any doctor. Some see him as a friend and equal, some as an authority figure, while others just see his color. It is equally valuable to note how Brooks responds to each individual and how it may differ from his attitude toward the members of his own family. How often does he permit himself to be himself? Rarely does a motion picture offer such a range of insights in the actions of a single character.

Patty (AKA The Shame of Patty Smith)
(1962)

Principal social theme: abortion

Handel Productions. No MPAA rating. Featuring: Dani Lynn, Merry Anders, Bruno VeSota, J. Edward McKinley, Carlton Crane, David McMahon, Jack Haddock, Bob Rudelson, Speer Martin, Sean Brian, Joe Conley, Leif Lindstrom, Sid Kane, Sherwood Keith, Phil Clarke, Adrienne Hayes, Sally Hughes, Ralph Neff, Barney Biro. Written by Leo A. Handel. Cinematography by Howard Schwartz. Edited by Stanford Tischler. Music by Ingram Walters. Produced by Leo A. Handel and Ib Melchior. Directed by Leo A. Handel. B&W. 92 minutes.

Overview

While on the surface a cheaply made exploitation film, *Patty* nevertheless presented a cogent case in the early 1960s for the legalization of abortion. The plot follows the ordeal of a single individual, Patty Smith, a young rape victim who finds herself pregnant and alone, and who eventually decides to get an abortion. Patty was circulated under various titles for some years, including *The Shame of Patty Smith, The Case of Patty Smith, Backroom Abortion,* and the most exploitive moniker, *Gang Rape.*

Synopsis

Patty opens in southern California as Allan Hunt (Carlton Crane) and Patty Smith (Dani Lynn) leave on a date and get involved in a minor fender bender with three tough young thugs. The driver refuses to give Allan his name or license and threatens him when he tries to read their plate number. Reluctantly, Allan drives off with Patty, but the thugs decide to follow them. When they stop at a secluded spot overlooking the ocean, they beat Allan and rape Patty. At this point, a rather pompous narrator appears speaking from behind a desk, announcing that this film will deal with illegal abortion, estimating that six hundred thousand to two million operations occur each year. He adds that approximately eight thousand of these women will die due to infection or complications because of the medical incompetence of those performing the procedure. He asks the viewer to consider the ordeal of a young woman like Patty Smith "as she travels from station to station of her

Calvary." After bringing Patty back to her apartment, Allan asks her if she wants to report the crime to the police, but she declines. A number of weeks later, Patty suspects that she is pregnant. Her roommate, Mary (Merry Anders), takes her to her own physician, Dr. Miller. After he confirms her suspicions, she asks him for his help in terminating her pregnancy. He gently but firmly declines, saying it is against the law. Patty explains that she cannot go home to her parents in the Midwest as they would not understand. He suggests she contact a social agency that could help her and set up an adoption for the child after its birth. Patty asks around and locates another doctor who would be willing to help her, Dr. Friddon, but he asks for an advance payment of six hundred dollars, beyond her means since she was just laid off from her job as a typist. A Catholic, Patty visits her local church. The priest, Father O'Brien, notices she is troubled and tries to counsel her. She says she needs an operation, and the priest offers to intercede for her to obtain a loan. When he learns it is for an abortion, he withdraws his offer, saying that abortion is murder whether she was raped or not.

Patty then contacts Allan, who has been avoiding her since the rape. He learns that she can get an abortion for $200. He gives her all he can afford, $60. Mary helps raise additional funds, and Patty pawns her only piece of jewelry of any value. She is told to contact Henry Colbert (Bruno VeSota) who runs a bar in the seedy side of town, Colbert functions as a middleman who screens clients for an abortion ring. After talking with Patty, Colbert arranges for the operation. He tells her to bring $200 in five-dollar bills and to wait in front of a local shoestore several nights later. Mary takes her to the spot, but when a man turns up, he says he is only authorized to take Patty. When she enters his car, he asks for the money, takes several bills, and tells her to give the rest to the nurse. He drives her to a massage parlor and tells her to report to the second floor. A chain-smoking nurse takes the rest of her money, saying the doctor will be ready for her shortly. The man she calls a doctor is actually her husband, an unemployed pharmacist. After the operation, the nurse gives her some pills. The driver takes her to a cabstand, advising her to go to the emergency room of the hospital if she has any problems. Mary puts her weary roommate to bed when she arrives home, and Patty takes the pills she was given by the nurse. When she starts to run a high fever, Mary calls Dr. Miller. Patty is taken to the hospital in an ambulance, telling the doctor about the location of the massage parlor as best as she can remember. Lt. Powell, a homicide detective who specializes in abortion cases, arrives at the hospital, as Patty falls into a coma. Dr. Neilson, handling her case, talks with Mary and Dr. Miller about how abortion is handled in Sweden, where the procedure is legal and safe. The next day, Miller accompanies Powell, helping him track down the abortionist with Patty's clues. They soon identify the club and rescue another girl just before the abortionist is set to operate. Patty revives briefly and has a vision of the various people she had encountered leading to her abortion. Mary consoles her before she dies. The narrator repeats his assertion that eight thousand women die from illegal abortions each year.

Critique

Exploitation films actually date back to the silent era, the first feature being *Traffic in Souls* (1913). These films grew in popularity during the 1930s. Many were built around social issues such as prostitution or drug addiction, but were presented in such a hyped and stilted fashion that completely distorted the topic. In fact, the social issues aspect of many of these films was window dressing to cover a quick flash of nudity or other risqué scenes. Some well-known examples were *Reefer Madness* (1936), *Cocaine Fiends* (1936), *Child Bride* (1937), *Escort Girl* (1941), *The Devil's Sleep* (1949), and Ed Wood's *Glen or Glenda* (1953). Most of these titles are known purely for their camp value. *Patty* is a cut above the usual exploitation fare. The theme is serious, and blatant distortions are kept to a minimum. The position of the script, clearly, is pro-abortion, yet arguments favoring adoption or stressing moral concerns of the issue are given a straightforward presentation. The doctors, priest, and policeman present their point of view in a clear fashion. Sometimes a piece of information, such as the fact that the number of legal abortions in Japan equals their birth rate, is simply laid out without any additional comment. The audience itself is left to decide whether that statistic is meaningful or not. *Patty* is also valuable for capturing a moment in history, 1962, when abortion was largely illegal and for presenting a balanced view of the situation at that time. The film can generate discussions comparing the status of the issue in the early twenty-first century.

The Perez Family
(1995)

Principal social theme: immigration

Goldwyn Pictures. R rating. Featuring: Marisa Tomei, Alfred Molina, Anjelica Huston, Chazz Palmintieri, Trini Alverado, Celia Cruz, Diego Walraff, Angela Lanza, Ranjit Chowdhry, Ellen Cleghorne, Vincent Gallo, Jose Felipe Padrone, Bill Sage, Lazaro Perez. Written by Robin Swicord based on the novel by Christine Bell. Cinematography by Stuart Dryburgh. Edited by Robert Estrin. Music by

Alan Silvestri, Arturo Sandoval, and Jellybean Benitez. Produced by Michael Nozik and Lydia Dean Pilcher. Directed by Mira Nair. Color. 112 minutes.

Overview

The Perez Family is set against the backdrop of the 1980 exodus from Cuba when Fidel Castro opened the port of Mariel to allow a large number of people, including political prisoners, criminals, and other detainees, to emigrate in a ragtag flotilla of boats, some barely seaworthy. The U.S. government granted most of them asylum. Popularly called the Mariel Boat Lift, this event electrified the Cuban community in Miami, where most of the refugees headed. This film concentrates on a group of immigrants sharing the last name Perez who pose as a family in order to receive a lower number on the list of those seeking American sponsors.

Synopsis

The film opens with a surreal, dream image of Juan Raul Perez (Alfred Molina) and his family. He is dressed in a white suit, watching his closest relatives walk into the sea. He awakens suddenly in a Cuban jail. He is dragged out of his cell by guards, who throw him down in the prison yard, threatening to shoot him. The scene switches to a television report about the release of political prisoners in Cuba. Carmelita (Anjelica Huston) watches the television in her luxurious home in Coral Gables, Florida, hopeful that her husband will be released. They have been separated for twenty years; she and her daughter, Teresa, were able to escape to America while her husband was imprisoned by the Communist regime. Elsewhere in Cuba, a young, beautiful sugarcane worker, Dorita Perez (Marisa Tomei) asks her supervisor if she can be permitted to join the boat convoy to America. A free spirit, she describes herself as resembling Cuba, "used by many, mastered by none." Raul and Dorita meet on one of the boats. They comment about how common the last name "Perez" is in Cuba. Raul tells her he looks forward to seeing his wife again after twenty years, and Dorita says how she looks forward to freedom in America. When they near the coast of Florida, Dorita jumps off the boat and swims ashore. The refugees gather on shore and are briefly questioned by American immigration officials. They are then transported to the Orange Bowl, where a refugee camp is set up.

Back at Coral Gables, however, Carmelita's brother, Angel Diaz, tells her that Raul has not been released, and he will never be able to come to America. In truth, Angel wants to keep her apart from Raul. He was initially responsible for Raul's arrest by the Communists. For years, he has been pocketing the money that Carmelita has been sending for her husband's benefit in prison. He does not want his twenty years of deceit to be exposed. Raul expects his wife to show up at the Orange Bowl to meet him, and is disappointed when she does not appear. Dorita, noting that he has not heard from her in over two years, suggests that she might have died. The manager of the refugee camp tells Dorita that as an individual, her number in the sponsor list is fairly high, but if she teamed up with other family members, they would be assigned a lower number. She becomes depressed when he tells her that John Wayne, her favorite film star, is no longer alive. At a camp film show, she sees a guard who resembles John Wayne and befriends him. He agrees to take her out on a date to a disco dance hall.

Carmelita becomes friendly with John Pirelli (Chazz Palmintieri), a federal agent doing research on the Mariel refugees. He and Carmelita are attracted to each other, and he asks her out on a date. Feeling she will never see her husband again, she agrees.

The refugees at the Orange Bowl learn that they will be transferred in a few weeks to a military base in the Midwest. Dorita persuades Raul to pose as her husband in order to get a lower number. She then persuades Felipe Perez, a streetwise young teen refugee, to pose as their son, and a mute elder to pose as Raul's father. The new "Perez family" is quickly sponsored by a Catholic mission, and they are provided work selling flowers on a busy street. By chance, Raul sees a newspaper advertisement for a furniture store featuring Angel, his brother-in-law. When he visits the store, Angel calls the police, claiming he is an impostor posing as Raul. He tracks down Carmelita's address, but observes her flirting with Pirelli outside her house, and he lacks the confidence to approach her. Felipe gets in trouble with a loan shark, who kills him when he cannot pay off. Raul and Dorita are heartbroken, as if they had lost a real son. Dorita has fallen in love with Raul.

Angel sees them selling flowers on the highway, and tracks him down at the mission. He visits Raul there and warns him to stay away. Raul finally realizes that it was Angel who had him arrested in Cuba. Angel's girlfriend, a popular singer named Luz, is angry that he is trying to keep Raul and Carmelita apart. Conspiring with Teresa, they arrange to have Carmelita and Raul attend the same dance at which Luz is hired to sing. Luz plans to make a surprise announcement from the stage reuniting them. Their scheme does not work exactly as planned, because Angel sees Raul at the dance and tries to shoot him. Instead, a guard shoots Angel, and Carmelita and Raul are finally reunited. Teresa is delighted to talk with her father, but Carmelita is hesitant. When alone, they talk honestly. Carmelita had been almost a child bride when they married, but now has to admit that she had even forgotten how her husband looked. Raul praises her for raising their daughter so well, and he is happy to see how American she is. They both reach the conclusion that too much time has passed for them to resume their marriage. Raul returns to Dorita, with whom he has fallen in love, and Carmelita feels free to continue her relationship with Pirelli.

Critique

The Perez Family is essentially a tribute to the vibrant Cuban American community in southern Florida. The film magnificently recreates the flavor and spirit of the community, laced with humor as well as tragedy. The title, of course, can be taken on many levels. Many of the refugees are named Perez, a very common name, so it almost serves as a metaphor for the boat people themselves. It also refers to the artificially constructed family that Dorita creates to save them from being shipped to a military base out of the area. Finally, it stands for the broken original Perez family, whose unity withered away due to the passing years as well as the poisonous influence of Carmelita's brother. Yet, in Teresa, the family continues as another generation, this time fully Americanized.

The film itself has numerous side plots, such as Felipe's attempts to be a hustler and make money, which end in his death by loan sharks. Then there is the mystery of Papi, the old man who continually climbs trees and flagpoles. It turns out that he thinks he can catch a glimpse of his homeland, Cuba, if he just manages to climb high enough. The new refugees love America, but are also traumatized by their past. For one brief moment, they are afraid they are going to be shot when they arrive at the Orange Bowl. Dorita personalizes Americans in the image of John Wayne. When she learns he is dead, she runs sobbing to Raul, saying her hero is dead just like Elvis Presley. Raul, hopelessly out of touch with recent events, mutters in response, "So many political assassinations." Later, as he grows more perceptive, Raul overhears two old-timers discussing the past, claiming it never got so hot in Cuba. He tells them he just came from Cuba, and it gets as hot. Then he looks around at the stores and the people and observes that Cuba is actually here, too. *The Perez Family* provides an excellent glimpse into the Latino heritage blending with American culture to become renewed and invigorated.

Philadelphia
(1993)

Principal social themes: AIDS, homosexuality

Tristar. PG-13 rating. Featuring: Tom Hanks, Denzel Washington, Jason Robards, Mary Steenburgen, Antonio Banderas, Charles Napier, Ron Vawter, Robert Ridgely, Lisa Summerour, Roger Corman, Joanne Woodward, Kathryn Witt, John

Bedford Lloyd, Anna Deavere Smith, Tracey Walter, Daniel von Bargen, Roberta Maxwell, David Drake, Paul Lazar, Obba Babatunde, Bradley Witford, Daniel Chapman, Ann Dowd, Holly Hickok, Chandra Wilson, Julius Erving, Robert Castle. Written by Ron Nyswaner. Cinematography by Tak Fujimoto. Edited by Craig McKay. Music by Howard Shore. Produced by Edward Saxon and Jonathan Demme. Directed by Jonathan Demme. Color. 119 minutes

Overview

Philadelphia was the first mainstream American film to focus on the issue of AIDS. The film also concentrated on homosexuality as commonly perceived in popular culture. *Philadelphia* became a popular success, a contender at the Academy Awards for the Best Picture of 1993. Tom Hanks won the Academy Award as Best Actor for his performance in this motion picture.

Synopsis

Philadelphia opens with several scenes depicting the successful career of Andy Beckett (Tom Hanks), an up-and-coming lawyer with one of Philadelphia's most prestigious law firms. In fact, Andy has just been handed control of one of the most important cases handled by the firm. The film jumps ahead several weeks, and Andy is unemployed and reaching out to various attorneys seeking representation in a wrongful firing lawsuit against his former employers. Joe Miller (Denzel Washington) is a hustling black attorney who specializes in accident suits. He has gained some notoriety for his television ads promoting his business. Andy consults Joe, who reacts negatively when he learns that Andy has AIDS. Joe tells his wife that he truly despises homosexuality and could never take the case. He later observes Andy in the reference room of the law library, and he feels outraged when he sees Andy treated unjustly by the library staff. He goes over to talk with Andy, discussing his case and eventually agreeing to represent him. Andy meets with members of his family, informing his brothers and parents that his lawsuit may result in bad publicity and notoriety. They encourage Andy to proceed with his suit no matter what the cost.

Months later, Andy's suit come to trial. The position of the firm is that they were unaware of Andy's condition or his sexual orientation. They claim he was fired because he was getting careless in his work, citing how he lost a brief that could have resulted in the loss of an important case. Andy suggests that his brief was deliberately removed from his desk and computer files by the firm so they could use it as an excuse to dismiss him. He explains that he admired Charles Wheeler (Jason Robards), the head of the law firm, but never revealed his homosexuality, particularly after hearing Wheeler and his partners chortling in the sauna over a series of sophomoric jokes ridiculing homosexuals. The night before Andy is due to take the stand, Joe and his wife attend a gay party thrown by Andy and Miguel Alvarez (Antonio Banderas), his lover. After the party, Joe tries to prep his client about his upcoming testimony, but Andy sinks into a pensive mood, suggesting he might not even survive the trial. He then plays for Joe his favorite opera aria in a recording by Maria Callas.

When he is sworn in at the trial, Andy speaks quietly, openly, and with eloquence. He insists that the other members of the firm had concluded that he had AIDS because of the numerous lesions that began to appear on Andy's face and neck. Melissa Benedict, a secretary in the office, had earlier been diagnosed with AIDS, and she was affected with lesions duplicating those on Andy. When cross-examined, Andy admits he contracted AIDS after getting picked up by another man at a gay porn theater. When questioned about the lesions appearing on his face. Andy admits that they cannot be seen from three feet away. Asking a follow-up question, Joe asks Andy to remove his shirt, and the lesions on his chest are large and numerous enough that the jury sees them clearly. After testifying, Andy collapses and is rushed to the hospital. The trial continues, and the jury decides in Andy's favor, awarding him a generous settlement. Joe visits Andy at the hospital, where he is bedridden, saying goodbye to his family. After they leave, Miguel sits alone with Andy, who tells him that he is now ready to die. Joe is phoned that night and informed that Andy has died. Joe attends a memorial party in Andy's memory. The film concludes while focusing on films of Andy's youth.

Critique

Philadelphia has been widely acclaimed as a frank and open film dealing with both AIDS and homosexuality. In actuality, the focus is on discrimination against people living with AIDS and homosexuals. In this context, Joe Miller (Denzel Washington) is actually the more important character in the film. Unlike Andy Beckett, it is Joe whose attitudes and personality change, as he transforms from a homophobe into a champion of both gay rights and the rights of individuals suffering discrimination to being HIV positive. When Andy first tells Joe he has AIDS, he backs away to the rear of his office, eyes widened in panic.

It is a brilliant touch that the most virulent gay-bashing on screen is delivered by Joe, in private to his wife and in public at the trail. Other acts of discrimination are largely conducted off screen. Even Wheeler's gay jokes are more insensitive than vicious. For most members of the viewing audience, it is Joe's progression that is the film's primary axis, even though Tom Hanks won the Academy Award for best performance. Some of the changes in Andy seem too abrupt, as he goes from being a wiseguy attorney in a fashionable suit to appearing as a street bum and martyr within two weeks. The script highlights the martyr scenario, from his name Beckett (recalling Saint Thomas Becket, the martyred Archbishop of Canterbury) to his favorite opera *Andre Chenier* (a martyr of the Reign of Terror during the French Revolution). Andy changes from wearing makeup to disguise his condition to actually highlighting it in one abrupt shift. At times, Andy even exasperates the patience of his lover, Miguel, such as when he decides to nobly skip his treatment one evening when the needle becomes clogged. The audience never really sees Andy's rage, and it is only suggested by Wheeler's smarmy attorney Belinda Conine, played excellently by Mary Steenburgen. The story touches on a great number of points, sometimes too briefly, such as the contrasting treatment of Melissa, who contracted AIDS from a blood transfusion, to Andy, who got it from a homosexual exchange of body fluids. Belinda's unspoken implication, subtle yet noxious, seems to be if your illness is derived from risky behavior, you are not entitled to any sympathy or consideration. On the other hand, the script sometimes throws in one too many clichés, such as the protester who proclaims the old chestnut, "It's supposed to be Adam and Eve, not Adam and Steve." Nevertheless, *Philadelphia* handles most of the social issues quite well, providing excellent opportunities for viewer discussion.

The Pride of Jesse Hallam
(1981)

Principal social themes: education/literacy

Konigsberg Company. No MPAA rating. Featuring: Johnny Cash, Brenda Vacarro, Eli Wallach, Glen Marley, Crystal Smith, Viola Borden, Michael Burnham, Tara Cash. Written by Roy Huggins. Cinematography by Gayne Rescher. Edited by Tony DeZarraga. Music by Johnny Cash. Produced by Sam Manners. Directed by Gary Nelson. Color. 107 minutes.

Overview

The Pride of Jesse Hallam was an exceptional film highlighting the problem of adult illiteracy and a man who finally decides to face the issue and learn to read and write. Noted singer and balladeer Johnny Cash is cast in the title role. The National Literacy Foundation assisting in the making of the telefilm, which debuted on CBS March 3, 1981.

Synopsis

Jesse Hallam (Johnny Cash) is a widower who sells his home in Kentucky to pay for an operation for his young daughter, Jenny, to be performed at the Children's Hospital in Cincinnati. Jesse rents a house and enrolls his son, Ted, in the local high school. After testing Ted, Marion Gallucci (Brenda Vacarro), the vice principal, recommends that Ted be sent to junior high instead. Jesse appeals to the principal, however, and persuades him to allow his son to remain in the tenth grade. Jesse, a former miner, has trouble finding a job, largely because of his inability to read, which he tries to cover up. He finally lands a job with an elderly greengrocer, Sal Gallucci (Eli Wallach), who is impressed by Jesse's familiarity with the quality of produce. Sal likes Jesse, but he figures out he is illiterate when he is unable to find the correct stall at the local farmer's market. Sal was also illiterate when he immigrated to America, and he decides to help his new employee tackle his problem. Jesse also has to face the problem of getting a driver's license in Ohio, which requires him to pass a multiple-choice test. Jesse tries attending a class to help adult students to read, but he finds that the process will take too long. Sal asks his daughter, Marion, to tutor Jesse privately. Jesse and Marion bury the hatchet over their past dispute about Ted, and they learn to work together using the special method that employs pictures to help students recognize letters and sounds. At the end of the first lesson, Jesse is able to read his first word, promise. Marion asks Jesse how he managed to cope for so many years. Jesse replies that he relied on his late wife and learned to bluff his way through most situations. He had managed to sign his name simply by memorizing it.

Jesse continues to make great progress in his lessons. Soon he is able to read a children's book to his daughter as she recovers in the hospital. Marion gives Jesse his first novel to read, *The Old Man and the Sea* by Hemingway. Jesse tries to take the written driving test, but gives up in frustration. Depressed while leaving the Motor Vehicle Department, he has an accident and is arrested when the police discover his Kentucky license has lapsed. Jesse becomes concerned that Ted fails to do well in school except for math. He suspects Ted is also illiterate. Instead of returning to Kentucky, Jesse decides to remain in Cincinnati, and Sal plans to make him a partner in his business. Together, Jesse and his son attend a remedial reading class. Making progress, Jesse decides to continue his education and obtain his high school diploma.

Critique

Johnny Cash is excellent as Jesse, coming across as both sincere and tenacious, a good man but one who is embarrassed to admit his limitations. The script brilliantly shows the obstacles that Jesse Hallam has to overcome simply to admit he is illiterate, having tried for years to hide his problem even from his own children. *The Pride of Jesse Hallam* explores the issue of adult illiteracy with understanding and compassion. Just enough adult-learning techniques are depicted to make the process understandable to the viewing audience. The plot never bogs down, maintaining a high interest level and good production values. Ted is also well portrayed by Glen Marley, showing the development of another functional illiterate. By the conclusion of the story, Jesse transcends his appreciation of the ability to read and comes to respect the value of education as a whole.

Prophecy
(1979)

Principal social themes: environmental issues, abortion

Paramount. PG rating. Featuring: Robert Foxworth, Talia Shire, Armand Assante, Richard Dysart, Victoria Racimo, George Clutesi, Evan Evans, Lyvingston Holmes, Tom McFadden, Charles H. Gray, Burke Byrnes, Mia Bendixsen, Johnny Timko, Graham Jarvis. Written by David Selzer based on his novel. Cinematography by Harry Stradling Jr. Edited by Tom Rolf. Music by Leonard Rosenman and Johannes Brahms. Produced by Robert L. Rosen. Directed by John Frankenheimer. Color. 101 minutes.

Overview

Prophecy was originally promoted as a straightforward monster movie. Although critics panned the film, largely due to the unconvincing creature and special effects, a number of reviewers cited it as a horror film with a genuine social conscience. Moreover, the ecological details about methyl mercury contamination portrayed in the film are accurate, informative, and far more frightening than the story's monster. In recent years, *Prophecy* has gained considerable popularity as an offbeat cult film.

Synopsis

Dr. Robert Verne (Robert Foxworth) is a crusading physician working with the Environmental Protection Agency (EPA). He is sent by them to northern Maine to issue an environmental report on forest lands claimed by both the local Indians and the Pitney Paper Company. He asks his wife, Maggie (Talia Shire), the lead cellist of the Washington Symphony, to accompany him. Maggie is looking for an opportunity to tell her husband that she is pregnant, afraid that he will insist on an abortion, because in principle, he is against bringing another child into the overcrowded world. The Vernes take up residence in a remote lakeside cabin in the disputed forest. They hear from Mr. Isley (Richard Dysart), manager of the paper mill, that the Indians are suspected of killing a number of lumberjacks who have disappeared in the forest. Dr. Verne fishes in the lake and is amazed when he sees an oversized salmon. That night, an enraged raccoon invades their cabin, and Dr. Verne kills it.

John Hawks (Armand Assante), the local tribal leader, invites the Vernes to tour the forest. M'Rai, an Indian elder, tells him how things grow to giant size in certain ponds. He also tells about the legend of Katahdin, a mythical monster who supposedly will arise someday to protect the Indians. Hearing about the high rate of deformity from Ramona, a midwife, Dr. Verne becomes suspicious that the paper mill is somehow polluting the land. Isley gives him a tour of the mill, which appears to be operating safely. However, Maggie picks up a silvery substance on her shoe that indicates use of methyl mercury, a chemical that was once used in the paper industry as a cheap caustic solution. Use of methyl mercury had been banned since 1956, when thousands of people suffered from environmental contamination in Minamata, Japan. Maggie is horrified to learn from her husband that the poison concentrates on fetal tissues whenever a pregnant animal (or human) eats any contaminated food. Since Maggie ate the fish from the lake, she believes her unborn child may have become infected.

When Dr. Verne takes blood samples from the Indian villages, Isley shows up with the police chief to arrest John Hawks for the murder of a family of hikers who were found torn to pieces. When the Indian flees, Dr. Verne and his wife fly by helicopter to a prearranged spot to meet him. Maggie finds a dying, mutated bear cub trapped in a net by a river. Dr. Verne considers this to be positive proof of methyl mercury pollution. He summons Isley and the police chief to meet them at a teepee shelter where he is trying to keep the cub alive. Maggie reveals her pregnancy to her husband, explaining her fears that her infant might be born a freak. Isley is stunned when he sees the baby monster, realizing that the people murdered in the forest were not harmed by the Indians but by a mutant bear. He confesses that the mill had used the forbidden chemical.

The monster, called Katahdin by M'Rai, launches its attack. The remainder of the film features the people fleeing the wrath of Katahdin. One by one, the police chief, the helicopter pilot, Isley, M'Rai, and John Hawks fall victim to the monster. Hawks wounds it with an arrow, and Dr. Verne manages to kill the creature, stabbing it through its eye. As Maggie and her husband fly home, another mutant bear is seen roaming through the forest below.

Critique

Minamata disease has become the official name of the illness to the central nervous system brought on by methyl mercury poisoning. The Chisso Corporation, a Japanese firm, dumped huge quantities of mercury into Minamata Bay, leading to an ecological disaster in the 1950s. The use of mercury has been curtailed since then, but as recently as 1998, Minamata disease has been detected in Brazil along the Amazon River, possibly caused by contamination from the local mining industry. The plot of *Prophecy*, unlike most horror films, has a sound, scientific basis. Also unlike many horror films, the script of *Prophecy* spends considerable time on the scientific data. Dr. Verne, for example, narrates the scientific data into a tape recorder. When his wife questions him about it, he restates the information in less technical terms, explaining exactly how the contamination goes through the food chain and impacts the ecosystem. Then Maggie replays the tape, so the audience is clearly and thoroughly briefed on this environmental issue. Besides the extent of this exposition, the material is highlighted by the passion and anger with which Foxworth plays the scene. Unfortunately, the rest of the film lacks the quality and verisimilitude of these scenes. The film's setting according to the novel is Millinocket, Maine, but the scenery is quite unlike this area of Penobscot County (*Prophecy* was actually shot in western Canada.). The name Katahdin comes from Mount Katahdin, Maine's highest point and the northern tip of the Appalachian Trail. There is a major paper mill in Millinocket known for over a century as Great Northern Paper, only recently changed to Katahdin Paper, but the logs are brought in by truck and rail, not by river. Also there has never been any case of Minamata disease in the United States. Richard Dysart makes a reasonable attempt at a Maine accent, but Armand Assante's accent in the film is a complete puzzlement.

The other social issue raised in the film, the question of whether or not Maggie should obtain an abortion due to possible contamination, is left unresolved. The second-rate special effects, sloppy editing, major plot gaffes, and the phony Maine backdrop made Stephen King proclaim *Prophecy* as his favorite entertaining "golden turkey," although he, too, was impressed by the film's utilization of authentic environmental concerns and accurate scientific data.

⊏⊤⊤⊐

Pump Up the Volume
(1990)

Principal social themes: censorship,
suicide/depression, homosexuality, education/literacy

New Line Cinema. R rating. Featuring: Christian Slater, Annie Ross, Robert
Schenkkan, Ellen Greene, Samantha Mathis, Scott Paulin, Cheryl Pollak, Mimi
Kennedy, Lala Sloatman. Written by Roy Huggins. Cinematography by Walt
Lloyd. Edited by Janice Hampton and Larry Bock. Music by Cliff Martinez.
Produced by Rupert Harvey and Sandy Stern. Directed by Allan Moyle. Color.
100 minutes.

Overview

Pump Up the Volume was a production that outgrew its teen film roots to find
a larger audience largely due to superior acting and directing and a clever,
well-paced script that deftly but realistically weaves numerous social issues
into its storyline. The film was credited with creating a boom of interest in
amateur radio in the early 1990s.

Synopsis

Mark Hunter (Christian Slater) is a secretive new student at Hubert H.
Humphrey High School in Paris Hills, Arizona. His father, Brian Hunter, has
just been appointed the new commissioner of the school district, which
necessitated the recent family move to Arizona from the East. Brian buys his
son a shortwave radio set so he can keep in touch with his old friends from
home, but Mark is unable to contact anyone. Instead, he starts broadcasting
a pirate radio signal at ten o'clock every night, sometimes for five minutes
but other times for hours.

Mark completely transforms behind the microphone, assuming a cocky,
brazen attitude as he plays censored recordings and rap music, and mocks
the conventions and peculiarities of his new school. He electronically alters
the sound of his voice for his broadcasts and uses the pseudonym "Happy
Harry Hardon" as his airname. He expects that perhaps a handful of students
would listen, but soon his show becomes a local student fad. Mark secretly
examines his father's files to expose poor judgments by school officials, such
as the guidance counselor. He questions the pattern of student expulsions
from the school. He sets up a drop box so listeners can write him, and he

telephones them on the air. One of his most devoted listeners is Nora (Annie Ross), a student who works at the school library. She writes passionate letters on red stationery, but never provides her phone number. When Mark returns a book *How to Talk Dirty and Influence People* by Lenny Bruce, Nora begins to suspect that Mark may be Happy Harry. She follows him one day and catches him opening Harry's mail drop box. Nora confronts Mark with her discovery, but he shyly backs off. Later Miss Emerson, Mark's English teacher, begins to suspect that Mark is the phantom broadcaster. When one student sends a letter threatening suicide, Mark calls him on the air and determines that it is not a prank. He takes him seriously, but does not try to talk him out of it. The next day, the student kills himself, and Mark is stunned and regretful. Nora encourages him, saying it was not his fault.

After the student's death, Mark wants to discontinue his broadcasts, but Nora convinces him that too many students are now depending on him. Later on the air he calls another student who wrote a heartfelt letter admitting he is a closet homosexual. Mark calls him and helps him talk through his problems. He also calls the guidance teacher on the air, and the counselor gloats that the call has been traced. However, when the police arrive, they discover that the phantom broadcaster had used a transmitter and had tapped into someone else's phone line. Mark's parents become suspicious and check out his radio room one evening, and are surprised to discover him with Nora. They are secretly delighted that Mark has a girlfriend. A news station decides to pick up and broadcast Harry's show nationwide. The high school principal becomes alarmed by the broadcasts of Happy Harry and tries a crackdown to discover his identity. She expels a number of students, including Nora. When Miss Emerson protests, she is also fired. The principal calls in the Federal Communications Commission (FCC) to find Harry's studio and shut him down. To confuse the FCC monitoring trucks, Mark rigs up his mother's jeep so he can broadcast while Nora drives him around. Miss Emerson turns over to Mark's father a file that proves the principal has been illegally expelling students with the lowest grade averages in order to inflate the school's ratings on test scores. Brian fires the principal. The FCC eventually captures Harry after he abandons his voice disguise. He pleads for students everywhere to take to the airways and speak up whenever the truth is suppressed. In response, a large number of student pirate radio stations begin to spring up across the country as the end credits roll.

Critique

Pump Up the Volume is a lively and energetic film that addresses a whole host of social issues in an innovative format. It is intriguing to watch Mark mature during the story in an excellent performance by Christian Slater. At first, Mark does his show simply out of boredom and for kicks. He merely plays at being a shock jock, spouting obscenity and doing outrageous bits such as pretending to masturbate while on the air. Soon, however, he starts to address his own problems, such as his chronic shyness. He becomes interested in the problems of the other students. He knows something sinister is going on at Hubert H. Humphrey High School, eventually learning that many students are being deprived of their education by the principal in order to boost test scores artificially. Ironically, his father, a dedicated educator, is on the same track, suspecting that something is wrong with the school administration and trying to learn the truth. In a way, Mark and his father are cut from the same cloth, although belonging to different generations. The one glaring error of the script is that they fail to bring them together at the climax of the film. The audience feels cheated when Mark is led away by the police, and his parents are not brought on the scene to show their reaction. Brian undoubtedly would have given his son some words of encouragement or support, given the background of school corruption against which they both were fighting. Another misstep is the presence of the head of the FCC, who personally comes to Arizona to track down Happy Harry. This seems somewhat unrealistic, but it allows the airing of his comments against free speech and censorship, which is the issue at the heart of the film. The segments dealing with suicide, homosexuality, identity crisis, and the right to education come across as sincere and are very well done.

Reversal of Fortune
(1990)

Principal social themes: end-of-life issues, addiction, suicide/depression

Warner Brothers. R rating. Featuring: Jeremy Irons, Glenn Close, Ron Silver, Annabella Sciorra, Uta Hagen, Fisher Stevens, Jack Gilpin, Christine Baranski, Stephen Mailer, Felicity Huffman, Mano Singh, Tom Wright, Bill Camp, Lisa Gay Hamilton, Christine Dunford, Julie Hagerty. Written by Nicholas Kazan based on the book by Alan Dershowitz. Cinematography by Luciano Tovoli. Edited by Lee Percy. Music by Mark Isham. Produced by Edward R. Pressman and Oliver Stone. Directed by Barbet Schroeder. Color. 120 minutes.

Overview

Reversal of Fortune is based on the true case of wealthy Newport heiress Sunny von Bülow, who went into a coma in 1980 and has remained in that state for the past twenty-two years. Amid rumors of attempted suicide, euthanasia, and murder, her husband Claus von Bülow was charged and convicted of attempted homicide based on evidence gather by private detectives working for Sunny's children from a previous marriage. The autocratic von Bülow contacted noted legal scholar Alan Dershowitz, whose extraordinary appeal led to the granting of a new trial and eventual acquittal for von Bülow. The film was a critical success, and actor Jeremy Irons won the Academy Award as Best Actor for his portrayal of von Bülow.

Synopsis

Reversal of Fortune has a very complex structure as many characters express their own reminiscences about Sunny von Bülow (Glenn Close) and how she wound up in a vegetative state. Several key scenes are repeated in alternate takes, for example, some depicting Claus von Bülow (Jeremy Irons) behaving either innocently or criminally in the same situation. There are various layers of issues that can also be interpreted differently. In short, the film is an intellectual challenge. Oddly enough, Sunny von Bülow herself narrates the proceedings from her "brain dead" coma, as the viewers periodically witness the extent of the treatment to maintain her shadowy existence.

Harvard legal scholar Alan Dershowitz (Ron Silver) is approached by Claus von Bülow to review his case after he is convicted of the attempted murder of his wife, Sunny. At first, Dershowitz seems convinced, like the public at large, that von Bülow was responsible for inducing his wife's coma. When he studies the case, he discovers that a basic legal principle had been violated, namely that most of the evidence against von Bülow was gathered by private detectives working for two of Sunny's grown children, Alexander and Ala, from a previous marriage. The defense was never allowed to review the notes of the private investigators. The district attorney's office merely accepted the filtered evidence presented to them and based their case on it. Dershowitz decided to file an appeal. At first, he discovers most of the legal apprentices working with him believe von Bülow is actually guilty, but as they uncover that more and more of the evidence was manufactured, their opinions change. Von Bülow appears before them for questioning, and he maintains his complete innocence. Sunny's younger daughter, Cosima, also believes in her father's complete vindication. The motives of Alexander and Ala are examined, including their desire to disinherit Claus and Cosima and to prevent anyone else from having any input in the care of the comatose Sunny. A potential witness secretly tapes his interview with Dershowitz and offers to provide him valuable testimony in exchange for money. When the lawyer declines, the tape is doctored and sent to the prosecutor's office, but this gambit fails.

In private, Dershowitz asks his client to recount in detail his personal recollections of Sunny's various drug addictions and her behavior before the onset of the coma. Dershowitz comes to believe fully that his client is innocent. He personally argues his brief before the Rhode Island Supreme Court, citing some of their own previous rulings regarding the introduction of new evidence in cases that are circumstantial in nature. When the prosecution responds by discussing the new evidence (the notes of the private attorney and inaccurate results reported by the medical lab), Dershowitz is confident of success. The court in fact sets aside the conviction and allows the defense access to the notes. This material completely undermines the prosecution's case, particularly any evidence dealing with insulin (which the prosecution had theorized was the murder weapon). The hostility of the testimony of Sunny's maid, Maria, was also exposed. Von Bülow was easily cleared in a second trial, but Sunny is left in legal limbo in her vegetative state.

Critique

Although Alan Dershowitz's book *Reversal of Fortune* concentrates on the legal case, the film touches on other matters through the narration of Sunny, which adds a sense of fantasy to the production. This device is similar to the one used in the Bela Lugosi thriller *Scared to Death* (1946), in which a corpse narrates the story from a slab in the morgue. Sunny's narration, in particular, stresses end-of-life issues with almost diametrically opposed results. She says she is brain dead and has no hope of recovery. Yet, by the fact the audience can hear her and follow her reasoning, she still appears to have cognition, which in reality she does not. The film can serve as a vehicle for the question of extending life medically when there is no consciousness or chance of recovery. Claus believes that she should be allowed to die. She was desperately unhappy, and when she was revived from a previous coma a year earlier, she seemed to resent it. If Claus did not actively kill her, could he have been guilty on some other level? Did he notice her collapse earlier than he admitted and chose to do nothing? Did he provoke her suicidal tendencies by discussing divorce? From the book and film, the evidence suggests not, but von Bülow was such an unlikable man that people wanted to think him guilty.

Jeremy Irons is brilliant in his portrayal, showing Claus as somewhat cold and formal but suave with a clandestine sense of black humor. Incidentally, von Bülow's mistress, played in the film by Julie Hagerty, was Alexandra Moltke, best remembered for her role as Victoria Winters in the gothic soap opera *Dark Shadows*. Exteriors for the show were filmed in Newport, just a few blocks away from Claredon Court, the lavish home of the von Bülows. Claus was related on his mother's side to the famous Cosima von Bülow, the daughter of Franz Liszt, and second wife of Richard Wagner. Sunny's youngest daughter was named in her honor.

Right of Way
(1983)

Principal social themes: end-of-life issues,
suicide/depression, aging

HBO. PG rating. Featuring: Bette Davis, Jimmy Stewart, Melinda Dillon, Priscilla Morrill, Louis Schaefer, Charles Walker, East Carlo, John Harkins, Edith Fields. Written by Richard Lees based on his play *Right of Way*. Cinematography by Howard Schwartz. Edited by Sidney M. Katz. Music by Brad Fiedel. Produced directed by George Schaefer. Color. 102 minutes.

Overview

Right of Way, a made-for-cable production, is best remembered for the historic pairing of two screen legends, Jimmy Stewart and Bette Davis, in their only joint screen appearance. The screenplay is a dramatic one showcasing their talents as an elderly couple who decide to commit suicide together after one of them is diagnosed with a terminal illness. The initial cut of the film was judged too disturbing, and the director changed it three times before HBO cleared it for broadcast. Nevertheless, the original ending, including the suicide of the two main stars, remained intact. Reaction to the film was positive, although with reservations. It attracted a large audience, becoming one of the highest rated cable films of all time.

Synopsis

Teddy and Miniature Dwyer, both in their early eighties, telephone their estranged forty-year-old daughter Ruda to come for a visit. She drives up from southern California and is startled to find their home in a dilapidated condition, with their four cats running wild. When Ruda tries to lecture them that they might be fined by the town for creating an eyesore, they tell her they do not care. Mini explains that she has been diagnosed with a rare blood disease and only has a few months left to live. Since the last stages of this condition are quite painful, Mini has decided to commit suicide. Teddy has no desire to live without her, and he informs Ruda that they intend to die together. Stunned, Ruda tries to talk them out of it, and finally walks out, checking into a hotel. She calls her mother's doctor to verify Mini's condition and then turns to the local social service agency for help. Mrs. Finter speaks with Ruda, and then visits the Dwyers herself. Speaking plainly, the elderly couple confirm Ruda's story. After Mrs. Finter files her report, the county authorities begin an investigation to declare the Dwyers unfit. Teddy is served with legal documents summoning them to a court hearing. They go to a lawyer, who refuses to take their case when they calmly tell him that they plan to commit suicide together. After leaving his office, Teddy and Mini decide they had better carry out their plans before they are placed in custodial care.

Ruda continues to visit them and finally tells them she now accepts their decision. She visits Mrs. Finter to see if the legal action can be halted, but the social worker explains that the matter is no longer in her hands but in those of the court. Teddy's hobby is reading poetry, and he selects a line of Spanish poetry to leave in their farewell note. Mini's avocation is doll-making, and she finishes her final doll, a perfect likeness of herself, which greatly moves Teddy when he sees it. They place all of Mini's dolls on their living room table with Teddy's note. They then withdraw to the garage. Teddy starts the car motor and attaches a hose from the exhaust pipe to the vehicle's interior. They sit in the car, embrace, and chat over old times. Ruda has a last-minute change of mind and returns to the house. After searching, she notices the four cats hanging around the garage door. Hearing the running motor, Ruda decides not to intervene. She returns to the house, takes the doll with her mother's likeness, and drives away.

Critique

Right of Way is a sober, almost gentle, love story that covers a whole range of social issues from aging and privacy to governmental authority over the lives of its citizens and the concept of death with dignity. Richard Lees' script is a potent one, raising a number of troublesome points but not providing any clear-cut solutions. It also deftly sidesteps several questions. Teddy and Mini are nonreligious, but they never discuss any philosophical or moral principals, which the story surely calls for (at least in passing). At one point, Mini tells her daughter that she rejects relying on anyone else but herself. This attitude of absolute self-reliance, however, is never examined or even discussed. Of course, Mini's decision to end her life is a logical one, since her condition is hopeless and she wants to avoid any artificial prolongation as she wastes away. It is a clear-cut example that illustrates end-of-life issues.

Teddy's decision, however, is more emotional and controversial, since he is physically well and has all of his mental faculties intact. Teddy does not see his choice as suicide but as an act of love to his ill wife, to accompany her and to make her last moments as easy as possible. He is a far more amiable character than the acerbic Mini, but it seems to touch a nerve whenever his decision is challenged, particularly by strangers. Incidentally, social workers are presented as meddlesome, remote, and insensitive in the drama. They do not seem to regard the Dwyers as people, merely a problem to be resolved. The lawyer, played by John Harkins, is even worse. He assures Teddy and Mini that their session with him is confidential, but then he spreads their story in the newspaper. At times it seems everyone wants to violate the Dwyers' rights (which is reflected in the film's title).

Viewers can also consider the film a case study of the limits of personal rights versus government intrusion. *Right of Way* avoids becoming maudlin. Mini and Teddy are largely nondemonstrative in their emotions. The performances of Jimmy Stewart and Bette Davis are exceptional, although the personal chemistry between the stars was reportedly strained. Stewart found Davis cold, arrogant, and uncooperative. Melinda Dillon is adequate as Ruda, which is somewhat confused, particularly since her final scene was revised three times. Perhaps this confusion served to represent the audience's traditional viewpoint, not wanting the main characters to die. One could argue that the final scene with Davis and Stewart is the most positive depiction of suicide in motion pictures. They both seem relaxed and content, untroubled by any fears or second thoughts. Their comfort with their final choice is a remarkable one that leaves a lasting impression on the audience.

Rock Hudson
(1990)

Principal social themes: AIDS, homosexuality

Konigsberg Productions. PG-13 rating. Featuring: Thomas Ian Griffith, Daphne Ashbrook, William R. Moses, Andrew Robinson, Thom Mathews, Michael Ensign, Diane Ladd, Joycelyn O'Brien, Don Galloway, Mathieu Carriére, Larry Dobkin, Jean Kasem, John Shepard, Julie Tesh, Diane Behrens, Ping Wu. Written by Dennis Turner based in part on the book *My Husband, Rock Hudson* by Phyllis Gates. Cinematography by Tom Sigel. Edited by Peter Parasheles. Music by Paul Chihara. Produced by Diana Kerew and Renee Palyo. Directed by John Nicolella. Color. 92 minutes.

Overview

Rock Hudson was probably the first person with AIDS who caught the attention of the average American. Previously, the disease was largely over-looked by the mainstream media, considered a condition only troubling the underground gay community. When it was announced that the disease had claimed the popular screen and television star, he personified the tragic illness in the mind of the general public worldwide. This biographical tele-film attempted to portray Hudson's life in frank terms, including his ho-mosexuality as well as his struggle with AIDS, secrets the actor tried to protect during his entire career.

Synopsis

Rock Hudson freely uses newsclips and photographs of the real Rock Hudson, even when his actual image clashes with that of Thomas Ian Griffith, the actor playing the title role. The picture begins as Roy Fitzgerald, a California truck driver, is signed and promoted by brilliant talent agent Henry Willson, who crafts a new persona for him, starting with a new name, Rock Hudson. Willson's efforts soon bear fruit, as Hudson is cast in a bit part in *Fighter Squadron* (1948) by famous director Raoul Walsh. Hudson is embarrassed when he misspeaks his only line, resulting in countless retakes. On the set, however, he strikes up a friendship with Tim Murphy, a member of the crew, and they soon become lovers. When they decide to share an apartment, Willson warns Rock that he must protect his career in public. He urges that Tim and Rock take along a couple of girls as dates when they want to go out together.

Rock's career starts to blossom as a contract player with Universal. Actual posters from Rock's films such as *Scarlet Angel* (1952) and *Sea Devils* (1953) represent his screen career. When he signs for the male lead in *Magnificent Obsession* (1954), Willson introduces the actor to his new secretary, Phyllis Gates, and he begins to date her. Soon Tim begins to get jealous and moves out, feeling that Rock is spending too much time acting as if he were straight. Shortly thereafter, Willson warns Rock that *Confidential Magazine* is about to expose him as a homosexual. To protect his career, Willson suggests that Rock marry Phyllis, which would provide him some cover. Phyllis is delighted, and Rock becomes a good husband. He hides his homosexuality from her and has discreet liaisons with men. On one occasion he visits a gay bar, however, and when news filters back to him, Willson warns his client that a single misstep would ruin his career. Becoming increasingly moody, Rock loses his temper and slaps Phyllis during an outing to the beach. She demands to know what is troubling him, and he confesses that he is a homosexual. After hearing of his numerous affairs, she decides to ask for a quiet divorce.

Years pass, and Rock becomes a superstar. News clips show the real life Hudson with Doris Day at a publicity event. Hudson buys a lavish estate and tells Willson that he intends to live as he pleases in his compound, but Willson still urges caution. After he argues with his agent over the creation of a production company to develop new projects, Rock decides to end his contract with him, holding a series of stag parties at his mansion in celebration. Rock accepts a dramatically different role in *Seconds* (1966), about a man who attempts to adopt a new identity. The movie is an artistic success, but a financial flop. Rock revives his career on television with a successful series, *McMillan and Wife.*

His wild lifestyle comes to a halt, however, after he suffers a massive heart attack. Upon recovering, Rock has a relationship with a new live-in lover, Marc Christian. When Rock discovers an oddly shaped mole on his neck, he gets a check up and is diagnosed with Kaposi's sarcoma, a form of cancer that is a symptom of AIDS. Stunned, Hudson decides to keep his condition a secret, only informing his secretary, Mark Miller, but not Marc. Hearing about an experimental treatment in France, Rock flies to Paris. He begins the treatment, which involves a series of injections on four consecutive days each week. After six weeks, Rock decides to abandon the treatment when he is offered a role on *Dynasty*, the leading television series. He appears on the show, but continues to lose weight. When Marc urges him to get tested for AIDS, Rock insists he is well. He continues to deteriorate, and Miller tells Marc that Hudson is dying from anorexia. Hudson returns to Paris and collapses. He is told that the disease has progressed too far for treatment. A press release is issued on July 25, 1985, with the news that Rock Hudson has AIDS. He tells his doctor that he wants to go home to die. His journey home is accompanied by a media frenzy. When alone, Marc sits by his bedside and asks why he kept his condition secret. Rock says he was frightened that he would lose Marc. Rock Hudson dies on October 2, 1985. Later Marc Christian, in a landmark case, wins a lawsuit against Hudson's estate because his lover had not informed him that he was infected with AIDS.

Critique

Rock Hudson offers scant coverage of the actor's film career, except for brief cameos by actors playing Raoul Walsh (Larry Dobkin), John Frankenheimer (Don Galloway), and Robert Stack (John Shepard). The focus instead is on Hudson's double life as a top movie star and a closet homosexual. Yet here the production only concentrates on several relationships, such as Tim Murphy and Marc Christian. His long association with actor George Nader, for example, is never even mentioned. His three-year marriage to Phyllis Gates is covered sympathetically, and the script has Rock proposing marriage to her before his agent alerts him about the tabloid press plan to expose his homosexuality. The screenplay portrays Hudson as a man eternally divided, almost wishing to be both straight and gay simultaneously. His secrecy after he knows he is infected with AIDS is painful to watch as he continues to lie to people he supposedly loves. Hudson's homosexuality is treated in an open fashion unusual for a television production. It shows Hudson embracing numerous lovers, sharing his bed and other small intimacies, although avoiding open mouth kissing. Thomas Ian Griffith, who is also a producer and writer, is not fully convincing as Hudson in the first half of the film, but he is riveting as the older Hudson, particularly in the scenes in which he succumbs to AIDS. Other cast members are excellent, particularly William R. Moses as Marc Christian and Andrew Robinson as Henry Willson. In real life, Willson was a homosexual, but this fact is not suggested in *Rock Hudson*. (Ironically, Robinson earlier starred in the title role of another telefilm, *Liberace* (1988), which portrayed the life of another major star and cultural icon with AIDS.) The last twenty minutes of *Rock Hudson* are especially poignant and well done. When he decides to break off his initial treatment in Paris, his doctor warns him that he is risking his life. His reply that his career is his life is a significant admission, demonstrating that both the public and the private Hudson are essential halves of his personality. The film's portrayal of Hudson's experiences as a person with AIDS can be seen as representative of typical patients. His first reaction is shock, then disbelief and denial, false hope, and finally acceptance. Sadly, he never realizes the importance of the announcement that he has AIDS, which brought world focus on the seriousness of the disease for the first time.

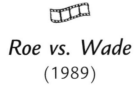

Roe vs. Wade
(1989)

Principal social themes: abortion, women's rights,
suicide/depression

Mannheim. No MPAA rating. Featuring: Holly Hunter, Amy Madigan, Terry O'Quinn, James Gannon, Kathy Bates, Chris Mulkey, Annabella Price, Dion Anderson, David Wohl, Micole Mercurio, and George Murdock. Written by Alison Cross. Cinematography by Tom Sigel. Edited by Elodie Keene and Joann Fogle. Music by Snuffy Walden. Produced and directed by Gregory Hoblit. Color. 96 minutes.

Overview

Roe vs. Wade is an oddly constructed telefilm, half a folksy character drama and half a dry, courtroom chess match that concentrates on the background and legal maneuvering behind the controversial Supreme Court decision that secured the rights of women to terminate a pregnancy. The two halves of the film do not always blend, but the picture provides a solid airing of the major arguments for and against abortion. *Roe vs. Wade* initially aired on NBC May 15, 1989.

Synopsis

Roe vs. Wade opens at a carnival in Texas, where Ellen Russell (Holly Hunter) works as a sideshow barker. She telephones her mother with news that she is pregnant. Her mother, who is custodian of Cheryl, Ellie's baby daughter, is unsympathetic, so Ellie moves in with her father, who is more supportive. She tells him that she wants an abortion, which is illegal in Texas. She visits a doctor and concocts a story that she was raped, but that makes no difference in terms of the state law. Eventually she is recommended to two lawyers, Sarah Weddington (Amy Madigan) and Linda Coffee, who need a plaintiff for a lawsuit in a test case to change the abortion restriction in the state. Ellie agrees to serve as plaintiff, signing her complaint on April 20, 1970, using the alias of Jane Roe in her suit against the district attorney of Dallas, Henry Wade, for enforcing the laws forbidding abortion. Meanwhile, Assistant Attorney General Jay Floyd (Terry O'Quinn) is assigned to represent the state in the case before the district court. After lively oral arguments, the court issues a compromise ruling, declaring abortion legal but not issuing an injunction to enforce their decision. The end result is that Ellen is still unable to receive an abortion. Her lawyers plan to ask the U.S. Supreme Court for injunctive relief, but they inform Ellie that the procedure would take over a year, far too late to help her. The story then divides between Ellie's personal life and the wrangling of the lawyers involved in the case. Disappointed, Ellie moves in with a friend (Kathy Bates) and awaits the birth of her child, which she gives up for adoption. She attempts suicide, but her father discovers her unconscious when he stops by for a visit, and he cares for her, thinking she has passed out from too many drinks. She recovers and tries to get on with her life.

Linda reluctantly has to pull out of the case due to her workload, leaving Sarah to handle it by herself with the help of Ron, her husband, and another lawyer volunteer. In his preparations for the Supreme Court, Floyd decides to concentrate on the humanity of the unborn fetus. As time to file the final brief nears, Ron suggests the use of several technical legal concepts besides a woman's right to privacy. The Fourteenth Amendment, for example, uses the phrase, "all person's born or naturalized," therefore not recognizing the fetus as having any rights. Miscarriages do not need death certificates. Floyd also prepares a technical argument, namely that the case is moot since due to the passage of time, "Jane Roe" is no longer pregnant. Since Sarah has only limited experience arguing before the bench, it is suggested that an experienced litigator, Terry Beaumont, be used to argue the case. Sarah decides to let Ellen make the decision as to who should represent her and travels to speak with her. Ellen insists that Sarah represent her. Before the Court, Sarah makes a strong, rational case and is responsive to queries from the Justices. Floyd, however, is thrown off stride when his moot case argument is rejected. He replies weakly to several questions by Justice Thurgood Marshall. In January 1973, the Court issues their ruling, a 7–2 compromise that basically legalizes abortion during the first six months of pregnancy. Ellen tells the friend she lives with that she is actually Jane Roe.

Critique

A curious mixture, *Roe vs. Wade* attempts to outline clearly the arguments in the legal battle that resulted in the famous Supreme Court decision. Fearing that a dry courtroom battle would not hold the viewer's interest, the script loads the personal story of Ellen with colorful but hokey touches that are somewhat fictionalized. Of these scenes, the most memorable one is her suicide attempt and her relationship with her father, who always treats her with respect. The legal portion of the film, however, remains basically accurate. Viewers interested in the issue of abortion will find this section of the film more meaningful. A number of intriguing arguments are brought to light, such as the fact that abortion was legal when the Constitution was originally drawn up and antiabortion laws by the states only started to appear in the nineteenth century. Both Terry O'Quinn and Amy Madigan are excellent as the opposing lawyers, both emotionally committed to their case and both believing that their position is the one that would actually save lives. The script respects both of their deeply felt attitudes, and since the film ends with a special acknowledgment to the real-life Sarah Weddington and Jay Floyd, they undoubtedly cooperated in the making of the picture. The scrawl at the end of the film refers to *Webster vs. Reproductive Services*, a later case that refined some of the loose ends of the *Roe vs. Wade* decision. Another provocative development is the changing attitude of the real-life Ellen Russell, who later adopted a pro-life viewpoint. A study of the reasons behind this shift would make an interesting study.

Separate but Equal
(1991)

Principal social theme: racism/civil rights

Republic/New Liberty. No MPAA rating. Featuring: Sidney Poitier, Burt Lancaster, Richard Kiley, Cleavon Little, Gloria Foster, Ed Hall, Lynne Thigpen, Henderson Forsythe, Thomas Hollis, Randle Mell, Hallie Foote, Mark Hammer, Jack Rothman, Mike Nussbaum, Albert Hall. Written by George Stevens Jr. Cinematography by Nic Knowland. Edited by John W. Wheeler. Music by Carl Davis. Produced by Stan Margulies and George Stevens Jr. Directed by George Stevens Jr. Color. 206 minutes.

Overview

Separate but Equal is a methodical, detailed telefilm that examines one of the most important legal cases decided by the Supreme Court in the twentieth century, a case involving civil rights and the concept of racial segregation. The production did not seem well tailored to a two-night presentation playing on ABC on April 7 and 8, 1991. It could have benefited from tighter editing in a lengthier one-night format, and it drew rather tepid ratings. Nevertheless, the film was of the highest quality and received many Emmy nominations; it won as the best drama special of the year.

Synopsis

In 1950, a legal case develops in South Carolina when a school is denied a bus to transport black students. The principal contacts the National Association for the Advancement of Colored People (NAACP) to accept the case, and their legal counsel Thurgood Marshall (Sidney Poitier) sees it as a good choice to challenge South Carolina's segregation law. In 1951, a lower court upholds the state's law. The case is appealed to the Supreme Court in 1952. Attorney John W. Davis (Burt Lancaster) is hired to defend the position of South Carolina. Davis's daughter advises him not to take the case as she believes it would make him seem to be a racist. The gentle, soft-spoken Davis insists he is only defending the valid legal principle of states' rights. The Chief Justice dies before a decision is reached, and the case is argued again in 1953. Earl Warren (Richard Kiley), the new Chief Justice, believes that segregation is wrong, but decides that a unanimous verdict is needed so that the Court can emphasize the importance of the issue. Warren spends many hours behind the scenes trying to persuade his colleagues to his viewpoint. When their decision is read, Thurgood Marshall is profoundly moved by the depth of the Court's decision. Back at home, John W. Davis is also struck by the fact that the court ruled unanimously, agreeing with his daughter that desegregation would be good for the country as a whole.

Critique

Separate but Equal is an exceptional production despite its unevenness and occasional slow spots. The film is most effective when it deals with the legal arguments involving civil rights and equal protection under the law. A prologue to the film notes that much of it was based on first-hand interviews with a number of the participants and that historical consultants were also employed. However, the story was padded out with personal subplots that in some cases were fictional, and these distracted from the overall effectiveness of the presentation. The film's greatest strength is the performances of the three leads. Burt Lancaster, in the last role of his career, is exceptional as John W. Davis, a lawyer's lawyer, who defends the law of South Carolina with quiet conviction, framing his arguments with intelligence and dignity, untinged by any sense of racial prejudice. Sidney Poitier, as Thurgood Marshall, has a far greater sense of passion in his presentation, presenting the human face behind the issue of civil rights in his ardent presentation. The give and take of these issues in the judicial setting are compelling, and both actors clearly demonstrate the respect and esteem that these historic figures felt for each other as they debated their case. Richard Kiley, as Earl Warren, has an even more crucial role, to craft a unanimous agreement from eight associate justices with different sets of values. His persuasiveness in bringing about this landmark civil rights decision is truly enlightening for anyone examining the issue of civil rights at this juncture of American society.

Sign of the Ram
(1948)

Principal social themes: suicide/depression, disabilities

Columbia. No MPAA rating. Featuring: Susan Peters, Alexander Knox, Phyllis Thaxter, Peggy Ann Garner, Ron Randell, Allene Roberts, Ross Ford, Diana Douglas, Margaret Tracy, Paul Scardon, Gerald Hammer, Doris Lloyd, Dame May Witty. Written by Charles Bennett based on the novel by Margaret Ferguson. Cinematography by Burnett Guffey. Edited by Aaron Stell. Music by Hans J. Salter. Produced by Irving Cummings Jr. Directed by John Sturges. B&W. 84 minutes.

Overview

Susan Peters was an up-and-coming star in the 1940s, who received an Academy Award nomination as Best Supporting Actress for her sixth film, *Random Harvest* (1942). Unfortunately, she had suffered a spinal injury in January 1945 when her gun accidentally discharged while she was on a duck-hunting trip. Resuming her career from a wheelchair, she starred in two stage plays. After reading Margaret Ferguson's novel *Sign of the Ram*, about a domineering paraplegic who tries to manipulate her son's fiancée into committing suicide, Peters interested producer Irving Cummings Jr. into making the dark, gothic film, which was quite successful. Peters later starred in a television series, *Miss Susan*, about the adventures of a wheelchair-bound lawyer. She died in 1952 after developing bronchial pneumonia.

Synopsis

Sherida Binyon (Phyllis Thaxter) is hired to work at Bastian, a remote estate in Cornwall, to be the secretary to Leah St. Aubyn (Susan Peters). Leah is the second wife of Mallory St. Aubyn (Alexander Knox), and stepmother to his three children, Logan (Ross Ford), Jane (Allene Roberts), and Christine (Peggy Ann Garner). On her first night at Bastian, Sherida learns many things. Leah is actually the popular sentimental poet Faith Hope. She is a paraplegic who lost the use of her legs many years earlier, just after marrying the widower Mallory, in the course of rescuing Logan and Jane who were caught in an undertow while swimming in the ocean. After the children were pulled to safety in Mallory's rowboat, Leah was dashed against the rocks, injuring her spinal column. Since then, Leah was practically worshipped by her husband and children, and she now completely dominates the family. Many years have passed, and since Logan and Jane are grown, Leah is having a more difficult time keeping them under her thumb. First, Dr. Crowdy, her physician, informs her that he intends to propose to Jane. Then Logan tells her of his plans to marry Catherine (Diana Douglas), a talented artist and adopted daughter of the local vicar. Leah becomes alarmed and concocts an elaborate lie to sabotage their plans. She warns Jane that Dr. Crowdy had told her he was afraid that she was taking his attentions far too seriously. Jane decides to refuse when the doctor asks her to attend the local dance. Later, Leah meets with Catherine, telling the naive girl that her real father had been insane, and since she carries his strain, she should never have children. As Leah hopes, Catherine is overwhelmed by this news, becoming deeply depressed. Shortly after, she attempts suicide, jumping into the ocean. Thanks to the quick intervention of Sherida, Catherine is rescued. Taking her back to the vicarage, Logan, Jane, and Dr. Crowdy puzzle out Leah's destructive schemes. Logan and Jane inform their father that they are leaving home and never intend to return.

Back at Bastian, Christine becomes alarmed by this turn of events, and because of Leah's comments, the young girl comes to the conclusion that Sherida is at fault. She takes Leah's sleeping pills and that night poisons Sherida's milk, believing her death will look like suicide. During the night, the housekeeper overhears Sherida moaning and alerts Mallory. When Dr. Crowdy arrives, they deduce that Christine poisoned her. Under her father's questioning, Christine admits her guilt, provoked by Leah. Mallory is outraged and turns against his wife, saying she has broken up their home. When Christine visits her room, she tells the paraplegic that she has decided to go to boarding school, and her father agrees. Leah wheels herself out the door into the fog, heading for the cliff behind the house. She hesitates for a moment at the edge. She then hears her husband call out her name. By the time he reaches the cliff, Mallory finds only her empty wheelchair. Leah has committed suicide, flinging herself over the edge.

Critique

Sign of the Ram is one of the most remarkable films of the late 1940s, an imaginative combination of the gothic, film noir, and psychological drama. The screenplay, remaining faithful to the Ferguson novel, takes a number of daring chances, even testing the motion picture code by fixating on the concept of suicide and its malevolent portrayal of a handicapped individual. Indeed, Leah's suicide is staged with a theatrical grandeur that the code normally found objectionable and distasteful. Dark and obsessive, the film runs quite counter to the traditional Hollywood product of the era. It almost seems that the censors overlooked their code in deference to Susan Peters, since the Hollywood community was strongly encouraging of her comeback effort. In fact, Peters's spellbinding, thoughtful performance is one of the most unique on screen. She manages to be beguiling, sweet, and charming on the surface, concealing a manipulative, conniving, and deceitful core. It is a reading of extraordinary depth, since even at her worst, Peters manages to endow her character with a degree of sympathy. Leah St. Aubyn is shown in a variety of complex moods, and the film even offers the actress an opportunity to display musical talents at the piano. (Years earlier, Peters starred as a concert pianist in *Song of Russia*.) *Sign of the Ram* is worth multiple viewings, if simply to study Leah's dialogue, which is often filled with cryptic meanings that can be taken at different levels. In fact, Leah is a deeply troubled woman on the verge of a breakdown.

The title is a reference to Leah's astrological sign. At one point, Dr. Crowdy observes that people born under her sign are endowed with strong willpower and are steadfast of purpose, letting nothing deter them from their goal. She sees Logan, Jane, and Christine as her own, since she suffered her accident saving the lives of two of them. Now, the inexorable march of time changes the circumstances since the two older children are determined to set out on their own, causing Leah to become depressed and suicidal since it is inevitable that her wishes are going to be thwarted. Everyone at Bastian, however, seems unaware of this. They are completely under Leah's spell, taking her actions at face value. The only one not taken in by Leah is the newest member of the household, her secretary, Sherida, superbly played by Phyllis Thaxter. Her character alone is able to observe the situation clearly, without any predisposition or prejudice. She does not overhear Leah's fluent manipulation of Catherine, but she is clearly aware of Leah's forceful powers of persuasion.

In Leah's skewed viewpoint, anything is justified or justifiable. She herself is on the brink of suicide, so why should she not push Catherine in that direction instead? It is no coincidence that Leah's suicide takes the same form as Christine's attempt, throwing herself into the sea. Leah also feels oppressed by the unseen presence of Mallory's first wife, whose photograph she addresses regularly whenever she is alone in her room. Even though Leah has replaced her, in her own mind she still feels in competition with the dead woman, much as did Joan Fontaine's character in *Rebecca* (1940). On the other hand, it seems apparent that Leah's bitter and venomous attitude is only partially due to her paralysis. To her, that is only a condition that can be mastered, whereas dealing with human emotions requires continual control.

Viewers studying this film should also consider the character of the local gossip, played to perfection by Dame May Witty. To what extent is she a vehicle for Leah's own ideas? Is she a disruptive influence, or does she serve as a sounding board for Leah? Why is the youngest daughter, Christine, so vulnerable and in danger of becoming warped by the influence of her stepmother, whom she adores? At times, Christine seems to be an alter ego for Leah, with the girl trying to anticipate the desires and needs of her invalid stepmother. The young girl's connection to reality seems tenuous, and at times she misjudges events completely, such as suspecting that Mallory is romantically interested in Sherida. Mallory himself is somewhat of an enigma. Why is he so ineffectual in dealing with his wife, whom he indulges shamelessly? Why does Leah take Mallory so much for granted that he is never the target of any of her machinations? The only real passion in Mallory seems to be for the flowers in his greenhouse. The only time he seems to touch Leah is when he announces that he plans to name his new hybrid in her honor. Since hybrids are sometimes considered botanical freaks, Mallory's tribute might give an ironical tinge to the story. By the end of the film, Mallory seems to be the only person who will be saddened by Leah's death. Yet he will undoubtedly recover as he did after the death of his first wife, making Leah's suicide seem an even more futile and insignificant gesture.

Sixth and Main
(1977)

Principal social themes: homelessness/poverty, addiction (heroin), suicide/depression, disabilities

Universal. No MPAA rating. Featuring: Leslie Nielsen, Roddy McDowall, Beverly Garland, Gammy Burdell, Joe Maross, Leo Penn, Sharon Thomas, Brad Stephens, Martin St. Judge, Ken Johnson, Bill Erwin, Ancel Cook, Lisa Todd, Phyllis Flax, Edwin Mills, D'Mitch Davis. Written by Chris Cain. Cinematography by Hilyard John Brown. Edited by Ken Johnson. Music by Bob Summers. Produced and directed by Chris Cain. Color. 95 minutes.

Overview

Originally conceived as a television film, *Sixth and Main* was considered a bit too sordid for the medium, and writer/director Christopher Cain decided to use his more graphic, alternate takes of various scenes when it was decided to release the film theatrically. In fact, the film did poorly on its initial release, but won a minor cult following when it became frequently shown on cable stations.

Synopsis

Monica Cord (Beverly Garland) is a wealthy socialite who is planning to write a book about the homeless. She observes the men who attend a rescue mission and shelter in downtown Los Angeles. Monica becomes intrigued by one particular derelict, a tall, quiet man known only as John Doe (Leslie Nielsen). His main friends among the transients are Doc, an unlicensed doctor; Skateboard, a legless tramp who operates a newsstand; and Peanut, a heroin addict and hooker. Monica secretly follows John and finds he lives in a battered trailer in a junkyard. She examines his shelter when he leaves and is startled to find it filled with handwritten manuscripts. She takes one and reads it. Amazed, she brings it to her friend Adair Callison, a noted book critic, who agrees it is a remarkable literary document. They go to the junkyard and seek out John. Monica offers to provide him a room and office in her own home so he can continue his writing. John responds by snatching his manuscript from her hands and setting it on fire. Stunned, Monica and Adair withdraw.

John's only interest seems to be flowers. He emerges from his solitude, however, when he overhears Peanut telling Doc that she is pregnant and needs an abortion. John breaks his silence and suggests that Peanut keep the baby and that he, Skateboard, and Doc will help take care of it. At first, Peanut thinks that it is a foolish idea, but then she has a change of heart. She asks Skateboard to serve as the father of the child. He agrees and takes the obligation seriously, insisting that Peanut kick her heroin habit. Doc makes a deal with John. He will deliver the baby if John will consent to Monica's proposal in order to provide the funds to raise the child. Reluctantly, John agrees. Peanut eventually gives birth in the hallway of an abandoned building at the corner of Sixth and Main Street. John takes up residence in Monica's mansion, but at first he refuses to abandon his street clothes. Monica throws a cocktail party to show off her new find. Eventually, he cleans himself up and slowly begins to write.

Doc turns up at the mansion to let John know that the baby has died due to heroin in his system. John goes on an alcoholic binge. When Monica, in a fury, strikes John, he hits her back. Adair knocks him out with a vase. When they take him to the hospital, John claims that he is already famous. He later disappears from the hospital. Adair does research and learns that the enigmatic derelict is actually John Christopher, one of America's major writers, a cult figure who presumably died ten years ago when his Bel Air mansion was destroyed in a fire. Adair and Monica return to the junkyard to find the trailer blazing in flames. Doc tells them he thinks John was inside. As the end credits roll, a mysterious figure can be seen walking away in the distance.

Critique

Sixth and Main is a fascinating sleeper film that combines a remarkable number of themes and issues in a ninety-minute package. Leslie Nielsen plays it straight as John Christopher, a celebrated writer who fakes his own death to live on the streets, filling his days smelling flowers, watching puppies in a pet store window, and scribbling out manuscripts just for his own amusement. The script never reveals what tragedy or pressures forced John to abandon his life and retreat to this hobo existence, but the other denizens of Skid Row do not find it peaceful. Doc is a bitter lush, drowning the memories of his failed medical career. Skateboard ekes out a marginal existence with a small magazine stand. Roddy McDowall must have studied Lon Chaney's memorable silent film roles to prepare for this convincing portrayal of a man born without legs and glides along on his small platform. McDowall brings a quiet sense of dignity to the role of Skateboard and manages to avoid any hint of self-pity, even in his line, "Does it have legs?" after the birth of the baby. Finally, Gammy Burdell is touching as Peanut, the fragile girl behind a tough exterior. Her struggle with the symptoms of withdrawal are very well handled. It is a fascinating premise to watch how these four destitute people form an alliance to raise a newborn child on the streets. Each of these individuals is ennobled by the effort, but when it fails, their world sinks back again into the dregs.

This film would be ideal for discussion, both in exploring the challenges of the homeless in raising children or debating the possible future of each character. For example, why did John choose to live as a homeless drifter? Did he actually commit suicide at the end of the film or merely faked it as he did in the past to disappear into obscurity? The screenplay is also filled with subsidiary issues, such as the dilemma of being pregnant and hooked on drugs. Then there are the bitter but honest truths present in Doc's long drunken diatribe against the American Medical Association. Another avenue for exploration is the character of Monica Cord, a limousine liberal who sees herself as a reformer. In fact, she simply wants to exploit the issue of homelessness.

Several flaws exist as well in *Sixth and Main*. The film's structure largely abandons Skid Row after the birth of Peanut's child (a brilliant and memorable sequence), and the scenes in Monica's mansion tend to wander and drag in comparison. The climax, when Monica slaps John and he fights back, however, is extremely well played. Christopher Cain's career suffered a setback after the completion of *Sixth and Main*, but by the mid-1980s, he was back in stride with such productions as *The Stone Boy* (1984) and *The Principal* (1987), also films with a social issues subtext.

Sleeping With the Enemy
(1991)

Principal social themes: spouse abuse, women's rights

Twentieth Century Fox. R rating. Featuring: Julia Roberts, Patrick Bergin, Kevin Anderson, Elizabeth Lawrence, Kyle Secor, Claudette Nevins, Tony Abatemarco, Marita Geraghty, Harley Venton, Graham Harrington, Sandi Shackelford, Nancy Fish, Bonnie Cook. Written by Ronald Bass based on the novel by Nancy Price. Cinematography by John W. Lindley. Edited by George Bowers. Music by Jerry Goldsmith, Leonard Bernstein, and Hector Berlioz. Produced by Leonard Goldberg. Directed by Joseph Ruben. Color. 98 minutes.

Overview

Sleeping With the Enemy is a thriller portraying a wife who fakes her death to escape from her abusive husband. Although far-fetched on several points, the film makes an interesting case portraying the desperate options that face a woman who is trapped in a violent marriage. Julia Roberts, one of the most popular actresses of the 1990s, makes a persuasive case in the leading role and attracted considerable attention to this picture.

Synopsis

Laura Burney is a virtual prisoner in a luxurious ultra-modern beach house on Cape Cod. Her husband, Martin Burney, a wealthy investment counselor, is an obsessive/compulsive control freak. He orders every detail of Laura's life, from her daily wardrobe to the positioning of cans in her pantry. His physical abuse for minor infractions is becoming increasingly brutal. Their lovemaking, always accompanied by the playing of the last movement from the Berlioz's *Symphonie Fantastique* on their CD system, has become an ordeal for her. When she decides to leave him, she realizes Martin will never let her go willingly. She plans an elaborate escape. Martin knows that Laura is terrified of the water, and every few months he forces her on a boat trip. She secretly leans to swim, and when their neighbor invites them for an evening sail, she slips out of the boat during a storm. She sneaks back to her home, grabs a few items, and heads off, tossing her wedding ring into the toilet. Meanwhile, Martin has summoned the police and Coast Guard to search for his wife, presumably lost at sea. Laura is declared dead, and Martin howls in despair, smashing the huge glass windows of his home. In disguise, Laura has hopped a bus to the

Midwest, finally settling in Cedar Falls, Iowa. She rents a house and tries to start a new life with a new identity.

Martin becomes suspicious of his wife's death, however, when he gets a condolence call from one of Laura's friends who mentions her efforts to learn to swim. He then finds her wedding ring in her toilet, unused since she had vanished. He begins to organize a search. Months earlier, Laura had told him that her mother, blind and paralyzed, had passed away at a nursing home in the Midwest. When he visits the nursing home, however, he learns that his wife had simply moved her to another home. He hires a team of detectives to locate the mother, and then he stakes out the new nursing home, waiting for Laura to appear.

Now using the name Sara Waters, Laura is befriended by her neighbor Ben, a drama teacher from the university. He helps her get a job at the school library. He soon realizes that Sara is in constant fear, and she slowly confides in him about her past. She confesses that she wants to visit her mother in the nursing home, but is afraid that Martin may have the institution under surveillance. Ben disguises her as a young man so she can visit her mother. When Martin learns the old lady had her first visitor, he interviews her, posing as a policeman. He tricks her into revealing that Laura has a new boyfriend who is a college drama professor. Martin tracks her down to Cedar Falls. He slips into her home while Laura and Ben have a moonlight picnic. When Laura returns home, she knows that something is wrong when she finds the cans rearranged in her kitchen cabinet and the *Symphonie Fantastique* playing on her CD player. Martin holds her at gunpoint before she can escape. Ben comes to the door and can detect something is wrong by the tone in Laura's voice. He breaks in and Martin knocks him out. Laura gets the gun away from Martin and calls the police, saying she just shot an intruder. She then kills Martin as he tries to persuade her to surrender to him.

Critique

Several plot loopholes weaken the impact of *Sleeping With the Enemy*, although it still makes an excellent launching point for discussions about the implications and trauma of spouse abuse. Laura did library research to consider her situation, and felt the legal course of informing the police and obtaining a restraining order to be inadequate protection. The psychological damage done to her also made it impossible for her to confide in another person. If she had followed that course, she might have received some practical advice. Completely isolated, Laura worked out the only feasible scheme that made sense to her. Her distress and isolation is undoubtedly the dilemma faced by many women in the nightmare of an abusive relationship. This is the core issue of *Sleeping With the Enemy*, which makes the film relevant as a social issue film. Even when the film later gets sidetracked into a traditional stalker thriller, this point remains central to the story. The screenplay disappoints, however, when it ignores other important concerns. How does Laura finance her escape? What is her mother's financial situation in the nursing home? How does she handle the other legal questions, such as her Social Security card or a driver's license. These issues could have been addressed in some fashion, but the screenplay simply ignores them.

Despite its flaws, the film remains powerful due to the strong performances by Julia Roberts and Patrick Bergin, who manages to avoid making Martin a complete monster by showing him to be a prisoner of his own madness. He even seems human when he reveals his own desperate attachment to Laura, best evident perhaps in the last scene of the film as he pleads with her. The picture is also graced with a splendid soundtrack by Jerry Goldsmith, influenced no doubt by the lyrical third movement of Sergei Rachmaninoff's *Second Symphony*. The scene in which Laura overhears Ben singing and dancing passages from *West Side Story* while tending his apple trees is also a magical moment. On the bad side, the film contains a silly montage sequence of Laura and Ben out on a date. This scene clashes in tone with the rest of the film. It is also a shame the film did not contain an epilogue showing whether Laura revealed the entire sequence of events to the police when they arrived. It could have also suggested whether she might have had a possible future with Ben.

Slender Thread
(1965)

Principal social theme: suicide/depression

Paramount. No MPAA rating. Featuring: Sidney Poitier, Anne Bancroft, Telly Savalas, Steven Hill, Ed Asner, Indus Arthur, Paul Newlan, Dabney Coleman, H. N. Wynant, Robert Hoy, Marjorie Nelson, Thomas Hill, Janet Dudley, Charlotte Stewart, Viola Harris, and John Napier. Written by Stirling Silliphant based on a magazine article by Shana Alexander. Cinematography by Loyal Griggs. Edited by Thomas Stanford. Music by Quincy Jones. Produced by Stephen Alexander. Directed by Sydney Pollack. B&W. 98 minutes.

Overview

Slender Thread is a dramatic portrayal of one evening shift at the Seattle Crisis Clinic, a 24-hour hot line for counseling people in trouble. It focuses on one particular case, a woman who takes an overdose of sleeping pills and calls to talk until the drugs take effect. The story covers the factors that compelled the woman to take this desperate step as well as the intense efforts to save her—from the volunteer manning the telephone at the Crisis Center to those of the police, the local hospital, and the telephone company. The production managed to interweave carefully the suspense elements in tracking down the woman with the general problems that might drive individuals to suicide.

Synopsis

Psychology student Alan Newell (Sidney Poitier) arrives for his evening shift as telephone monitor at the Seattle Crisis Center. He hopes it will be a quiet evening, so he can catch up with his studies for an upcoming test at the university. Dr. Coburn (Telly Savalas) asks Alan if he could leave him alone tonight since the psychiatrist wants to spend the evening with his son. He leaves his phone number with him in case of emergency. At first, things are routine, the only call being from an inebriated barber who just wants to shoot the breeze. His next call, however, is a matter of life and death. A woman (Anne Bancroft) confesses that she is planning to kill herself and just took a large quantity of barbiturates. At first she refuses to tell him her name, but as she continues to ramble on, she mentions her name is Inga. Alan tells Inga he needs to get a cup of coffee, and calls the phone company switchboard to trace the woman's call and to summon Dr. Coburn back to the center. Meanwhile, he begins to gain Inga's confidence and asks her to explain to him what went so wrong that she decided to attempt suicide. Alan learns that her marriage is in crisis since her husband, Mark (Steven Hill), a commercial fisherman, learned that he was not the biological father of their twelve-year-old son Christopher. In fact, Inga tried to drown herself months earlier, when her husband opened a letter from an attorney that granted Chris a small inheritance from his actual father. Mark became less hostile after her suicide attempt, but their rift was never completely healed. After Mark returned from his next extended fishing trip, they made an effort to reconcile, but Inga feels it was a failure. Alan is relieved when Dr. Coburn returns, but the psychiatrist refuses to take his place on the phone, saying it would be too difficult for Inga to switch to another person, and she would probably hang up. With the sketchy details gathered about Inga's previous suicide attempt, Coburn contacts the police to track down her identity from hospital records. Once the cops establish her last name is Dyson, they visit her home address and learn from the sitter that she supposedly went on an overnight trip, and her husband is on his regular fishing run. They put out an all points bulletin to locate her car and radio her husband to return to port immediately. The phone trace finally reports that the call is coming from Hyatt House, a large hotel. Alan continues talking with Inga, who is becoming increasingly sluggish and lethargic. Coburn estimates that only a short time remains to save her. At one point Inga asks Alan to laugh. He forces himself at first, and finally, he and

Coburn start to guffaw convulsively. The police begin searching Hyatt House, which is fully booked due to a convention, checking out each room. Inga becomes incoherent and passes out. Mark Dyson arrives at the crisis center, and he starts to call out to her over the phone. Finally, they hear sounds of someone breaking in the door. Moments later, a policeman comes on the line and informs Alan and Mark that Inga is still breathing. The medics are working on her and believe she will survive. After the phone line is disconnected, Alan stares at the receiver. The police rush Mark to the hospital where Inga will be taken. Coburn and the others congratulate Alan for saving the woman's life. He lets out a shout of triumph, and then sits back in a chair, relieved, as the end credits run.

Critique

The Slender Thread is very successful in striking the right tone. Part of this is due to the excellent location footage in and around Seattle, at police stations, hospitals, and telephone relay centers. The approach is semidocumentary, but also with a gritty edge like traditional film noir. The cast provides the film's main thrust. Sidney Poitier is excellent in the starring role, which is race neutral. Anne Bancroft is a bit too old to be the thirty-year-old Inga, but she carries off her difficult role quite well. Telly Savalas is totally convincing as the overworked psychiatrist. The script is very well balanced between the action, battling the clock to save Inga in time, and the flashback sequences depicting the background of Inga's troubles. The main theme of the film is kept front and center throughout by a large sign on the wall of the clinic directly behind Poitier. It reads, in large block letters: "EVERY TWO MINUTES SOMEONE ATTEMPTS SUICIDE IN THE U.S.A." The irony is that actual suicide calls to the hot line appear to be a rarity. Most phone callers are either hoaxes or depressed individuals wanting to talk out their problems. Volunteers, such as Alan Newell, fill out a form as they receive calls, mostly a series of standard questions for later follow-up if people require additional treatment or referral. The crisis center operates with a shoestring staff mostly of volunteers. At one point, alone in the center, Alan cries out to Inga that the night she places the most important call of her life, fate swindles her by having only a barely trained amateur on hand. However, as the film proceeds, the audience sees the large number of professionals, technicians, doctors, medics, policemen, and others, who back Alan up, unknown even to him. Their efforts, a network of caring individuals doing their jobs, provide a somewhat reassuring subtext to the entire film.

A Small Killing
(1981)

Principal social themes: aging, homelessness/poverty

Motown Productions. No MPAA rating. Featuring: Jean Simmons, Ed Asner, Sylvia Sidney, Matthew Faison, Kent Williams, Andrew Prine, Mary Jackson, John Steadman, Anne Ramsey, Nicholas Guest, Doug Johnson, Noel Conlin, Barbara Edelman, J. Pat O'Mally. Written by Burt Prelutsky based on the novel *The Rag Bag Clan* by Richard Barth. Cinematography by Howard Schwartz. Edited by Richard E. Rabjohn. Music by Fred Werner. Produced by Peter Nelson and Arnold Orgolini. Directed by Stephen Hilliard Stern. Color. 96 minutes.

Overview

A Small Killing was a modest telefilm that combined a murder mystery with a sympathetic portrayal of the elderly poor. Largely shot on location in the Skid Row district of Los Angeles, the picture gathered considerable buzz, particularly after Jean Simmons was cast in the leading role. CBS broadcast the film on November 24, 1981, to critical acclaim and decent ratings. The network briefly considered transforming the film into a series, but dropped the idea when the stars indicated that they would not be interested.

Synopsis

Margaret Lawrence (Jean Simmons) is a sociology professor preparing a report on aging for a congressional committee. She interviews Sadie (Sylvia Sidney), an observant and streetwise bag lady. When Sadie is found murdered, the Los Angeles police contact Margaret since Sadie had her business card. At the police station, she meets Simon Shrabner (Ed Asner), an officer who works undercover in the Skid Row district. Margaret believes that the police will give solving Sadie's death low priority since they believe that the elderly woman was killed because she worked as a courier for a drug dealer. She volunteers to pose as a bag lady, both to understand the lifestyle and to see if she can learn who killed Sadie. When he learns that Margaret is adamant about the idea, Si agrees to work with her on the streets.

After a few days, Margaret makes friends with other aged men and women who pick through garbage to survive. Margaret spends her nights at a cheap hotel. A stranger approaches her and asks if she wants to make some extra dollars. She agrees and he pays for a telephone to be installed in her room. She is then given a series of test runs, picking up a package in a garbage can one day and delivering it on the following day. Si keeps her under observation and they develop a relationship. Eventually, the police start picking up the couriers who leave the packages, which contain drugs. Margaret and Si enlist other elderly street people to help in their efforts. One of the packages left for Margaret contains a bomb. A belligerent bag lady confronts Margaret, delaying her pick up and the bomb explodes before she reaches it. Margaret goes into hiding at Si's apartment, knowing the drug dealers have marked her for death. A ragpicker recruited by her locates a suspicious package that helps lead the police to the drug lord. Sadie's killer spots Margaret, and pursues her, but Si arrives in time and rescues her. As the film concludes, Margaret and Si have fallen in love and decide to marry.

Critique

Unlike a number of other films, *A Small Killing* deftly merges the criminal plot with both character development and social issues. Jean Simmons makes a passionate plea of concern for the aged even before the opening credits, as her character states that senior citizens face more discrimination in housing, employment, and day-to-day living than any other minority group. Ed Asner, however, approaches his role in a less serious vein, making the tone of his performance rather mocking and humorous. In his pan-handler disguise, Simon is simply not believable. His opening scene features him wiping car windshields while looking for a handout. Sylvia Sidney, much as Lucille Ball in *Stone Pillow*, plays her role straight and makes an effective case as she describes garbage-picking as a viable option for the elderly poor since Americans often throw away items of value. The brief bond forged between Sadie and Margaret is remarkably well handled. When Margaret assumes the role of a bag lady, her first day is rather uncertain, but she soon becomes convincing and credible in her masquerade. These scenes are quite good, with a serious shading to some of the surface humor. Most of the scenes with the other members of the elderly poor are also laudable, with the exception of J. Pat O'Mally, who comes across as too corny. Viewers should observe that most of these people are not actually homeless, living in modest rooms or apartments rather than on the street full time. *A Small Killing* manages to portray the lowliness of their lifestyle and how helping Margaret and Si made them feel needed, even important.

The plot also demonstrates how most people, going along on their daily business, either ignore or simply never notice the elderly poor, making them practically invisible. When Margaret is asked the purpose of her street interviews, she says she wants to pass more laws to help the elderly. She is told in response that the laws never seem to touch them. At first, Margaret is silent, but finally replies that more useful laws are needed. In this exchange, the professor has actually learned something meaningful. This is only one of many exceptional moments in *A Small Killing* that make it special. The final scene of the film, unfortunately, is the weakest, since it is played entirely for laughs. Margaret and Si's new friends attend their wedding dressed in formal attire, but O'Mally returns to his hobo ways as he takes out a bag to swipe the shoes that were tied to Si's automobile.

Soylent Green
(1973)

Principal social themes: environmental issues, censorship, suicide/depression

MGM. No MPAA rating. Featuring: Charlton Heston, Edward G. Robinson, Leigh Taylor-Young, Chuck Connors, Joseph Cotton, Brock Peters, Celia Lovsky, Paula Kelly, Lincoln Kilpatrick, Whit Bissell, Mike Henry, Roy Jenson, Stephen Young, Leonard Stone, Dick Van Patton. Written by Stanley R. Greenberg based on the novel *Make Room! Make Room!* by Harry Harrison. Cinematography by Richard H. Kline. Edited by Samuel E. Beetley. Music by Fred Myrow, Ludwig van Beethoven, Edvard Grieg, and Peter Ilyich Tchaikovsky. Produced by Walter Seltzer and Russell Thatcher. Directed by Richard Fleisher. Color. 99 minutes.

Overview

Soylent Green was one of a number of science fiction films that addressed environmental issues by depicting possible futures in which life on Earth is threatened because of ecological disasters. Some of these titles include *Silent Running* (1971), *Doomwatch* (1972), and *Waterworld* (1995). *Soylent Green*, however, is considered the most effective of these endeavors, largely due to the powerful performances by Joseph Cotton, Charlton Heston, and Edward G. Robinson, who gave one of the most poignant and moving death scenes in all cinema filmed just months before his actual demise.

Synopsis

It is the year 2022. Civilization is in a state of near collapse due to many factors including global warming, the breakdown of industry, and overpopulation. Former college professor Sol Roth (Edward G. Robinson) now works as an information specialist for a state detective named Thorn (Charlton Heston) in New York City. The population of 40 million New Yorkers are anxious and restless, concerned about cutbacks in the food supply, particularly the popular staple known as Soylent Green. Thorn is assigned to solve the murder of William Simonson (Joseph Cotton), one of the wealthiest men in the city and a member of the board of Soylent, the organization that controls the world's food supply. Simonson apparently offered no resistance to his killer, who bludgeoned him to death, Thorn is amazed at the size of Simonson's apartment, which he shared with his bodyguard, Tab Fielding (Chuck Connors) and a female companion (Leigh Taylor-Young), who is regarded as "furniture" and comes with the apartment. Thorn steals some food from Simonson's refrigerator, including a salad, apples, and a steak. Roth prepares their supper with these ingredients and explains that such meals were once the norm.

Thorn asks Roth to investigate Simonson's past. He learns that he was obsessed and depressed by some terrible secret. Simonson told his secret to a priest, and when Thorn confronts him, the priest seems on the verge of collapse. Fielding, apparently a member of a secret security force, later kills the priest. Roth consults a group of elders, former scholars led by a woman (Celia Lovsky). They deduce the terrible secret known by Simonson. Roth, depressed by the knowledge, leaves a note for Thorn and heads for a suicide clinic. Thorn breaks into the chamber where Roth is spending the last moments of his life listening to classical music and watching a film of a luxurious world when there were green fields, clean oceans, forests, and wildlife. Thorn is thunderstruck that the earth was ever so beautiful. Roth tells him Simonson's secret: All life on Earth is dying, even the plankton in the sea. Roth dies peacefully.

Thorn follows Roth's body as it is loaded onto a truck and transported to a processing plant. There, the detective sees the process by which the corpses are turned into the food wafers known as Soylent Green. Fielding and other troops hunt Thorn, but, although wounded, he manages to fight and kill them. As he is carried to the infirmary, Thorn tells the secret to his supervisor. He continues to shout, "Soylent Green is people," and he is overheard by a crowd who are disturbed by the news.

Critique

Unlike many other apocalyptic films, *Soylent Green* is both memorable and effective. The film deals with environmental issues in several ways. The montage sequence that opens the picture shows historic pictures of the development of the automotive industry, an endless flow of cars off the assembly lines, the billowing of clouds of pollutants out of factory smoke-stacks, and traffic jams with exhaust rising into the atmosphere. Soylent Green was definitely ahead of the curve in promoting the dangers of the greenhouse effect. The other half of the equation is the runaway population explosion, straining the natural resources of the planet until it can no longer support life.

The breakdown of society is depicted in many ways. With industry and technology stalled, old machines simply break down and cannot be repaired due to lack of parts. Many products that are commonplace to the viewing audience, such as strawberries, apples, and shower stalls, are regarded as remarkable luxuries to the characters in the film. In one ironic line, Heston sneaks a puff on a cigarette from a girl in Simonson's apartment building and remarks, "If I were rich enough, I would smoke two, maybe three of these every day." Of all the losses, the most poignant are those of the ordinary scenes of nature, forests, oceans, flocks of birds, and schools of fish that are revealed in the deathbed documentary viewed by Edward G. Robinson. Obviously, all such images are forbidden for public viewing and permitted only as a treat for the dying after they drink poison. This censorship had to be in place for some time, with all films and books with scenes of nature destroyed so the public would not be reminded how the earth was devastated by the governments of the nations of the world. Finally, suicide, or "leave-taking," has been transformed into a celebratory ritual. Those choosing to die are catered to, provided with their favorite color scheme, favorite music, and a full twenty-minute film showing the wonders of the planet before the environment was devastated by pollution, climate change, and abuse. Robinson's and Heston's reactions to this cinerama presentation, accompanied by music from Beethoven's *Pastoral Symphony*, are remarkable and unforgettable. In some ways, *Soylent Green* stresses the frail beauty and importance of nature with more impact than any other film in history.

Stand and Deliver
(1987)

Principal social themes: education/literacy, racism/
civil rights

Warner Brothers. PG rating. Featuring: Edward James Olmos, Lou Diamond Phillips, Rosana de Soto, Andy Garcia, Will Gotay, Ingrid Oliu, Virginia Paris, Vanessa Marquez, Mark Eliot, Patrick Raca, Lydia Nicole, Daniel Villarreal, Carmen Argenziano, James Victor, Michael Goldfinger, Rif Hutton, Betty Carvalho, Karla Mintana. Written by Ramon Menendez and Tom Musca. Cinematography by Tom Richmond. Edited by Nancy Richardson. Music by Craig Safan. Produced by Tom Musca. Directed by Ramon Menendez. Color. 105 minutes.

Overview

Stand and Deliver is an exceptional motivational story based on the incredible success of mathematics teacher Jaimie Escalante. Since 1982, he prepared a number of average students from Garfield High School, a rundown urban school in a poor area of East Los Angeles, to pass the very difficult Advance Placement Test in Calculus. Edward James Olmos worked closely with the real-life Jaimie Escalante to capture his style and technique of motivating students.

Synopsis

Jaimie Escalante is a successful computer expert who decides to leave his high-paying job to take a teaching position at Garfield High School in East Los Angeles. When he reports to work, he learns that budget cuts have eliminated funding for school computers. Instead, he is asked to teach basic math, and he agrees. His students, all Hispanics, seem uninterested and even frightened of basic math. Jaimie experiments with new techniques to stimulate them. For example, he dresses like a chef and slices up apples, which he distributes to the class. He uses them as props to explain fractions. Some of his students are gang members, but Jaimie inspires one of them, Angel Guzman (Lou Diamond Phillips), into becoming one of his best students. At teacher meetings, Jaimie notices that the teachers are discouraged. The test scores are Garfield are low, and the administration is afraid the school might lose its accreditation. To inspire morale, Jaimie proposes a radical idea. He asks to prepare his math class to take the national Advance Placement Calculus Test, one of the most challenging of all preparatory tests that can earn early college credits for students who pass. Success in this area would capture the attention of the state. The head of the math department is aghast because calculus is not even taught at Garfield. She resigns when Jaimie's idea is approved. He convinces eighteen students to enroll in this special project. He asks them to sign contracts to attend extra classes with him before and after regular school hours to prepare for the test.

The students begin to make exceptional progress. Jaimie overextends himself, however, when he starts to teach evening literacy classes for adults and suffers a heart attack. A substitute teacher carries on for him, and Jaimie returns to work sooner than expected, ignoring his doctor's suggestion to take several weeks of rest. Jaimie continues to drill his students, sometimes in unorthodox ways, but they all seem to respond. When they take the test, the results are extraordinary. All eighteen pass with flying colors, the highest number of successful students from any school in southern California. The national board that oversees the test, however, sends each student a letter that questions the results. They suspect cheating. A two-person investigating team grills all of the students. Jaimie and the students are insulted by this turn of events. Jaimie calls on the investigators, accusing them and the board of racism (in spite of the fact that one investigator is black and the other Hispanic). The students volunteer to take the test again, but are only given twenty-four hours to prepare. Jaimie runs an all-night review session to help. The two investigators administer the test, which is more difficult than the original exam. Nevertheless, all the students pass. As Jaimie walks proudly down the school corridor after hearing the results, an end scrawl reveals that each year, an increasing number of Garfield High School students take Jaimie's challenge seminar, and by 1987, the success rate is amazing, as a total of eighty-seven students take and pass the Advance Placement Calculus test.

Critique

Stand and Deliver is a unique film, concentrating its efforts on making the simple act of learning seem like an exhilarating adventure. Although widely acclaimed, several teachers' organizations voiced criticism of the film since the hero, Jaimie Escalante, enters the educational system as a virtual outsider, whose accomplishments far exceed those of dedicated teachers who devote a lifetime to their craft. Since the story and Escalante's achievements are true, these complaints ring hollow. Some of Escalante's approaches to teaching are undoubtedly unconventional, but they merit study. He praises math to his class as "the great equalizer" before which no student has any advantage despite their ethnic background. In fact, Escalante tries to install a sense of pride since many Hispanics have Indian blood in their backgrounds and the Mayans invented the concept of zero, an idea that eluded both the Greeks and Romans. He also tries to form his mathematical examples on relevant topics that might engage the students and make the subject seem exciting.. He uses humor, pep talks, biting satire, and games to raise the enthusiasm of his class. However, he is also very demanding, using frequent quizzes and insisting that his students come to class prepared. If any of his students need help, Escalante is also willing to take an extra step to aid them. When a promising student announces that her parents are planning to take her out of school, he visits them to plead her case in person. He manages to gain the students' respect, and they respond by studying hard and achieving far beyond their normal level. They also respond in other unexpected ways. When Jaimie's car is stolen, Angel and his old gang members track it down and repair the car so it seems better than new. There are drawbacks as well to Escalante's methods and personality. He sometimes loses patience and drives some people too hard (including himself). His own family often feels neglected when Jaimie becomes too obsessed with his work. His temper, when aroused, is terrible. He even threatens the investigators when he feels his students are being discriminated against because of their ethnic background. Edward James Olmos gives a dynamic performance as Jaimie, warts and all. His single-minded dedication to excellence is refreshing and an inspiration.

Stone Pillow
(1985)

Principal social theme: homelessness/poverty

CBS. No MPAA rating. Featuring: Lucille Ball, Daphne Zuniga, William Converse-Roberts, Stephen Lang, Susan Batson, Anna Maria Horsford, Stefan Schnabel, Josephine Nichols, Peter Phillips, Rebecca Schull, Imogene Bliss, Michael Champagne, Gloria Cromwell, Pat MacNamara, Matthew Locricchio, Edward Seamon, Ray Sera, Gary Singer, Patrick Kilpatrick. Written by Rose Leiman Goldenberg. Cinematography by Walter Lasally. Edited by Andy Blumenthal. Music by Georges Delerue. Produced and directed by George Schaefer. Color. 96 minutes.

Overview

The final starring film role of Lucille Ball's career was a startling choice, a realistic drama about an elderly bag lady and her determination to cope and survive on the streets of New York City. *Stone Pillow* was broadcast on November 5, 1985, receiving good to excellent ratings and is considered one of the finest portrayals ever done of the plight of the homeless. A few reviewers, however, panned the film in a critical backlash, calling Ball a late convert to social concerns.

Synopsis

Carrie Lang (Daphne Zuniga) is an idealistic young social worker who wants to understand the growing phenomenon of homelessness. While visiting the Hargrove Shelter, she meets Florabelle, a feisty, streetwise old woman who agrees to show Carrie the truth about life on the streets. Through an episodic series of events, Carrie learns to see the world through Florabelle's eyes, learning her habits, such as rubbing vinegar on her feet to toughen them up, and her routines. A genuine bond develops between the two women, but when apart, Carrie returns to her apartment, and Florabelle returns to her life on the streets.

Critique

Stone Pillow was filmed entirely on location in Manhattan during the late spring of 1985, and on several occasions Lucille Ball almost passed out due to heat and exhaustion. She was largely unrecognizable in the role, which was an asset while the film was being shot. There is little humor in Ball's performance, which is realistic, honest, and convincing. Filming at the Port Authority Bus Terminal was done largely in the middle of the night, illustrating the difficulty of the shoot. Several homeless people reportedly were used as extras during the shooting, which added to the verisimilitude of the production. The storyline of *Stone Pillow* was almost plotless at times, since the project was largely conceived as a character portrait rather than a drama. There was little chemistry between Daphne Zuniga and Lucille Ball, both on screen and off, but this did not seem to harm the film.

Stone Pillow raised a number of thorny issues, including the rights of the homeless, their freedom of choice, their mental health, the influence of drugs and alcohol, and the question of if and when city authorities should intervene in their care. The only time the police seem to act is to hustle them away from one location, only to have them recongregate in a different spot. For the most part, average people try to ignore them. One of the aims of *Stone Pillow* is simply to encourage people to take notice. In simple but dramatic fashion, *Stone Pillow* shines a spotlight on this harrowing lifestyle.

Storm Center
(1956)

Principal social themes: censorship, education/literacy

Columbia. No MPAA rating. Featuring: Bette Davis, Brian Keith, Paul Kelly, Kim Hunter, Joe Mantell, Kevin Coughlin, Joseph Kearns, Sallie Brophy, Howard Wierum, Curtis Cooksey, Howard Wendell, Kathryn Grant, Edward Platt, Michael Raffetto, Burt Mustin. Written by Daniel Taradash and Elick Moll. Cinematography by Burnett Guffey. Edited by William A. Lyon. Music by George Dunning. Produced by Julian Blaustein. Directed by Daniel Taradash. B&W. 85 minutes.

Overview

Storm Center, intended as an unpretentious protest against censorship and the Red-baiting virus of the early 1950s, itself became the center of a critical storm after the Legion of Decency created a special classification outside their usual rating of a film's moral content to denounce the picture for presenting "a warped, oversimplified" view of American life. Other groups, such as the Motion Picture Industry Council, fired back, calling the Legion's attack "a form of censorship" itself. The controversy provided a profitable publicity boost during the film's initial run, but later caused the film to be broadcast rarely on television. In any case, *Storm Center* was remarkably successful in raising concerns over the issue of censorship.

Synopsis

Mrs. Alicia Hull (Bette Davis), a middle-aged widow, has served as the library director of a small, midwestern community for the past twenty-five years. Despite her school-marmish ways, she is well liked, particularly by the children who frequent the library. One youngster in particular, a boy named Freddie Slater (Kevin Coughlin), adores her and reads with enthusiasm every book she recommends, from the classics to Greek mythology. One day the Town Council summons her to an informal meeting held at a local restaurant. They approve her request to expand the library by building a new wing dedicated to children's books. After the vote, they add a small request. They ask her to remove one title from the library shelves, a controversial book called *The Communist Dream*, which has been the target of a few letters of complaint. Mrs. Hull herself considers the book to be a rather preposterous attempt at propaganda. Reluctantly, the librarian agrees in order to please the council. Later, she considers the principle of freedom of thought and the issue of censorship, and she decides not to discard the book.

When she informs the council, they summon her to a formal meeting. Alicia makes a strong argument that censorship is against American beliefs. After all, the library also circulates *Mein Kampf* by Adolf Hitler, a hateful volume, but when it is read and understood, the ideas in it repel the reader. The same, she believes, is true about *The Communist Dream*. She reminds the council that a similar volume praising Western democracies would not be allowed behind the Iron Curtain, and that is why American values are stronger. Paul Duncan (Brian Keith), one of the council members, questions Mrs. Hull about having belonged to several organizations that were determined to be Communist fronts. She replies that when she learned their true beliefs, she resigned from those groups. Nevertheless, Duncan says she has proven that she can be duped and insists in the future that the Town Council review her book purchases. Mrs. Hull still refuses to discard the book, and after she leaves, the Town Council takes a vote to fire her. She is replaced by her assistant, Martha Lockridge (Kim Hunter), who is also Duncan's fiancée. Moreover, Duncan publishes his beliefs that the library director has been tainted by Communist doctrines. A protest rally is sponsored at the local church, but when Mrs. Hull sees how cantankerous the issue has become, she decides not to fight and asks that nothing be done on her behalf.

Instead of calming the firestorm, Mrs. Hull's withdrawal leads most of the town's citizens into believing Duncan's slander. She becomes ostracized. Worst of all, her young friend, Freddie Slater, turns against her. Slater's uneducated father, who dislikes reading and books in general, tells his son that Mrs. Hull has filled the library with subversive poison for twenty-five years. When Freddie has a series of nightmares, his father blames the library books. The atmosphere in the town has become so poisonous that Mrs. Hull decides to abandon her hometown and move. Finally, the disturbed Freddie sneaks into the library one night and sets fire to the place. In a short time, the building goes up in flames. The whole town watches in shock, and they all, including Martha, turn against Duncan. Mrs. Hull is asked to stay and help rebuild the library. She agrees, promising never to back down on her principles again.

Critique

Despite the criticism that *Storm Center* is a contrived film, the issue of library censorship has been a continuing one, and every year attempts have been made to ban particular books from library stacks. Most of these battles, however, have been fought in public school libraries rather than town libraries as in *Storm Center*, but at times they, too, have become battlegrounds. The second Town Council meeting provided a clear discussion of the topic, both pro and con. Students examining censorship should carefully evaluate these arguments. They should compare Mrs. Hull's points with those of the American Library Association, which promotes events such as "Banned Book" weeks to effectively highlight the issue. Why did so many of the town's citizens turn against the librarian? Why did Freddie's father use the incident to poison his son's mind against reading and education?

This film was the first directorial effort of Daniel Taradash, who was best known as a screenwriter, having won the Academy Award for his script for *From Here to Eternity* (1953). Bette Davis was somewhat criticized for her rather smug and mannered interpretation, but Kevin Coughlin's performance as Freddie received strong praise. (The young Coughlin later met a tragic early death, having been struck by a car.) The scene in which the library is burned has been cited as one of the most powerful sequences of the 1950s, and, oddly enough, many of the titles that are shown in flames are classics that themselves have been targets of censorship at one time or another. In a sense, the scene is a symbolic visual allegory of censorship itself. The climax of *Storm Center* inspired similar scenes in *Fahrenheit 451* (1966), based on a Ray Bradbury novel, in which the firemen from an oppressive future society seek to burn each and every book since they all are considered to be subversive.

Storm Warning
(1950)

Principal social themes: hate groups, racism/civil rights, spouse abuse

Warner Brothers. No MPAA rating. Featuring: Ginger Rogers, Ronald Reagan, Doris Day, Steve Cochran, Hugh Sanders, Lloyd Gough, Raymond Greenleaf, Ned Glass, Walter Baldwin, Lynn Whitney, Stuart Randall, Sean McClory, Gene Evans. Written by Daniel Fuchs and Richard Brooks. Cinematography by Carl Guthrie. Edited by Clarence Kolster. Music by Daniele Amfitheatrof. Produced by Jerry Wald. Directed by Stuart Heisler. B&W. 93 minutes.

Overview

Storm Warning is a powerful film with many unforgettable images, including Ginger Rogers getting bullwhipped, Doris Day getting shot, and Ronald Reagan singlehandedly breaking up a Ku Klux Klan rally. In fact, Warner

Brothers downplayed the film after its release because of its controversial nature, and for some reason, the picture received few television broadcasts, even after the election of Reagan in 1980 when the ban on his films was lifted due to the fair and equal coverage provisions of the election law. This is unfortunate, since *Storm Warning* is one of the most effective social issue films of the early 1950s, even challenging certain aspects of the McCarthy movement.

Synopsis

Marsha Mitchell (Ginger Rogers) is a fashion model on tour in the South with a clothing salesman. When their bus passes through Rock Point late at night, she informs her employer that she plans to get off and visit her sister Lucy (Doris Day), who is recently married. She then plans to rejoin him the following evening on their next stop. When she leaves the bus at 10 P.M., the nervous terminal attendant behaves in a strange manner, anxious to close up. The diner across the street also closes up, and the taxi driver brushes her off after giving her directions to the Valley Cafe and Recreation Center, where her sister works as a night waitress. Marsha decides to walk through the deserted streets. Hearing a commotion, she ducks into a doorway and watches a group of men in white sheets pursuing a man. A shot rings out and the man falls dead. Two of the Klan members remove their hoods, and Marsha sees them clearly, including the man who fired the shot. After they leave, she hastens to the Recreation Center and meets her sister. Lucy tells her sister that she is pregnant, but is stunned into silence when Marsha reports that she has just witnessed a murder.

The police arrive at the crime scene and identify the victim as Walter Adams, a reporter who had been investigating the KKK. Adams was being held in protective custody at the jail when the Klan overpowered the guard on duty, but the reporter broke free and they chased him. The owner gives Lucy the night off, and she brings her sister home to ask her husband, Hank Rice (Steve Cochran), what Marsha should do. Startled, Marsha recognizes Hank as the unmasked KKK man who fired the shot. Hank reluctantly admits to Lucy that he is a member of the Klan, and he went with them reluctantly. They had planned only to frighten Adams, but things got out of hand. Burt Rainey (Ronald Reagan), the county prosecutor, assumes control of the investigation of the murder. He is curious why the bus station and diner closed early. Everyone is afraid to speak with him. He tracks down Marsha, who admits to being a witness but does not reveal that she saw two of the men unmasked. Burt plans to subpoena her as a witness at the coroner's inquest. Hank alerts Charlie Barr (Hugh Sanders), the local Klan leader, that his sister-in-law had witnessed the murder. Barr visits Marsha, and she recognizes him as the other unhooded man. He threatens her not to reveal that she even saw the Klan at the scene of the crime or there will be consequences.

At the inquest, Marsha claims she saw nothing. The jury decides that Adams was killed by assailants unknown. Burt is flabbergasted, and later shoves Marsha in frustration when she leaves the courthouse. The members of the Klan celebrate at the cafe, and Hank gets drunk as he imitates the reading of the verdict over and over again. Barr orders Hank to speed Marsha's departure from Rock Point. Foolishly, Hank tries to kiss Marsha as she packs her bags. Lucy witnesses his attack and announces that she's leaving him. With this development, Marsha says she will tell Burt Rainey everything. Hank kidnaps Marsha and takes her to the Klan rally. Lucy alerts Burt about Marsha's peril. Many of the citizens of Rock Point, decked out in sheets, attend the rally, some even bringing their children. Those without hoods wear an eye mask. Charlie Barr, the grand wizard of the local clan, orders Marsha to be beaten with a bullwhip. Burt Rainey, with Lucy and a handful of men, invade the rally and ridicule their costumes as Halloween nonsense. Burt shames some of them into leaving, and he frees Marsha. Barr identifies the killer as Hank, who grabs a gun and starts shooting. Lucy is struck and collapses dead. The KKK members flee in panic, despite Barr's pleas to stand together. Burt arrests Barr and leads him away. The last remnant of the rally, a burning cross, collapses to the ground in the film's final shot.

Critique

Storm Warning, like numerous other film noir pictures, is filled with significant social implications. The impact of the last scene is riveting, giving the picture a remarkable hard-edge style typical of the genre. Two flaws undercut the main theme, however. First, none of the black victims of the Klan are ever portrayed on screen. In fact, even references to the black citizens of Rock Point are indirect and oblique, such as when Barr proclaims the good the Klan does by keeping elements of the population in line. Second, the fact that Barr and Faulkner, his partner, are embezzlers detracts from the plot, since their victim of their theft is the Ku Klux Klan itself. The audience would approve of the Klan getting bilked by their local leadership. The script never openly indicates in which state Rock Point is located. Following Marsha's itinerary, the last city they visited was Atlanta, so Rock Point is west of Atlanta heading toward the Mississippi River. On the other hand, the portrayal of the working methods of the Klan are well illustrated by the film, particularly how they intimidate nonmembers into following their orders. The Klan rally is chilling, especially when children (in miniature Klan get-ups) populate the crowd. The illustration of how the KKK is able to blend in with and influence society is aptly demonstrated. The relationship of Hank and Lucy is another carefully crafted element of the plot, as the man's true nature is slowly revealed to his wife as he becomes more and more abusive. The production values of *Storm Warning* are excellent. The lead, Marsha Mitchell, was originally to be portrayed by Lauren Bacall, who chose to bow out of the production to accompany Humphrey Bogart, her husband, to Africa where he made *The African Queen* (1951). Ginger Rogers is less suited to the part, but she still was able to make it her own, a woman with tremendous fortitude who refuses to back down after a certain point is crossed. Ronald Reagan gives one of the strongest performances of his career, showing genuine depth in the part. When Burt walks into the KKK rally, he tries to defuse it with folksy charm, a ploy that works very well until Hank loses his cool and starts shooting. Doris Day is also exceptionally strong as Lucy, and her killing, one of the few times a pregnant woman is murdered on camera, is one of the most unforgettable screen deaths of the 1950s.

Richard Brooks, the author of the screenplay, went on to become a major director as well. Many of his films became noted for their approach to social issues, including *Crossfire* (1947) and *Elmer Gantry* (1960) as a writer and *The Blackboard Jungle* (1955) and *In Cold Blood* (1967) as a director.

The Straight Story
(1999)

Principal social theme: aging

Walt Disney Pictures. G rating. Featuring: Richard Farnsworth, Sissy Spacek, Harry Dean Stanton, Jane Galloway Heit, Jennifer Edwards-Hughes, John Farley, Kevin Farley, Anastasia Webb, James Cada, Matt Guidry, Russ Reed, Bill McCallum, Everett McGill, Jack Walsh. Written by John Roach and Mary Sweeney. Cinematography by Freddie Francis. Edited by Mary Sweeney. Music by Angelo Badalamenti. Produced by Mary Sweeney and Neal Edelstein. Directed by David Lynch. Color. 111 minutes.

Overview

The Straight Story is one of the few mainstream efforts by the brilliant, but unconventional director David Lynch. It is based on a true episode in the life of Alvin Straight, an elderly Iowa retiree who traveled three hundred miles on a riding lawn mower to reconcile with his brother, who had suffered a stroke. The film is filled with many small adventures and encounters that illustrate the challenges and dilemmas of aging. Veteran actor Richard Farnsworth, the former stunt double of Roy Rogers, dominates the film in an unforgettable performance. It took an extraordinary effort for Farnsworth to complete the film since he was ill with terminal cancer. He received an Academy Award nomination for Best Actor, the oldest actor to receive a nomination. Farnsworth took his own life a year after completing *The Straight Story*.

Synopsis

Alvin Straight, a cantankerous senior citizen living in Laurens, Iowa, with his daughter Rose, suffers a fall and cannot get up. He visits his doctor, who advises that he change his ways, quit smoking, and start using a walker. Alvin disregards the advice. He receives word that his brother Lyle, with whom he had not spoken in over ten years, has suffered a stroke. With his eyesight too poor to maintain his driver's license, Alvin decides to take to the road and have one last adventure, planning to visit his brother and bury the hatchet. He plans to travel the three hundred mile distance to Mount Zion, Wisconsin, on his riding mower, hitching up a wagon in tow. At first Rose tries to dissuade him, but knowing that her father never changes his mind once it is made up, offers him her support. Setting off, Alvin only manages to travel twenty miles before the mower breaks down, and he has it hauled back to town. He visits Tom, the local tractor dealer, and asks him for a good used riding mower. Tom sells him his own personal rider, and Alvin sets off again.

Alvin's journey is encapsulated in a series of montages and encounters with a great variety of people. A runaway teenager, for example, stops by Alvin's fireside, and he shares his supper of wieners with her. They talk, and Alvin explains why the concept of family is important. He helps convince the girl to return home and ask her family for their help with her pregnancy. Alvin spends another night in a motorcycle camp, and the bikers chat with him about how it feels to be old. After five weeks, Alvin almost has a bad accident in Clermont, Iowa, when the mower overheats traveling downhill, breaking the drive belt. Dan Reardon and his wife, Darla, invite Alvin to bunk in their garage while his machine is being repaired. They even offer to drive him the last lap of his journey to Mount Zion. Alvin is appreciative of the offer, but he explains that this journey is something he has to finish on his own terms. He calls Rose to forward his Social Security check so he can pay for the mower repair. He negotiates the cost from $247.80 down to $180, and then heads off again. He feels a genuine moment of triumph when he reaches and crosses the Mississippi River into Wisconsin. When he sets up his camp outside a graveyard, the local priest brings him supper. He and Alvin discuss the purpose of his trip, to reconcile with his brother. The priest recalls seeing Lyle after his stroke at the local hospital. The next day, Alvin's mower breaks down just outside Lyle's farm, and a neighbor tows him the last mile. Using two canes, Alvin walks up to his brother's porch. He calls out his name, and Lyle appears, coming out of his door using a walker. (Curiously enough, Alvin refused to use a walker when his doctor suggested he should.) They stand and look at each other for a few moments, before his brother asks him to sit.

Lyle stares at the mower, amazed that Alvin drove it the entire distance to visit him. They sit together for a while until the sun sets, casting their gaze up to the night sky full of stars. Before the end credits, a title card appears, saying "In Memory of Alvin Straight (1920–1996)."

Critique

The Straight Story has an unusual sense of verisimilitude since it was shot on the exact Iowa roads that the real Alvin Straight traveled in 1992, when he undertook his unusual quest. Some critics have dubbed Straight the "Don Quixote of America" because of his outlandish scheme. The movie is also an unusual variant of the road film, a popular American subgenre including such varied efforts as *It Happened One Night* (1934), *Easy Rider* (1969), and *Thelma and Louise* (1991). By its very nature, these films are episodic and present different slices of Americana through the people that Alvin encounters. Although some of the people he meets are indifferent or preoccupied (such as the commuter woman whose car just struck a deer), most individuals he comes across are good-natured and try to be helpful. Alvin manages to touch most of them with his quiet dignity and sense of determination in spite of his diminished capacity.

Along the way, we learn additional facts about Alvin and his life. Many of these observations have to do with aging. At one point, Alvin comments that the worst part about getting old is remembering when you were young. We also learn about a calamity in the life of his daughter, Rose, when the state, feeling she could not be a fit mother, took away her baby. When he is laid up for repairs in Clermont, Alvin befriends a local elder, and they share their tragic experiences during World War II. Alvin recounts how he accidentally killed an American scout who was sneaking back across the enemy lines. Alvin later expresses his overwhelming desire to set things right with his brother, Lyle. He states that only a brother can understand exactly who you are. As one approaches the end of life, such empathy is critical for peace of mind. Until he meets the priest in Wisconsin, he does not know if his brother had recovered from his stroke.

Few films have examined aging in such a simple, honest, and unsentimental fashion. The film's observations about aging are bittersweet, tinged with regrets and sorrow as well as an undercurrent of dignified acceptance. The final scene, in which Alvin and Lyle sit side by side looking up at the stars, is truly sublime, one of cinema's golden moments.

The Suicide's Wife
(1979)

Principal social themes: suicide/depression,
homosexuality

Factor/Newland Productions. No MPAA rating. Featuring: Angie Dickinson, Peter Donat, Gordon Pinsent, Zohra Lampert, Todd Lookingland, Don Marshall, Majel Barrett, Walt Davis, Martin Rudy, Luana Anders, Alan Frost. Written by Dennis Nemec based on the novel by David Madden. Cinematography by Michael Marguiles. Edited by Dan Cahn. Music by David Raksin. Produced by Alan Jay Factor. Directed by John Newland. Color. 96 minutes.

Overview

The issue of suicide is examined in a different light in this film, which explores the effects on the individuals left behind, in this case the suicide's wife and son, and how they cope with the upheaval in their lives. This film is almost a mystery, since no note was left explaining the act, and the wife struggles to learn why her husband killed himself. A quiet and reflective picture, *The Suicide's Wife* debuted on the CBS television network on November 7, 1979.

Synopsis

Professor Wayne Harrington (Peter Donat) is a secretive and unassuming college English teacher. For the past nine years, he has been unable to find his niche, transferring from campus to campus in the California University system and unable to gain tenure. His wife, Diana (Angie Dickinson), is largely unaware of his problems as he seldom confides in her. His relationship with his teenage son, Mark (Todd Lookingland), is good, but not really warm or close. When Wayne is summoned by the head of the English department, he emerges from the meeting looking distraught. He does not tell his wife anything about this encounter, instead taking the next day off as a holiday, spending it with Diana and Mark, telling them at times how much he loves them. The next morning, he takes a gun and shoots himself in his study at home, leaving no note. Diana rushes into the room in disbelief. Mark is brought home from his high school by a policeman, who only tells him that he is needed back at home due to a crisis. After Wayne's body is removed from the scene, Diana and Mark are thunderstruck, unable to communicate with each other. Diana is haunted because she never suspected that her husband was troubled or depressed.

Diana is called to the college to remove her husband's effects from his office. She meets Professor Alan Crane (Gordon Pinsent), another member of the English Department who seems genuinely sympathetic. Diana is startled to find a hardcover book, *In Quest of the Pearl Poet* written by her husband. She was aware that Wayne had worked on a manuscript, but never knew it was published. (The "Pearl Poet" was an unknown medieval writer to whom several notable works are attributed, such as *Patience, Pearl*, and possibly *Sir Gawain and the Green Knight*.) Diana takes the book to Alan and asks him to evaluate it. He invites her to dinner, and she accepts. Alan reluctantly describes the book as dry and unsubstantial, largely concerned with technique instead of the thematic heart of the poems. Diana spends the night with Alan, touched by his sympathy and warmth. Mark grows increasingly distant from his mother, disapproving of her relationship with Alan and blaming her for his father's death.

When she discovers that Wayne withdrew most of their savings, $6,000, for some unknown reason, Diana is stunned. It turns out that Wayne ordered 1,500 copies of *In Quest of the Pearl Poet* from a vanity press. Apparently it was part of his plan to gain tenure. She notes that Wayne's book is dedicated to three people, herself, Mark, and a third person, unknown to her, named Anson Keller. She asks Alan to track down this individual. He turns out to be a homosexual student who befriended Wayne. Anson tells Diana that he and Wayne were not lovers, but he did confide in him, telling him all his problems. He reveals the reason for the suicide: The college had fired Wayne. Diana, who wondered if she was in any way responsible for Wayne's act, now understands the truth. Mark, however, still holds his mother to blame for the suicide.

Diana decides to leave California and move to the Midwest to live with her sister. Alan is sorry to see Diana go, and they part on friendly terms. Mark is upset, particularly when Diana sells off his father's possessions. He fakes his own suicide at the beach, and Diana panics when her son is reported missing while swimming in the deep surf. Mark observes his mother's reaction from a safe spot behind the beach. When she sees him, she drags him home and they have a confrontation. Diana explains everything that she learned about Wayne's death, and Mark starts to come to terms with it. He agrees that they both need a fresh start.

Critique

The Suicide's Wife is a carefully crafted examination of the issue of suicide from the point of view of the survivors, particularly the intense feelings of guilt, responsibility and shame. Diana has a series of follow-up shocks, such as when her husband's insurance claim is denied due to a suicide clause.

Except for Alan, Diana finds it difficult to discuss her husband's death since everyone seems artificially sympathetic. She begins to feel that others blame her for the act. Mark also undergoes the cruelty of his schoolmates. The day he returns to class, another student pantomimes shooting himself, which leads to a fight. Unlike his mother, Mark seems to have no outlet for his feelings of anger and rage over the loss of his father, which he secretly interprets as a personal rejection. Other seldom-explored aspects of suicide are also considered in the plot. Did Wayne ever contemplate the effect of his death on his family? Since the medieval poem *Pearl* deals with loss (the death of a daughter), why was Wayne unable to anticipate their pain? What factors made it impossible for him to communicate with them? Both Diana and Mark are walking wounded, victims of psychological trauma, and neither have the traditional family ties that can allow them to heal. Why did they initially fail to comfort each other? How did their friends let them down? The script leaves many open questions that viewers could consider on their own.

John Newland does a superb job in directing *The Suicide's Wife*, never overplaying his hand or sounding a false note. Angie Dickinson and Todd Lookingland both deliver credible performances of far greater depth than what is typically found in a telefilm.

Suspect
(1987)

Principal social themes: homelessness/poverty, disabilities, depressioin/suicide

Tri-Star. R rating. Featuring: Liam Neeson, Cher, Dennis Quaid, John Mahoney, Joe Mantegna, Philip Bosco, E. Katherine Kerr, Fred Melameo, Lisabeth Bartless, Paul D'Amato, Aaron Schwartz. Written by Eric Roth. Cinematography by Billy Williams. Edited by Ray Lovejoy. Music by Michael Kamen. Produced by Daniel A. Sherkow. Directed by Peter Yates. Color. 121 minutes.

Overview

Peter Yates's excellent legal thriller has an unusual backdrop as a homeless deaf and dumb veteran is arrested as a scapegoat in a political murder of a Justice Department secretary. The accused man's background as a homeless man on the streets of Washington, D.C., facing a daily battle for survival, is effectively highlighted in the script.

Synopsis

The film opens a few days before Christmas as Supreme Court Justice Charles Lowell commits suicide after handing an envelope with a cassette tape to Elizabeth Quinn in his private chambers. Shortly afterward, Quinn, a Justice Department secretary, is found murdered in a parking lot along the Potomac River. A vagrant, Karl Anderson (Liam Neeson), who lives in a culvert, is discovered with Quinn's purse; he is arrested for her murder. When he appears in court, the indigent man seems dazed and nonresponsive. The judge orders a psychiatric evaluation and appoints Kathleen Riley (Cher) from the Public Defender's office to serve as his counsel. After trying to interview the disheveled man, Riley is struck by him when she tries to leave the cell. After he is restrained, the lawyer discovers that her client is deaf and dumb. Through writing, Karl tells her that he saw another derelict named Michael near Quinn's body before he came upon it. The Public Defender's office hires a detective in an attempt to find Michael. When the detective tries to question the homeless men hiding in an abandoned building, he is stabbed. This more or less terminates the search for Michael.

Justice Helms (John Mahoney), a candidate for the Supreme Court vacancy, asks to be assigned to try the Anderson case, believing it would be a relatively speedy trial. Riley requests a delay to allow more time to find Michael, but Helms turns down her motion. Eddie Sanger (Dennis Quaid), a congressional lobbyist for the dairy industry, is selected to serve on the jury. He believes that the system is railroading the defendant. For example, he notices that the wounds on Quinn's body indicate her attacker was right-handed. During a court break, the juror telephones Riley to ask if Karl Anderson is left-handed. Later, Riley points out her client's left-handedness in court. In the court parking lot, she confronts Eddie, warning him that contact between them is forbidden since it is considered to be jury tampering. On his own, however, Eddie investigates the crime scene, talking to various derelicts. When he encounters a bag lady who has found a clue, Eddie tries to buy it, but instead she asks him to trade his shoes for it. Later, Eddie mails his various finds to Riley. He then calls her to arrange a clandestine meeting, at which they encounter Michael, who stabs the juror. Riley takes him to her apartment to treat his wound, and they become emotionally involved.

Later, Eddie finds Michael's hideout and discovers that he has been killed. The juror finds a key on the vagrant's body and turns it over to Riley. They conclude the key had belonged to Quinn and track down the file case it unlocks in the dead woman's office, The case is now empty, but it once contained old case files of Justice Lowell. When Judge Helms spots Eddie doing research in the same law library as Riley, he decides to sequester the jury. Riley finds a cassette in Quinn's car that contains a confession from Justice Lowell that he had once accepted a bribe. He planned to commit suicide in atonement, but he had also informed the others involved in the case that Quinn had uncovered the evidence of their crime. The next day in court, Riley accuses Judge Helms as Quinn's murderer, which he did in order to protect his career. A mistrial is declared, and Karl Anderson is set free.

Critique

Suspect provides an excellent study of the plight of the homeless neatly entwined into its story. In her opening statement, his lawyer calls Karl "an American nightmare." She sketches his history as a veteran of the Vietnam War who had a breakdown because of his reservations about killing. He later became deaf from meningitis and lost his ability to speak due to traumatic stress. He divorced his wife since he could no longer support her and retreated to the streets, in which every day is a life-or-death struggle. By the time he was arrested, he had spent years in isolation and became more of an animal than a man. The issue of homelessness is dramatically portrayed in various ways. In another courtroom speech, Riley notes how people train themselves not to see the homeless, to completely disregard and ignore them. It is a poignant but accurate description. In this case, it becomes too easy to use one of the homeless as Quinn's killer, even though no trace of the dead woman could be linked to Karl or his knife. Until the discovery of Justice Lowell's tape, *Suspect* makes a potent illustration of the vicious cycle of homelessness. This focus changes during the last twenty minutes of the movie, as the emphasis switches to exposing the real murderer. Yet the scenes involving the homeless make such a powerful statement that it never seems to be window dressing but instead provides the heart of the film.

Karl's disabilities add another layer of social relevance to the production. Since Karl was totally isolated on the streets, he never learned to communicate by sign language. The system totally failed him as he fell through the cracks and was driven into homelessness due to his disabilities. The question of suicide is also of great importance. Lowell chooses death before dishonor, yet his decision sets up the tragedy to follow after he gives his taped confession to Quinn. By telling Helms of his plans, he unwittingly set up her murder. Viewers might debate the eventual fate of Karl Anderson at the end of the story. He is just as impoverished and handicapped as he was at the start of the film. If Quinn's murder never occurred, he would have likely frozen to death or been killed in a struggle with other derelicts. Ironically, his trial undoubtedly would ensure that he would receive treatment, shelter, and eventually rehabilitation since he is intelligent and has abilities. What he lacked was hope, which he had given up when he surrendered himself to a life on the streets. By the end of the film, he had regained this essential ingredient.

Sybil
(1976)

Principal social themes: child abuse,
suicide/depression

Lorimar. PG rating. Featuring: Sally Field, Joanne Woodward, Brad Davis, Martine Bartlett, Jane Hoffman, Charles Lane, Jessamine Milner, William Prince, Natasha Ryan, Tommy Crebbs, Penelope Allen, Camila Ashlend, Paul Tulley, Elizabeth Anne Beesley, Harold Pruitt. Written by Stewart Stern based on the book by Flora Rheta Schreiber. Cinematography by Mario Tosi. Edited by Michael S. McLean, Rita Roland, and Robert Pickarts. Music by Leonard Rosenman. Produced by Jacqueline Babbin. Directed by Daniel Petrie. Color. 198 minutes, original version; 132 minutes revised version.

Overview

Sybil is a meticulous adaptation of an amazing true-life case of a woman who had sixteen different personalities, the result of traumatic childhood abuse. The film starred Sally Field in the title role, and Joanne Woodward as her psychiatrist. Woodward previously won an Academy Award for portraying a victim of multiple personalities in *The Three Faces of Eve* (1957), another true story. *Sybil* won Emmy Awards for best screenplay, film score, leading actress (Field), and most outstanding special drama. Joanne Woodward and Natasha Ryan (Sybil as a child) were also cited for their outstanding work. Originally shown over two nights on NBC (November 14–15, 1976), the film was revised and edited for overseas theatrical release, syndicated broadcasts, and video release.

Synopsis

Sybil Dorsett is a strange young woman working as a substitute teacher in New York City. She becomes incoherent while having a cut on her arm treated at a hospital emergency room. The psychiatrist on duty, Dr. Cornelia Wilbur, examines her and finds her talking and behaving as if she were a nine-year-old child. She suddenly returns to normal, and when the doctor questions her, she admits to having had blackout spells most of her life. Sybil agrees to continue treatment. She asks her father, Williard Dorsett, for financial assistance when he visits New York with his new wife. Instead, he suggests that Sybil return to live at home.

A crisis develops when a stranger called Vicky telephones Dr. Wilbur in the middle of the night saying that Sybil is in a hotel room in Harlem contemplating suicide. The doctor finds her in a depressed state, again reverted to a childlike persona. Dr. Wilbur realizes that Sybil is suffering from multiple personality syndrome. At her next appointment, Sybil arrives in the character of Vicky, a confident and self-assured thirteen-year-old. Dr. Wilbur encounters other personalities through hypnosis: Vanessa, an accomplished pianist; Peggy, the troubled nine-year-old; Marsha, depressed and suicidal; even an old woman who is a surrogate grandmother. Through treatment, the psychiatrist discovers that Sybil's deceased mother, Hattie, was behind the fragmentation of her personality. When she was growing up in rural Wisconsin, Sybil suffered terrible abuse as a child from her mother, who treated her daughter normally in front of her father and others, but mistreated her continually when they were alone, pushing her downstairs, burning her hand on the stove, and locking her in a storage bin in the barn. Each of Sybil's personalities has different memories of the abuse, except for Sybil herself.

Another crisis develops when Sybil starts dating Richard, a street musician. After cooking Christmas dinner for Richard and Matt, his young son, Sybil starts acting irrationally. Hearing her say the name "Dr. Wilbur," Richard calls the doctor, who warns him about her condition and tells him that she may become suicidal in the persona of Marsha. Richard prevents Sybil from jumping off the roof. When Dr. Wilbur arrives, he overhears Sybil telling her that she is in love with Richard but would prefer not to see him again until she is cured. Shortly afterward, Richard moves away. As Dr. Wilbur makes progress in treating Sybil, she encounters resistance just before she plans to leave for Chicago for a medical lecture. Sybil claims that she is faking, that there are no other personalities. After her Chicago conference, Dr. Wilbur drives to Sybil's hometown in Wisconsin. She searches through her old house and finds purple crayon markings in the storage bin in the barn, confirmation that Sybil's original story under hypnosis was true. The psychiatrist consults with Dr. Quinoness, the local physician, who reveals a series of shocking events from Sybil's medical records. He confesses his shame in having taken no action at the time.

Returning to New York, Dr. Wilbur convinces Sybil to confront her most frightening memories. She recalls how her mother gave her enemas, forcing her to hold the water while her mother played Dvorak's *New World Symphony* on the piano. When the water leaked out, her mother would tie her up and poke at her genital area with knives and hooks. Screaming, Sybil spoke aloud of her rage about the abuse she suffered. By reliving this most painful event, Sybil accepts all of Peggy's memories, and the personalities merge. After this breakthrough, Sybil, with Dr. Wilbur's help, is able to join with all of her other "selves" and become a whole person again.

Critique

Sybil was one of the most compelling examinations of child abuse on film, demonstrating that recovery from such trauma is almost a lifelong process. The picture uncovers numerous issues for study. How could Sybil's mother behave in such a monstrous fashion? She obviously knew her behavior was wrong because she concealed it from her husband and others. Her worse abuse of her daughter was mercurial, performed while she quoted old proverbs and nursery rhymes. Actress Jane Hoffman is brilliant as Frieda Dorsett, the mother, in one of the most terrifying performances of the 1970s. The only individual who could have intervened was Dr. Quinoness, since he had seen the proof of the child's mistreatment. Charles Lane brings considerable depth to his portrayal of Quinoness, haunted by his memory of his inaction. Joanne Woodward as Dr. Wilbur, also shows considerable compassion by not rebuking Dr. Quinoness during this scene, seeing that his torment is genuine. In terms of prevention, this scene is key to the film, especially since Sybil's father, Willard Dorsett, seems to have been blind to the abuse, observing little outside his strict religious platitudes. Still, as a parent, he should not be exonerated for his inattention. It is harder to blame Sybil's grandmother, crippled in a wheelchair, for any responsibility. She was largely confined to the upper floor of the house and played lovingly with Sybil whenever the child visited her room. Yet actress Jessamine Milner portrays the grandmother as having some suspicions. When Hattie trips Sybil on the stairway, she calls out, "What was that?" She does not seem fully satisfied with Hattie's reply that Sybil had another of her clumsy falls. Could Sybil have asked her grandmother for help? It appears that her mother frightened her into silence lest she be punished for lying. Her suicidal impulse, blaming herself for the treatment she receives from her mother, is another crucial aspect of the story. This is only swept away when Dr. Wilbur unleashes the adult Sybil's outrage against her dead mother. One interesting point, in 1998, psychologist Robert Rieber wrote a report casting doubt on Dr. Wilbur's multiple personality analysis, based on a taped discussion between the doctor and the book's author, Flora Schreiber. Since both Wilbur and Schreiber are both deceased, they could not respond to the criticism. Other psychiatrists found Rieber's arguments to be weak. Dr. Leah Dickstein, of the University of Louisville, was in contact with the actual patient "Sybil," who confirmed the book as being entirely factual. In any case, the film remains a powerful one. *Sybil* is above all a testament to the human spirit, that this fragile young girl managed to find a way to survive despite the worst imaginable abuse.

Ten Rillington Place
(1971)

Principal social themes: capital punishment, abortion

Columbia Pictures. PG rating. Featuring: Richard Attenborough, John Hurt, Judy Geeson, Pat Heywood, Andre Morell, Isobel Black, Robert Hardy, Geoffrey Chater, Sam Kydd, Bernard Lee, Gabrielle Daye. Written by Clive Exton based on the book *Ten Rillington Place* by Ludovic Kennedy. Cinematography by Denys Coop. Edited by Ernest Walter. Music by John Dankworth. Produced by Leslie Linder and Martin Ransohoff. Directed by Richard Fleisher. Color. 111 minutes.

Overview

John Christie was one of the most notorious British serial killers, most of his crimes being committed in his lodging at Ten Rillington Place. One of his most audacious feats was his murder in 1949 of Beryl Evans and her baby, framing her illiterate husband Tim Evans for the crime, who was tried and hanged. Years later, after Christie was exposed as the killer, the execution of Tim Evans became one of the primary factors behind the abolishment of the death penalty in Great Britain in 1971, the same year as this film's release. The script is closely based on the most detailed book on the case, written by Ludovic Kennedy, who also served as technical advisor for the production. The original location of the events, Rillington Place, was scheduled for demolition, allowing a unique opportunity for the filmmakers to shoot the movie in the actual building where Christie had killed, buried, and walled up many of his victims. *Ten Rillington Place* is considered one of the most effective true-crime pictures ever made. As a document of how the death penalty can be mistakenly applied to an innocent man, the film itself has come to be regarded as one of the most powerful arguments against capital punishment.

Synopsis

The picture begins with a 1944 sequence during a London blackout. Christie, a local air raid warden, invites a young woman to his flat under the pretense of treating her bronchitis. He induces her to inhale gas through a homemade device, rendering her unconscious, after which he rapes and kills her. The scene sets up Christie's method, how he puts his victims at ease with his calm reassurance. He feigns medical knowledge with an air of complete confidence, and only at the last instance do his victims realize that they have been deceived.

The scene switches to 1949, as Tim Evans, a truck driver of low intelligence, his wife Beryl, and their baby daughter, Geraldine, take up residence on the third floor of Ten Rillington Place. Christie, as caretaker of the building, befriends them. He soon learns that the tenants are very short of money and that they are quarreling since Beryl is pregnant again. Christie tells Beryl that he is knowledgeable about "terminations," and when she asks for his help, he agrees. Before Tim leaves for work on the morning of the planned abortion, Christie obtains Tim's permission, warning him that the procedure can be dangerous. Christie sends his wife out on an errand. He proposes to operate on Beryl on the floor of the kitchen, placing a blanket down for her comfort. She fights back when he tries to administer the gas, and he knocks her out with his fist and kills her. When Tim comes home that evening, Christie tells him that Beryl died due to septic poisoning. He warns Tim not to involve the police, convincing him that it would mean prison for both of them if word of the abortion attempt reached the authorities. He convinces Tim to flee, telling him that he will look after Geraldine and put her up for adoption. Instead, he strangles the child as soon as Tim leaves. Several days later, a confused Tim attempts to report to the police, but his story is incoherent. The police investigate and discover the bodies of Beryl and the baby behind the wall of a water closet just off the back yard. The police accuse Tim of double homicide, and he has a breakdown, signing a confession. During the trial, Tim tells the truth, that Christie had committed the murders, although he can provide no motive. Christie serves as the main witness for the prosecution, and Tim Evans is convicted and sentenced to death. He is hanged at the prison, still proclaiming Christie as the murderer.

Christie's wife suspects that her husband is the real killer. She attempts to leave him, but he kills her and puts her body beneath the floorboards. Christie goes on a killing spree, placing his victims' remains in the walls or burying them in the backyard of Ten Rillington Place. Too impoverished to afford the rent, Christie is forced to abandon the flat, and the new residents, alerted by the foul odor, discover the decomposing bodies. Christie is apprehended by a policeman as he wanders aimlessly along the banks of the Thames. An end scrawl proclaims that Christie was tried and executed, and that Timothy Evans was officially exonerated, and his remains were reburied in hallowed ground.

Critique

Ten Rillington Place adopts a low-key, almost understated tone to this film, giving it a very matter-of-fact and documentary tone. It does not try to manipulate the audience in its approach to the social themes of capital punishment or abortion, allowing the situation itself to address these issues.

The only implied criticism is that the police are shown as only willing to make a minimum effort in this case. They never show the slightest interest in investigating Christie. At one point, a dog unearths a body part in Christie's backyard, which the killer hastily shoves back into the ground as the police search the premises. It is the one moment of black humor in a rather somber and tragic proceeding.

The cast of the production is exceptional. Richard Attenborough as Chrisite speaks in a soft whisper (and we later learn during the Evans trial that Christie suffered from hysterical muteness for three years after World War I). His performance is multilayered as well as one of depth. For instance, when the death sentence against Timothy Evans is read in court, Christie is unexpectedly moved to tears. Ultimately, Attenborough's Christie is a cold, inhuman, confidence man who drifts from killing to killing with no real design or purpose. John Hurt does not portray Tim Evans as a sympathetic character. He is at times cruel, stubborn, and quick to anger, but nevertheless he is not a murderer. Judy Geeson is the most likable character in the film, and she is clearly the predestined victim in the tragic series of events. Pat Heywood, on the other hand, plays Christie's wife as a shadow, an enigma. It is unclear why she remains silent while Tim is on trial, and only later plans to desert her husband, when it is too late. Her killing is the only one of Christie's crimes that seems to have a motive, but the audience feels no sympathy for her because of her silence.

Ten Rillington Place makes an excellent sounding board for students researching the issue of the death penalty. It is a crystal clear example of the misapplication of justice and that the legal system, no matter how fair, will produce mistakes. The film serves as a perfect example of one of the major arguments questioning the moral foundation of capital punishment.

Trial
(1955)

Principal social issues: hate groups, racism/civil rights, immigration

MGM. No MPAA rating. Featuring: Glenn Ford, Dorothy McGuire, Arthur Kennedy, Rafael Campos, Katy Jurado, John Hodiak, Juano Hernandez, Robert Middleton, John Hoyt, Elisha Cook, Paul Guilfoyle, Ann Lee, Richard Gaines, Barry Kelley, Whit Bissell, Percy Helton. Written by Don M. Markiewicz based on his Harper Prize novel. Cinematography by Robert Surties. Edited by Albert Akst. Music by Daniele Amfitheatrof. Produced by Charles Schnee. Directed by Mark Robson. B&W. 105 minutes.

Overview

Trial is an intense and fascinating film dealing with a Mexican teenager in California who is accused of murder on a technicality. His case becomes a cause celebre for various political movements. Arthur Kennedy won an Academy Award for Best Supporting Actor for his role as attorney Barney Castle.

Synopsis

In 1947, law professor David Blake (Glenn Ford) learns his university position is at risk because he never practiced law. His department chairman suggests that he take the summer off to work in a law office as a volunteer to gain actual court experience. David approaches various firms, which dismiss his offer. Attorney Barney Castle is also dubious, but finally decides to use David to defend Angel Chavez (Rafael Campos), a teenage Mexican who trespassed on a restricted beach and was discovered kissing a teenage girl who unexpectedly collapsed and died. She suffered from a heart condition, but since her death might have been caused inadvertently by Chavez, he is charged as being responsible for her death. The southern California town has a history of hostility against Mexican immigrants. DA Armstrong (John Hodiak) offers a plea bargain deal with a two-year sentence, but Barney rejects it, insulting Armstrong. The DA replies that Chavez will then face a first-degree murder charge. David agrees to serve as defense attorney.

A hate group organized by a prominent local citizen (John Hoyt) attempts to lynch Chavez, but David persuades the local jailer, Fatty Sanders (Robert

Middleton), to calm the mob by vowing he will see that the boy is executed legally. Sanders gains time until the National Guard arrives, and he becomes a hero, appearing on the cover of *Look* magazine. Barney's legal secretary, Abbe (Dorothy McGuire), assists David when Barney heads to the East Coast with the Chavez's mother to raise money for the "Angel Chavez Defense Fund." The murder case is to be held in the court of Ted Motley, a stern black judge with a reputation for favoring the prosecution. When David interviews the first group of potential jurors, the detective hired by the defense discovers that the police had already pre-interviewed the entire panel. Saying the jury pool is tainted, David moves that the entire panel be dismissed, and Motley agrees to the motion. This legal victory is touted by the national press. Barney asks him to appear at a rally in New York City that weekend. David goes, reluctantly, and is shocked to learn that the organizations raising money are largely Communist fronts. They cheer him as a hero, but when David tries to speak at the rally, his microphone is cut off and the band drowns him out. Returning to California, David confronts Abbe, who has fallen in love with him, and she admits that Barney is a Communist whose only interest in Chavez is to raise money for his radical friends. David returns Abbe's love, and decides to concentrate on saving Chavez.

David is called to appear before the state legislature's Committee on UnAmerican Activities. He demands a postponement until the Chavez trial is finished. The DA completes his case, which David believes is a weak one. He intends to rest his case, but Barney returns and takes over the defense. He insists that Chavez take the stand. Since Chavez's mother believes in Barney, David has no choice but to call the boy to testify. Under the DA's cross-examination, Chavez makes some incriminating statements. The jury finds Chavez guilty. David plans a special plea to save the boy's life, but Barney dismisses him, wanting Chavez to be a martyr and hopefully foment more racial incidents. Outraged, David appeals to Motley to allow him to speak as a friend of the court. The judge agrees, and David explains how he became the dupe of left-wing hate groups. He knows that the state law will force Motley to apply the death penalty, but he points out a technical loophole that Motley can apply to the case since Chavez is under age. The DA unexpectedly joins David in his request to the judge. Barney, however, defies and insults the judge. Motley uses the loophole and sentences Chavez to an indefinite term at a juvenile center, to be freed on recommendation of the warden. The judge also sentences Barney to a two-month term for contempt of court. David leaves the court with Abbe, believing that justice has been served.

Critique

During the late 1940s and early 1950s, a number of Hollywood films reflected the anti-Communist hysteria, inspired in part by the activities of

Senator Joseph McCarthy and his controversial hearings. McCarthy was eventually censured by the Senate in 1954. Some of these films, such as *Red Menace* (1949) or *I Married a Communist* (1950), were entirely fictional, while others, including *I Was a Communist for the FBI* (1951) and the television series *I Led 3 Lives* (1953–1956) were based on fact. Today, these productions are interesting largely as a study of the era or purely for camp value.

Trial is generally considered apart from these typical Red-baiting films, since it takes a more balanced and realistic approach, criticizing the hate movements of both the left and the right that try to exploit a controversial case for their own purposes. The first hate group to appear is the vigilante force controlled by the local rabble-rouser played by John Hoyt. Ironically, this group is thwarted in their crude lynch mob attempt not by a rational appeal but by fear that their community would suffer economically if their plan succeeded. The Communist hate group, on the other hand, is far more subtle. Their manipulation of events is actually hidden for the first half of the film. The actual agenda of lawyer Barney Castle, brilliantly depicted by Arthur Kennedy, is disguised. Once he detects the powder keg that could be ignited by the Chavez case, he springs into action, acquiring law professor David Blake as the perfect dupe, an idealist who believes Chavez to be innocent. In fact, David is apolitical, an advocate for justice but not for any cause. It is not until he is summoned to the huge rally in New York City that he realizes the Chavez Defense Fund is a front for Communist money-laundering. Glenn Ford is excellent as the naive Blake, particularly when he finds himself as the keynote speaker at a Communist rally. He refuses to read the speech, washing his hands of it and rushing back to California to defend his client. The Communist groups are a myriad of different organizations and causes that are merely covers for a massive money-making scheme to fund the party organization. Later, David refuses to testify before the California House Committee on UnAmerican Activities, believing that they are also seeking to exploit him. Elisha Cook, who serves as the process server for the committee, admits as much to the lawyer, implying the politicians are only interested in political theater, not in exposing the truth about Communist infiltration. Unless David intends to plead the Fifth Amendment or offer himself as a victim for the chairman's accusations, the committee would have no interest in his appearance. Both the Communist radicals and the Red-baiters are depicted as abhorrent phonies with hidden, self-serving agendas. They both use the emotion of hate to achieve their goals. If the Communists seem worse, it is only because they are somewhat more ruthless, willing to sacrifice Chavez to further their cause. The script carefully shows how the boy's mother is duped by the Communists until she hears David's final plea before the judge. DA Armstrong, well-played by John Hodiak, has his own moment of self-awareness of his part in the tragedy of the Chavez case. When he asks the judge to mitigate the sentence, he successfully undercuts both the left-wing and right-wing exploiters of the case. In addition, *Trial* clearly demonstrates how hate groups can manipulate the social ills of the community, racism and the hostility toward the Mexican immigrant workers. In some ways, this theme is one of the central messages of the film. The plot also highlights the unequal application of the law. If a white youth were in the same situation as Chavez, it is unlikely he would ever have been charged. As David pointed out, it had never been proved that the girl's collapse was caused by Chavez's embrace instead of the strain of climbing the stairway. David certainly should have placed a rebuttal witness on the stand to discuss the nature of the girl's heart defect. His most serious error, however, was not to ask for a change in venue after the first jury pool had been tainted. In another jurisdiction, away from the racism of the local court, Chavez would not have been convicted.

As a case study, *Trial* offers unusual areas for discussion, including the hard-nosed black judge who seems to favor the prosecution from the bench. It also cleverly exposes the sometimes hidden agendas of hate groups.

Ultimate Betrayal
(1993)

Principal social theme: child abuse/spouse abuse

Hearst Entertainment. PG-13 rating. Featuring: Marlo Thomas, Mel Harris, Eileen Heckert, Ally Sheedy, Kathryn Dowling, Henry Czerny, Donna Goodhand, David B. Nichols, Joanne Vannicola, Justin Louis, Chandra Muszak, Kim Schraner, Brett Pearson, Valerie Buhagiar, Nigel Bennett, John David Wood. Written by Gregory Goodell. Cinematography by Dick Bush. Edited by Sharyn L. Ross. Music by Chris Boardman. Produced by Julian Marks. Directed by Donald Wrye. Color. 94 minutes.

Overview

Ultimate Betrayal is generally regarded as one of the best depictions of the cycle of abuse, seen from the viewpoint of four adult sisters who were not only beaten as children but suffered sexual molestation by their father. This film attempts to deal with this highly inflammatory material in a sober, non-sensational manner. Groups of survivors of abuse have utilized screenings of *Ultimate Betrayal* in their counseling sessions. *Ultimate Betrayal* was originally broadcast on the Lifetime Cable Network.

Synopsis

All four of the grown Rodgers children are experiencing continual psycho-logical problems. Sharon (Marlo Thomas) has become cold and unloving toward her family and is unable to sleep except in the closet or in a parked car. The others frequently strike their own children, and Mary (Ally Sheedy) plans to sue her father to help pay for her therapy bills that exceed $400 a month. Mary's potential suit upset the other sisters, who start to recall more and more of the abuse they suffered as children. Consulting lawyer Dana Quinn, they learn of new rules regarding "delayed discovery" that would permit lawsuits of events occurring over thirty years earlier. Due to pressure from her husband, Mary decides not to proceed, but two other sisters, Sharon and Susan (Mel Harris) decide to file suit. Beth (Kathryn Dowling) decides not to join the suit, but to testify for her sisters at the trial. Their father, Ed Rodgers, a retired FBI agent, comes to the deposition and denies all charges. When the trial begins, however, the father chooses not to appear, and neither does his attorney. The judge allows the trial to continue. The two Rodgers brothers, Steve and John, later appear in court and ask to be permitted to defend their father. The judge denies their request, and the trial proceeds.

All four of the sisters take the stand and provide testimony about the abuse they each suffered. Their depositions are emotionally charged, yet restrained. These incidents are depicted in flashbacks. For example, whenever their father mowed the lawn, he would put Sharon in charge of a stick patrol to gather every fragment of wood. Inevitably Ed would find a twig, leading to a thrashing for one or more of the children. Their mother was also a victim of abuse, but she would do nothing to protect them. However, once in a while, the mother also was an abuser. When teenage Susan became pregnant, Ed was surprisingly considerate and supportive, but her mother turned against her vehemently. Ed's sympathy for his daughter vanished, and Susan was sent away to have her baby; her parents had no contact at all with her during this difficult time. The four daughters felt relieved and strengthened by telling their experiences, bur they are also frustrated that Ed was not present to hear and acknowledge their suffering. Nevertheless, they now feel that they can get on with their lives. At the conclusion of the trial, the court awards Sharon and Susan a judgment for 2.3 million dollars, over twice the amount they requested. However, the sisters were unable to collect since Ed, along with his assets, had completely disappeared. Due to publicity from the case, the "Child Abuse Accountability Act" was introduced in Congress that would address other cases similar to this one.

Critique

Based on a true case, *Ultimate Betrayal* is an emotionally draining and riv-eting viewing experience. The production is multilayered, considering the question of abuse from various angles. The problem is clearly portrayed as a vicious circle, the father's abuse spreading out to his wife, children, and eventually grandchildren. Ed Rodgers is depicted as somewhat of an enigma. The origin of his behavior is not explored (except for Sharon's observation that he was unloved by everyone), only the tragic results. He never acknowledges the abuse, either consciously or unconsciously, and this is all the more puzzling because he had been considered an expert on child abuse in his law enforcement work. He was also an advocate who spoke in support of the rights of abused children. Yet at the same time, he instigated the worst possible abuse within his own family. As for his sexual molestations, the script suggests that it was triggered when his wife ended their sexual relationship and he moved to a basement bedroom. In the film, Ed is seen only in the flashback memories of his children, except for at the deposition, where he appears elderly, tired, and apparently perplexed by the charges leveled against him. He then disappears, and it is surprising that he manages this deception so completely, given his notoriety. One would imagine that any good detective would be able to track him down. The mother is another enigma. She divorces Ed after the children are grown, but never interfered or threatened to do so while her children were being beaten and molested. When questioned before the trial, the mother tells her children that she did indeed helped them through her prayers, a rather feeble rationalization.

The abuse pattern of the children is covered as well, including their sudden irrational anger and their instinctive resort to violence. The script of *Ultimate Betrayal* wisely avoids the side issue of repressed memory syndrome. The memories of the Rodgers sisters are portrayed as actual memories, not artificially derived from hypnosis. The accuracy of memories stimulated by this method has been scientifically questioned, and in some cases these memories have been proven false. Most of the experiences discussed in the court case were shared by two or more of the sisters.

The hostility of Steve and John, the Rodgers brothers, is another tragic element of the plot. According to the sisters, the brothers suffered the worst of the beatings. David and John admit they were hit, but claim it was not excessive. On the other hand, they deny their sisters were ever molested. Since they never witnessed it, they would rather regard their sisters as liars than accept that their father was perverted. Their stance can stimulate additional discussion from viewers. The story does not suggest that the children of Steve and John are abused. This suggests that the main trauma suffered by the sisters was due to the molestation rather than the physical abuse. It is also instructive to compare the pattern of abuse in *Sybil* to that in *Ultimate Betrayal*. The mother in *Sybil* provided psychological torment in addition to physical punishment. In *Ultimate Betrayal*, the father created an atmosphere of fear without any mind games. Sharon felt she could hold off her father's wrath by doting on him, being his favorite, and to some extent this worked, as she was the least abused of the Rodgers offspring, never having been struck after the age of two. Finally, should the father's disappearance be regarded as an admission of guilt? Is there any chance he was mentally ill and unaware of the extent of his monstrous behavior?

The Unfaithful
(1947)

Principal social theme: divorce

Warner Brother. No MPAA rating. Featuring: Ann Sheridan, Lew Ayers, Zachary Scott, Eve Arden, Steven Geray, John Hoyt, Jerome Cowan, Peggy Knudsen, Douglas Kennedy, Jane Harker, Marta Mitrovich, Claire Meade. Written by David Goodis and James Gunn. Cinematography by Ernest Haller. Edited by Alan Crosland Jr. Music by Max Steiner. Produced by Jerry Wald. Directed by Vincent Sherman. B&W. 109 minutes.

Overview

While some sources call *The Unfaithful* a remake of the 1940 Bette Davis film *The Letter*, it is more properly a complete revision of the earlier Somerset Maugham story, redressed to highlight the issue of divorce and the psychological trauma experienced by wives during the years their husbands were in the armed forces. *The Unfaithful* is one of those rare dramas in which characters and their motivations carry more impact than the plotline.

Synopsis

The plot of *The Unfaithful* is somewhat complex, and this synopsis will simplify it. The story opens in 1947 as Los Angeles housewife Christine Hunter (Ann Sheridan) receives a phone call from her husband, Bob (Zachary Scott), telling her that he will be returning from his business trip the following morning, and she proposes to meet him at the airport. She reminds him that his cousin Paula (Eve Arden) is throwing a party that evening, and she will reluctantly attend. Paula is celebrating because she just obtained a divorce. When her former husband (and Chris's cousin) Roger shows up to disrupt the party, Chris tries to calm him down. Bob's best friend, divorce attorney Larry Hannaford (Lew Ayers) is guest of honor at the party, but he decides to drive the inebriated Roger home as a good deed. When Chris gets home, a man hiding near the front door barrels his way into the house with her. The camera remains outside, as it appears that a struggle breaks out and Chris screams.

The next day, Bob is puzzled when Chris does not meet him at the airport. He calls home and is startled when the police answer the phone and tell him there has been an accident. Grabbing a cab, Bob arrive home to find the place overun with cops and a dead body lying in the living room. A servant explains that early in the morning she heard a scream, came downstairs, and found Mrs. Hunter standing over the dead man. Bob rushes upstairs to find Chris with Larry and a doctor. She tells them and the police that an intruder assaulted her after asking for her jewelry. They struggled in the dark, and Chris stabbed him with a Japanese knife, a war souvenir that Bob kept in the living room. Lieutenant Reynolds (John Hoyt) asks her to come to the police station that afternoon to sign a statement. When they arrive at Reynolds' office, however, they are confronted by the wife of the dead man, who was a relatively unknown sculptor named Michael Tanner. The grieving woman accuses Chris of murder. Chris insists the man was a stranger to her. At his office, Larry receives an unusual phone call from Martin Barrow (Steven Geray), an art dealer, who asks for an outrageous sum to sell him a sculpture by Tanner, claiming it is a bust of Christine Hunter. Considering it blackmail, Larry rejects the offer. He later questions Chris in private, who breaks down and admits she knew Tanner and that they had a brief affair years earlier while her husband was overseas in the armed forces. Larry implores her to tell this fact to her husband and the police. Chris asks Larry to remain silent, saying she will tell Bob at a time of her choosing. Meanwhile, Chris and Larry expect the blackmailer to contact them again. Instead, Barrow has brought the statue to Tanner's wife. She wants to turn it over to the police. Barrow objects and suggests they instead approach Chris' husband. Barrow calls Bob and brings him to Tanner's apartment to see the statue. He is thunderstruck and too numb to respond to their blackmail. When the police see Bob leaving Tanner's apartment, they investigate, arresting Barrow and Mrs. Tanner for blackmail. Bob arrives home and confronts his wife about the statue. She tells him everything, admitting her past relationship with Tanner. She claims it ended years earlier, that she never expected Tanner's visit nor his assault. Larry arrives and tries to intervene, but Chris had fallen into despair, and Bob is in shock from this discovery. Bob tells them that he plans to buy the statue and then divorce Chris. The police arrive, however, and arrest Chris for murder.

The trial is a public sensation. The district attorney tries to convince the jury that Chris planned the crime. On the stand, Chris tells the truth, admits the affair, but claims that Tanner assaulted her that evening, and she killed him in self-defense. The physical evidence supports her story, and Larry's closing statement to the jury is decisive. Bob attends the trial and is moved by Chris' testimony. While waiting for the verdict, he visits his cousin Paula, who dislikes Chris. Paula, however, makes a strong argument in favor of Chris and her reasons for not admitting the brief affair. The jury acquits Chris of murder, and she plans to move away after the trial. Larry speaks to them, making an ardent plea to reconsider their divorce plans. Bob relents and asks Chris to stay, at least long enough to talk over the idea of reconciliation. She agrees, and the film ends as Larry leaves them, saying this is one occasion in which he hopes to forgo a fee in a divorce case.

Critique

Although *The Unfaithful* covers many different topics, it is the issue of divorce that is the central theme. In fact, the opening narration presents divorce as one of the central concerns of modern times. The earlier film, *The Letter* (1940) was quite different. Taking place on a plantation in the tropics, Leslie Crosbie (Bette Davis) deliberately kills her lover in a jealous rage, then stages the crime to look like an act of self-defense. She does not love her husband and merely uses the lawyer to further her own schemes. On the other hand, Ann Sheridan's Chris loves her husband, tells the truth about being attacked, and does not try to manipulate her lawyer whom she treats as her friend. The interesting thing about *The Unfaithful* is the level of tension it maintains around Chris's efforts to save her marriage. The script of *The Unfaithful* (cowritten by film noir icon David Goodis) has little action and is very talkative, yet the speeches are invariably compelling and potent. When Chris describes how her affair occurred, it presents a poignant picture of the loneliness and isolation felt by innumerable wives on the homefront during the war years. Chris only knew Bob two weeks before their marriage, and he was sent overseas soon thereafter. She had not received a letter from him in months and fell prey to the, at first, innocuous advances of Michael Tanner, who asked her to pose for him. After succumbing to his advances, she received six letters from her husband that were delayed, and she broke off with Tanner. He would not accept it easily, however, and kept turning up to see if Chris had changed her mind.

Zachary Scott, who usually plays a screen rogue, was an unusual choice to play the aggrieved husband, a part that could easily descend into bathos. Scott, however, walks a delicate line, managing his emotions closely but convincingly. His lines about the hurt and pain in discovering the unfaithfulness of his wife is another of the film's highlights. Lew Ayers also plays his part well, but he never drops his professional manner in dealing with Bob or Chris. His eloquent speech about the nature of marriage and divorce, although delivered over fifty years ago, still seems relevant. Likewise, Eve Arden, as the catty Paula, puts aside her flippant attitude to level with Bob about his shallowness and the hypocrisy of the "male ego" in denying the depth of his wife's love. Almost unspoken, the relationship of Michael Tanner and his wife is also worth examining. Mrs. Tanner never knew the extent of her husband's unfaithfulness, and her rage takes the form of an irrational hatred of Chris. Played by Marta Mitrovich, Mrs. Tanner makes an unusual counterbalance to the hurt and pain experienced by Bob. The exceptional character actor Steven Geray is unforgettable as the slimy blackmailer, Barrow, who has the exceptional talent of always making wrong choices. The dark and moody photography and the exceptional music score by Max Steiner add considerably to the film's effectiveness. In terms of the social issue of divorce, *The Unfaithful* is remarkably perceptive without becoming preachy or pompous, a rare achievement.

*The Unspoken Truth (**AKA** Living the Lie)*
(1995)

Principal social themes: women's rights, suicide/depression, child abuse/spouse abuse

Frankovich Productions. PG rating. Featuring: Lea Thompson, Patricia Kalember, James Marshall, Robert Englund, Dick O'Neill, Sharon Shawnessey, Karis Paige Bryant, Mona Lee Fultz, Gary Carter, Norman Bennett, Jeanne Evans, Gail Cronauer, Guich Koock. Written by J. A. Mitty. Cinematography by Neil Roach. Edited by Martin Nicholson. Music by Mark Snow. Produced by Norman I. Cohen and Donna Ebbs. Directed by Peter Werner. Color. 95 minutes.

Overview

An extraordinary complex story, this telefilm gained such acclaim that it received theatrical distribution after its debut on television, a unique accomplishment. The story focuses on two families so dominated by the father that in one, a daughter abandons her role as mother to her own daughter, and in the other, a wife takes the blame for a murder committed by her husband. The essence of the story is how these two women regain their rights, both legally and emotionally, and regain control of their lives. *The Unspoken Truth* originally premiered on the Lifetime Cable Network.

Synopsis

The storyline of *The Unspoken Truth* is rather intricate and told in a sophisticated manner with numerous flashbacks and unexpected revelations. This abbreviated synopsis presents the story in a straightforward, chronological fashion. Thomas Cleary (Dick O'Neill), "Da," is the authoritative head of his family living in Texas. When his daughter, Margaret (Patricia Kalember), becomes pregnant, he sends her to Ireland to give birth. Instead of placing her daughter Brianne up for adoption, Margaret brings the child back to America. Da agrees to raise the child only if he and his wife are listed as the parents, and Margaret agrees to pose as Brianne's sister. When Da's wife dies, he marries again. Margaret marries Ernest Trainer (Robert Englund), a kind and supportive husband. Brianne (Lea Thompson) grows up and marries Clay Hawkins (James Marshall), a domineering hellraiser. They have a daughter, Lily. Clay never provides a good home for them, and Brianne works to make ends meet.

Years pass, and Clay gets into a barroom brawl. He goes home and returns to the bar with two loaded guns in his truck. Brianne tries to calm him down. Dale Modell, the man who fought with Clay, comes over to the truck and continues the argument. He tries to grab Clay's gun and is shot dead in the struggle. Clay is arrested, and he convinces Brianne to say that it was she who killed Dale Modell. At the trial, both Brianne and Clay are convicted of murder and sentenced to life imprisonment. Da has a heart attack and dies. Lily is placed in the custody of Clay's mother, an unpleasant and harsh woman. Brianne appeals for a new trial, but is turned down by a stern female judge. Clay continues to control Brianne even though they are both imprisoned. Lily is miserably unhappy living with Clay's mother. Margaret breaks her promise to Da and announces that she is Brianne's mother. Since the maternal grandmother is given preference over the paternal grandmother in custody cases, Margaret then claims the right to raise Lily. With her daughter's happiness at stake, Brianne defies Clay and support's Margaret's claim. Margaret manages to snatch Lily, and the court grants her custody. Lily swears an affidavit that Clay beat both her and her mother. Brianne is granted a new trial because she was a victim of battered woman's syndrome, which explains her perjury. Brianne is eventually cleared of the murder, divorces Clay, and reunites with her mother and daughter.

Critique

The script of *The Unspoken Truth* is a tangle of numerous social concerns, but the central issue appears to be women's rights, both in legal terms and strictly human terms, revolving around Margaret Cleary Trainer and her daughter Brianne Cleary Hawkins. Margaret is first bullied by her father to abandon her identity as a mother and live a lie, posing as her daughter's sister. She only asserts her legal rights when her granddaughter is mistreated. Brianne in many ways had been manipulated and repressed since birth. It is not surprising that her choice of a husband was a control freak like her grandfather, but she was not prepared for the physical abuse that backed up her husband's authority. Brianne would have opposed Clay, however, if she had known that her daughter was experiencing similar abuse. Clay's method of domination even when they are both imprisoned is insidious, using their daughter as a pawn. The script also provides a case study of battered woman's syndrome, demonstrating how Clay forced his wife to confess to his own criminal act. Viewers might find it interesting to compare the two judges who oversee Brianne's case. Other individuals worth comparing are Da and Clay, Clay and his mother, and the prosecuting and defense attorneys. What do their attitudes demonstrate about the issues of abuse and women's rights?

Among the many flawed and troubled characters in *The Unspoken Truth*, two stand out for close study: Ernest Trainer and Lily Hawkins. Ernest is a powerful and positive role model as Margaret's husband, a gentle man who is a pillar of support for his wife and granddaughter. Brilliantly played by Robert Englund, the actor best remembered for his role as the monstrous Freddie Kruger in the *Nightmare on Elm Street* series, this performance manages to portray sincere and undemanding love. Karis Paige Bryant is exceptional as Lily, a remarkably poised and intelligent young girl who manages to get to the heart of the matter with her observations. Her testimony when she is questioned by the lawyers seems refreshing among all the deceptions and fabrications in the story. That Clay's daughter should demonstrate such integrity and compassion is ultimately a tribute to her upbringing by Brianne.

Walking on Water
(2002)

Principal social themes: end-of-life issues, AIDS, homosexuality

Fortissimo. R rating. Featuring: Vince Colosimo, Maria Theodorakis, Nathaniel Dean, Judi Farr, Nicholas Bishop, David Bonney, Daniel Roberts, Anna Lisa Phillips, Timothy Jones. Written by Roger Monk. Cinematography by Robert Humphreys. Edited by Reva Childs. Music by Antony Parlos. Produced by Liz Watts. Directed by Tony Ayers. Color. 90 minutes.

Overview

Walking on Water is an independent Australian film about a person with AIDS who asks his friends to euthanize him when his health begins to fail, rather than be transferred to a hospital to die. The film focuses on the repercussions of this decision on these individuals after his death.

Synopsis

As the film opens, interior decorator Gavin Siddons (David Bonney) collapses in his house. He is helped into bed by his lover Charlie (Vince Colosimo) and his business partner Anna (Maria Theodorakis), who both live with him. Gavin tells them that the time has come to carry out their arrangement. They had agreed to help Gavin die with dignity in his own bed at the time of his own choosing, not in any institution. Anna notifies Margaret (Judi Farr), Gavin's mother, and Simon (Nathaniel Dean), his brother, who fly to Sydney later that day. Simon's wife and daughter also come. Anna and Charlie explain Gavin's last desire, to die with dignity. Other friends arrive and everyone gathers at his bedside as he takes his leave of them. Charlie prepares an injection of morphine and other drugs. Gavin's breathing becomes labored, but he does not die. He is given a second shot, and he finally appears to expire. People begin to leave. A few minutes later, however, Gavin revives. Desperate, Charlie places a plastic bag over Gavin's head until his breathing permanently stops. Badly shaken, Charlie leaves the room, and Anna calls the funeral home. Two female attendants show up and place the body in a plastic bag. They have difficulty carrying the body down to their van, and Charlie offers to assist.

After the vehicle leaves, everyone sits around, some in silence, some crying, and others watching television. Gavin had given Anna instructions about the arrangements for the funeral, and Margaret feels a little irritated by her take-charge attitude. She tells her to check Gavin's will before she starts giving away all his things. At the funeral, Anna takes charge again, tearing apart the floral bouquet on the casket because Gavin had insisted that there be no baby's breath in the arrangement. After the service, Margaret flies back home with her daughter-in-law and granddaughter, but Simon stays to help settle affairs. When Charlie goes for a walk, he returns to find Simon and Anna making passionate love. In private, he berates Anna, saying that Simon is married. She replies that he could not understand, that Simon is so similar to his brother except that he is not a homosexual.

Charlie, Anna, Simon, and two friends go to the ocean, walk down a breakwater (inspiring the title *Walking on Water*), and bring Gavin's ashes to the ocean. They speak their own brief remembrances and smear some of the ashes on their faces. They accidentally drop the entire container into the ocean, then bring it home and dry it in the microwave. Gavin's will leaves his house equally to Charlie and Anna, who have become enemies. Simon returns home to his wife and child. Arguments flare up between Charlie and Anna. She asks to buy out his share of the house, finally condemning him for the spectacle of Gavin's demise, particularly the smothering with a plastic bag. Charlie is thunderstruck, and returns to the ocean, thinking about throwing himself in. Anna seeks him out and apologizes. They both recall that their dying friend asked them to watch out for one another. They finally agree to sell Gavin's home.

Critique

Walking on Water is a rather different film, completely poker-faced in execution, yet with elements of black comedy. The primary focus of the film is the psychological burden of Gavin's euthanasia request. His lengthy death scene is almost excruciating, as every person in the room breathes in synchronization with the dying man. Charlie simply cracks when Gavin apparently revives. The guilt weighs on all of them, yet the film sidesteps how the death certificate was arranged so they were not accused of murder. Each of Gavin's friends and lovers is haunted by his killing, some sinking into depression or drugs (like Charlie), while Anna acts out her fantasies about Gavin, using his brother as a prop. Simon's motivations are more obscure, but apparently he saw the lovemaking as a ritual in his brother's memory. The script is filled with pained vignettes from each of the characters, even Margaret who steals objects from her son's house that she was too proud to accept as gifts from Anna. The hostility and rivalry between the various characters is intense. Gavin's ritual of the ashes at the beach bears a similarity to the funeral of Donny in *The Big Lebowski* (1998), when John Goodman tosses his ashes into the wind and they blow back, coating his face and body. At one point, Charlie places the container with Gavin's ashes on his friend's car, and he has to snatch it back as the car pulls away. None of these events seems the slightest bit absurd or amusing to the characters themselves, even as most of their actions have unintended consequences. Even the reconciliation at the end between Anna and Charlie seems illusionary, as they are really just leaving to go their separate ways. They can no longer stand to be near each other since each of them reminds the other of Gavin and their sense of guilt.

The War of the Roses
(1989)

Principal social themes: divorce, spouse abuse

Twentieth Century Fox. R rating. Featuring: Michael Douglas, Kathleen Turner, Danny DeVito, Marianne Sägebrecht, Sean Austin, Heather Fairfield, Peter Donat, J. D. Spradlin, Dan Castellaneta, Gloria Cromwell, Danitra Vance, Harland Arnold, Shirley Mitchell. Written by Michael Leeson based on the novel by Warren Adler. Cinematography by Stephen H. Burum. Edited by Lynzee Klingman. Music by David Newman. Produced by James L. Brooks and Arnon Michan. Directed by Danny DeVito. Color. 116 minutes.

Overview

The War of the Roses is a seething black comedy that can be viewed as either a satiric allegory about divorce and materialism or a darker psychological study of the elusive nature of love and the basic incompatibility of the sexes. This film may require several viewings to unearth subtle details, and do not be surprised if your viewpoint shifts with additional viewings.

Synopsis

The film opens as divorce lawyer Gavin D'Amato (Danny DeVito) explains to his new client how some divorce cases can spiral completely out of control. As an example, he tells him the story of another member of his law firm, Oliver Rose (Michael Douglas) and his wife Barbara (Kathleen Turner). They met years earlier at an auction in Nantucket Island, rivals in a bid for a seventeenth-century Japanese carving of a Shinto goddess. Barbara won the auction, and Oliver struck up a conversation with her. She was a gymnast and he a law student. They get married after a whirlwind affair, have twins, and settle down together. After several years, Oliver's career begins to take off. Barbara locates an elegant house that they bought and soon filled up with their collection of china and figurines. Eventually, Oliver begins to take Barbara for granted, and she feels neglected in the marriage. Barbara finally starts her own business as a caterer. By the time their children leave for college, their marriage is an empty shell.

A crisis comes when Oliver is rushed to the hospital from a business lunch. He believed he was dying from a heart attack, and he scrawled off a passionate letter saying farewell to his wife. It turns out he was only suffering from a hernia, but Oliver was hurt that Barbara did not come to the hospital when she was told he was ill. When he gets home, they have a confrontation. Barbara explains that when she thought that Oliver might be dying, she began to feel unexpectedly happy. Oliver is stunned, and a fight develops when Barbara continues with the confession that the only emotion she has for her husband is a desire to punch his face. She does so, and asks for a divorce. Gavin represents Oliver in the case. As a settlement, Barbara demands that she be ceded the house and all its contents lock, stock, and barrel. Outraged, Oliver vows that he will never yield to her. Gavin proposes to Oliver that he remain in the house until the divorce is settled, using an obscure point of law as precedent. Oliver and Barbara work out a complicated scheme of dividing the house into her zone, his zone, and shared zone. While their children are home from college, the system barely works, but when they leave in the fall, the arrangement falls apart. When their housekeeper needs some medicine one night, Oliver accidentally runs over Barbara's cat with his car. He does not tell Barbara, and when she finds out, she locks Oliver in the steam room, almost killing him. Oliver gets his revenge by ruining Barbara's reception with her clients, ruining her prepared meal and causing a scene. Barbara retaliates by destroying Oliver's sports car. Barbara invites Oliver to a peace conference, at which she serves him paté. Oliver proposes a reconciliation, while Barbara begs her husband to simply leave the house. When he refuses, she tells him the paté was made from his dog. (It was not.) A battle royal develops in which most of their priceless collection of china is smashed. Oliver offers to cede everything to Barbara if she will give him the Japanese carving she won at the auction where they met. Barbara refuses. Performing an acrobatic move, Barbara unexpectedly winds up on their chandelier. Oliver tries to rescue her, but ends up stranded with her. Gavin arrives and tries to save them by getting a ladder. He is too late, however. The chandelier crashes to the floor, killing them. With his dying gesture, Oliver reaches out to Barbara, but with her last effort she pushes his hand away. As Gavin concludes his lengthy story for his client, he is pleased that the man takes his advice and decides to try for a reconciliation.

Critique

In analyzing *The War of the Roses*, the flaws of both the husband and wife are both obvious and human. Boiled down to the essence, Barbara simply has no love left for Oliver, and he cannot accept that. The divorce is her solution, and he wants to oppose it. The point of the story, according to Gavin at the end of the film, is that there may not be such a thing as a civilized divorce unless both parties want out. As a satire, *The War of the Roses* exaggerates the situation, yet the points of contention can be seen as genuine. Oliver believes he loves Barbara, but he gives her little in terms of human warmth and affection. He does not cheat on her, but on the other hand he does not show her any respect. As long as the children were growing up, the marriage stayed intact. When they left the nest, Barbara came to realize how entirely empty her life had become. On the other hand, Oliver did nothing of consequence to earn his wife's wrath. In terms of physical abuse, Barbara, the trained gymnast, is the aggressor. In fact, his hernia was the result of a body scissors applied by Barbara. There are numerous other clues that indicate which spouse may be at fault in the breakup of the marriage. Oliver sees it somewhat as a game and never appreciates the depth of his wife's anger or the fact that she really does not love him. For Barbara, it is a life or death struggle, and if it takes Oliver's death to end the marriage, that is the price she is willing to pay. Gavin sees the hopelessness of Oliver's position, but when he tells him he cannot win ("It is only a matter of how badly you lose"), Oliver fires him.

As an allegory, the film is excellent even when it seems to go over the line. In fact, it is no more absurd than the reality of many divorce scenarios. If anything, the divorce lawyer, Gavin, becomes an advocate of reason in matters of divorce. In the framework story, he would rather lose a client than generate a divorce, unless it is the last resort. *The War of the Roses* also manages to capture the emotional trauma of divorce, which can strip both parties of their humanity, leaving only rage and despair.

West Side Story
(1961)

Principal social themes: violence/gangs, immigration

United Artists. No MPAA rating. Featuring: Natalie Wood, Richard Beymer, Russ Tamblyn, Rita Moreno, George Chakiris, Simon Oakland, Ned Glass, William Bramley, Tucker Smith, David Winters, Tony Mordente, Jose de Vega, John Astin. Written by Ernest Lehman based on the musical play by Arthur Laurents, Jerome Robbins, Stephen Sondheim, and Leonard Bernstein. Cinematography by Daniel Fapp. Edited by Thomas Stanford. Music by Leonard Bernstein. Produced by Saul Chaplin and Robert Wise. Directed by Robert Wise and Jerome Robbins. Color. 151 minutes.

Overview

West Side Story, one of the most remarkable and successful musicals in cinema history, is basically a retelling of Shakespeare's *Romeo and Juliet* transferred to the rundown area of the Upper West Side of Manhattan and the feuding families replaced by rival street gangs, the Sharks and the Jets. Modern-day social issues permeate not only the plot but also the lyrics of the songs, making *West Side Story* unique in terms of the theme of this book. Critically acclaimed, *West Side Story* gained an impressive ten Academy Awards, including the Best Motion Picture of 1961.

Synopsis

Two street gangs, the Jets and the Sharks, confront each other over control of a small cluster of blocks on New York's West Side. The Sharks consist of Puerto Ricans who have recently moved to the city. Riff (Russ Tamblyn), leader of the Jets, enlists his friend Tony (Richard Beymer), the original founder of the Jets, to challenge the Sharks to a rumble to settle their differences. They plan to extend the challenge that evening at a local dance. Bernardo (George Chakiris), leader of the Sharks, brings his sister, Maria (Natalie Wood), newly arrived in America, to the dance. He intends her to be a date for his pal Chino, but Maria has no interest in him. She spots Tony at the dance, and the two of them fall in love at first sight. Bernardo is angry when he catches Maria dancing with Tony. Angrily, he accepts Riff's challenge for a rumble. Later, Tony and Maria meet on the fire escape outside her window, and they declare their love for one another, despite the fact they come from different cultures.

When Bernardo and Riff meet for a war council at Doc's candy store, Tony intervenes and gets the leaders to agree to a fair fight—no weapons—between the best men from each gang. The next day, when Tony meets Maria at the bridal shop where she works, Anita (Rita Moreno), Bernardo's girlfriend, learns of their liaison, but agrees to keep quiet. Maria asks Tony to try to stop the planned fight. Tony heads to the scene of the battle, and tries to get the fight called off, but Riff and Bernardo get into a knife fight. Tony interferes, and Riff is stabbed. Dying, he hands his knife to Tony, who kills Bernardo as a full-fledged rumble breaks out. Chino heads off to tell Maria of her brother's death, but is stunned when she seems more concerned about Tony. Chino gets a gun and vows to kill Tony. Meanwhile, Maria hides Tony in her room, deciding to elope with him. When Tony goes to Doc's candy store to borrow money from the owner, Maria packs her bags. Lt. Schrank (Simon Oakland), investigating Bernardo's death, visits Maria to question her. Maria sends Anita to warn Tony that she will be delayed. Instead, Anita is terrorized by the Jets when they encounter her at the store. Angry, she leaves a message for Tony that Maria was shot by Chino and is dead. When

Tony hears this, he despairs and heads out into the night, hoping that Chino will kill him as well. Calling for Chino, Tony is startled to see Maria walking past the playground. They rush to greet each other, but Chino interferes and shoots Tony. The members of the two gangs come running at the sound of the shot and watch Tony die in Maria's arms. She cries out in anger at all of them. The police arrive and arrest Chino. Three members of the Jets pick up Tony's body, but when they falter, two members of the Sharks help them carry him off.

Critique

West Side Story created a Broadway sensation as a stunning amalgamation of Shakespeare, musical theater, and the theme of street gangs and violence among modern youths. Not since *The Cradle Will Rock* did social concerns figure so prominently in a work of musical theater. Dancing was stressed in the original stage production, often including a dynamic stylization of street fighting. The film tried to preserve this element of the production, as choreographer Jerome Robbins was hired as a co-director to film the vibrant dance routines. Much of the film was shot in the streets of New York in the neighborhood where Lincoln Center was scheduled to be built. After the buildings were vacated, the film was shot on location shortly before the structures were to be razed. This setting provided the film with a unique background far more interesting than any soundstage production. The sequence of the songs was shifted in Ernest Lehman's script. Stephen Sondheim provided a number of new lyrics, in some instances making them less suggestive than the stage version, but at other times, such as in "America," altering the rationale of the song. In the stage version, "America" was sung by the Puerto Rican girls, mocking one member of their group who preferred her original island home to Manhattan. In the screen treatment, the Puerto Rican girls still sing of their preference for life in New York, but their boyfriends sing instead of the climate of racism they encounter in America. A number of songs, particularly "Officer Krupke," have incredible lyrics that both illustrate and satirize the social issues of urban youth and the problems of juvenile delinquency, police harassment, drugs, alcoholism, prostitution, child abuse, spouse abuse, venereal disease, lack of education, unemployment, ghetto crime, and street violence.

Other points worth examining are the attitudes of the police. Both the Sharks and the Jets cover up for each other when questioned by Lt. Schrank. Both gangs it seems respect a code of the streets. Yet they also have a nihilism that foreshadows the gangs portrayed in *Colors*. The end of the film does not portray a reconciliation between the gangs as much as a temporary revulsion at the consequences of their violence. How long this truce will last remains an open question.

The Whales of August
(1987)

**Principal social themes: aging, end-of-life issues,
disabilities**

Alive Films. PG rating. Featuring: Bette Davis, Lillian Gish, Vincent Price, Ann Sothern, Harry Carey Jr., Frank Grimes, Frank Pitkin, Mike Bush, Margaret Ladd, Tisha Sterling, Mary Steenburgen. Written by David Berry based on his play *The Whales of August*. Cinematography by Mike Fash. Edited by Nicolas Gaster. Music by Alan Price. Produced by Mike Kaplan and Carolyn Pfeiffer. Directed by Lindsay Anderson. Color. 90 minutes.

Overview

The Whales of August is a quiet, elegiac character study of two elderly widows, sisters who have spent their summers in a house overlooking the ocean on a Maine island. One of them, blind and cantankerous, expects to die in several months, while her sister wants to concentrate on enjoying life as long as she can.

Synopsis

The film opens at the turn of the century as three young ladies, Sarah, Libby, and Tisha, hold a vigil on a cliff near their summer home to watch for passing whales that make an appearance every August. They excitedly take turns watching through a pair of binoculars. The scene shifts forward half a century to August 1950, and all three women are elderly widows. Sarah (Lillian Gish) looks after her sister Libby (Bette Davis), now blind, in their summer home, while their friend Tisha (Ann Sothern) now resides on the island year round. Sarah is finding it increasingly difficult to care for Libby, who has become cantankerous, opinionated, and very bossy. Sarah also wonders if her sister is becoming senile. Instead of returning home to Philadelphia, Sarah is considering an offer to move in with Tisha and get a paid companion to care for Libby. Mr. Maranov (Vincent Price), an elderly Russian emigre, asks permission to fish along their shore front, promising to share his catch with them. Handyman Joshua Brackett (Harry Carey Jr.) stops by to work on their plumbing. Sarah is interested in his suggestion to install a picture window overlooking the ocean, but Libby rejects the idea, saying they are too old to make any changes. She says that she expects to die soon.

Tisha informs them that Hattie, another elderly island resident, had just died. Maranov had been her guest, and now he needs a new place to stay. When Maranov brings them their fish, Sarah invites him to return for dinner. Libby insists that she will not eat the fish, so Sarah agrees to substitute a pork chop for her. She is upset that Sarah invited Maranov for supper. Maranov arrives with a bouquet of handpicked flowers, and Sarah lights candles at their dining room table, but after their meal, Libby makes it clear that Maranov would not be welcome as a guest in the house. Sarah and Maranov pause to watch the moonlight on the ocean as he prepares to leave. She asks if he might return the next morning, to join her in her vigil for the whales. Kissing Sarah's hand, he graciously declines, not wanting to upset Libby again. Later that evening, Sarah celebrates her forty-sixth wedding anniversary by herself, sitting at a table with a glass of wine, flowers, and a photograph of her late husband. Libby has a nightmare in which Sarah has abandons her. When she tries to talk again about death, Sarah insists that they talk about life instead.

The next morning, Tisha stops by with the realtor who is going to sell Hattie's house. She thought that Sarah might be interested in putting her summer house on the market, but Sarah says she plans to keep it. Libby is in a more mellow mood and apologizes to Sarah for being so blunt with Mr. Maranov. When Joshua stops by, Libby tells him to install the picture window that Sarah wanted. Sarah then walks Libby down to the cliff, telling her sister there is no sign of any whales. Libby replies that it is possible they might still appear as the film closes.

Critique

Lillian Gish was ninety-three when she appeared in *The Whales of August*, making her the oldest actress to appear as the lead in a feature film. Bette Davis was seventy-eight, Vincent Price was seventy-five, and Ann Sothern, who received an Academy Award nomination as Best Supporting Actress for her role, was seventy-seven. The entire production was shot on location on Cliff Island, off the coast of Falmouth, Maine. The production values of the film were high, featuring gorgeous cinematography, first-class performances, and a poetic script by David Berry, based on his stage play. Yet some reviewers criticized the picture for being slow moving and plotless, missing the point that the film is a reverie about aging and the end of life. The heart of the film is the dialogue between Lillian Gish and Vincent Price as he takes his leave of her after supper. She asks if he believes a person can live too long? He replies it is not possible, even when she insists they have outlived their time. "One's time is all one's time, even to the end," he responds, comparing each moment of life to an elusive treasure like the moonbeams that dance across the waters. Each of the characters of the film represents a contrasting attitude toward aging. Sarah is "busy, busy" with housework, hobbies, and entertaining friends. Libby is reclusive, brooding, and bitter. Tisha is resigned to her increasing limitations but remains positive in attitude, and Maranov tries to savor each moment for whatever transitory delights he can find. Each of them is sustained to a great degree by their memories. Libby insists that memories never fade, but Sarah insists that they do. Libby's blindness, although central to the story, is not overplayed. It even provides a moment of gentle humor. When Tisha handpicks a bunch of berries to share with her friends, Libby greedily scoops handfuls out of the bowl. Noticing this, Tisha quietly moves the container, and the next time Libby reaches for them, she grabs only empty air.

The relationship between Libby and Sarah is a complex one. For example, Sarah owns the house, but Libby appears to make all the decisions. Sarah does not mind deferring to her on these matters or the choice of programs to hear on the radio, but she is upset by her negativity and pessimism. Libby's nightmare seems to dispel some of her gloom. When she insists that the picture window be installed, it seems a reaffirmation of life. Her last line in the film also reflects this attitude, as she holds out hope that Sarah may yet see the whales.

When Innocence Is Lost
(1997)

Principal social theme: women's rights

Hearst Entertainment. PG rating. Featuring: Keri Russell, Jill Clayburgh, Roberta Maxwell, Vincent Corazza, Charlotte Sullivan, Deborah Grover, Alan Jordan, Shelley Thompson, Kris Holdenreid, Barry Flatman, Jonathan Potts, Dabe Nichols, Julie Khaner, John Bourgeois, Neil Dainard. Written by Deborah Jones. Cinematography by Laszlo George. Edited by Michael S. Murphy. Music by Dennis McCarthy. Produced by Sandra Saxson Brice. Directed by Bethany Rooney. Color. 92 minutes.

Overview

When Innocence Is Lost is a telefilm by Hearst Entertainment, which specializes in small-budget social issue films made directly for cable stations such as Lifetime and USA. They are often based on true-life events, although the personal background of the characters is frequently fictionalized. *When*

Innocence Is Lost is considered one of their best efforts, covering the case in which a single college student lost custody of her daughter to the family of the father. The key issue was the young woman's use of day care. The judge felt the child would be better cared for by the father's parents instead of "strangers," sparking a controversial battle over a woman's right to raise her own child and receive an education.

Synopsis

Erica French (Keri Russell) is a high school student who gives birth to a baby girl. Her divorced parents, Susan and Matt, and the parents of the father, Scott Stone (Vincent Corazza), another student, have persuaded Erica to give the child up for adoption. After Erica sees the baby, she changes her mind and decides to raise the child herself. She names her Molly and brings her home. Erica finishes her senior year, graduating as the top student. Meanwhile, her mother (Jill Clayburgh) and her younger sister help Erica take care of the baby. The young father never sees Molly until his family runs into Erica at the local mall. Scott becomes enchanted with the baby and starts paying regular visits. He refuses, however, to offer any financial support. Molly sues Scott for support and is awarded a payment of $12 a week by the court, but Scott is also granted visitation rights three days a week.

Erica is offered a scholarship at Cornell University, fifty miles from her hometown. She plans to have Molly live with her on campus, and place Molly in a nearby daycare facility while she attends class. Scott is angry when he hears these plans, believing that he and his parents should take care of Molly. He sues for total custody, attempting to build a case that Erica is an unfit mother. The court battle becomes contentious, and the judge eventually rules in favor of Scott and the Stone family, since he believes Molly would be better cared for by blood relatives rather than strangers. Women's groups are enraged at the verdict, and Erica approaches a prestigious attorney whom she hears talking about the case on television. The women's rights expert agrees to file her appeal, and the case becomes a nationwide rallying point. The appeals court overturns the original ruling, stating that Erica's reliance on day care cannot be held against her, and Erica retains custody of Molly. After a celebratory conclusion with Molly's friends and family, a voiceover epilogue reveals that a subsequent court three years later required Molly to live in the same city as her father to accommodate his part-time custodial rights, forcing Erica to leave college.

Critique

When Innocence Is Lost provides an unusually thoughtful presentation of a complicated and controversial social issue that touches many bases, the legal ramifications of single parenthood, the rights of parents, and a woman's right to complete education. The film is ideal to stimulate debate and discussion among viewers over many points. Without being heavy-handed, the screenplay continually contrasts the treatment of the sexes. In court, Scott is treated almost gingerly by Erica's male attorney, but Scott's female attorney attacks Erica with no holds barred. Earlier in the story, Scott twice physically assaulted Erica, but this is never brought up at the trial. Neither is the fact that Scott is continually late in paying his $12 a week child support for Molly. Erica, however, is berated because Molly had a playground accident, even though she was on the scene to help. The male judge in the case seems to have no appreciation or respect for the birth mother's rights. Matt, Erica's own father, seems absent for most of the proceedings, making only a token appearance after her case is won. This is not to say that there are no positive male role models in the film. Dave, Susan's companion, and Kevin, Erica's college boyfriend, are both supportive and helpful.

When Innocence Is Lost can be seen as providing a few mixed messages, given the consequences of a series of decisions by Erica, such as not having an abortion, not giving the baby up for adoption, trying to involve the father in raising Molly, and wanting to complete her education. Erica tries to be responsible at each step, but encounters nothing but opposition and heartache. The only positive factor is Molly, a beautiful, intelligent child to whom she is completely devoted. In these terms, each of Erica's alternate choices would have been the easier path. Society neither recognizes nor rewards her efforts, and the legal system seems to work against her, not only trampling on her rights, but also penalizing her for wanting to finish her education. The judge, for example, prefers the Scott's lifestyle. He has no further educational goals, as opposed to Erica who wants to become a lawyer. Which parent could provide a more financially secure future? The epilogue does not explain if the same judge handled the case three years later, which awarded Scott joint custody and required Erica to live in the same city as Scott. This ruling also seems unjust, forcing Erica to withdraw from college. In essence, this is another violation of her rights, justifying Scott's pronouncement that one cannot be both a mother and a full-time student. Yet, the inverse of this premise, that one could not be both a father and a full-time student, would be dismissed as a ridiculous concept.

Whose Life Is It Anyway?
(1981)

Principal social themes: end-of-life issues,
suicide/depression, disabilities

MGM. R rating. Featuring: Richard Dreyfuss, John Cassavetes, Christine Lahti, Bob Balaban, Kenneth McMillan, Kaki Hunter, Thomas Carter, Alba Oms, Janet Eilber, Kathryn Grody, George Wyner, Mel Stewart, Charles Gross, Ward Costello, Jeffrey Combs. Written by Brian Clark and Reginald Rose based on a play by Brian Clark. Cinematography by Mario Tosi. Edited by Frank Morriss. Music by Arthur B. Rubinstein. Produced by Lawrence P. Bachman. Directed by John Badham. Color. 118 minutes.

Overview

Whose Life Is It Anyway? is a very literate picture built around a specific premise. A brilliant man is injured in an accident. Transformed into a helpless paraplegic, he decides that his life is in fact over, and his existence is being artificially prolonged without his permission. He undertakes a legal battle to assert control of his own destiny, even if his choice is for his life to end. Perhaps no other film focuses the spotlight on this subject to such an extent, while at the same time attempting to be both balanced and open-minded. While both an artistic and critical success, *Whose Life Is It Anyway?* was largely shunned by the general filmgoing public as a "downer."

Synopsis

Ken Harrison (Richard Dreyfuss) is a brilliant young sculptor living in Boston, where his career is beginning to take off. His life changes drastically when he is involved in an automobile accident, which cripples him due to a spinal cord injury. He has become totally physically helpless, incapable of any movement below his neck, and also dependent on dialysis to survive. In the emergency ward, Ken becomes the patient of Dr. Michael Emerson (John Cassavetes), a passionate physician and teacher who regards death as a personal adversary who must be fought on a patient-by-patient basis.

In a way, Ken is an ideal patient, witty, clever, and continually joking with the nurses, orderlies, and other members of the hospital staff. After six months, Ken begins to become more irritable, as the extent of his disabilities begins to dawn on him. He finally asks Dr. Emerson if there might be any chance for an improvement in his condition. When he learns there is not, Ken assumes a new attitude. He asks Pat, his girlfriend, to cease her daily visits. He tells her that he is touched by her love and devotion, but that it is too painful for him to see her because it reminds him of who he was and what he has become. Tearfully, she agrees to his request. Ken refuses to try any rehabilitation services, such as learning to use a reading machine. He starts to resent the power and control Dr. Emerson has over him, particularly when the doctor injects him with sedatives against his wishes. He finally contacts his insurance lawyer, Carter Hill (Bob Balaban) and asks for his help in gaining his discharge from the hospital. When Dr. Emerson learns of Ken's efforts, he contends that Ken is not fit to make any decisions because he is depressed due to his condition. Other staff members become involved in the emerging struggle. Dr. Claire Scott (Christine Lahti), a physician fond of Ken, visits Pat and asks for her help to break through Ken's emotional wall, but instead Pat says she respects Ken's decision. Claire takes one of Ken's sculptures, a hand modeled after Adam from the Sistine Chapel painting by Michelangelo, and brings it to him in the hospital. John, an orderly, sneaks Ken in a wheelchair to the basement, so he can hear his steel drum band. Ken's attorney asks for a writ of habeas corpus, for Ken to be discharged from the hospital. A hearing is held at the hospital, and the issue is thoroughly examined. The judge decides that Ken is of sound mind and grants his request. Dr. Emerson tells Ken that he will not have to leave the hospital if he chooses, and they will respect his wish to discontinue dialysis. No attempt would be made to revive him when he slips into a coma. Ken is returned to his bed. He looks at his sculpture of the hand and smiles as the end credits roll.

Critique

Whose Life Is It Anyway? is a quality production on all levels, both well acted and well photographed with a rather briskly moving screenplay. A strong effort is made to keep the tone of the proceedings light and optimistic, a rather difficult challenge given the storyline. The musical soundtrack, for example, is always upbeat. Ken, as portrayed by Richard Dreyfuss, is always a fun individual, with an endless stream of wisecracks and clever asides. This makes his arguments in favor of ending his life that much more powerful. At one point, he asks the judge, if he denies his request, to come back and see him in five years to see the results of his decision; it is one of the most potent lines in the film.

The reviews of the picture were largely positive, and a few critics even suggested that Ken would change his mind and not choose to die (simply because Dr. Emerson noted he was free to change his mind). This interpretation appears unlikely, since Ken's decision seemed irrevocable and unwavering. This brings out what may be the most serious flaw in the screenplay: No one is permitted to engage with Ken about his rationale in a meaningful way. No one challenges Ken when he dismisses an idea. If someone suggests he could learn to write a book, Ken responds that if he wanted to be a writer, he would have been, but he chose to be a sculptor. The logic is rather weak here, and the film suffers because there is never a cogent plea for life. Nevertheless, the issues involving medical intervention, the right to die, and freedom of choice are all given strong and logical presentations without any maudlin sidetracks. To this extent, the film is rather unique in its viewpoint. It is also interesting to note that the film has an "R" rating apparently due to the subject matter alone, since the film shows no violence (outside the car accident), no sex (except for an innocent flashback), and no bad language. The ratings board simply concluded that you needed to be mature enough to deal with the film's subject matter.

Woman on the Beach
(1947)

Principal social themes: disabilities, spouse abuse, suicide/depression

RKO. No MPAA rating. Featuring: Joan Bennett, Robert Ryan, Charles Bickford, Nan Leslie, Walter Sande, Irene Ryan, Glenn Vernon, Frank Darien, Jay Norris. Written by Frank Davis and Jean Renoir based on the novel *None So Blind* by Mitchell Wilson. Cinematography by Leo Tover and Harry Wild. Edited by Roland Gross and Lyle Boyer. Music by Hans Eisler. Produced by Jack J. Gross. Directed by Jean Renoir. B&W. 73 minutes.

Overview

Woman on the Beach is a controversial film noir, an intense psychological drama about the world's leading artist, recently blinded, who is obsessed with his condition and takes out his frustrations on his beautiful wife. A Coast Guard officer, recuperating from injuries suffered during the war, is drawn into their quiet conflict, and they become locked in an odd symbiotic relationship. This was the last American film by the French screen legend Jean Renoir. Critically panned when first released, the film later developed a cult following by many who consider it an existential masterpiece.

Synopsis

Lieutenant Scott Burnett (Robert Ryan) is assigned to a remote Coast Guard station (presumably in eastern Long Island) after being released from a military hospital. He is not fully recovered, however, suffering from both mental distress and recurring nightmares. He thinks he might be cured if he got married, but Eve, his fiancée, a local girl who runs a small shipbuilding business, is reticent when he suggests an immediate marriage. Scott thereafter ignores Eve (Nan Leslie), abandoning the idea of marriage. He tries to lose himself in his work, patrolling the local beaches on horseback. He meets a woman on the beach, Peg (Joan Bennett), who is gathering firewood. He helps her carry the wood back to her isolated cottage, where she lives with her husband, Tod Butler (Charles Bickford), considered to be the world's most famous artist. He learns that Butler has become blind. Scott is perplexed by the painter, who seeks him out as a friend yet seems to ridicule him at the same time.

Scott becomes drawn to Peg, and they develop a relationship. She explains that her husband controls her, since it was she who was responsible for her husband's condition, having injured him in a drunken fight. Scott is familiar with the rehabilitation of the blind, as he shared a hospital room with a sailor who had lost his sight. He starts to believe that Tod is faking his blindness. When Peg admits that she would leave Tod if he could see, Scott takes the artist on a dangerous excursion on a rocky cliff overlooking the ocean. He unexpectedly leaves Tod, suggesting he find his own way home. Scott expected this would force the artist to reveal that he still has sight. Instead, Tod falls over the cliff and is hurt. Scott rescues him, relieved that his wounds are only superficial. Oddly enough, Tod forgives him after he confesses that he was obsessed with the idea that Tod was not really blind.

The artist shows Scott his hidden treasure, a large closet filled with his paintings. Since his blindness, the value of his work has skyrocketed. Peg wants him to sell some of them so that they would not have to live in poverty, but Tod refuses and beats her when she pushes the point. Scott offers to take Tod deep-sea fishing, a desire the artist had previously expressed. Since it is a blustery day, Peg suspects that Scott intends to kill her husband, and she alerts the Coast Guard to watch out for their boat. At sea, Scott demands that Tod promises to release Peg or he will never return to shore. When Tod refuses, Scott tries to scuttle the boat, intending to kill them both, but they are rescued by the Coast Guard. When Tod returns home, he decides to burn his paintings. He sets them ablaze, setting fire to the cottage as well. Peg calls Scott, who arrives just in time to lead them to safety. Tod tells Scott that he had clung to his art as he had clung to Peg. He had to destroy the paintings to set both her and himself free. The artist then asks Peg for one last favor, to drive him to New York City. She embraces Tod and leads him away, as Scott watches the fire as it continues to burn.

Critique

As Jean Renoir recounted in his autobiography, he believed that the story of *None so Blind*, the original title of this film, would be simple, but found it became more and more complex as he wrote it and later directed it. In fact, the relationship of the three main characters, each disabled in their own way, is one of the most intricate ever portrayed on the screen. Tod Butler is filled with contradictions. On the one hand, he appears to have accepted his loss of sight extremely well and manages his daily activities so easily that most observers would think he is not blind. *Woman on the Beach* even explores the various degrees of blindness. Tod is supposed to be totally blind, without any ability to even detect light. At other times, he is in total denial. For example, he holds out a painting to Scott and describes all the details of the portrait, the brushwork, and so forth, but Scott has to eventually tell Tod that he is describing the wrong painting, that he is actually holding a still life. Tod is also suicidal, deliberately putting himself in situations where his life is in danger. He walks over the cliff instead of asking for Scott's help. He encourages Scott to take him fishing, knowing that a storm is brewing. Tod has a complicated love/hate relationship with Peg, almost encouraging her to have affairs and then proving his dominance by cutting them off. Peg is handicapped by her sense of guilt over her husband's blindness, and it is this that gives him his power over her. Scott is unbalanced due to shell shock. He lacks the ability to make any rational judgment, and both Tod and Peg seem to exploit this. In truth, he has become an unwitting pawn in their marriage struggle.

The film's conclusion suggests that the destruction of the paintings has resolved their crisis (although selling the art would have been a far more lucrative way to resolve the problem). It is also interesting to note that the painting Tod most wanted to destroy was his portrait of Peg. This also seemed to be the painting that Peg most wanted to save. Since this film centered on art and a great painter, commentators have speculated whether this film contains any secret insight into the director's own relationship with his father, the impressionist master, Pierre-Auguste Renoir. In his book, Jean Renoir's comments are very circumspect about the entire project. Undoubtedly, *Woman on the Beach* contains some of the most harrowing depictions of disabilities, particularly the scene in which Scott leads Tod to the rocky bluff. The performances by the actors in this picture are hypnotic. Robert Ryan portrays Scott as both fragile and desperate, unable to come to terms with his condition. Knowing his handicap, the audience does not judge his actions in the same light as it would an ordinary screen protagonist. Joan Bennett handles her part with equal aplomb. At times she seems a figure from classical mythology, a siren leading other men to their doom. At other times, she is a confused waif, driven mad by her isolation and her inability to relate to her husband. Charles Bickford is both moving and enigmatic as Tod. Renoir instructed Bickford to regard his character as a man facing a vast and empty void. Could this concept by Renoir be regarded as a metaphor for any individual facing a major disability? In his autobiography, Renoir claimed that the point he was trying to make in *Woman on the Beach* might have been too obscure, but it was something that he felt that needed to be said. As for the audience, there is ample room for speculation about what this film may or may not reveal about Renoir's attitude toward his own father.

Index

[*Note.* Numerals refer to actual pages. In the case of topics identified as "social themes" however, only the first page of each film entry is noted.]

Abatemarco, Tony, 222

Abcon, Theodor, 82

Abortion (social theme), 3–4, 37, 50, 125, 188, 198, 211, 252

Aboulela, Amir, 101

Absolution (1981 film), 10

Abuse. *See* Child abuse; Spouse abuse

Academy Awards, 2, 6, 19, 22, 26, 76, 85, 101, 108, 112, 120, 123, 136, 152, 154, 162, 184, 194, 195, 204, 216, 242, 249, 255, 272, 275

Acovone, Jay, 66

Acquired immunodeficiency syndrome. *See* AIDS

An Act of Murder (1948 film), 10

Acuff, Eddie, 32

Adam: His Song Continues (1986 film), 9

Adam's Rib (1949 film), 17

Aday, Marvin Lee. *See* Meat Loaf

Addiction to alcohol (social theme), 4, 47, 154, 164, 176

Addiction to drugs (social theme), 4, 8, 78, 152, 162, 164, 173, 203, 219

Addiction to gambling (social theme), 4–5, 146, 173

Adler, Mark, 93

Adler, Warren, 269

Adolfi, John G., 160

Advise and Consent (1962 film), 13

Affleck, Ben, 107, 108

Affleck, Casey, 107

The African Queen (1951 film), 241

Agar, John, 56

Aging (social theme), 5, 78, 85, 135, 206, 227, 241, 274

Ai, Catherine, 117

AIDS (social theme), 5–6, 13, 23, 68, 87, 193, 208, 266

Air pollution, 91

Akst, Albert, 255

Albertson, Eric, 137

Albertson, Jack, 173

Alcoholics Anonymous (AA), 176–77

Alda, Alan, 23, 25, 47

Alexander, Richard, 170

Alexander, Shana, 224

Alexander, Stephen, 224

Algren, Nelson, 162

Alimony (1949 film), 9

Allan, Ross, 180

Allen, Corey, 142

Allen, Dede, 19

Allen, Irwin, 90

Allen, Karen, 66

Allen, Millie, 34

Allen, Penelope, 249

Allen, Woody, 144

Allman, Sheldon, 128

Alonso, Maria Conchita, 54

Alonzo, John A., 59

Alton, John, 40
Alverado, Trini, 190
Alzheimer's disease, 87, 136, 137
Amarilly of Clothesline Alley (1919 film), 12
The Amboy Dukes (novel), 17
"America" (song), 273
America, America (1963 film), 13, 19–21
American Graffiti (1973 film), 17
American History X (1998 film), 11, 13, 14, 16, 21–23
American Library Association (ALA), 238
American Medical Association (AMA), 221
An American Tail (1986 film), 14
Amfitheatrof, Daniele, 238, 255
Anchia, Juan Ruiz, 93
And the Band Played On (book), 24
And the Band Played On (1993 film), 5, 12, 23–26
Anders, Luana, 244
Anders, Merry, 188, 189
Anders, Rudolph, 185
Anderson, Cheryl, 87
Anderson, Dion, 211
Anderson, Kevin, 222
Anderson, Lindsay, 274
Anderson, Mary, 47
Anderson, Richard, 57
Anderson, William, 114
Andre Chenier (opera), 196
Andrews, Dana, 7
Andrews, Giuseppe, 21
Andrews, Tina, 59
Andrus, Mark, 26
Angels With Dirty Faces (1938 film), 6
Anorexia. *See* Eating disorders
Anti-Catholicism, 33, 95, 122
Anti-Semitism, 14–15, 29–30, 86, 93–95, 138
Antonio, Lou, 19
Antrim, Harry, 40
Anwar, Tariq, 93
Apfel, Oscar, 160
Appalachian Trail, 200
Arden, Eve, 261, 263

Are These Our Children? (1943 film), 16
Argenziano, Carmen, 232
Ari, Robert, 144
Arledge, John, 111
Arliss, George, 160
Armstrong, Henry, 174
Armstrong, Robert, 7
Arnold, Harland, 269
Arrest and Trial (television series), 58
Arroyave, Karina, 149
Arthur (1981 film), 4
Arthur, Indus, 224
As Good As It Gets (1997 film), 9, 12, 26–29
Ashbrook, Daphne, 208
Ashe, Arthur, 25
Aslend, Camila, 249
Asner, Ed, 140, 141, 224, 227, 228
Asparagus, Fred, 55
Assante, Armand, 198–200
Astin, John, 271
Atlas, Larry, 66
Attack on Terror: The FBI vs. the Ku Klux Klan (1975 film), 11
Attaway, Ruth, 59
Attenborough, Richard, 252, 254
Aubrey, Juliet, 135
Audley, Eleanor, 45
Augustus, Sherman, 55
Auschwitz, 100
Austin, Sean, 269
Austin, Stephanie, 140
Austin-Olsen, Shaun, 93
Autobiography of Miss Jane Pittman (1974 film), 14
Avildsen, John G., 149
Avnet, Jon, 42
Ayala, Corina Catt, 62
Ayers, Lew, 261, 263
Ayers, Tony, 266
Aykroyd, Dan, 85, 87
Ayres, Rosalind, 101
Azaria, Hank, 62, 63, 65

Babatunde, Obba, 194
Babbin, Jacqueline, 249
Babcock, Todd, 101

Bacall, Lauren, 240
Bach, Johann Sebastian, 50
Bachman, Lawrence P., 279
Backroom Abortion. See Patty
Backus, Jim, 167, 170
Bacon, Irving, 111
Badalamenti, Angelo, 241
Badham, John, 279
Bailey, John, 26, 135–27
Bailey, Raymond, 123, 124
Baker, Art, 178
Baker, David Aaron, 144
Baker, Joby, 142
Baker, Terence, 73
Balaban, Bob, 62, 279, 280
Baldwin, Walter, 238
Balk, Fairuza, 21
Ball, Lucille, 228, 234, 235
Bancroft, Anne, 224–26
Banderas, Antonio, 193, 195
Bangor Daily News (newspaper), 79
Baranski, Christine, 203
Barber, Ellen, 137, 138
Bardette, Trevor, 111
Bargen, Daniel von, 194
Barker, Clive, 101
Barnes, Charles, 133
Barnes, George, 32
Barr, Tony, 40
Barrat, Robert, 32
Barrett, Edith, 146
Barrett, Majel, 244
Barry, Julian, 152
Barry, Raymond J., 71
Barth, Richard, 227
Bartless, Lisabeth, 246
Bartlett, Martine, 249
Bartlett, Robin, 149
Basehart, Richard, 16, 95–97
Basehart, Stephanie, 97
Bass, Ronald, 222
Bassin, Roberta, 130
Bates, Kathy, 52, 78, 81, 211, 212
Batista, Henry, 45
Batson, Susan, 234
Battered women's syndrome, 42–45,
    265

Battle Stripe. See The Men
Bauchau, Patrick, 23
Baye, Nathalie, 23
Beach, Michael, 149
Beatty, Bruce, 54
Beaumont, Charles, 133, 135
Beck, Stanley, 152
Becker, Dixie, 90
Becker, Harold, 82
Becker, Terry, 57
Becket, St. Thomas, 196
Beddoe, Don, 146
Bedoya, Alfonso, 40
Beesley, Elizabeth Anne, 249
Beethoven, Ludwig van, 60, 61, 229,
    231
Beetley, Samuel E., 229
Behrens, Diane, 208
Bel Geddes, Barbara, 95, 96
Belafonte, Shari, 140
Bell, Christine, 190
Bellayer, Harry, 185, 187
The Bells of St. Mary's (1945 film), 10
Bender, Lawrence, 107
Bender, Russ, 57
Bendixsen, Mia, 198
Benedict, Richard, 173
Benitez, Jellybean, 191
Bennet, Michael, 25
Bennett, Charles, 216
Bennett, Joan, 281–83
Bennett, Nigel, 258
Bennett, Norman, 264
Benny, Jack, 15
Benz, Julie, 26
Berenger, Tom, 29
Beresford, Bruce, 85, 87
Bergin, Patrick, 222, 224
Bergman, Henry, 170
Bergman, Ingrid, 10, 16
Bergmann, Alan, 34
Beristain, Gabriel, 78
Berkeley, Xander, 125
Berlinger, Warren, 37
Berlioz, Hector, 222
Berneis, Peter, 47
Bernstein, Elmer, 162, 164

Bernstein, Leonard, 222, 271
Berry, David, 274, 275
Besser, Joe, 157
Betrayed (1988 film), 11, 14, 29–31
Betts, Jack, 101
Between Two Worlds (1944 film), 16
Bevis, Leslie, 140
Beymer, Richard, 271, 272
Beyond a Reasonable Doubt
  (1956 film), 7
Bickford, Charles, 281–84
The Big Knife (1955 film), 16
The Big Lebowski (1998 film), 268
The Bigamist (1953 film), 9
Bigger than Life (1956 film), 10
Biggs, John, 90
Bikel, Theodore, 123
Bill (1981 film), 9
A Bill of Divorcement (1932 film), 9
A Bill of Divorcement (1940 film), 9
Binns, Edward, 57
Birch, Paul, 92
Birney, Meredith Baxter, 140
Biro, Barney, 188
Biroc, Joseph F., 98
Birth of a Nation (1915 film), 11, 14
Bishop, Nicholas, 266
Bissell, Whit, 229, 255
Black, Isobel, 252
Black Legion (1936 film), 11, 13, 32–33
Black Like Me (book), 34
Black Like Me (1964 film), 2, 14, 34–37
Black Swan (1942 film), 60
Black Tuesday (1955 film), 6
Blackboard Jungle (1955 film), 17, 241
Blacklisting, 8
Blades, Ruben, 62, 63
Blair, Betsy, 29
Blake, Amanda, 25
Blake, Robert, 128, 130
Blaustein, Julian, 236
Bleckner, Ross, 26
Blind Spot (1947 film), 4
Blindness, 9, 274–76, 281–84
Bliss, Imogene, 234
Blitzstein, Marc, 62–65
Bloom, John, 73

Blossier, Patrick, 29
Blue Denim (1959 film), 3, 37–40
Blue Jeans. See Blue Denim
Blum, Mark, 130, 132
Blumenthal, Andy, 234
Blystone, Stanley, 170
Boardman, Chris, 258
Boardwalk (1979 film), 5
Bock, Larry, 201
Bogart, Humphrey, 32, 33, 130, 241
Bogdanovich, Peter, 164, 167
Bogosian, Eric, 78, 79
Bolster, Anita, 154
Bond, Ward, 111
Boni, Gabrielle, 130
Bonneville, Hugh, 135, 136
Bonney, David, 266, 267
Booke, Sorrell, 34
Booth, Ned, 98
Boothe, Powers, 66
Borchert, William, 176
Borden, Viola, 196
Border Incident (1949 film), 13, 40–42
Borzage, Frank, 2
Bosco, Philip, 246
Boston, Meredith Strange, 176
The Bottom of the Bottle (1956 film), 4
Bourgeois, John, 276
Bowden, Dorris, 111
Bowers, George, 222
Bowery Boys (film series), 16
Boxoffice (magazine), 37
Boy Slaves (1939 film), 16
Boyd-Perkins, Eric, 180
Boyer, Lyle, 281
The Boys in the Band (1970 film), 13
Boys Town (1938 film), 16
Bracht, Frank, 59
Brackett, Charles, 37, 154
Bradbury, Ray, 238
Bradford, Richard, 130, 132
Bradley, Christopher, 87
Brahms, Johannes, 198
Bram, Christopher, 101
Bramley, William, 271
Branagh, Kenneth, 15
Brando, Marlon, 11, 17, 167–69

Brandon, Henry, 32
Brandt, William, 90
Braselle, Keefe, 157, 159
Braverman, Bart, 45, 47
Breaking Up Is Hard To Do
   (1979 film), 9
Brecher, Egon, 32
Brecht, Bertolt, 65
Breen, Joseph, 7, 8
Brennan, Eileen, 125
Brenner, Alfred, 142
Brezner, Larry, 104
Brian, Sean, 188
Brice, Sandra Saxson, 276
The Bride of Frankenstein (1935 film),
   101–4
Bridge to the Sun (1961 film), 15
British Board of Film Censors, 8
Broadbent, Jim, 135, 136
Brock, Stanley, 34
Brodine, Norbert, 76
Brokaw, Tom, 132
Broken Blossoms (1919 film), 15
Brooke, Tyler, 76
Brooks, Avery, 21–23
Brooks, James L., 26, 269
Brooks, Randy, 54
Brooks, Richard, 128, 130, 238, 241
Brophy, Sallie, 236
Broun, Heywood Hale, 34
Brown, Charles D., 111
Brown, Hilyard John, 219
Browne, Roscoe Lee, 34, 35
Brubaker, Judy, 47
Bruce, Lenny, 152–54, 202
Bryan, William Jennings, 7
Bryant, Karis Paige, 264, 266
Bryant, Nana, 146–47
Bryar, Paul, 157
Buckley, John, 180
Buddy Buddy (1981 film), 16
Buhagiar, Valerie, 258
Bui, Timothy Linh, 117
Bui, Tony, 117
Bukowski, Bobby, 125
Bulimia. *See* Eating disorders
Bülow, Claus von, 204–6

Bülow, Cosima von, 204, 206
Bülow, Sunny von, 204-6
Burdell, Gammy, 219, 221
Burke, Delta, 68, 69
Burkley, Dennis, 130, 132, 164
Burnham, Michael, 196
Burnham, Terry, 142
The Burning Bed (1984 film), 8, 9, 12,
   17, 42–45
The Burning Cross (1947 film), 11
Burns, George, 5
Burns, Ralph, 152
Burress, Hedy, 125
Burton, Richard, 10, 13, 15, 73, 75
Burum, Stephen H., 269
Burwell, Carter, 24,101, 104
Buscemi, Steve, 82
Bush, Dick, 258
Bush, Grand, 54
Bush, Mike, 274
Butler, Nancy, 59
Butler, Samuel, 37
Butts, Larry, 137
Byars, Taylor, 133
Byrnes, Burke, 198

Cada, James, 241
Cagney, James, 6
Cahn, Dan, 244
Cain, Christopher, 219, 221
California Split (1974 film), 5
Callahan, James, 42
Callas, Maria, 195
Camp, Bill, 203
Campbell, Graeme, 68
Campbell, Robert, 45
Campbell, William, 45–47
Campos, Raphael, 255
Cannes Film Festival, 59
Capital punishment (social theme),
   6–7, 45, 57, 71, 123, 128, 252
Capote, Truman, 2, 128, 130
The Cardinal (1963 film), 3, 11
Carey, Harry, Jr., 164, 274
Carey, Macdonald, 37, 38
Cariani, John, 144
Carlo, East, 206

Carpenter, John, 62
Carr, Howie, 52
Carr, Marian, 45
Carradine, John, 111, 112, 114
Carriére, Mathieu, 208
Carroll, Leo G., 15
Carruth, Milton, 147
Carta, Jennifer, 144
Carter, Dan T., 137
Carter, Gary, 264
Carter, Harry, 57
Carter, John, 149
Carter, Thomas, 279
Carvalho, Betty, 232
The Case of Patty Smith. See Patty
Cash, Aaron, 125
Cash, Johnny, 196, 197
Cash, Tara, 196
Cassavetes, John, 279
Castellaneta, Dan, 269
Castle, Robert, 194
Castro, Fidel, 191
Catholic Legion of Decency, 8, 236
Cell 2455 Death Row (book), 45
Cell 2455 Death Row (1955 film), 2, 6, 45–47
Celli, Teresa, 40
Censorship (social theme), 7–8, 62, 104, 152, 201, 229, 236
Centers for Disease Control and Prevention (CDC), 24, 25
Chakiris, George, 271, 272
Champagne, Michael, 234
Chan, Charlie, 6, 15
Chaney, Lon, Sr., 9, 14, 221
Chaplin, Charlie, 4, 8, 12, 14, 15, 170–73
Chaplin, Saul, 271
Chapman, Daniel, 194
Chapman, Margaret, 180
Chappell, John, 50
Charles, Lewis, 173
Charlie Chan in London (1934 film), 6
Charly (1968 film), 9
Chater, Geoffrey, 252
Cheadle, Don, 54
Cheech and Chong (comedy team), 4

Cher, 125, 126, 164–66, 246, 247
Chessman, Caryl, 45–47
Cheyenne Autumn (1964 film), 15
Chicago Calling (1951 film), 4, 12, 15, 47–49
Chihara, Paul, 208
Child abuse (social theme), 8–9, 42, 68, 78, 82, 107, 130, 249, 258, 264
Child Bride (1937 film), 190
Children of a Lesser God (1986 film), 9
The Children Nobody Wanted (1981 film), 12
The Children of Times Square (1986 film), 9
The Children's Hour (1961 film), 13
The Children's Hour (play), 13
Child's Play (1972 film), 10
Childs, Reva, 266
Chinatown (1974 film), 9
Chinh, Khu, 117
The Choice (1981 film), 3, 50–51
Chowdhry, Ranjit, 190
Christian, Marc, 210, 211
Christie, John, 252–54
Christine, Virginia, 120, 122, 167
Christopher, John, 180
Christopher Strong (1933 film), 17
Churgin, Lisa Zeno, 71
Cider House Rules (1999 film), 4
City Across the River (1944 film), 16
City Girl (1931 film), 2
City Lights (1931 film), 8
A Civil Action (book), 52
A Civil Action (1998 film), 2, 11, 52–54
Civil rights (social theme), 14–15, 21, 29, 34, 59, 85, 93, 120, 133, 137, 149, 185, 214, 232, 238, 255
Clanton, Ronny, 137
Clark, Brian, 279
Clark, Cliff, 167
Clark, Joe, 149–51
Clark, Susan, 50
Clarke, Frank, 180
Clarke, Phil, 188
Class, Buck, 37
Clayburgh, Jill, 276, 277
Cleghorne, Ellen, 190

Clemenson, Christian, 23
Clements, Stanley, 157, 159
Clennon, David, 24, 29
Cliff Island (Maine), 275
Clive, Colin, 103, 104
Close, Glenn, 89, 203, 204
Clutesi, George, 198
Cocaine Fiends (1936 film), 190
Cocaine Traffic (1914 film), 4
Cochran, Steve, 238, 239
Cocoon (1985 film), 5
Cohen, Norman I., 264
Cohen, Scott, 144, 145
Coleman, Dabney, 224
Colichman, Paul, 101
Colick, Lewis, 82
Coll, Ivonne, 149
Colleano, Mark, 73
Collins, Phil, 23
Colors (1988 film), 16, 54–56, 142, 144, 273
"Colors" (song), 55, 56
Colosimo, Vince, 266, 267
Comanor, William, 82
Combs, Jeffrey, 279
Common Threads: Stories from the Quilt (1989 film), 6
The Communist Dream (book), 236, 237
Communist movement, 12, 62–65, 98, 100, 138, 172–73, 191, 257
Como, Perry, 105
Compulsion (1959 film), 2, 6, 7, 13, 57–59
Condon, Bill, 101
Confessions of a Nazi Spy (1939 film), 11
Confidential (magazine), 209
Conklin, Chester, 170
Conley, Joe, 188
Conlin, Noel, 227
Connors, Chuck, 229, 230
Conrack (1974 film), 10, 12, 14, 59–61
Conroy, Pat, 59–61
Conte, John, 162
Conti, Bill, 29, 149
Contner, James, 66
Converse-Roberts, William, 234
Conway, Curt, 146

Cook, Ancel, 219
Cook, Bonnie, 222
Cook, Donald, 160
Cook, Elisha, 255, 257
Cook, Fiedler, 137
Cooksey, Curtis, 236
Coolidge, Philip, 123
Cooney, Kevin, 125
Coop, Denys, 252
Cooper, Jeanne, 133
Cooper, Miriam, 14
Copeman, Michael, 93
Corazza, Vincent, 276, 277
Corey, Jeff, 95, 128
Corley, Nick, 144
Corman, Gene, 134
Corman, Roger, 1, 133–35, 193
The Corn Is Green (1945 film), 10, 110
Cornell University, 277
Cornthwaite, Robert, 90, 92
Cort, Bud, 23
Cortese, Joe, 21
Costa-Gavras, Constantin, 29
Costello, Ward, 279
Cotton, Joseph, 229, 230
Coughlin, Father Charles, 94
Coughlin, Kevin, 236, 238
Coulouris, George, 180, 181, 184
Courtney, Alex, 23
Cowan, Jerome, 261
Cowen, Ron, 87
Cox, Richard, 66
Crabtree, Brian, 180
Cradle Will Rock (1999 film), 7, 12, 62–65
The Cradle Will Rock (opera), 62–65, 273
Crane, Carlton, 188
Craniodiaphyseal dysplasia.
   See Lionitis
Crawford, Broderick, 178–80
Crawford, Joan, 17
Crebbs, Tommy, 249
Crime School (1938 film), 16
The Criminal Code (1930 film), 6
The Crimson Kimono (1960 film), 15
Cromwell, Gloria, 234, 269

Cromwell, James, 130
Cronauer, Adrian, 104, 107
Cronauer, Gail, 264
Cronin, Hume, 5, 59, 60
Crosland, Alan, Jr., 261
Cross, Alison, 211
Cross of Fire (1989 film), 11
Crossfire (1947 film), 14, 241
The Crowd (1928 film), 2
Crowley, Pat, 142
Cruising (1980 film), 12, 66–68
Crump, Owen, 176
Cruz, Celia, 190
Cukor, George, 102
Cummings, Irving, Jr., 216
Cunningham, Sarah, 34
Cuong, Phu, 117
Curtis, Dick, 47
Curtis, Tony, 147
Cusack, Joan, 62, 63
Cusack, John, 62, 63, 65
Czerny, Henry, 258

da Silva, Howard, 40, 41, 65, 95, 96,
    154–156
Dainard, Neil, 276
Dall, John, 13
Dalzell, Dennis, 140
D'Amato, Paul, 246
Damon, Matt, 107, 108
Dance Hall Racket (1953 film), 153
D'Angelo, Beverly, 21
Dangerous Child (2002 film), 8, 9, 68–70
Dankworth, John, 252
Danna, Jeff, 117
Danna, Michael, 117
Darien, Frank, 111, 281
Dark Shadows (television series), 205
Darktown Jubilee (1915 film), 14
Darnell, Linda, 185
Darr, Lisa, 101
Darrow, Clarence, 7, 57–59
Darwell, Jane, 111, 112
Davenport, Nigel, 180, 181, 184
Davidovich, Lolita, 101, 130, 131
Davis, Bette, 5, 10, 17, 160, 206, 208,
    236, 238, 261, 263, 274, 275

Davis, Brad, 249
Davis, Carl, 214
Davis, D'Mitch, 219
Davis, Frank, 281
Davis, Gene, 66
Davis, Harry, 19
Davis, John W., 214–15
Davis, Ossie, 95, 185
Davis, Walt, 244
The Day After Tomorrow (2004 film), 11
Day, Doris, 210, 238, 239, 241
Daybreak (1948 film), 6
Daye, Gabrielle, 252
The Days of Wine and Roses
    (1962 film), 4
De Grasse, Robert, 47
de Havilland, Olivia, 17
De Vol, Frank, 120, 122
de Wilde, Brandon, 37, 38, 40
Dead End Kids. See Bowery Boys
Dead Man Walking (1995 film), 6,
    71–72
*Dead Man Walking: An Eyewitness
    Account of the Death Penalty in the
    United States* (book), 71
Dead Poets Society (1989 film), 16
Deafness, 9, 160, 185, 246–48
Deakins, Roger A., 71
Dean, James, 17
Dean, John A., 90
Dean, Nathaniel, 266, 267
The Death of Grass (novel), 180
Death Trap (1982 film), 13
DeCamp, Rosemary, 178
Decoy (1947 film), 7
Dee, Ruby, 185
Dee, Sandra, 146
DeGarmo, Denise, 140
DeHaven, Gloria, 170
DeLaire, Diane, 45
Delerue, Georges, 234
Delgado, James, 157, 159
DeLine, Donald, 82
The Delinquents (1957 film), 17
DeMille, Cecil B., 8
Demme, Jonathan, 194
DeMunn, Jeffrey, 29

Dench, Judi, 135, 136
Denton, Christa, 42
Depardieu, Gerard, 114, 115
Depression (social theme), 15–16, 47,
    78, 87, 95, 101, 117, 146, 154, 160,
    178, 201, 203, 206, 224, 229, 244,
    246, 249, 264, 279, 281
Dern, Laura, 93–95, 164, 166
Dershowitz, Alan, 203–5
Desk Set (1957 film), 17
Detective Story (1951 film), 3
Devil's Doorway (1950 film), 15
The Devil's Harvest (1941 film), 4
The Devil's Sleep (1949 film), 190
DeVito, Danny, 269
Devlin, Joe, 178
DeWitt, Jack, 45
DeZarraga, Tony, 196
Dickinson, Angie, 244, 246
Dickstein, Dr. Leah, 251
Dies, Martin, 63
Different from the Others (1919 film), 13
A Different Story (1978 film), 13
Dignam, Arthur, 101
Dilello, Richard, 55
Dillman, Bradford, 57, 59
Dillon, Melinda, 206, 208
Director's Guild Award, 88, 131
Disabilities (social theme), 9, 26, 140,
    160, 164, 167, 185, 216, 219, 246,
    274, 279, 281
Disney, Walt, 84, 241
Displaced Persons law, 98
Divorce (social theme), 1, 9, 42, 68, 73,
    76, 82, 95, 261, 269
Divorce American Style (1968 film), 9
Divorce His/Divorce Hers (1973 films),
    9, 73–76
The Divorce of Lady X (1938 film), 9
Divorce Wars (1982 film), 9
The Divorcee (1930 film), 2, 9, 76–78
Dobkin, Larry, 208, 210
Dodd, Bo, 133
Dodsworth (1936 film), 9
A Dog's Life (1918 film), 172
Dolores Claiborne (1995 film), 2, 4, 5, 8,
    10, 15, 17, 78–81

Domestic Disturbance (2001 film), 8, 9,
    17, 82–85
Don Quixote, 243
Donat, Peter, 244, 269
Donat, Robert, 10
Donato, Marc, 68, 69
Dondi (1961 film), 14
Don't Change Your Husband
    (1918 film), 9
Doomwatch (1972 film), 11, 229
Doran, Mary, 76,77
Dostoevsky, Fyodor, 5
Douglas, Diana, 216, 217
Douglas, Michael, 269
Douglas, Paul, 95–97
Dowd, Ann, 194
Dowling, Doris, 154
Dowling, Kathryn, 258, 259
Dr. Cook's Garden (1971 film), 10
Dr. Kildare (film series), 9
Dracula's Daughter (1936 film), 13
Dragonwyck (1946 film), 4
Drake, David, 194
Dreamboat (1952 film), 15
Dreams Don't Die (1982 film), 12
Dreyfuss, Richard, 10, 279, 280
Driver, Minnie, 107, 108
Driving Miss Daisy (1989 film), 5, 10,
    14, 85–87
Drucker, Gary, 82
The Drunkard (play), 4
A Drunkard's Reformation
    (1908 film), 4
Dryburgh, Stuart, 190
Dubov, Paul, 45, 157, 159
Dudley, Anne, 22
Dudley, Janet, 224
Dudley, Paul, 173
Dukes, David, 23, 101
Dunford, Christine, 203
Dunne, Philip, 37, 40
Dunning, George, 236
Dunsmore, Rosemary, 68
Duong, Don, 117
Duryea, Dan, 47, 48
Duvall, Robert, 52–56
Dvorak, Antonin, 250

Dynasty (television series), 210
Dysart, Richard, 164, 198–200

An Early Frost (1985 film), 5, 12, 15,
    87–90
East Side Gang. See Bowery Boys
Eastside High School (Paterson, New
    Jersey), 149–51
Easy Rider (1969 film), 17, 243
Easy Street (1917 film), 172
Eating disorders, 4,
    140–42, 176
Ebbs, Donna, 264
Edelman, Barbara, 227
Edelman, Gregg, 114
Edelstein, Neal, 241
Edson, Richard, 104
Education (social theme), 10, 42, 59,
    85, 107, 149, 196, 201, 232, 236
Edwards, Vince, 45
Edwards-Hughes, Jennifer, 241
Eidelman, Cliff, 125
Eilber, Janet, 279
Eisler, Hans, 281
Eldridge, Florence, 76
Elegy for Iris (book), 135
Elfman, Danny, 52, 78, 80, 107
Eliot, Mark, 232
Elliott, Alison, 130, 131
Elliott, Paul, 24
Elliott, Robert, 76
Elliott, Ross, 47
Elliott, Sam, 164, 165
Ellis Island (miniseries), 14
Ellis, Juney, 37
Elmer Gantry (1960 film), 241
Eltz, Theodore von, 76
Elwes, Cary, 62, 63
Emhardt, Robert, 133, 134
Emmy Awards, 43, 88, 131, 249
The Emperor's Club (2002 film), 10
End-of-life issues (social theme),
    10–11, 78, 101, 135, 164, 178, 203,
    206, 279, 266, 274
Engel, Roy, 47
Englund, Robert, 264–66
Ensign, Michael, 208

Environment (1971 film), 11, 90–93
Environmental issues (social theme),
    11, 52, 90, 114, 180, 198, 229
Environmental Protection Agency
    (EPA), 52, 53, 198
Erdman, Richard, 167–70
Erickson, Leif, 95, 146
Erman, John, 88
Ermey, R. Lee, 71
Erving, Julius, 194
Erwin, Bill, 219
Escalante, Jaimie, 232–34
Escoffier, Jean Yves, 62, 107
Escort Girl (1941 film), 190
Essex, Harry, 157
Estrin, Robert, 55, 190
Eszterhas, Joe, 29
Euthanasia. *See* End-of-life issues
Evans, Evan, 198
Evans, Gene, 238
Evans, Jeanne, 264
Evans, Tim, 252–54
Evdemon, Nikos, 68
Executive Decision (1996 film), 12
Exton, Clive, 252
Ex-Wife (novel), 76
Eyre, Richard, 135

The Face of Rage (1983 film), 18
Factor, Alan J., 244
Fahrenheit 451 (1966 film), 238
Fairfield, Heather, 269
Faison, Matthew, 227
Faith, Percy, 105
Falmouth (Maine), 275
Fapp, Daniel, 271
Fargas, Antonio, 59
Farley, John, 241
Farley, Kevin, 241
Farmer, Virginia, 167
Farnsworth, Richard, 241, 242
Farr, Judi, 266, 267
Fash, Mike, 274
Father of the Bride (1950 film), 121
Father of Frankenstein (novel), 101
Faustus (play), 63
Fawcett, Farrah, 42, 43

Faylen, Frank, 95, 111, 154–156
Fear in the Night (1947 film), 16
Federal Bureau of Investigation (FBI), 29–30, 257
Federal Communications Commission (FCC), 202
Federal Theater Project (FTP), 62–64
Feinberg, Greg, 101
Feldshuh, Tovah, 144
Ferguson, Margaret, 216, 217
Ferrero, Martin, 101
Ferzetti, Gabriele, 73
Fetterman, Richard, 42
Fiedel, Brad, 206
Field, Chelsea, 130, 131
Field, Grace, 37
Field, Sally, 249
Fields, Edith, 206
Fields, W. C., 4
Fifth Symphony (Beethoven), 60–61
Fighter Squadron (1948 film), 209
Finkel, Abem, 32
The First Wives' Club (1996 film), 9
Fish, Nancy, 222
Fisher, Theodore, 90
Fitzpatrick, Richard, 107
Flatman, Barry, 276
Flavin, James, 128
Flax, Phyllis, 219
Fleischer, Richard, 57
Fleisher, Richard, 229, 252
Flick, Pat C., 32
Flight of the Bumble Bee (musical composition), 60
Flint, Helen, 32
Flower Drum Song (1961 film), 14
Flowers in the Attic (1987 film), 9
Floyd, Susan, 82
The Flying Deuces (1939 film), 16
Flynn, Miriam, 130
Focus (2001 film), 2, 11, 14, 93–95
Focus (novel), 93
Fogle, Joanne, 211
Fonda, Henry, 5, 111, 112
Fontaine, Joan, 218
Fontaine, Lilian, 154
A Fool There Was (1914 film), 1

Foolish Wives (1922 film), 8
Foote, Hallie, 214
Foran, Dick, 32
Forbstein, Leo, 160
Ford, Brendan, 125
Ford, Glenn, 255
Ford, John, 111, 114
Ford, Ross, 178, 216
Foreman, Carl, 167
Forestal, Sean, 180
Forsythe, Henderson, 214
Forsythe, John, 128
Forte, Joe, 45
Fosse, Bob, 152
Foster, Barry, 73
Foster, Diane, 173, 174
Foster, Gloria, 214
Fourteen Hours (1951 film), 9, 12, 15, 95–97
Fox, Crystal R., 85
Fox, Michael, 98
Fox, Robert, 135
Foxworth, Robert, 198
Francis, Freddie, 241
Frank, Harriet, Jr., 59
Frank, Joanna, 19
Frankenheimer, John, 198, 210
Frankenstein (1931 film), 101
Fraser, Brendan, 101–3
Frederick, Lynne, 180, 181, 184
Freeman, Al, Jr., 34
Freeman, Kathleen, 98
Freeman, Morgan, 85, 87, 149, 150
Freeman-Fox, Lois, 24
Friedkin, William, 66–68
Friedman, Hillel, 144
Friends (television series), 146
From Here to Eternity (1953 film), 238
The Front (1976 film), 8
Front Page Woman (1935 film), 6
Frost, Alan, 244
Frost, David, 184
Frye, Vergil, 42
Fuchs, Daniel, 238
Fujimoto, Tak, 194
Fuller, Tex, 180

Fultz, Mona Lee, 264
Furlong, Edward, 21–23

Gable, Martin, 95, 96
Gaines, Richard, 255
Gainey, Michael, 37
Gallaudet, John, 128
Gallo, Vincent, 190
Galloway, Don, 208, 210
Gamblers Anonymous, 176
Gammell, Robin, 125
Gandolfini, James, 52, 54
Gang Rape. See Patty
Gangs (social theme), 16–17, 21, 54,
    107, 142, 157, 271
Garcia, Allan, 170
Garcia, Andy, 232
Garcia, Rodrigo, 130
Gardos, Eva, 164
Garfield High School (East Los
    Angeles), 232–34
Garland, Beverly, 219
Garner, Jack, 176
Garner, James, 176, 177
Garner, Peggy Ann, 216
Garralaga, Martin, 40
Garver, Kathy, 173
Gasman, Vittorio, 98
Gaster, Nicolas, 274
Gates, Phyllis, 208–10
Gazzara, Ben, 87–89
Gebert, Gordon, 47, 48
Geer, Will, 34, 36, 128, 130
Geeson, Judy, 252, 254
Gehringer, Linda, 26
Geigerman, Clarice F., 85
Gentleman's Agreement (1947 film),
    14, 94
George, Kent, 101
George, Laszlo, 276
Geraghty, Marita, 222
Geray, Steven, 261
Gere, Richard, 23, 25
Gerringer, Robert, 34
Gerstad, Harry, 167
Gertsman, Maury, 173
Getty, Estelle, 164

Giallelis, Stathis, 19
Gibson, Mel, 15
Gidding, Nelson, 123
Gilfillan, Sue Ann, 87
Gilpin, Jack, 203
Gilroy, Tony, 78
Gish, Lillian, 12, 274, 275
Glass, Ned, 238, 271
The Glass Wall (1953 film), 12, 13, 14,
    98–100
Gleason, Jackie, 4
Gleason, Joanna, 125
Glen or Glenda (1953 film), 190
Glenn, Roy, 120
Glover, John, 87–89
Goddard, Paulette, 170
Godfather (film series), 14, 152
Gods and Monsters (1998 film), 10, 13,
    15, 101–4
Going in Style (1979 film), 5
Gold, Carolyn, 85
Goldberg, Leonard, 222
Goldemberg, Rose L., 42
The Golden Chance (1915 film), 8
Golden Globe Awards, 26, 131
Goldenberg, Rose Leiman, 234
Goldfinger, Michael, 232
Goldsmith, Jerry, 222, 224
Goldwyn, Samuel, 1
Golm, Lisa, 173
Good Morning Miss Dove (1955 film), 10
Good Morning, Vietnam (1987 film), 7,
    104–7
Good Will Hunting (1997 film), 8, 10,
    12, 16, 107–11
Goodbye Mr. Chips (1939 film), 10
Goodell, Gregory, 258
Goodhand, Donna, 258
Gooding, Cuba, Jr., 26, 27
Goodis, David, 261, 263
Goodman, John, 268
Goodman, Jules Eckert, 160
Gorcey, Leo, 16
Gordon, Bruce, 142
Gordon, Leo, 133, 134
Gordon, Michael, 147
Gotay, Will, 232

Gough, Lloyd, 238
Gould, Elliott, 21
Gould, Terry, 68
Gowland, Gibson, 8
Grace Quigley (1985 film), 5
Graff, Wilton, 57
Graham, Barbara, 123, 124
Graham, Fred, 40, 185
Grahame, Gloria, 98, 99
Granger, Farley, 13
Grant, David Marshall, 23
Grant, Kathryn, 45, 236
The Grapes of Wrath (1940 film), 2, 12, 111–14
Grapewin, Charley, 111
Grasse, Robert de, 167
Gray, Charles H., 198
Gray, Linda, 66
The Great Dictator (1940 film), 8
Great Northern Paper, 200
The Great Sinner (1949 film), 5
Greed (1925 film), 8
Green Card (1990 film), 3, 11, 13, 114–17
Green Dragon (2002 film), 2, 13, 15, 117–120
The Green Mile (1999 film), 6
Greenberg, Jerry, 21
Greenberg, Stanley, R., 229
Greene, David, 50
Greene, Ellen, 201
Greenleaf, Raymond, 173, 238
Greenlee, Laura, 125
Greenstreet, Sydney, 7
Greenwald, Robert, 42
Greer, Dabbs, 123
Grieg, Edvard, 229
Griffin, John Howard, 34
Griffith, Ava, 73
Griffith, D. W., 1, 4, 8
Griffith, Thomas Ian, 208, 211
Griggs, Loyal, 224
Grimes, Frank, 274
Grinde, Nick, 76
Grody, Kathryn, 279
Gross, Charles, 42, 279
Gross, Jack J., 281

Gross, Roland, 281
Grover, Deborah, 276
Grubbs, Gary, 42
Guess Who's Coming to Dinner? (1967 film), 14, 120–22
Guest, Nicholas, 227
Guffey, Burnett, 216, 236
A Guide to Apocalyptic Cinema (book), 11
Guidry, Matt, 241
Guilfoyle, Paul, 111, 255
Guillaume, Robert, 149
The Gulag Archipelago (book), 184
Gunn, James, 261
Gunton, Bob, 78
Guthrie, Carl, 238
Guttman, Ronald, 24, 114

Hackford, Taylor, 78
Haddock, Jack, 188
Hadjidakis, Manos, 19
Hagen, Uta, 203
Hagerty, Julie, 203, 205
Haines, William Wister, 32
Hale, Louise Closser, 160
Hall, Albert, 29, 214
Hall, Conrad L., 52, 128
Hall, Ed, 214
Hall, Huntz, 16
Hall, Philip Baker, 62
Hall, William, Jr., 85
Hallelujah, I'm a Bum (1933 film), 12
Haller, Ernest, 261
Halop, Billy, 16
Hamill, John, 180, 181
Hamilton, John, 167
Hamilton, Linda, 18
Hamilton, Lisa Gay, 203
Hamlet (play), 15
Hamm, Jon, 144
Hammer, Gerald, 216
Hammer, Mark, 214
Hammer, Victor, 149
Hampton, Janice, 201
Hancock, Herbie, 55
Handel, Leo A., 188
Hanks, Tom, 193, 194

Hannah, Bob, 85
"Happy Days Are Here Again" (song), 81
Hard to Handle (1933 film), 12
Hard Luck (1921 film), 16
Hardy, Oliver, 16
Hardy, Robert, 252
Harker, Jane, 261
Harkins, John, 206, 208
Harmon, John, 146
Harper Prize, 255
Harper, Robert, 176
Harr, Jonathan, 52
Harrington, Graham, 222
Harris, Brad, 173
Harris, David, 137, 138
Harris, Mark, 101, 152
Harris, Mel, 258, 259
Harris, Richard A., 130
Harris, Robert H., 19
Harris, Viola, 224
Harrison, Doane, 154
Harrison, Harry, 229
Harrison, Rex, 13
Harrison, Susan, 142
Harvard University, 204
Harvey (1950 film), 4
Harvey, Paul, 32
Harvey, Rupert, 201
Haskell, Eddie, 39
The Hatchet Man (1932 film), 15
Hate groups (social theme), 11–12, 21, 29, 32, 93, 133, 137, 185, 238, 255
A Hatful of Rain (1957 film), 4
Hathaway, Henry, 95
Hatton, Raymond, 128
The Haunting (1999 film), 9
Hauser, Cole, 107
Havrilla, Joann, 85
Hawke, Ethan, 15
Hawtrey, Kay, 93
Hayden, Harry, 32
Hayes, Adrienne, 188
Hays, Lora, 34
Hays Office (motion picture code enforcement), 4, 7–8
Hays, Will H., 7

Hayward, Susan, 123, 124
Haze, Jonathan, 45
Headly, Glenne, 24
Health Maintenance Organization (HMO), 29
Heard, John, 29
Hearst, William Randolph, 65
The Heart Is a Lonely Hunter (1968 film), 9
Hearts of the World (1918 film), 8
Heche, Anne, 125, 126
Heckert, Eileen, 258
Hedaya, Dan, 52, 54
Heim, Alan, 21, 152
Heimbeinder, Susan, 62
Heisler, Stuart, 22, 238
Heit, Jane Galloway, 241
Helen Keller, The Miracle Continues (1984 film), 9
Hellman, Lillian, 13
Helmsley, Estelle, 19
Helton, Percy, 255
Heming, Violet, 160
Hemingway, Ernest, 197
Henry, Mike, 229
Hepburn, Katharine, 5, 17, 120–22
Hereford, Kathryn, 142
Herlihy, James Leo, 37
Hermann-Wurmfeld, Charles, 144
Hernandez, Juano, 255
Herrmann, Bernard, 37, 40
Heston, Charlton, 229–31
Heyman, Barton, 71
Heywood, Pat, 252, 254
Hickman, Darryl, 111
Hickock, Dick, 128–30
Hickok, Holly, 194
Hicks, Russell, 95
Higgins, John C., 40
High School Hellcats (1958 film), 17
Hill, Arthur, 137–39
Hill, Steven, 224, 225
Hill, Thomas, 224
Hinds, Samuel S., 32
Hines, Alan, 68
The Hippie Revolt (1968 film), 17
Hitchcock, Alfred, 13

Hitler, Adolf, 14, 22, 31, 237
Hobbie, Duke, 128
Hoblit, Gregory, 211
Hodiak, John, 255, 257
Hoffman, Dustin, 152, 153
Hoffman, Jackie, 144
Hoffman, Jane, 249, 251
Hold Back the Dawn (1941 film), 14
Holdenreid, Kris, 276
Holiday, John "Doc," 184
Hollis, Thomas, 214
Holmes, Dennis, 142
Holmes, Lyvingston, 198
Holmes, William, 160
The Holocaust (1978 miniseries), 15
Holt, Patrick, 180
Homans, Robert, 111
Home of the Brave (1949 film), 14
Home Sweet Homeless (1988 film), 12
Homelessness (social theme), 12, 42,
    47, 59, 62, 78, 98, 107, 111, 170,
    219, 227, 234, 246
Homosexuality (social theme), 8,
    12-13, 23, 26, 62, 66, 87, 95, 101,
    144, 193, 201, 208, 244, 266
Honess, Peter, 82, 125
Hood, Don, 87-89
Hooper, Geoffrey, 180
Hope, Barclay, 68
Hopkins, Jermaine, 149
Hopkins, John, 73
Hopper, Dennis, 55, 56, 142
Hornbeck, William, 123
Horner, James, 135
Horsford, Anna Maria, 234
Horton, Edward Everett, 5
Horton, James Edwin, 137-39
Horton, Thomas, 59
Hough, Paul, 128
Houghton, Katharine, 120, 122
House of Games (1987 film), 5
House UnAmerican Activities
    Committee, 63-65
Houseman, Arthur, 4
Houseman, John, 10, 63-65
How to Talk Dirty and Influence People
    (book), 202

Howell, Maude T., 160
Hoy, Robert, 224
Hoyt, John, 146, 148, 255, 257, 261,
    262
Huddlestone, David, 34
Hudson, Rock, 25, 208-11
Huffman, Felicity, 203
Huggins, Roy, 147, 196, 201
Hughes, Barnard, 62
Hughes, Sally, 188
Human Rights Commission, 99, 100
Human Wreckage (1923 film), 4
Humphrey, Hubert H., 201, 203
Humphreys, Robert, 266
Hunnicutt, Arthur, 40
Hunt, Helen, 26-28, 146
Hunt, Marsha, 37
Hunter, Holly, 211, 212
Hunter, Jeffrey, 95, 142
Hunter, Kaki, 279
Hunter, Kim, 236, 237
Hunter, Nita, 167
Hurry Sundown (1967 film), 14
Hurt, John, 252, 254
Hussein, Waris, 73
Huston, Anjelica, 23, 190, 191
Hutton, Rif, 232

I Accuse My Parents (1944 film), 16
I Hate Your Guts. See The Intruder
I Led 3 Lives (television series), 257
I Married a Communist (1950 film),
    257
I Never Sang for My Father
    (1970 film), 5
I Want to Keep My Baby (1976 film), 18
I Want to Live! (1958 film), 6, 123-25
I Was a Communist for the FBI (1951
    film), 257
I Was a Fugitive from a Chain Gang (1932
    film), 12
Ice-T, 55, 56
If These Walls Could Talk (1996 film), 3,
    125-7
Iley, Barbara, 87
Imhof, Roger, 111
The Immigrant (1917 film), 14, 172

Immigration (social theme), 13–14, 19, 21, 32, 40, 98, 114, 117, 190, 255, 271
In Cold Blood (book), 128
In Cold Blood (1967 film), 2, 6, 128–30, 241
In Quest of the Pearl Poet (book), 245
In the Gloaming (2000 film), 89
In the Heat of the Night (1967 film), 14
In the Matter of Karen Ann Quinlan (1977 film), 10
Indictment (1995 film), 8, 130–33
Ingraham, Lloyd, 170
Inherit the Wind (1960 film), 7
The Interns (1962 film), 4
Intolerance (1916 film), 1
Intruder in the Dust (1949 film), 14
The Intruder (1962 film), 11, 14, 133–35
The Intruder (novel), 133, 135
The Invisible Man (1933 film), 101
Iris (2001 film), 5, 10, 135–37
Iris: A Memoir (book), 135
The Iron Curtain (1948 film), 12
Irons, Jeremy, 203–6
Irving, George, 76
Isham, Mark, 203
Islam, 20–21
Islamic radical movement, 12
It Happened One Night (1934 film), 243
It's a Wonderful Life (1946 film), 16
The Italian (1915 film), 13
Ivanek, Zeljko, 52

Jacek, Scott, 87
Jackman, Fred, Jr., 45
Jackson, Charles R., 154, 156
Jackson, Mary, 227
Jackson, Mick, 130
Jackson, Selmer, 111
Jacobson, Peter, 52
Jaffe, Sam, 5
James, Clifton, 34
James, Jesse, 26, 101
James, Peter, 85
James, Walter, 170
Janssen, Famke, 1

Jarvis, Graham, 198
Jenkins, Ken, 24
Jennings, Peter, 132
Jenson, Roy, 229
Jessye, Eva, 34
Jesus Christ, 2, 72, 114
Jewell, Hollis, 111
Jill (Brussels Griffon), 26, 28
John, Elton, 25
Johnny Belinda (1948 film), 9
Johnny Stool Pigeon (1949 film), 4
Johnson, Bridgit, 26
Johnson, Dots, 185
Johnson, Doug, 227
Johnson, Georgann, 140
Johnson, George Clayton, 133
Johnson, Helen, 76
Johnson, Ken, 219
Johnson, Mark, 104
Johnson, Nunnally, 111
Jones, Cherry, 62, 63
Jones, Deborah, 276
Jones, Dickie, 32
Jones, Jennifer, 10
Jones, Marsha, 47
Jones, Quincy, 128, 224
Jones, Robert C., 120
Jones, Simon, 114
Jones, Timothy, 266
Jordan, Alan, 276
Jordan, Bobby, 16
Josephson, Julien, 160
Jubinville, Kevin, 93
Judge Horton and the Scottsboro Boys (1976 film), 2, 11, 14, 137–39
Juergensen, Heather, 144–46
Julius Caesar (play), 64
Jurado, Arthur, 167–70
Jurado, Katy, 255
Jurgensen, Randy, 66

Kalember, Patricia, 264, 265
Kaler, Sylvia, 85
Kamen, Michael, 246
Kander, John, 88
Kane, Frank, 142
Kane, Sid, 188

Kaplan, Mike, 274
Karam, Elena, 19
Karloff, Boris, 6, 102, 104, 161
Karlson, Phil, 142
Kartlian, Buck, 45
Karyo, Tcheky, 24
Kasdan, Lawrence, 26
Kasem, Jean, 208
Katahdin Paper Company, 200
Kate's Secret (1986 film), 9, 17, 140–42
Katz, Sidney M., 206
Katz, Stephen M., 101
Katz, Virginia, 101
Kaun, Bernhard, 32
Kaye, Tony, 21
Kazan, Elia, 19
Kazan, Nicholas, 203
Keach, Stacy, 21, 22
Kearns, Joseph, 236
Keaton, Buster, 4, 12, 16
Keefer, Catherine, 125
Keene, Elodie, 211
Kefauver, Estes, 157, 158
Keith, Brian, 10, 236, 237
Keith, Robert, 95
Keith, Sherwood, 188
Kellaway, Cecil, 120, 122
Keller, Helen, 9
Kelley, Barry, 173, 255
Kelley, DeForest, 167, 168
Kelly, Grace, 95, 96
Kelly, Paul, 236
Kelly, Paula, 229
Kennedy, Arthur, 255
Kennedy, Douglas, 261
Kennedy, John, 59
Kennedy, John F., 154
Kennedy, Ludovic, 252
Kennedy, Mimi, 201
Keosian, Jessie, 114
Kercheval, Ken, 137
Kerew, Diana, 208
Kerr, E. Katherine, 246
Key Witness (1960 film), 16, 142–44
Khaner, Julie, 276
Kiely, Mark, 101
Kiley, Richard, 214

Kilik, Jon, 62
Kill Me While You Can (1977 film), 47
The Killing of Sister George (1968 film), 13
Kilpatrick, Lincoln, 229
Kilpatrick, Patrick, 234
Kimball, Edward, 170
King, Marlene, 125
King, Martin Luther, Jr., 86, 87
A King in New York (1957 film), 15
King, Stephen, 2, 78, 200
Kinnear, Greg, 26–28
Kinskey, Leonid, 162
Kirby, Bruno, 104
Kirk, Jon, 71
A Kiss Before Dying (1956 film), 16
Kissing Jessica Stein (2001 film), 12, 144–46
The Klansman (1974 film), 11
Kleyla, Brandon, 101
Kline, Kevin, 10
Kline, Richard H., 229
Klingman, Lynzee, 269
Knight, Shirley, 26, 125, 130, 131, 133
Knight, Ted, 142
Knowland, Nic, 214
Knox, Alexander, 216
Knudsen, Peggy, 261
Kolster, Clarence, 238
Koock, Guich, 264
Koppel, Ted, 132
Korean War, 126, 167
Kovacs, Laszlo, 164
Kraike, Michel, 147
Kramer, Stanley, 120, 121, 167
Krane, Jonathan, 82
Krasner, Milton, 185
Kruger, Freddie, 266
Krugmar, Lou, 123
Ku Klux Klan (KKK), 11, 14, 30–33, 95, 134, 135, 138, 139, 238–41
Kupferman, Meyer, 34
Kuras, Ellen, 125
Kurtz, Swoosie, 23
Kurtz, Walter, 133
Kydd, Sam, 252

La Pierre, Georganne, 125
Ladd, Diane, 208
Ladd, Margaret, 274
The Lady Gambles (1949 film), 4, 15, 146–49
Lafayette, John, 87
Lafferty, Perry, 88
Lahti, Christine, 279, 280
Lamblon, Anne, 21
Lampert, Zohra, 244
Lancaster, Burt, 214, 215
Lanchester, Elsa, 102, 104
Lander, Rosalyn, 73
Lane, Charles, 249, 251
Lane, Rusty, 123
Lang, Stephen, 234
Lanza, Angela, 190
Larner, Stevan, 50
Lasally, Walter, 234
Laselles, Kendrew, 93
The Last Mile (1932 film), 6
"The Last Song" (song), 25
Lau, Wesley, 123
Laufer, Jack, 24
Laurents, Arthur, 271
Laurie, Piper, 10
Law and Order (television series), 58
Lawrence, Elizabeth, 222
Lazar, Paul, 194
Le, Hiep Thi, 117
Le Sainte, Ed, 170
Leaf, Paul, 137
Lean on Me (1989 film), 10, 14, 149–51
"Lean on Me" (song), 151
Leavitt, Sam, 120, 162
Lederer, Suzanne, 137, 138
Lee, Ann, 255
Lee, Bernard, 252
Lee, Gracia, 59
Lee, Harper, 139
Lees, Richard, 206, 207
Leeson, Michael, 269
The Legion of Terror (1937 film), 11
Lehman, Ernest, 271, 273
Leigh, Jennifer Jason, 78, 79, 81
Lein, Jennifer, 21
LeMat, Paul, 21, 42, 43

Lembeck, Harvey, 95
Lemmon, Jack, 16
Lenin, Vladimir, 64, 65
Lenny (1974 film), 3, 4, 7, 152–54
Lenny (play), 152
Lenny Bruce Performance Film (documentary), 153
Leonard, Robert Z., 76
Leopold, Nathan, 13, 57
Lerner, Carl, 34
Lerner, Gerda, 34
Lesbianism, 13, 144–46
Leslie, Nan, 281, 282
The Letter (1940 film), 261, 263
Levin, Meyer, 57
Levine, Ted, 29
Levinson, Barry, 104
Lewis, Paul, 55
Leyton, Drue, 6
Liberace, 25, 161, 211
Libertini, Richard, 29
The Life of David Gale (2003 film), 7
Light that Failed (1939 film), 9
Ligon, Tom, 137
Li'l Abner (1940 film), 113
Lincoln, Abraham, 23, 64
Linder, Leslie, 252
Linder, Stu, 104
Lindfors, Viveca, 178, 180
Lindley, John W., 222
Lindon, Lionel, 123
Lindstrom, Leif, 188
Lionitis, 164–167
Lipman, Daniel, 88
Liszt, Franz, 206
Litel, John, 32
Literacy (social theme), 10, 42, 59, 85, 107, 149, 196, 201, 232, 236
Lithgow, John, 52, 53
Little, Cleavon, 214
The Living End (1992 film), 6
Living the Lie. See The Unspoken Truth
Lloyd, Doris, 216
Lloyd, Harold, 12, 16
Lloyd, John Bedford, 194
Lloyd, Kathleen, 50

Lloyd, Walt, 201
LoBianco, Tony, 13
Lock, Gerry, 57
Locricchio, Matthew, 234
Loeb, Richard, 13, 57
Loeffler, Louis R., 162
Lofthouse, Christopher, 180
Logue, Donal, 24
London, Jason, 125
Long, Jesse, 101
Longtime Companion (1990 film), 6
Look (magazine), 256
Lookingland, Todd, 244, 246
Lord, Daniel A., 7
Lord, Justin, 50
Lord, Robert, 32
The Lords of Discipline (novel), 59
Lorimer, Louise, 57
Lost Boundaries (1948 film), 14
The Lost Weekend (1945 film), 4, 15,
    147, 154–57, 175Ä
Louis XVI (king of the French), 7
Louis, Justin, 258
Lovejoy, Frank, 157–159
Lovejoy, Ray, 246
Lovsky, Celia, 229, 230
Lucas, Wilfred, 170
Ludwig, Jerold L., 88
Ludwig, Salem, 19
Lugosi, Bela, 4, 205
Luguet, Andre, 160
Lukens, Victor, 34
Lummis, Dayton, 173
Lundsford, Beverly, 133
Luong, Kathleen, 117
Lupino, Ida, 18
LuPone, Patti, 85
Lustig, Aaron, 125
Lux Video Theater (television series), 161
Lynch, David, 241
Lynley, Carol, 4, 37, 40
Lynn, Dani, 188
Lyon, William A., 236
Lyons, Phyllis, 125

MacDonald, C. P., 59
MacDonald, Joe, 95

MacDonald, Wallace, 45
MacDowell, Andie, 114, 115
MacDuff, Tyler, 45
MacFadyen, Angus, 62, 63
MacLeod, Gavin, 57, 123
MacNamara, Pat, 234
Macy, William H., 52, 54, 93, 95
The Mad Doctor (1941 film), 15
Mad at the World (1955 film), 16,
    157–59
Mädchen in Uniform (1931 film), 13
Madden, David, 244
Madigan, Amy, 211–13
Maganini, Elena, 125
Magnificent Obsession (1954 film), 209
Maguire, Charles H., 19
Mahoney, John, 29, 246, 247
Mailer, Stephen, 203
Make Room! Make Room! (novel), 229
Make Way for Tomorrow (1937 film), 5
Malatesta, Fred, 170
Malnick, Susan, 152
Malthusian theory, 91
Maltin, Leonard, 30
Man at the Crossroads (mural), 63–65
Man on the Ledge (1955 film), 97
The Man Who Played God (1932 film), 9,
    15, 160–61
The Man With the Golden Arm (1956
    film), 4, 162–64
Man, Frankie, 152
Mancina, Mark, 82
Mandel, Johnny, 123
Mankiewicz, Don M., 123
Mankiewicz, Joseph L., 185
Mankofsky, Isadore, 42
Mann, Abby, 130
Mann, Anthony, 40
Mann, Hank, 170
Mann, Myra, 130
Mann, Paul, 19
Manners, Sam, 196
Mantegna, Joe, 246
Mantell, Joe, 236
March, Fredric, 4, 10
Margaret (princess of England), 102
Marguiles, Michael, 244

Margulies, Stan, 214
Mariel Boat Lift, 191–93
Marjorowski, Rachel, 107
Markiewicz, Don M., 255
Marks, Julian, 258
Marks, Owen, 32
Marks, Richard, 26
Marley, Glen, 196, 198
Marley, John, 19, 123
Marley, Peverell, 178
Marlowe, Christopher, 63–65
Marokwitz, Mitch, 104
Maross, Joe, 219
Marquez, Vanessa, 232
The Marriage of a Young Stockbroker
    (1971 film), 9
Marriott, John, 34
The Marrying Kind (1952 film), 9
Marsh, Linda, 19
Marsh, Mae, 111
Marshall, Don, 244
Marshall, E. G., 57, 58
Marshall, James, 264, 265
Marshall, Kris, 135
Marshall, Thurgood, 213–15
Martin, D'Urville, 34
Martin, Speer, 188
Martin, Steve, 24
Martindale, Margo, 71
Martinez, Cliff, 201
Mask (1985 film), 4, 9, 10, 164–67
Maslin, Kristy Jacobs, 144
Mason, James, 10
Massachusetts Institute of Technology
    (MIT), 108
Massen, Osa, 178
Masters, Ben, 140
Mastro, Michael, 144
Masur, Richard, 24, 42, 43
Mathews, A. E., 5
Mathews, Dakin, 24
Mathews, Thom, 208
Mathis, Samantha, 201
Matinee (1993 film), 92
Max, Norman, 176
Maxwell, Frank, 133, 134
Maxwell, Jenny, 37

Maxwell, Roberta, 71, 194, 276
May, Anthony, 180, 181, 184
Mayer, Louis B., 1
Mayo, Archie, 32
McCallum, Bill, 241
McCarrol, Robert, 93
McCarthy, Dennis, 276
McCarthy, Joseph, 173, 239, 257
McClory, Sean, 238
McCoy, Dr. Leonard, 168
McDowall, Roddy, 219, 221
McFadden, Tom, 198
McGavin, Darren, 162–164
McGill, Everett, 241
McGlynn, Pauline, 135
McGraw, Charles, 40, 128
McGreevey, John, 137
McGuire, Dorothy, 255, 256
McHugh, Kitty, 111
McKay, Craig, 194
McKellen, Ian, 23, 25, 101, 103
McKenna, David, 21
McKenzie, Matt, 101
McKinley, J. Edward, 188
McKinney, Myra, 170
McLarnin, Jimmy, 174
McLean, Michael S., 249
McLiam, John, 128
McMahon, David, 188
McMartin Case, 131–133
McMillan and Wife (television series),
    210
McMillan, Kenneth, 279
McNally, Stephen, 146–148, 185, 187
McNulty, Faith, 42
McQuarrie, Murdoch, 170
McQueen, B. J., 93
McRobbie, Peter, 24
Meade, Claire, 261
Meadows, Arlene, 93
Meat Loaf, 93–95
Meehan, John, 76
Mein Kampf (book), 237
Mejia, Geraldo, 54
Melameo, Fred, 246
Melchior, Ib, 188
Melkan, Barbara, 185

Mell, Randle, 214
Mellor, William C., 57
Melnick, Peter Rodgers, 130
Meltzer, Lewis, 162
The Men (1950 film), 9, 167–70
Menendez, Ramon, 232
Mental illness, 9, 154
Mental retardation, 9
Merande, Doro, 162
Mercurio, Micole, 164, 211
Merriman, Ryan, 68, 69
Metty, Russell, 147
Meyer, Emile, 162–164
Meyers, Stanley, 73
Michaels, Deena, 42
Michaels, Jana, 125
Michaels, Sidney, 142
Michan, Arnon, 269
Micheaux, Oscar, 14
Middleton, Charles, 111
Middleton, Robert, 255, 256
Miles, Vera, 137
Milford, Penelope, 42
Milland, Ray, 6, 154–57, 160, 175
Millard, Helene, 76
Millbern, David, 101
Miller, Allan, 66
Miller, Arthur, 2, 93, 95
Miller, Robert A., 93
Miller, Walter, 111
Millinocket (Maine), 200
Mills, Edwin, 219
Mills, Shirley, 111
Milner, Jessamine, 249, 251
Milner, Martin, 57
Minamata disease, 200
Miner, Jan, 152
Miners, Bruce, 180
Mintana, Karla, 232
Mintner, Kelly, 164
The Miracle of Kathy Miller
    (1982 film), 10
The Miracle Worker (1962 film), 9
Miss Susan (television series), 216
Missing Children: A Mother's Story (1982
    film), 9
Mitchell, Cameron, 97, 173–75

Mitchell, Grant, 111
Mitchell, James, 40
Mitchell, Shirley, 269
Mitchell, Thomas, 4
Mitrovich, Marta, 261, 264
Mitty, J. A., 264
Modern Times (1936 film), 12, 170–73
Modine, Matthew, 23, 25
Moffett, D. W., 87, 88
Mohammed, 21
Molina, Alfred, 190, 191
Moll, Elick, 236
Moll, Gretchen, 62
Moltke, Alexandra, 205
Monk, Roger, 266
Monkey on My Back (1957 film), 4,
    173–75
Monoson, Lawrence, 164
Monsieur Verdoux (1947 film), 8
Montalban, Ricardo, 40, 41
Montgomery, Ed, 123, 124
Montgomery, Robert, 76, 77
Moore, Demi, 125
Moore, Dudley, 4
Moore, Millie, 140
Moore, Muriel, 85
Moorehead, Agnes, 95, 96
Moosekian, Duke, 140
Moran, Frank, 147
Mordente, Tony, 271
Moreland, Jane, 59
Moreno, Rita, 271, 272
Morgan, Ira, 170
Morganthau, Kramer, 117
Morrill, Priscilla, 206
Morris, Chester, 76, 77
Morris, Gouverneur, 160
Morriss, Frank, 279
Morrissey, John, 22
The Mortal Storm (1940 film), 14
Morton, Gary, 152
Moses, William R., 208, 211
Moss, Arnold, 40
The Mother and the Law. See Intolerance
Mother Machree (1928 film), 14
Motion Picture Association of
    America (MPAA), 3, 8

Motion Picture Industry Council,
  236
Mount Katahdin (Maine), 200
Mowbray, Alan, 6
Moyle, Allan, 201
Mozart, Wolfgang Amadeus, 110
Mr. Holland's Opus (1995 film), 10
Mrs. Doubtfire (1993), 9
Mrs. Wiggs of the Cabbage Patch (1934
  film), 12
Mueller, Henry, II, 34
Mulkey, Chris, 211
Mulvehill, Charles, 78
Murder or Mercy (1974 film), 10
Murdoch, Iris, 135–37
Murdock, George, 211
Murnau, F. W., 2
Murphy, George, 40, 41
Murphy, Michael S., 276
Murphy, Richard, 57
Murray, Bill, 62, 63
Musca, Tom, 232
The Musketeers of Pig Alley (1912 film), 1
Mussolini, Benito, 63
Mustin, Burt, 236
Muszak, Chandra, 258
Muth, Ellen, 78
My Husband, Rock Hudson (book),
  208
My Left Foot (1989 film), 9
My Name Is Bill W. (1989 film), 2, 4,
  176–77
My Son John (1952 film), 12
Myrow, Fred, 229
Mystic River (2003 film), 9

Nadel, Arthur H., 47
Nader, George, 210
Nagel, Conrad, 76
Naile, Joanne, 50
Nair, Myra, 191
Nanus, Susan, 125
Napier, Charles, 193
Napier, John, 224
Narcotic (1933 film), 4
Nash, Johnny, 142
Natheaux, Louis, 170

National Association for the
  Advancement of Colored People
  (NAACP), 138, 214
National Literacy Foundation, 196
National Security Agency, 109
Nayfack, Nicholas, 40
Nazi movement, 11, 22, 31, 62, 98, 100
Neame, Christopher, 180
Neeson, Liam, 246, 247
Neff, Ralph, 188
Neft, Else, 98
Nelson, Craig T., 125
Nelson, Marjorie, 224
Nelson, Peter, 227
Nelson, Tracy, 140, 141
Nemec, Dennis, 50, 244
Nervig, Conrad, 40
Neuwirth, Bebe, 114
Never Weaken (1921 film), 16
Nevins, Claudette, 222
New World Symphony (Dvorak), 250
New York Daily News (newspaper),
  100
New York Herald Tribune (newspaper),
  134
New York Times (newspaper), 37, 134
Newlan, Paul, 224
Newland, John, 244, 246
Newman, Alfred, 111, 185
Newman, David, 269
Newman, Lionel, 57
Newman, Walter, 162
Nguyen, Cu Ba, 104
Nguyen, Long, 117
Nguyen, Phuoc Quan, 117
Nguyen, Trung, 117
Nichols, Dabe, 276
Nichols, David B., 258
Nichols, Josephine, 234
Nicholson, Jack, 26–28
Nicholson, Martin, 264
Nicole, Lydia, 232
Nicolella, John, 208
Nielsen, Leslie, 219, 220
Night Unto Night (book), 178
Night Unto Night (1947/1949 film), 10,
  15, 178–80

Nightmare on Elm Street (film series), 266

Nitzsche, Jack, 66

Nixon, Richard M., 11

No Blade of Grass (1970 film), 2, 11, 180–84

No Man Stands Alone (book), 173

No Way Out (1950 film), 9, 11, 14, 185–87

Noble, William, 37

Nolan, William F., 133

None So Blind (novel), 281, 283

Nora Prentiss (1947 film), 6

Nordling, Jeffrey, 24, 25

Norris, Bruce, 52

Norris, Jay, 281

North, Alan, 149

North, Alex, 104

Norton, Edward, 21–23

Norton, Jim, 21

Not of This Earth (1957 film), 92

Nourse, Allen, 45

Novak, Kim, 162, 164

Novikoff, Rashel, 152

Nozik, Michael, 191

Nussbaum, Mike, 214

Nye, Carrie, 73

Nyswaner, Ron, 194

O Brother, Where Art Thou? (2000 film), 11

Oakland, Simon, 123, 271, 273

O'Brien, Joycelyn, 208

O'Brien-Moore, Erin, 32

Obsessive/compulsive disorder, 4, 26

O'Connor, Kevin J., 101

Odell, Deborah, 68

O'Donnell, Cathy, 157

"Officer Krupke" (song), 273

O'Hagen, Michael, 101

O'Herlihy, Cornelia Hayes, 101

O'Laughlin, Gerald S., 128

The Old Dark House (1932 film), 101

The Old-Fashioned Way (1934 film), 4

The Old Man and the Sea (novel), 197

Old Wives for New (1918 film), 9

Oldring, Peter, 93

O'Leary, Matt, 82

Oliu, Ingrid, 232

Oliver, Ted, 170

Oliver, Thelma, 34

Oliver Twist (novel), 109

Olivier, Laurence, 10, 15

O'Mally, J. Pat, 227, 228

Olmos, Edward James, 232, 234

Omens, Woody, 88

Oms, Alba, 279

On Dangerous Ground (1951 film), 9

On Golden Pond (1981 film), 5

One AM (1916 film), 4

One Flew Over the Cuckoo's Nest (1975 film), 9

One More Spring (1935 film), 12

One Third of a Nation (1938 film), 12

One on Top of the Other (1971 film), 7

O'Neil, Ed, 66

O'Neill, Dick, 264, 265

Ontiveros, Lupe, 26

Opium (1918 film), 4

O'Quinn, Terry, 87–89, 211–13

O'Reare, James, 59

Orgolini, Arnold, 227

Orpheus (1949 film), 16

Orth, Frank, 154

Osterwald, Bibi, 26

Oswald, Richard, 13

Our Daily Bread (1934 film), 2

Our Gang (film series), 16

The Outsider (1961 film), 15

Overpopulation, 91, 230–31

Pacino, Al, 66

Padrone, Jose Filipe, 190

Page, Robert W., 59

Paget, Debra, 95

Palance, Jack, 16

Palmintieri, Chaz, 190, 192

Palyo, Renee, 208

Panic in Needle Park (1971 film), 4

Papa's Delicate Condition (1963 film), 4

The Paper Chase (1973 film), 10

Paralyzed Veterans of America (PVA), 168–170

Paraplegia, 9, 167–170, 216

Parasheles, Peter, 208
The Parent Trap (1961 film), 9, 84
Parfitt, Judy, 78, 79, 81
Paris, Jerry, 98, 99
Paris, Virginia, 232
Park Row (1952 film), 7
Parker, Eleanor, 162, 164
Parlos, Antony, 266
Parrott, Ursula, 76
Parting Glances (1986 film), 6
Pascal, Jefferson, 180
Pasteur Institute (Paris), 25
Pastoral Symphony (Beethoven), 231
A Patch of Blue (1965 film), 9
Patience (poem), 245
Patrick, Mervyn, 180
Patterson, Pat, 93
Patty (1962 film), 3, 188–90
Paulin, Scott, 201
Pawley, William, 111
The Pawnbroker (1965 film), 14
Paxton, Bill, 87
Paxton, John, 95
Paxton, Tajamika, 117
Paymer, David, 93, 95
Payne, Jonathan, 68
Pearl (poem), 245, 246
Pearl Poet (medieval author), 245
Pearson, Brett, 258
Penn, Leo, 219
Penn, Sean, 54–56, 71, 72
Percy, Lee, 203
The Perez Family (1995 film), 13,
    190–93
Perez, Lazaro, 190
Perkins, Anthony, 25
Perkins, Voltaire, 57
Peroni, Geraldine, 62
Perrine, Valerie, 152
Persky, Lisa Jane, 50
Personal Best (1982 film), 13
Peter and the Wolf (musical
    composition), 28
Peters, Brock, 229
Peters, Susan, 216–18
Petersen, Lenka, 34
Petrie, Daniel, 176

Petriem, Daniel, 249
Pfeiffer, Carolyn, 274
Pfeiffer, Rachel, 52
Phelan, Anna Hamilton, 164
Philadelphia (1993 film), 5, 6, 12,
    193–96
Philbin, Phil, 152
Philips, Ethan, 114, 149
Phillips, Anna Lisa, 266
Phillips, Lou Diamond, 232
Phillips, Mackenzie, 140
Phillips, Peter, 234
Phoenix, Liberty, 140
Phoenix, Summer, 140
Piazza, Ben, 164
Pickarts, Robert, 249
Pickford, Mary, 8, 12
Pilcher, Lydia Dean, 62, 191
Pillsbury, Sarah, 24
Pine, Larry, 71
Pinkett, Jada, 125
Pinsent, Gordon, 244, 245
Pirandello, Luigi, 90
Pitkin, Frank, 274
Pitts, Zasu, 8
Platt, Edward, 236
The Player (1992 film), 7
Plimpton, George, 107
Plotnick, Jack, 101
Plowman, Melinda, 47
Plummer, Christopher, 78, 79
Plummer, Glenn, 54
Pogany, Gabor, 73
Poitier, Sidney, 10, 120–22, 185–87,
    214, 215, 224–26
Pokorny, Diana, 130
Pollack, Sydney, 52, 224
Pollak, Cheryl, 201
Polo, Teri, 82
Port of New York (1949 film), 5
Portnow, Richard, 104
Potts, Jonathan, 276
Pounder, C. C. H., 125
Poverty (social theme), 1, 12, 42, 47,
    59, 62, 78, 98, 107, 111, 170, 219,
    227, 234, 246
Power, Tyrone, 60

Pratt, Roger, 135
Prejean, Sister Helen, 71
Prelutsky, Burt, 227
Preminger, Otto, 3, 4, 162
Presley, Elvis, 105, 193
Pressman, Edward R., 203
Pressure Point (1962 film), 11
Preston, Robert, 10, 146–148
Previn, André, 40
Price, Alan, 274, 275
Price, Alonzo, 32
Price, Annabella, 211
Price, Nancy, 222
Price, Vincent, 274, 275
The Pride of Jesse Hallam (1981 film), 10, 196–98
Priest, Dan, 34
The Prince of Tides (novel), 59
Prince, William, 249
The Principal (1987 film), 221
Prine, Andrew, 227
Prokofiev, Serge, 28
Prophecy (1979 film), 3, 11, 198–200
Prosky, Robert, 71, 114
Pruitt, Harold, 249
Public Defender's Office, 247
Pulitzer Prize, 85, 113
Pump Up the Volume (1990 film), 7, 10, 12, 15, 201–3

Quadriplegia, 9
Quaid, Dennis, 246, 247
Qualen, John, 111
Quiet Earth (1985 film), 11
Quigley, Martin, 7
Quillan, Eddie, 111
Quinlan, Karen Ann, 10
Quinlan, Kathleen, 52
Quinn, Aidan, 87, 88

Rabjohn, Richard E., 227
Raca, Patrick, 232
Rachmaninoff, Sergei, 224
Racimo, Victoria, 198
Racism (social theme), 14–15, 21, 29, 34, 59, 85, 93, 120, 133, 137, 149, 154, 185, 214, 232, 238, 255

Radd, Ronald, 73
Raffetto, Michael, 236
The Rag Bag Clan (novel), 227
A Rake's Progress (engravings series), 147
Raksin, David, 244
Ramis, Harold, 26
Ramos, Rudy, 54
Ramsey, Anne, 227
Rand, John, 170
Randall, Stuart, 238
Randell, Ron, 216
Randolph, Amanda, 185
Randolph, Barbara, 120
Random Harvest (1942 film), 216
Ransohoff, Martin, 252
Rape and Marriage (1980 film), 18
Rashomon (1950 film), 75
Rathbone, Basil, 15
Rathbone, Nigel, 180
Rather, Dan, 132
Ravetsch, Irving, 59
Raymond, Robin, 98
Reagan, Ronald, 25, 178–80, 238, 239, 241
Rear Window (1998 film), 9
Reaves-Phillips, Sandra, 149
Rebecca (1940 film), 218
The Rebel Set (1959 film), 17
Rebel Without a Cause (1955 film), 17
The Red Kimono (1925 film), 12
Red Menace (1949 film), 257
Redford, Robert, 52, 54
Redgrave, Lynn, 101, 103
Redgrave, Vanessa, 62
Reed, Russ, 241
Reefer Madness (1936 film), 4, 156, 190
Reeve, Christopher, 9, 89–90
Reeves, Richard, 98
Regeneration (1915 film), 1
Regina, Paul, 50
Reiner, Ira, 132
Reinhardt, John, 47
Reinhardt, Max, 162
Reinhardt, Ray, 176
Remar, James, 66
Remick, Lee, 18

Rennie, Guy, 152
Renoir, Jean, 281–84
Renoir, Pierre-Auguste, 283
Rescher, Gayne, 196
Reversal of Fortune (book), 203, 205
Reversal of Fortune (1990 film), 4, 10,
    15, 203-6
Reynolds, Adeline de Walt, 5
Reynolds, Cecil, 170
Reynolds, William, 37, 57
Ricci, Brian, 107
Richard, Wendy, 180
Richards, Addison, 32
Richards, Beah, 120
Richards, Paul, 173
Richardson, Nancy, 232
Richardson, Sy, 54
Richmond, Tom, 232
Ridgely, John, 40
Ridgely, Robert, 103
Ridges, Stanley, 185
Riener, Robert, 251
Right of Way (1983 film), 5, 10, 15,
    206-8
Right of Way (play), 206
Riley, John C., 78
Riley, Thomas, 178
Rimsky-Korsakov, Nikolai, 60
Der Ring des Nibelungen (opera cycle),
    183
Riot on Sunset Strip (1967 film), 17
Ritch, Ocee, 133
Ritt, Martin, 59
Rivera, Diego, 62–65
Rivera, Geraldo, 132
Roach, Hal, 16
Roach, John, 241
Roach, Neil, 176, 264
Robards, Jason, 193, 194
Robbins, David, 62, 71
Robbins, Jerome, 271, 273
Robbins, Tim, 62, 65, 71
Roberts, Allene, 216
Roberts, Daniel, 266
Roberts, Julia, 222, 224
Roberts, Steve, 82
Robespierre, Maximilien, 7, 58–59

Robinson, Andrew, 165, 166, 208, 211
Robinson, Ann, 98
Robinson, Edward G., 229- 31
Robinson, J. Peter, 140
Robinson, Jackie, 186
Robinson, Peter Manning, 68
Robson, Mark, 255
Rock Hudson (1990 film), 5, 12, 208–11
Rockefeller, Nelson, 62–65
Rockwell, George Lincoln, 11
Roe, Jane. *See* Russell, Ellen
Roe vs. Wade (1989 film), 3, 15, 17,
    211-13
Roemheld, Heinz, 47
Rogers, Ginger, 238, 239, 241
Rogers, Roy, 241
Roland, Rita, 249
Rolf, Tom, 198
Rolle, Esther, 85
Romance in Manhattan (1934 film), 14
Romeo and Juliet (play), 273
Rooney, Bethany, 276
Roots (1977 miniseries), 14
Roots: The Next Generation (1979 mini-
    series), 11
Rope (1948 film), 13
Rose, Reginald, 279
Rose, William, 120
Rosen, Robert L., 198
Rosenman, Leonard, 198, 249
Rosenthal, Laurence, 176
Ross, Annie, 201, 202
Ross, Barney, 4, 173–75
Ross, Jeremy, 42
Ross, Sharyn L., 258
Roth, Eric, 246
Roth, Gene, 47
Rothman, Jack, 214
Rowe, Phoebe, 133
Rowlands, Gena, 87, 88
Rozakis, Gregory, 19
Rozsa, Miklos, 154, 156
Rubell, Paul, 176
Ruben, Joseph, 222
Rubinek, Sol, 24, 25
Rubinstein, Arthur B., 279
Rudelson, Bob, 188

Rudin, Scott, 52, 135
Rudley, Herbert, 7
Rudy, Martin, 244
Ruehl, Mercedes, 130, 131
Ruginis, Vyto, 68, 69
Ruman, Sig, 40
Ruschetski, Larry, 90
Russ, William, 21, 66
Russell, Ellen, 212, 213
Russell, Keri, 276, 277
Russell, Lewis L., 154
Ryan, Irene, 281
Ryan, Mitchell, 50
Ryan, Natasha, 249
Ryan, Robert, 281–283
The Ryan White Story (1989 film), 6

Sacco and Vanzetti case, 137
The Sadist (1963 film), 17
Safan, Craig, 232
Sage, Bill, 190
Sägebrecht, Marianne, 269
Saldana, Theresa, 18
Salem, Pamela, 101
Salem witch trials, 131
Salter, Hans J., 216
Samaha, Elie, 117
Samaritan: The Mitch Snyder Story (1986 film), 12
Samuels, Lesser, 185
Samurai (1945 film), 15
Sande, Walter, 281
Sanders, Hugh, 238, 239
Sandman, Lee, 152
Sandoval, Arturo, 190
Sands of Iwo Jima (1949 film), 56
Sanford, Erskine, 178
Sanford, Isabel, 120
Sanford, Midge, 24
Sanford, Stanley, 170
Santiago-Hudson, Ruben, 82
Sarandon, Susan, 62, 63, 71, 72
Sarsgaard, Peter, 71
Satan Bug (1965 film), 16
Saturday Review (magazine), 134
Savalas, Telly, 224–26
Savoca, Nancy, 125

Sawtell, Paul, 173
Sawyer, Joseph, 32
Saxon, Edward, 194
Sayre, Joel, 95
Scalia, Pietro, 107
Scardino, Don, 66
Scardon, Paul, 216
Scared to Death (1946 film), 205
Scarlet Angel (1952 film), 209
Schaefer, George, 206, 234
Schaefer, Louis, 206
Schallert, William, 37
Scharwid, Diana, 125
Schenkkan, Robert, 201
Schiffer, Michael, 55. 149
Schlichtmann, Jan, 52–54
Schnabel, Stefan, 234
Schnee, Charles, 255
School integration, 133, 135
Schraner, Kim, 258
Schreder, Carol, 42
Schreiber, Flora Rheta, 249, 251
Schroeder, Barbet, 203
Schull, Rebecca, 234
Schulman, Arnold, 24
Schwartz, Aaron, 246
Schwartz, Howard, 188, 206, 227
Schweitzer, Michael, 68
Sciorra, Annabella, 203
Scola, Kathryn, 178
Scopes monkey trial, 7
Scott, Zachary, 261, 263
Scottsboro: A Tragedy of the American South (book), 137
Sea Devils (1953 film), 200
Seamon, Edward, 234
Sears, Fred F., 45
Sears, Zelda, 76
Second Symphony (Rachmaninoff), 224
Seconds (1966 film), 210
Secor, Kyle, 222
Seeger, Mindy, 140
Seeger, Susan, 140
Seidelman, Arthur Allen, 140
Seitz, John F., 154
Sellers, Peter, 194
Seltzer, Walter, 229

Selzer, David, 198
Seminole (1953 film), 15
Separate but Equal (1991 film), 14, 214–15
Sera, Ray, 234
Seresin, Michael, 82
Serling, Rod, 105
Sertees, Bruce, 152
The Seventh Sign (1988 film), 6
Sex and the City (television series), 146
Shackelford, Sandi, 222
Shadows (1922 film), 14
Shakespeare, William, 15, 64, 272, 273
Shalhoub, Tony, 52, 54
Shame! See The Intruder
The Shame of Patty Smith. See Patty
Shane, Maxwell, 98
Sharpe, Karen, 157
Shatner, William, 133–35
Shawnessey, Sharon, 264
Shearer, Norma, 76, 77
Sheedy, Ally, 258, 259
Shefter, Bert, 173
Shelton, Sloane, 149
Shepard, John, 208, 210
Sher, Lawrence, 144
Sheridan, Ann, 32, 261, 263
Sheridan, Jamey, 62, 63
Sherkow, Daniel A., 246
Sherman, Vincent, 261
Shilts, Randy, 24
Shipman, Nina, 37
Shire, Talia, 198, 199
Shore, Howard, 194
Shore, Roberta, 37
Showalter, Michael, 144
Shulman, Irving, 17
Sidney, P. J., 34
Sidney, Sylvia, 87, 227, 228
The Siege (1998 film), 12
Siegel, Don, 178, 180
Siegel, Saul, 95
Sigel, Tom, 208, 211
Sign of the Ram (1948 film), 2, 9, 15, 216–19
Sign of the Ram (novel), 216, 217
Silence of the Heart (1984 film), 16

Silent Running (1972 film), 11, 229
The Silent Voice (play), 160
Silliphant, Stirling, 224
Silva, Trinidad, 54
Silver, Ron, 203, 204
Silvera, Frank, 142, 143
Silvestri, Alan, 190
Simmons, Jean, 227, 228
Simmons, Rudd, 71
Simon, Robert, 57
Simpson, Geoffrey, 114
Simpson, Ivan, 160
Simpson, Robert, 111
Simpson, Russell, 111
Sinatra, Frank, 162–64
Sincerely Yours (1955 film), 161
Sinclair, Madge, 59, 60
Sinclair, Ronald, 133
Sinese, Gary, 176, 177, 234
Singh, Mano, 203
Singh, Parkie, 50
Sir Gawain and the Green Knight (poem), 245
Siskel, Gene, 9
Sixth and Main (1977 film), 4, 9, 12, 15, 219–21
Skarsgård, Stellan, 107, 108
Skinner, Frank, 147
Skokie (1981 film), 14
Skybell, Steven, 62
Slater, Christian, 201, 202
Slavin, Neal, 93
Sleep My Love (1948 film), 16
Sleeping with the Enemy (1991 film), 8, 17, 222–24
Slender Thread (1965 film), 15, 224–26
Slifer, Elizabeth, 98
Sling Blade (1996 film), 9
Sloane, Everett, 167–170
Sloatman, Lala, 201
Small, Edward, 173
A Small Killing (1981), 5, 12, 227–29
Smash-Up (1947 film), 4
"Smile" (song), 172
Smith, Anna Deavere, 194
Smith, Bud, 66
Smith, Charles Martin, 23, 25

Smith, Cheryl, 50
Smith, Crystal, 196
Smith, Juney, 104
Smith, Katherine, 133
Smith, Lois, 71, 114
Smith, Mildred Joanne, 185
Smith, Perry, 128–30
Smith, Tucker, 271
Smith, Yeardley, 26
The Snake Pit (1948 film), 9, 154
Snow, Mark, 264
Snyder, William, 157
Social reformers, 2, 221
Sol, Alex, 21
Solo, Robert H., 55
Solzhenitsyn, Alexander, 184
Sommer, Edith R., 37
Sondheim, Stephen, 271, 273
Song of Russia (1943 film), 218
Sonnier, Elmo Patrick, 71
Soon, Surgit, 180
Sorvino, Paul, 66
Sothern, Ann, 274, 275
Soto, Rosana de, 232
Soul Man (1986 film), 37
Sova, Peter, 104
Soylent Green (1973 film), 7, 11, 15, 229–31
Spacek, Sissy, 125, 126, 241
Spacey, Kevin, 1, 7
Sparrows (1926 film), 8
Spellbound (1944 film), 15
Spelling, Aaron, 24, 157, 159
Spelman, Sharon, 140
Spencer, Dorothy, 95
Spencer, Douglas, 98
Spinell, Joe, 66
Spinella, Stephen, 23
Spiro, Jordana, 125
Spottiswoode, Roger, 24
Spouse abuse (social theme), 8, 42, 68, 78, 82, 222, 238, 258, 264, 269, 281
Spradlin, J. D., 269
"The Squire of Gothos" (*Star Trek* episode), 47
St. Batholomew's Day massacre, 2
St. Jacques, Raymond, 34

St. John, Howard, 167
St. Judge, Martin, 219
Stack, Robert, 210
Stadlen, Lewis, J., 137, 138
Stagecoach (1939 film), 4
Staircase (1969 film), 13
Stand and Deliver (1987 film), 10, 14, 232–34
Stanford, Thomas, 224, 271
Stang, Arnold, 162, 163
Stanler, John, 125
Stanton, Dan, 104
Stanton, Don, 104
Stanton, Harry Dean, 241
Stanton, Paul, 32
Stanwyck, Barbara, 146–48
A Star Is Born (1937 film), 4
Star trek (television series), 47, 135, 168
Starger, Martin, 164
Steadman, John, 227
Steenburgen, Mary, 193, 196, 274
Stein, Herman, 133
Stein, Sam, 170
Steinbeck, John, 2, 111–13
Steiner, Max, 261, 264
Stell, Aaron, 216
Stepanek, Brian, 144
Stephens, Brad, 219
Stephens, Harvey, 45
Sterling, Tisha, 274
Stern, Sandy, 201
Stern, Stephen Hilliard, 227
Stern, Stewart, 249
Stevens, Andrew, 117
Stevens, Craig, 178
Stevens, Fisher, 203
Stevens, George, Jr., 214
Stevens, Leith, 98, 157
Stevenson, Housely, 146
Stevenson, Michael, 42
Stewart, Charlotte, 224
Stewart, Jimmy, 4, 5, 206, 208
Stewart, Mel, 279
Stewart, Paul, 128
Stillman, Karen, 68
Stockdale, Carl, 76

Stockwell, Dean, 57, 59
Stokes, Frank, 90
Stokowski, Leopold, 50
Stoltz, Eric, 164–66
The Stone Boy (1984 film), 221
Stone, George E., 162
Stone, Leonard, 229
Stone, Oliver, 130, 203
Stone Pillow (1985 film), 12, 234–35, 228
Storey, Ruth, 128
Storm Center (1956 film), 7, 10, 236–38
Storm Warning (1950 film), 8, 11, 14, 238–41
The Story of Mankind (1957 film), 90
Stradling, Harry, Jr., 198
Straight, Alvin, 241–43
The Straight Story (1999 film), 5, 241–243
Strange Holiday (1942 film), 11
Strathairn, David, 78, 79
Strauss, Robert, 162
Street Angel (1928 film), 2
Strock, Herbert L., 98
Stroheim, Erich von, 8
The Struggle (1931 film), 4
Sturges, John, 216
Sugarman, Alvin M., 85
Suicide (social theme), 15–16, 47, 78, 87, 95, 101, 117, 146, 154, 160, 178, 201, 203, 206, 211, 216, 219, 224, 229, 244, 246, 249, 264, 279, 281
The Suicide's Wife (1979 film), 12, 15, 244–46
Sukapatana, Chintara, 104
Sullivan, Charlotte, 276
Sullivan, Elliott, 146
Sullivan's Travels (1941 film), 12
Sully, Frank, 111
Summerour, Lisa, 193
Summers, Bob, 219
Sunrise (1927 film), 2
Suplee, Ethan, 21
Supreme Court (Alabama), 138
Supreme Court (Rhode Island), 205
Supreme Court (U.S.), 3, 37, 129, 212–16, 247

Surina, Daniela, 73
Surties, Robert, 255
Surviving (1985 film), 16
Suspect (1987 film), 3, 9, 12, 15, 246–48
Sutton, Juana, 170
Swann, Robert, 29
Swayze, Patrick, 117, 119
Sweeney, Mary, 241
Swicord, Robin, 190
Sybil (book), 249, 251
Sybil (1976 film), 8, 15, 249–51
Symbol of the Unconquered (1920 film), 14
Symphonie Fantastique (Berlioz), 222, 223
Synanon (1965 film), 4

Tamblyn, Russ, 271, 272
Tandy, Jessica, 5, 85, 87
Tannen, Charles, 111
Tannenbaum, Julius, 34
Taradash, Daniel, 236, 238
Taritero, Joseph, M., 50
Tarzan, 168
Taylor, Elizabeth, 73–75
Taylor, Vaughn, 37, 128
Taylor-Young, Leigh, 229, 230
Tchaikovsky, Peter Ilyich, 229
Teagarden, Jack, 98–100
Teal, Ray, 167
Teenage gangs. *See* Gangs
Ten Rillington Place (book), 252
Ten Rillington Place (1971 film), 2, 3, 6, 252–54
Tender Is the Night (1962 film), 9
Term of Trial (1962 film), 10
Terry, Karen, 180
Terry, Phillip, 154, 155
Tesh, Julie, 208
Tess of the Storm Country (1922 film), 12
Thalberg, Irving J., 76
Thatcher, Russell, 229
Thaxter, Phyllis, 216, 218
Thelma and Louise (1991 film), 243
Theodorakis, Maria, 266, 267
These Three (1936 film), 13

Thesiger, Ernest, 5, 103, 104
They Came to Blow Up America (1943 film), 11
They Made Me a Criminal (1939 film), 16
They Won't Forget (1937 film), 14
Thigpen, Lynne, 149, 214
The Thing (1950 film), 92
–30– (1959 film), 7
This Child Is Mine (1985 film), 18
Thomas, Clarence, 152
Thomas, Henry, 130, 131, 133
Thomas, Marlo, 258, 259
Thomas, Sharon, 219
Thomas, Wallace, 137
Thompson, Lea, 264, 265
Thompson, Sada, 130, 131
Thompson, Shelley, 276
Thomson, H. A. R., 180
The Three Faces of Eve (1957 film), 249
Thurman, Sammy, 128
Tilbury, Zeffie, 111
Tillman, Greg, 144
Time (magazine), 155
Timko, Johnny, 198
Tiomkin, Dimitri, 167
Tisch, Steve, 42
Tischler, Stanford, 157, 188
To Be or Not To Be (1942 film), 15
To Find a Man (1972 film), 4
To Kill a Mockingbird (1962 film), 14, 139
To Sir With Love (1967 film). 10
Tobacco Road (1941 film), 12
Todd, Beverly, 149
Todd, Lisa, 219
Toes, Malcolm, 180
Toland, Greg, 111
Tomei, Marisa, 190, 191
Tomlin, Lily, 23
Torey, Jose, 40
Torn, Angelica, 82
Toronto Film Festival, 93
Torre, Nick, 90
Torres, Liz, 140
Tors, Ivan, 98

Tory, Guy, 21
Tosi, Mario, 137, 249, 279
Toth, Andre de, 173
Totheroh, Rollie, 170
Toussaint, Lorraine, 125
Tover, Leo, 37, 281
Tovoli, Luciano, 203
Tracy, Margaret, 216
Tracy, Spencer, 17, 120-22
Traffic in Souls (1913 film), 1, 190
Tran, Billinjer, 117
Tran, Jennifer, 117
Tran, Tung Thanh, 104
La Traviata (opera), 157
Travolta, John, 52–54, 82
Treasure of Sierra Madre (1948 film), 130
Tree, Dorothy, 167
Trial (1955 film), 11, 13, 14, 255–58
Trial of Earth. See Environment
The Trials of Oscar Wilde (1960 film), 13
Trombetta, Leo, 117
"The Trouble With Tribbles" (*Star Trek* episode), 47
Tryon, Tom, 3
Tubb, Barry, 164
Tulley, Paul, 249
Turkel, Joe, 98, 157, 159
Turner, Dennis, 208
Turner, Kathleen, 269
Turturro, John, 62, 63
Twain, Norman, 149
21 Hours in Munich (1976 film), 12
Two Seconds (1932 film), 6
Tyler, Harry, 111
Tyler, Tom, 111

Uhry, Alfred, 85
Ulrich, Skeet, 26
Ultimate Betrayal (1993 film), 8, 258-61
The Unfaithful (1947 film), 9, 261-64
United Nations, 99, 100
University of Louisville, 251
The Unspoken Truth (1995 film), 8, 15, 17, 264-66
Urla, Joe, 130, 131

Vacarro, Brenda, 196, 197
The Vagabond (1916 film), 172
Van Effenterre, Joële, 29
Van Patten, Joyce, 95
Van Patton, Dick, 229
Van Sant, Gus, 107
Van Trees, James, 160
Van Zandt, Phil, 146
Vance, Danitra, 269
Vannicola, Joanne, 258
Varsi, Diane, 57
Vaughan, Dorothy, 32
Vaughn, Vince, 82
Vawter, Ron, 193
Vega, Jose de, 271
Vega$ (television series), 47
Veidt, Conrad, 13
Veiller, Anthony, 173
Venton, Harley, 222
The Verdict (1946 film), 7
Vernon, Glenn, 281
Vertigo (1958 film), 40
VeSota, Bruno, 188, 189
The Victim (1962 film), 13
Victims for Victims (1984 film), 18
Victor, James, 232
Vidor, King, 2
Viera, Asia, 68
Vietnamese Conflict, 104–7, 118
A View from the Bridge (1962 film), 13
The Villain Still Pursued Her
    (1940 film), 4
Villarreal, Daniel, 232
Vincent, Virginia, 123
Violence (social theme), 16–17, 21, 54,
    107, 142, 157, 271
Vivino, Floyd, 104
Vogan, Emmett, 32
Voight, Jon, 59
Voyage of Terror, the Achille Lauro Affair
    (1990 film), 12

Waara, Scott, 130
Wade, Dixie, 42
Wagner, Cosima, 206
Wagner, Lindsay, 18, 123
Wagner, Max, 111

Wagner, Richard, 183, 206
Wahrman, Wayne, 52
Wald, Jerry, 238, 261
Walden, Snuffy, 211
Waldis, Otto, 40
Walk East on Beacon (1953 film), 12
Walker, Charles, 54–55, 206
Walker, Ernest, 252
Walker, Gerald, 66
Walker, Rudolph, 73
The Walking Dead (1936 film), 6
Walking on Water (2002 film), 4, 10, 12,
    266–68
Wallace, Jean, 180, 181, 184
Wallach, Eli, 196, 197
Waller, Eddy, 111
Walraff, Diego, 190
Walsh, J. T., 104, 105
Walsh, Jack, 241
Walsh, Martin, 135
Walsh, Raoul, 209, 210
Walsh, Sydney, 87
Walter, Tracey, 194
Walters, Ingram, 188
Walton, Douglas, 6
Wanger, Walter, 123
War and Remembrance (1988
    miniseries), 15
The War of the Roses (1989 film), 2–3, 8,
    9, 269–71
Ward, Joan, 180
Ward, Richard, 34, 36
Warfield, Marsha, 164
Warner, Jack, 160
Warner, Mark, 78, 85
Warner, Rick, 176
Warren, Earl, 214–15
Warren, Jennifer, 50
Warren, Ruth, 185
Washington, Denzel, 193–95
The Water Is Wide (novel), 59
Water pollution, 52–54, 91
Watermelon Man (1970 film), 14
Waterworld (1995 film), 11, 229
Watson, Bruce, 137
Watson, Emily, 62, 63
Watts, Liz, 266

Waxman, Franz, 101, 104, 178
The Way of All Flesh (novel), 37
Way Down East (1920 film), 12
Wayne, John, 56, 192, 193
Waynes, Damon, 54
We Who Are About to Die (1936 film), 6
Weaver, Fritz, 176, 177
Weaver, Randy, 31
Webb, Anastasia, 241
Webb, Clifton, 15
Webb, Jack, 167–70
Webber, Ben, 144
Webster, Ferris, 142
Webster vs. Reproductive Services case, 213
Wedgeworth, Ann, 114
Weintraub, Jerry, 66
Weir, Peter, 114
Welcome Home, Bobby (1986 film), 13
Welk, Lawrence, 105
The Well (1951 film), 14, 154
Well of Loneliness (1934 film), 13
Welles, Orson, 7, 57–59, 62–65
Wellman, Harold E., 142
Welsh, Kenneth, 93, 94
Wendell, Howard, 236
Werner, Fred, 227
Werner, Peter, 264
West, Sam, 135
West Side Story (1961 film), 3, 13, 16, 224, 271–73
West, Timothy, 135
Westfeldt, Jennifer, 144, 146
Weston, Celia, 71
Weston, Jack, 123
Wexler, Haskell, 19, 55
Whale, James, 101–4
The Whales of August (1987 film), 5, 9, 10, 274–76
The Whales of August (play), 274, 275
What Dreams May Come (1998 film), 16
Wheeler, John W., 214
When Innocence Is Lost (1997 film), 17, 276–78
Whibley, Burnell, 180
Whitaker, Forest, 104, 117, 119
The White Caps (1906 film), 8

White, Karen Malina, 149
White, Ryan, 25
Whitehead, O. Z., 111
Whitmore, James, 34–36
Whitney, Lynn, 238
Who'll Save Our Children? (1978 film), 9
Whose Life Is It Anyway? (1981 film), 9, 10, 15, 279–81
Why Change Your Wife? (1920 film), 9
Why Must I Die? (1960 film), 123
Whytock, Grant, 173
Wide-Eyed in Babylon (book), 156
Widmark, Richard, 185–87
Wierum, Howard, 236
Wiest, Dianne, 18
Wigan, Gareth, 73
Wilbur, Dr. Cornelia, 249–51
Wilbur, Crane, 173
Wild Boys of the Road (1933 film), 12
Wild, Ernst, 73
Wild, Harry, 281
The Wild One (1953 film), 17
Wilde, Cornel, 180–84
Wilder, Billy, 154, 156
Wildman, Valerie, 130
Wilets, Bernard, 90
William, Timothy, 13
Williams, Billy, 246
Williams, Daniel, 90
Williams, JoBeth, 176, 177
Williams, John, 59
Williams, Kent, 227
Williams, Robin, 104, 105, 107–9
Williamson, Nicol, 15
Willingham, Noble, 104
Wilson, Chandra, 194
Wilson, Mary Louise, 114
Wilson, Mitchell, 281
Wilson, Rita, 125
Wilson, Scott, 71, 128, 130
Wilton, Penelope, 135
The Wind (1928 film), 12
The Winds of War (1983 miniseries), 15
Winfield, Paul, 59, 60
Winger, Debra, 29
Winkler, Irwin, 29
Winn, Hugh, 76

Winslett, Kate, 135, 136
Winters, David, 271
Winwood, Estelle, 5
Wise, Robert, 123, 271
Witford, Bradley, 194
Witt, Kathryn, 193
Witty, Dame May, 216, 218
Wizard of Oz (1939 film), 105
Wohl, David, 211
Wolcott, Charles, 142
Wolfe, Ian, 5, 185
Wolff, Frank, 19
Woman on the Beach (1947 film), 2, 8, 9, 15, 281–84
A Woman Rebels (1936 film), 17
Woman of the Year (1942 film), 17
Women in Chains (1972 film), 17
Women's rights (social theme), 17–18, 42, 78, 82, 140, 211, 222, 264, 276
The Women's Room (1980 film), 18
Wong, B. D., 24
Wood, Charles, 135
Wood, Edward D., Jr., 90, 190
Wood, John David, 258
Wood, Natalie, 271, 272
Woodruff, Largo, 50
Woods, James, 130, 133, 176, 177
Woodward, Joanne, 193, 249, 251
Works Progress Administration (WPA), 62, 64
World Trade Center, 146
World War I, 13, 101, 176
World War II, 11, 98, 167, 173–75, 243
Worth, Marvin, 152
Wotan, 92, 183
Wright, Howard, 45
Wright, John, 176

Wright, Teresa, 167–70
Wright, Tom, 203
Wright, Will, 185
Wrye, Donald, 258
Wu, Ping, 208
Wuhl, Robert, 104
Wurmfeld, Eden H., 144
Wurmfeld, Esther, 144
Wyatt, Gregory, 137
Wylie, Philip, 178
Wyman, Jane, 154–156
Wynant, H. N., 224
Wyner, George, 279

Yarbo, Lillian, 178
Yates, Peter, 246
Yellen, Sherman, 88
Young, Collier, 157
Young, Mary, 154
Young, Stephen, 229
Youth gangs. *See* Gangs
Yulin, Harris, 62, 63, 125

Zabriskie, Grace, 42
Zaillian, Steven, 52
Zanuck, Darryl F., 57, 111, 160, 185
Zanuck, Lili Fini, 85
Zanuck, Richard D., 57, 85
Zaremba, John, 45, 142
Zea, Kristi, 26
Zeppieri, Richard, 68
Ziegler, Joseph, 93
Zimmer, Hans, 26, 28, 85, 114
Zinnemann, Fred, 167
Zinner, Peter, 128
Zions, Brad, 144
Zuniga, Daphne, 234, 235

About the Author

CHARLES P. MITCHELL has served as Director of three Maine libraries and also as Chairman of the Southern Maine Library District. He has taught film appreciation courses and been a regular columnist and reviewer of books and film for numerous periodicals. He is the author of several film books, including *A Guide to Charlie Chaplin Films* (Greenwood 1999), *A Guide to Apocalyptic Cinema* (Greenwood 2001), and *The Complete H. P. Lovercraft Filmography* (Greenwood 2002).